MW00845277

China and Cybersecurity

CHINA AND CYBERSECURITY

Espionage, Strategy, and Politics in the Digital Domain

Edited by Jon R. Lindsay,
Tai Ming Cheung,

and

Derek S. Reveron

OXFORD
UNIVERSITY PRESS

OXFORD
UNIVERSITY PRESS

Oxford University Press is a department of the University of
Oxford. It furthers the University's objective of excellence in research,
scholarship, and education by publishing worldwide.

Oxford   New York
Auckland   Cape Town   Dar es Salaam   Hong Kong   Karachi
Kuala Lumpur   Madrid   Melbourne   Mexico City   Nairobi
New Delhi   Shanghai   Taipei   Toronto

With offices in
Argentina   Austria   Brazil   Chile   Czech Republic   France   Greece
Guatemala   Hungary   Italy   Japan   Poland   Portugal   Singapore
South Korea   Switzerland   Thailand   Turkey   Ukraine   Vietnam

Oxford is a registered trademark of Oxford University Press
in the UK and certain other countries.

Published in the United States of America by
Oxford University Press
198 Madison Avenue, New York, NY 10016

© Oxford University Press 2015

All rights reserved. No part of this publication may be reproduced, stored in
a retrieval system, or transmitted, in any form or by any means, without the prior
permission in writing of Oxford University Press, or as expressly permitted by law,
by license, or under terms agreed with the appropriate reproduction rights organization.
Inquiries concerning reproduction outside the scope of the above should be sent to the
Rights Department, Oxford University Press, at the address above.

You must not circulate this work in any other form
and you must impose this same condition on any acquirer.

Library of Congress Cataloging-in-Publication Data
China and cybersecurity : espionage, strategy, and politics in the digital domain /
edited by Jon R. Lindsay, Tai Ming Cheung, Derek S. Reveron.
    pages cm
Includes bibliographical references and index.
ISBN 978-0-19-020126-5 (hardback) — ISBN 978-0-19-020127-2 (paperback)
1. Cyberterrorism—China.   2. National security—United States.   3. Security, International.
4. International cooperation.   I. Lindsay, Jon R., editor.   II. Cheung, Tai Ming, editor.
III. Reveron, Derek S., editor.
HV6773.15.C97C45 2015
355.3'43202854678—dc23
2014046287

CONTENTS

PART III: National Cybersecurity Policy

PART IV: Practical and Theoretical Implications

ACKNOWLEDGMENTS

This project began as a pair of conferences at the University of California Institute on Global Conflict and Cooperation (IGCC) in La Jolla, California, in the spring of 2012. Cybersecurity was by then already a hot topic in Beijing and Washington, DC, but interest—and diplomatic tension—escalated throughout the following year with allegations of industrial espionage by the Chinese military and classified National Security Agency documents leaked by Edward Snowden. As this book was going through the final editing process, the US Department of Justice indicted five alleged members of the Chinese People's Liberation Army for involvement in industrial espionage. China responded with angry incriminations and retaliation against US firms in China. Further drama is surely inevitable. The relentless pace of current events has both challenged our contributors through the course of many revisions and strengthened our belief in the need for an objective analysis of the political and institutional foundations of cybersecurity in China.

This project has benefited from the generous support of IGCC; work supported by, or in part by, the U.S. Army Research Laboratory and the U.S. Army Research Office through the Minerva Initiative under grant #W911NF-09-1-0081; and Office of Naval Research Grant N00014-14-1-0071. Research for the chapter by Xu Jinghong was supported in part by the National Social Science Fund of China (11BXW042), the China Postdoctoral Science Foundation (20110490507), the Fundamental Research Funds for the Central Universities (2011RC1113), and the Social Science Fund of BUPT (2011BS03).

As in any project like this, many people have been vital in bringing this book to fruition. The conferences that initiated this project benefited from smooth management by Heidi Serochi and Marie Thiveos. Lynne Bush provided expert copyediting and book project management at IGCC. Brett Silvis standardized the figures and tables. Steven Glinert, Elizabeth Martin, Joseph Miller, Lauren Reed, and Taylor Roberts provided research assistance in locating sources and providing translations. Fan Yang provided expert translation help on the Chinese chapters. Scott Parris and Cathryn Vaulman at Oxford University Press were most helpful in shepherding the project through to completion and demonstrating patience as new revelations in the press necessitated additional revision. Eswari Maruthu and Richard Isomaki were a pleasure to work with throughout the final copy-editing process. We would also like to thank the anonymous peer reviewers for their detailed and valuable feedback on all of the chapters.

CONTRIBUTORS

Fred H. Cate is a Distinguished Professor and C. Ben Dutton Professor of Law at the Indiana University Maurer School of Law. He is the former director of the university's Center for Applied Cybersecurity Research—a National Center of Academic Excellence in both Information Assurance Research and Information Assurance Education—and director of the Center for Law, Ethics, and Applied Research in Health Information. Cate is a senior policy advisor to the Centre for Information Policy Leadership at Hunton & Williams LLP. Previously, he served as chair of the International Telecommunication Union's High-Level Experts on Electronic Signatures and Certification Authorities, counsel to the Department of Defense Technology and Privacy Advisory Committee, reporter for the third report of the Markle Task Force on National Security in the Information Age, and as a member of the National Academy of Sciences Committee on Technical and Privacy Dimensions of Information for Terrorism Prevention, Microsoft's Trustworthy Computing Academic Advisory Board, and the Federal Trade Commission's Advisory Committee on Online Access and Security. A regular speaker before industry groups and witness before congressional committees, Professor Cate is the author of more than 150 articles and books and one of the founding editors of the Oxford University Press journal *International Data Privacy Law*.

Tai Ming Cheung is director of the University of California Institute on Global Conflict and Cooperation. He is in charge of the Institute's Minerva project "The Evolving Relationship Between Technology and National Security in China: Innovation, Defense Transformation, and China's Place in the Global Technology Order." He is a longtime analyst of Chinese and East Asian defense and national security affairs. Cheung was based in Asia from the mid-1980s to 2002, covering political, economic, and strategic developments in greater China. He was also a journalist and political and business risk consultant in northeast Asia. Cheung received his Ph.D. from the War Studies Department at King's College, London University in 2006. His latest book, *Fortifying China: The Struggle to Build a Modern Defense Economy*, was published by Cornell University Press in 2009. He is an associate professor in residence at the School of International Relations and Pacific Studies at UC San Diego, where he teaches courses on Asian security and Chinese security and technology.

Duan Haixin is a professor in the Network and Information Security Lab of Tsinghua University and member of CCERT and CERNET Network Center. Professor Duan received his Ph.D. from Tsinghua University in computer science. His research interests include network intrusion detection, DNS security, and anonymous communication.

Nigel Inkster served for thirty-one years in the British Secret Intelligence Service (SIS). He had postings in Asia, Latin America, and Europe and worked extensively on transnational security issues. He was on the board of SIS for seven years, the last two as assistant chief and director for operations and intelligence. He graduated from St. Johns College Oxford with a First Class degree in Oriental Studies and is a Chinese speaker. He joined the International Institute for Strategic Studies (IISS) in March 2007 as director for transnational threats and political risk, dealing with transnational terrorism, international organised crime, intelligence, and cybersecurity. He is also responsible for the IISS Armed Conflict Database, which monitors some sixty-five armed conflicts worldwide. He has written, spoken, and broadcast on a range of transnational security issues.

Zhuge Jianwei is an associate professor at the Network and Information Security Lab of Tsinghua University, China. Before he joined Tsinghua, he was an associate professor at Peking University. He received his Ph.D. in computer science at Peking University in 2006, under the supervision of famous Chinese computer scientist Xuan Wang, where he received an IBM PhD Fellowship, a Microsoft Fellowship, and a PKU Young Investigator Award. Zhuge's research interests include network security, network measurement, and system security. He has made more than twenty presentations or at well-known international conferences, including AsiaCCS, FIRST, ICICS, IAW, and WEIS, and publications in first-class journals in China including *Chinese Journal of Computers, Journal of Software,* and *Journal on Communications*. Based on Google Scholar, his papers have been cited more than six hundred times, and the h-index of his publications is 13. He teaches several classes for graduate and undergraduate students at Tsinghua, and is the author of a textbook titled *Network Hacking and Defense: Technology and Practice.*

Xu Jinghong is a professor of communication at the School of Digital Media and Design Arts, Beijing University of Posts and Telecommunications (BUPT), vice director of the interdisciplinary Center of Social Network Information Management and Service at BUPT, and a postdoctoral scholar at the Chinese Academy of Social Sciences (CASS) Institute of Law. From 2012 to 2013 he was a Fulbright Visiting Scholar at the Center for Global Communication Studies, Annenberg School for Communication, University of Pennsylvania. Xu's research focuses on new media communication, media ethics, media policy and law, cyber culture, information law, Internet law, Internet governance, online privacy, online public opinion, and digital copyright law. He holds a B.A. in English, an M.A. in journalism, and Ph.D. in communications. The research for Xu's chapter was supported in part by National Social Science Fund of China (11BXW042), by the China Postdoctoral Science Foundation (20110490507), by the Fundamental Research Funds for the Central Universities (2011RC1113), and by the Social Science Fund of BUPT (2011BS03).

Jon R. Lindsay is an assistant professor of digital media and global affairs at the University of Toronto Munk School of Global Affairs as of July 2015, an Oxford Martin Associate with the Oxford Global Cyber Security Capacity Centre, and a nonresident research scholar with the University of California, San Diego. He was formerly an assistant research scientist at the University of California Institute on Global Conflict and Cooperation and assistant adjunct professor at the School of International Relations and Pacific Studies, UC San Diego. His research examines the impact of technology on international security and has appeared in leading academic journals such as *International Security, Security Studies, Journal of Strategic Studies*, and *Technology and Culture*. He is the co-Principal Investigator for a Department of Defense Minerva Initiative project on technological complexity and deterrence strategy. He holds a Ph.D. in political science from the Massachusetts Institute of Technology and an M.S. in computer science and B.S. in symbolic systems from Stanford University. He is served as an officer in the US Navy with assignments in Asia, Europe, Latin America, and the Middle East.

Gu Lion is a threat researcher at Trend Micro, Inc., a provider of top-ranked client, server, and cloud-based security solutions that protect data in physical, virtualized, and cloud environments. His research focuses on malware analysis, mobile security, and the underground cybercriminal economy.

He holds a bachelor of electronic information engineering from Tianjin University of Technology.

Xu Lu is an assistant researcher at the Internet Governance and Law Research Center and tutor at the International School of the Beijing University of Posts and Telecommunications. Her research specializes in intellectual property protection law, e-commerce law, and cyber law. She is involved in a number of research projects of the national, provincial, and ministerial levels.

Sarah McKune is a senior researcher at the Citizen Lab, Munk School of Global Affairs, University of Toronto. Her work focuses on targeted cyber-threats against human rights organizations, regulation of surveillance technologies, including sanctions and export controls, and international cybersecurity initiatives. McKune is a lawyer with a background in international human rights law. Prior to joining the Citizen Lab, she worked at the nongovernmental organization Human Rights in China (HRIC), where she focused much of her effort on international advocacy. She was the principal drafter and researcher of the HRIC white paper "Counter-terrorism and Human Rights: The Impact of the Shanghai Cooperation Organization." Her previous experience also includes work as a litigation associate at the New York office of Morrison & Foerster LLP, and teaching English in China. McKune obtained her J.D. from the University of Michigan Law School in 2002, and her B.A. in international relations from Michigan State University in 1999.

Joe McReynolds is a research analyst at Defense Group Inc.'s Center for Intelligence Research and Analysis. His public research interests primarily center on China's approach to computer network warfare and defense science and technology development. McReynolds has previously worked with the Council on Foreign Relations and the Pacific Council for International Policy, and is a graduate of Georgetown University's School of Foreign Service and Graduate Security Studies programs. He speaks and reads Chinese and Japanese, and has lived and studied in Nagoya, Guilin, and Beijing.

Kevin Pollpeter is deputy director of IGCC's Project on the Study of Innovation and Technology in China (SITC). Prior to working at IGCC, Pollpeter was deputy director of the East Asia Program at Defense Group Inc. (DGI) and an analyst at Rand. Pollpeter's research focuses on the Chinese military and Chinese military-related research and development and science and technology issues. In particular, Pollpeter focuses on the Chinese space program. Pollpeter has authored or coauthored numerous publications on the Chinese military and national security issues. His publications include "Controlling the Information Domain: Space, Cyber, and Electronic Warfare," in Ashley J. Tellis and Travis Tanner, *Strategic Asia 2012–2013: China's Military Challenge*, and a monograph entitled *Building for the Future: China's Progress in Space Technology during the Tenth Five-Year Plan and the U.S. Response*. He has also written frequently for *China Brief*. Pollpeter has also coauthored many works, including *Dangerous Thresholds: Managing Escalation in the 21st Century* and *Entering the Dragon's Lair: Chinese Anti-access Strategies and Their Implications for the United States*. Pollpeter received his master's degree in international policy studies from the Monterey Institute of International Studies and his bachelor's degree in China studies from Grinnell College. He is currently pursuing a Ph.D. at King's College London.

Derek S. Reveron is a professor of national security affairs and the EMC Informationist Chair at the US Naval War College in Newport, Rhode Island, and a faculty affiliate at the Belfer Center of Science and International Affairs, John F. Kennedy School of Government, Harvard University. He specializes in strategy development, nonstate security challenges, intelligence, and US defense policy. He has authored or edited ten books, most recently *US Foreign Policy and Defense Strategy: The Evolution of an Incidental Superpower* (Georgetown University Press, 2015), *Cyberspace and National Security: Threats, Opportunities, and Power in a Virtual World* (Georgetown University Press, 2012) and *Human Security in a Borderless World* (Westview Press, 2011). He received a diploma from the Naval War College and an M.A. in political science and a Ph.D. in public policy analysis from the University of Illinois at Chicago.

Taylor Roberts is a James Martin Fellow at the University of Oxford's Global Cybersecurity Capacity Centre, located at the Oxford Martin School. Presently, he is focusing on researching and developing maturity metrics for measuring cyber policy and cyber defense. He also works with cybersecurity experts in government, industry, and civil society in order to provide a comprehensive maturity model of international cybersecurity capacity building. He holds a master's in Pacific international affairs from the School of International Relations and Pacific Studies at UC San Diego.

Robert Sheldon holds a 2013–2014 Mike Mansfield Fellowship for advancing understanding and cooperation in U.S.-Japan relations. Previously, he was senior policy analyst for military and security affairs at the U.S.-China Economic and Security Review Commission, where he focused on trends in Chinese computer network operations, Chinese information technology and telecommunications firms, and China's Internet policies. His interests include cybersecurity, foreign policy, defense, and Asian security issues. Sheldon holds an M.A. in security policy studies and a B.S. in computer and digital forensics. His chapter represents his own views and not necessarily those of any organization with which he is or has been affiliated.

Mark A. Stokes is the executive director of the Project 2049 Institute. Previously, he was the founder and president of Quantum Pacific Enterprises, an international consulting firm, and vice president and Taiwan country manager for Raytheon International. He has served as executive vice president of Laifu Trading Company, a subsidiary of the Rehfeldt Group; a senior associate at the Center for Strategic and International Studies; and member of the Board of Governors of the American Chamber of Commerce in Taiwan. A twenty-year US Air Force veteran, Stokes also served as team chief and senior country director for the People's Republic of China, Taiwan, and Mongolia in the Office of the Assistant Secretary of Defense for International Security Affairs. He holds a B.A. from Texas A&M University, and graduate degrees in international relations and Asian studies from Boston University and the Naval Postgraduate School. He is a fluent Mandarin speaker.

Li Yuxiao is the dean of the International School of the Beijing University of Posts and Telecommunications, where he also directs the Internet Governance and Law Research Center. His research specializes in Internet governance, cyber law, new media communication, cyber culture, intellectual property protection, and network integration. Li is in charge of a key cross-discipline subject in Beijing on Internet governance and is the chief editor of a national key book series on Internet governance and cyber law. He is the executive director of the Beijing Communication Legal System Research Board, a member of China's Service Trade Professional Committee, a member of the Online Game Expert Committee of the Ministry of Culture, and an International Cooperation Expert with the Ministry of Science and Technology. Li has also been a visiting scholar in the UC Berkeley School of Law.

Ye Zheng is a senior colonel in the Chinese People's Liberation Army. He is the senior research scientist and Ph.D. advisor in the PLA Academy of Military Science and a member of the PLA consultation Committee for Strategic Planning and a member of China Association for Military Science. He is the author of numerous monographs and papers on contemporary topics in military strategy and international relations. His books, *On Informationalized Warfare*, *Science of Army Campaigns*, and *Information Warfare Course*, were published by the Beijing Military Science Publishing House.

ABBREVIATIONS

2/PLA	PLA GSD Second Department, Intelligence Analysis
3/PLA	PLA GSD Third Department, Signals Intelligence
4/PLA	PLA GSD Fourth Department, Electronic Warfare
APT	advanced persistent threat
ATM	automatic teller machine
BNCC	Beijing North Computing Center
C4ISR	command, control, communication, computers, intelligence, surveillance, and reconnaissance
CCP	Chinese Communist Party
CDF	cumulative distribution function
CDSTIC	China Defense Science and Technology Information Center
CIA	US Central Intelligence Agency
CILG	Cybersecurity and Informatization Leading (Small) Group
CMC	Central Military Commission
CNA	computer network attack
CNCERT/CC	Chinese National Computer Network Emergency Response Technical Team and Coordination Center
CND	computer network defense
CNE	computer network exploitation
CNITSEC	China Information Technology Security Evaluation Center
CNNIC	China Internet Network Information Center
CNO	computer network operations
COMINT	Communications Intelligence
CSIS	Canadian Security Intelligence Organization
CSDN	China Software Developer Network
DDoS	Distributed Denial of Service
EEA	US Economic Espionage Act of 1996
ECM	Electronic Countermeasures
ELINT	Electronic Intelligence

EU	European Union
EW	Electronic Warfare
FBI	US Federal Bureau of Investigation
GAD	PLA General Armament Department
GDP	gross domestic product
GSD	PLA General Staff Department
HUMINT	human intelligence
IAD	information analysis and dissemination
IANA	Internet Assigned Name Authority
ICANN	Internet Corporation for Assigned Names and Numbers
ICT	information and communication technology
ID/CCP	Investigation Department of the Central Committee of the Chinese Communist Party
IDAR	Introduce, Digest, Assimilate, Re-innovate
INEW	integrated network electronic warfare
IP	intellectual property or Internet protocol
ISP	internet service provider
IT	information technology
LSG	Leading Small Group
MIIT	Ministry of Industry and Information Technology
MLP	Medium- and Long-Term National Science and Technology Development Program (2006–20)
MLPS	multilevel protection scheme
MPS	Ministry of Public Security
MSS	Ministry of State Security
MUCD	military unit cover designator
NGO	nongovernmental organization
NISEC	National Information Security Engineering Technology Center
NSA	US National Security Agency
NTLM	Windows NT Local Area Network Manager
PLA	Chinese People's Liberation Army
PLAAF	Chinese People's Liberation Army Air Force
POS	point of sale
PRC	People's Republic of China
RAT	Remote Access Tool
R & D	research and development
RDA	research, development, and acquisition
RMB	renminbi (China's currency)
SASTIND	State Administration for Science, Technology, and Industry for National Defense

S & T	science and technology
SCADA	Supervisory Control and Data Acquisition
SCO	Shanghai Cooperation Organization
SIGINT	signals intelligence
SIIO	State Internet Information Office
SILG	State Informatization Leading (Small) Group
SNISCG	State Network and Information Security Coordination Group
SOE	state-owned enterprise
SVM	support vector machine
TRB	Technical Reconnaissance Bureau
UK	United Kingdom
USD	United States dollar
USITO	US Information Technology Office
XUAR	Xinjiang Uyghur Autonomous Region

China and Cybersecurity

CHAPTER 1

Introduction

China and Cybersecurity: Controversy and Context

JON R. LINDSAY

The information revolution has been a mixed blessing for China and the world. On one hand, computer networks have enhanced economic productivity, national security, and social interaction. In 2009 alone the Internet contributed to 2.6% of gross domestic product (GDP) growth in China and 3.8% in the United States. The Internet contribution to GDP growth from 2004 to 2009 averaged 21% for mature industrialized countries like the United States and Germany and a more modest 3% for high-growth industrializers like China and India, which suggests that the Internet is poised to become even more important as China matures.[1] China has leveraged information technology to integrate its firms into the global economy and modernize its infrastructure, and increasing Internet penetration has helped to boost export-led growth.[2] China's pursuit of "informatization" is not only remaking industrial sectors but also guiding the transformation of the Chinese People's Liberation Army (PLA) from a backwards conscript force into a formidable regional power. China has one of the fastest growing Internet populations in the world with 600 million users or "netizens" as of 2013, a quarter of them from rural regions.[3] To the degree that civil society exists in China at all, it exists on the Internet, even as the government censors content online. By 2012 nearly a quarter of the global Internet population (23%) was in China, more than double the next largest Internet nation, the United States (10%), and more than the entire

European Union (15%).[4] Cyberspace continues to be an important enabler of China's emergence as a great power in the twenty-first century.

On the other hand, the cutting edge of technology is a double-edged sword. Valuable information infrastructure and the data stored on it are lucrative targets for thieves, spies, and soldiers. Estimates of losses to financial theft and fraud online range from the absurdly high (a trillion dollars a year worldwide) to the more plausible (tens of billions of dollars per year). The losses are considerable in any case, even if they amount to only a fraction of the Internet's overall contribution to productivity.[5] Losses to espionage are much harder to estimate. The theft of intellectual property or negotiating positions can impose direct costs on competitiveness, and organizations pay indirect costs to defend against theft and reassure customers. Political espionage imposes even more intangible military and diplomatic costs, for it can be invaluable in a crisis or merely one policy input among many. China, like many other advanced industrial states, is both the source and target of extensive cyber exploitation, which includes financial crime and espionage. More destructive cyberattacks against critical infrastructure remain rare, thankfully. The only significant case so far is the disruption of Iranian uranium enrichment, allegedly by the United States and Israel.[6] Nonetheless, many strategists in China and the West foresee worse dangers on the horizon. Even as cyber technology creates prosperity, it facilitates cybercrime, espionage, and, potentially, cyberwarfare.

Political discourse on cybersecurity in English-speaking countries has recently been dominated by the pessimists. President Barack Obama writes that "the cyber threat to our nation is one of the most serious economic and national security challenges we face."[7] This growing worry about the vulnerability of cyberspace to espionage or disruption is motivated to no small extent by concerns about China's economic and military development. As reported in the *Washington Post*, a National Intelligence Estimate from early 2013 described China "as the country most aggressively seeking to penetrate the computer systems of American businesses and institutions to gain access to data that could be used for economic gain."[8] In the United Kingdom, the director-general of MI5 sent a confidential letter to three hundred corporate executives expressing "concerns about the possible damage to U.K. business resulting from electronic attack sponsored by Chinese state organizations, and the fact that the attacks are designed to defeat best-practice IT security systems."[9] Australia barred Chinese telecommunications giant Huawei from bidding on its national broadband network out of concerns that covert "back doors" might be installed.[10] Following shortly thereafter, a US congressional report recommended exclusion of Huawei and ZTE altogether from sensitive systems.[11] Annual reports by the US China Security and Economic Review Committee regularly highlight threats posed by Chinese military development of cyberwarfare capabilities and aggressive cyber exploitation of foreign governments, corporations, and nongovernmental organizations.[12]

Yet Western accounts of this threat tell only one side of the story. Chinese leaders are also quite concerned about cyber insecurity. President Xi Jinping stresses "the importance and urgency of internet security and informatization" and describes the dual goals of security and development as "two wings of a bird and two wheels of an engine. . . . No internet safety means no national security. No informatization means no modernization."[13] Xi's predecessor, Hu Jintao, observed during a keynote address to the Eighteenth Communist Party National Congress, "We should attach great importance to maritime, space, and cyberspace security."[14] Chinese authors frequently note that China is also a victim of foreign cyberattacks, predominantly from the United States, citing staggering statistics of tens or hundreds of thousands of attacks and compromised machines per month. The director of China's National Computer Network Emergency Response Technical Team and Coordination Center (CNCERT/CC) asserted, "We have mountains of data, if we wanted to accuse the U.S., but it's not helpful in solving the problem."[15]

To a Chinese audience, American allegations of cyber threats from China often sound like "a thief crying stop thief."[16] Documents leaked to the press by former US intelligence contractor Edward Snowden provided dramatic public evidence that Western intelligence services were penetrating Chinese networks aggressively. Some of Snowden's documents suggest that the National Security Agency (NSA) burrowed into the Shenzhen headquarters of Huawei in order to exploit the routers and switches used by a third of the world's Internet population.[17] These revelations created considerable resentment in China in light of earlier American and Australian allegations of Huawei collusion with Chinese intelligence. Furthermore, Chinese government agencies and corporations rely heavily on technology from American firms like Microsoft and Intel, and some Internet infrastructure like the Internet Corporation for Names and Numbers (ICANN) is located on American soil. This dependency feeds a sense of vulnerability in China, and development of cyberwarfare capacity by the United States only exacerbates the fear. Indeed, some of the most sophisticated malware discovered to date, such as the Stuxnet and Flame infections of computers in the Middle East, appears to have been developed in American labs.[18] According to a scholar at the China Institute of Contemporary International Relations, "the United States holds the power of determining anyone's life or death in cyberspace, and has the capability of dominating cyber information."[19] Chinese observers perceive American cyber behavior to be hypocritical, unfair, and reckless.

As rhetorical accusations and computer attacks flow back and forth across the Pacific, cybersecurity becomes a source of diplomatic mistrust.[20] The growing preoccupation with cybersecurity in large and influential countries like the United States and China reflects both their deepening dependence on shared global information infrastructure and their growing willingness to exploit it for political or economic gain in competition with one another. Future frictions between China and other nations are inevitable as technological progress, pursued on economic grounds, offers new ways and means, both subtle and overt, for sovereign states to enhance their prosperity and security. Nevertheless, a state's choices in the pursuit of wealth and power are constrained by domestic politics, historical choices, and cultural viewpoints. Failure to understand or acknowledge these constraints can heighten the potential for mistrust and miscalculation.

BEYOND THE HEATED RHETORIC

This book investigates how China both generates and copes with Internet insecurity through close attention to its domestic institutions and processes. An exploration of China, a critical case it its own right, also presents an opportunity to examine the effect of cybersecurity on politics more generally. In a discussion all too prone to hype and exaggeration, empirical perspectives—and multiple perspectives—are sorely needed.

There are many obstacles to a clear understanding of cybersecurity in general. Secrecy surrounds the nature and extent of cyber operations conducted by governments and nonstate actors alike. Because cyber exploitation depends on deception—hackers misuse machines for purposes other than intended and take advantage of the trust of gullible users—perpetrators are loathe to advertise their activity.[21] Meanwhile the victims often withhold evidence of intrusion in order to protect reputations (Mandatory disclosure requirements levied by regulators such as the Securities and Exchange Commission can alleviate this problem somewhat but not completely.). Beyond the paucity of facts, however, a greater problem is how to interpret the facts when they do become available, particularly in the case of China. The strategic significance of the information revolution and the rise of China are both topics of tremendous debate among scholars. Technological optimists believe that the Internet improves democracy while pessimists fear that cyber conflict is inevitable. Political optimists believe China's growth deepens global liberalism, while pessimists fear a resurgence of great power conflict. Given uncertainty and disagreement about both of these trends, it is almost inevitable that there is confusion and controversy about their intersection.

Specialists in the interdisciplinary fields of cybersecurity and China studies make different assumptions about which factors are important and how they should be studied. There is a large technical literature on computer network security, as well as an emerging discussion of the economic incentives and market failures that shape the problem.[22] Unfortunately, the international political context is often lost in the focus on technology and crime. In the security studies subfield of international relations there are only a few university press publications on cybersecurity, but most neglect economic themes. Likewise, defense policy analysts have directed more effort to the problem of large-scale disruption of critical infrastructure rather than long-term cyber espionage campaigns.[23] Few titles on cybersecurity focus on China in any depth, or they focus on only one aspect of the problem.[24] Studies of Chinese military modernization often discuss cyberwarfare in the broader context of China's "informatization" strategy, but they usually have little to say about civilian cybersecurity policy or civil-military integration in China, even though most of the relevant technology is created and used by civilians.[25] In the China studies field, examinations of the effects of new media tend to focus on its ability (or inability) to promote democracy and civil society, or the extent of state censorship and control efforts.[26] This addresses only a subset of the cybersecurity problem, overlooking its industrial and strategic dimensions. Studies of China's information technology sector assess its innovativeness and developmental obstacles, but they tend to neglect cybersecurity as an area of innovation in its own right or Chinese innovation policy as an influence on cybersecurity.[27] There is vibrant discussion about cybersecurity in openly available Chinese-language sources, but this has been relatively inaccessible to Western audiences.

This volume aims to fill literature gaps in both cybersecurity and China studies. It brings together contrasting perspectives in order to sensitize scholars and policymakers to the alternative interpretations that are available. Much like cybersecurity itself, this book is a thoroughly interdisciplinary and international endeavor. Seven of our authors hail from China and have expertise in computer science, economics, or public policy. The other authors are from the United States, Canada, or the United Kingdom, and they have spent considerable time working and studying in China or have an expertise in cybersecurity. Their contributions to this volume highlight Chinese perspectives on cyberthreats and policies, often missing in English-language treatments, and provide empirical and evaluative depth. The result is an integrated and comprehensive analysis of China and cybersecurity. Importantly, however, our contributors do not always agree with one another. As Li Yuxiao and Xu Lu stress in their chapter, it is important for Chinese and Western academic experts to study this topic together, even when they do not agree on everything, in order to improve trust and understanding in an area of great mutual concern. While this volume cannot hope to have the final word on this topic, it does aim to advance a productive dialogue.

Early versions of many chapters were first presented in 2012 in La Jolla, California, during a pair of conferences sponsored by the University of California Institute on Global Conflict and Cooperation and the United States Naval War College. Lively discussions among the participants revealed multifaceted problems that resisted simple interpretation. In China as in other countries, complicated economic trade-offs and fragmented regulatory systems give rise to inconsistent policies and uneven enforcement. China has invested considerable resources into controlling political content through Internet filtering and monitoring, but ironically, it has neglected network security against predation by financially motivated Internet criminals and other hackers. While there is increasing evidence that state-sponsored espionage from China is on the rise, its economic impact on strategic competition remains more uncertain. For good reasons, both Chinese and Western policymakers distrust one another's accounts of the true scope of their activities and intentions in cyberspace. Thus there is no one single Chinese view on cybersecurity or cyberwarfare, just as there is no one Western view. These debates continue to evolve.

The remainder of this introduction provides an overview of Chinese national policy and institutions for managing cybersecurity. It then summarizes the organization of this volume and the content of its chapters. As will become apparent, cybersecurity is shaped by the strategic interaction of many different actors and defies any simple interpretation or morality tale.

CHINA'S CYBERSECURITY SYSTEM

The promise and peril of cyberspace is a function of its ubiquity. Nearly every type of government agency, commercial firm, and social organization benefits from information technology and might be harmed to some degree through its abuse. A large and heterogeneous set of actors have a stake in any cybersecurity policy, but they often have very different political interests. Commercial firms use networks to enhance trade, expand market share, and catalyze innovation. Intelligence agencies exploit the Internet for surveillance of foreign and domestic threats. Civil society groups press for open networks and online privacy protection. Militaries seek opportunities to disrupt an adversary's command-and-control systems while protecting their own. Users want easy access to news, entertainment, and shopping. All of this diversity creates tangled policy trade-offs and collective action problems. Cyber defense is challenging, in part, because of failure among stakeholders to agree on adequate technical standards and protocols, or to persuade network managers to implement agreements, or to raise Internet hygiene levels among millions of users. The complexity of intra- and intergovernmental relations in any advanced industrial nation complicates efforts to define and enforce cybersecurity policy. China is no exception, and its idiosyncratic domestic politics only exacerbate the challenges.[28]

China has a centralized one-party government, but in practice it is fragmented functionally and regionally. The Politburo of the Chinese Communist Party (CCP) is led by an elite subset known as the Standing Committee (currently seven members). The CCP defines policy guidance through a system of issue-specific "Leading Small Groups" that may or may not meet regularly. The membership of Standing Group elites in any given group is a measure of its importance. The State Council, staffed by Politburo members at the senior levels, runs China's sprawling state bureaucracy. It is responsible for implementing policy, regulating state-owned enterprises and commercial industry, and carrying out day-to-day government operations. The PLA, China's large and modernizing military, is subordinate to the Party rather than the state and is a powerful political entity in its own right. Senior Chinese leaders often hold multiple positions in these various organizations or on the coordinating committees that span them. Furthermore, China's provincial governments enjoy substantial de facto autonomy and compete among one another for patronage from CCP elites. Chinese cybersecurity policy must be understood within this context. The speed of technological innovation in cyberspace is considerably faster than the speed of policy coordination in China, as in any other country. Yet the considerable complexity and lack of transparency in the Chinese system complicates the usual challenges of defining and implementing national cyber policy.[29]

A number of Leading Small Groups touch on cybersecurity, such as those dealing with national security, politics and law, science and technology, etc. After the Eighteenth National Party Congress, Xi Jinping (chairman of the Central Military Committee, general secretary of the CCP, and president of the Chinese state) consolidated power and began to reorganize parts of the government. This included a new Leading Small Group on cybersecurity (CILG), which will be discussed further below. Prior to 2014, however, the State Informatization Leading Group (SILG) and the State Council Informatization Office had primary responsibility for cyber policy. Formed in 2001, the SILG was chaired by the CCP premier and guided the overall development of China's national information technology infrastructure or "informatization" (*xinxihua*). A SILG subcommittee, the State Network and Information Security Coordination Group (SNISCG), was created to manage security policy in particular. The foundation of China's national cybersecurity policy was a 2003 SILG opinion (known informally as "Document 27") that described a number of initiatives, including a multilevel protection scheme (MLPS) for critical infrastructure, cryptography for trusted systems, information security monitoring systems, crisis management processes, support for research and development in security, definition of technical standards, expanded professional education, and guaranteed funding for implementation. The opinion focused on defensive measures and was silent on offensive uses of cyberspace, much like national cyber policy documents in other countries.[30]

A flurry of more detailed policy guidance and statutory support followed over the next few years elaborating on Document 27's focus areas. However, SNISCG activity appeared to decline after 2008, and State Council oversight was temporarily disbanded as CCP leadership focused on other issues like the Beijing Olympics and the global financial crisis. Yet throughout the next decade, the funding guaranteed by Document 27 enabled the agencies charged with implementation to grow and defend their turf from one another or prospective newcomers. The Chinese information security industry grew significantly from 3.4B RMB in 2003 to 17.9B RMB in 2011.[31] Domestic firms in the information security market include Huawei (secure routers and switches), Venustech (intrusion detection and threat management systems), Qihu 360 (antivirus), Leadsec (firewall), and Westone (encryption).[32] The profitability of these firms does not readily translate into strong cybersecurity for China, however, because of discombobulated oversight from at least six different regulators, including the Development and Reform Commission and the food safety regulator. This has resulted, in the opinion of one Chinese industry analyst, in a "lack of overall planning," the "decentralization of decision-making power," and "lack of adequate communication."[33]

Figure 1.1 depicts the tangle of official institutions that play a role in the management of Chinese cybersecurity policy.[34] At the center of the figure are CCP entities including the new Cybersecurity and Informatization Leading Group (CILG) chaired by Xi Jinping, which likely subsumed SILG and SNISCG in early 2014. The CCP State Secrets Protection Bureau manages all classified information and has been increasingly active in

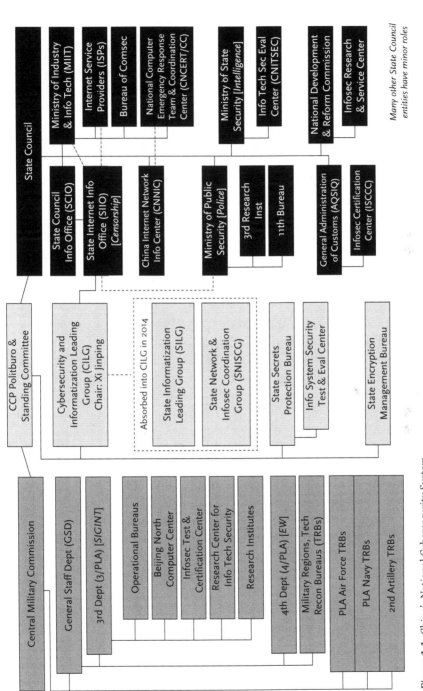

Figure 1.1 China's National Cybersecurity System

Many other State Council entities have minor roles

cybersecurity policy since the 2009 revision of the State Secrecy Law. The CCP State Encryption Bureau is in charge of encryption for the government, military, and industry. Chinese efforts to enforce compliance with indigenous encryption standards—at first demanding access to all foreign commercial encryption codes and later exempting those without encryption as a "core function"—have been a recurring source of friction with foreign firms in China.[35]

Shown on the left side of figure 1.1, the PLA is obviously a crucial player in China's overall cybersecurity system with its responsibility for military signals intelligence (SIGINT) and electronic warfare, but some PLA organs also undertake industrial espionage. Mark Stokes' chapter in this volume describes PLA entities such as the operational bureaus and research institutes of the Third Department of the General Staff Department (the Chinese version of the NSA), the Fourth Department in charge of electronic warfare, and the technical reconnaissance bureaus of the Military Regions and PLA service arms. It is unknown just how well these secretive units coordinate with one another or with their own chain of command. If PLA bureaucratic politics in other arenas is any guide, however, much friction and uncooperative turf protection is likely. The PLA also maintains a network of research universities that perform information security research. These and other Chinese universities may support civilian "cyber militias," which, in the judgment of Robert Sheldon and Joe McReynolds in their chapter, play a more defensively oriented and peripheral role in the PLA's cyber posture. Additionally, the PLA also has some regulatory roles in civilian sectors like transportation that enable it to demand idiosyncratic certification for civilian technologies purchased for those areas.

Most of the sprawling apparatus for managing civilian cybersecurity falls under the State Council on the right side of figure 1.1. The Ministry of Industry and Information Technology (MIIT) housed the administrative offices of the SNISCG, but its influence on overall cybersecurity policy seems to have dwindled since 2008. Notably, the administrative office for the new CILG is not in MIIT, but in the State Internet Information Office (SIIO), which coordinates Internet censorship. Moreover, the Minister of SIIO is a former Secretary-General of the Xinhua News Agency and SIIO vice directors include vice ministers of MIIT and the Ministry of Public Security. These changes highlight the importance of information control, not just technical network defense, in the Chinese notion of cybersecurity. Since the reorganization, SIIO is also referred to as the Cyberspace Administration of China (CAC).[36] MIIT is still important but it now has more of an operational rather than a leadership role. MIIT runs CNCERT/CC, which is responsible for emergency response to serious public computer infections and publishes a yearly report of cyberattacks against China, the source of statistics frequently quoted by officials to highlight Chinese vulnerability.[37] CNCERT/CC works closely with the China Internet Network Information Center (CNNIC), which manages Chinese Internet domain names. MIIT also regulates China's six Internet service providers (ISPs), which in turn are expected to monitor and filter content on their networks according to censorship guidelines established by the State Council Information Office and the SIIO.[38]

A distinguishing characteristic of the Chinese concept of information security (*xinxi anquan*) is that it emphasizes Internet content as much as, if not more than, technical network security (*wangluo anquan*). The siting of the new CILG administrative office in SIIO (i.e., Cyberspace Administration) highlights the importance of this dual notion. By contrast, the more restricted Western notion of cybersecurity emphasizes the technical threats to computer functionality. A former chairperson of the SILG Advisory Committee for State Informatization described information security as "an absolute necessity to ensure sustainable, healthy IT application," "a key component of the national security system," and "necessary for social stability and socialist cultural and ideological development" (i.e., to combat "reactionary, superstitious, violent, and pornographic information" on the Internet).[39] This emphasis has resulted in more focused national effort to build up censorship and surveillance infrastructure (colloquially known as "the Great Firewall of China") than to coordinate technical standards and enforcement mechanisms. As a result China tends to put more coherent effort into defense against the imagined perils of "terrorism, separatism, extremism" than in to defense against economic cybercrime and technical exploitation by foreign intelligence services.

The Ministry of Public Security (MPS) is responsible for investigating computer crimes, primarily through its Eleventh Bureau, and for mandating compliance with the MLPS regime initiated by Document 27. The MPS Third Research Institute conducts information security research through a number of bases such as the National Research Center for Anti-Computer Invasion and Virus Prevention.[40] The Ministry of State Security (MSS), as discussed in Nigel Inkster's chapter, is China's foreign intelligence service. MSS has considerable technical cyber expertise, which it puts to use through the China Information Technology Security Evaluation Center (CNITSEC) to conduct vulnerability testing and software reliability assessment. Notably, Microsoft turned over the source code to its Windows operating system to CNITSEC for review in 2003.[41] It is unknown whether MSS access to Windows code has aided Chinese cyber exploitation activities.

Additional regulatory oversight is vested with the Ministry of Commerce, which regulates import and export technology; the General Customs

Administration, which runs an Information Security Certification Center; the State Asset Supervision and Administration Commission, which oversees state-owned enterprises; the National Development and Reform Commission, and still others yet.[42] Even the General Administration of Sports might need to be consulted in a cybersecurity emergency because it regulates the video game industry![43] As in so many other policy areas in China, executive authority is fragmented across a number of bureaucratic agencies, each with its own requirements. With so many actors jostling for overlapping roles and missions, there is little hope for consistent policy. This inefficiency is passed on in turn to technology firms and users.

Private firms in China must contend with multiple compliance standards and certification requirements, and these are selectively enforced. This creates the potential for China to use security policy to justify technical trade barriers or the harassment of foreign firms. A recurring question for foreign firms in China, and for trade ministries or industry groups dealing with China, is whether ostensible security measures in any given case are actually a cover for protectionist motives. The US Information Technology Office (USITO), the industry advocate for American computer and telecommunications firms in China, concludes that Chinese policies "systematically favor products and services of Chinese companies over those of foreign invested companies . . . in a number of areas ranging from the development of national standards and conformity assessment, to competition policy and local favoritism in government procurement."[44] Not surprisingly, China often levies the same charge against other countries, especially following accusations by the United States and Australia of linkages between Chinese intelligence and Huawei, which both countries used to justify exclusion of the Chinese telecommunications giant from government bids.

After several years of relative neglect, bureaucratic deadlock, and increasing international controversy about cyberthreats, Chinese leaders have recently begun to pay attention to cybersecurity again. In July 2012, the State Council released an opinion updating Document 27. While reiterating familiar themes like the need to improve encryption, expertise, and regulation, it also stressed securing critical infrastructure control systems and Internet user privacy protection. Probably not coincidentally, the previous year saw international media reports of US/Israeli use of Stuxnet against Iran as well as some major compromises of Chinese websites (mentioned in the chapter by Zhuge Jianwei, Gu Lion, Duan Haixin, and Taylor Roberts). The new opinion was candid about the challenges facing China: "the broadband information infrastructure development gap with developed countries has widened; the level of government information sharing and business collaboration is not high; the core technology is controlled by others; . . . insufficient strategy coordination; weak critical infrastructure protection capability; mobile Internet and other technologies pose serious challenges."[45] It is important to recognize that many of these problems are the result of China's tangled system of cyber policy implementation, not a lack of previous guidance.

US-China cybersecurity relations hit a nadir in 2013, galvanizing the attention of senior leaders in both countries. In January major American newspapers accused China of hacking into their computers to harass reporters and obstruct reporting about Chinese officials.[46] In February the cybersecurity firm Mandiant published a major exposé on Chinese economic espionage, implicating a specific PLA unit in Shanghai.[47] US officials ramped up the rhetorical pressure by "naming and shaming" the Chinese state for its support of cyber espionage. Then in dramatic fashion, Edward Snowden took the wind out of their sails. After leaking highly classified documents about NSA cyber espionage programs to journalists, Snowden fled to Hong Kong in June, where he gave an interview to local reporters alleging that the NSA had hacked Chinese universities, telecommunications firms, and submarine cables. The revelation of extensive NSA surveillance via US Internet firms (described in China as "Prism-gate" after the name of one of the compromised NSA programs) undermined in one stroke Washington's efforts to take the moral high ground against Chinese espionage and American firms' efforts to cultivate a reputation for independence from Washington. Moreover, the Snowden bombshell dropped just days before Xi Jinping's first meeting as president of China with President Obama, stealing media headlines from a carefully orchestrated event. Further Snowden revelations, culminating in allegations of deep penetrations by the NSA into Huawei, reinforced Chinese bitterness over American espionage, even as media reporting of Chinese espionage dwindled (both because senior Chinese leaders clamped down on PLA activity after the Mandiant report and Western journalists became more interested in reporting on the Snowden files).[48] American attempts to articulate the difference between the political-military targets of US cyber espionage and the economic targets of Chinese espionage, or between Internet control as practiced by China and metadata collection as practiced by the NSA, have tended to fall on deaf ears.[49]

With US-China cybersecurity tensions mounting and with Xi Jinping seeking to tighten the reins on Party discipline, official Chinese media announced the creation of the CILG in February 2014. The CILG is chaired by Xi Jinping with Premier Li Keqiang and Standing Committee member Liu Yunshan as vice chairs, with nineteen other Politburo or ministerial-level officials as members (table 1.1). It is potentially notable that ten of the eleven Politburo members are also on Xi Jinping's new Leading Group for the Comprehensive Deepening of Reform, an indication that the new Chinese president sees cybersecurity as an important aspect of consolidating CCP authority in the wake of internal corruption scandals and tense relations with the United States.[50]

Cybersecurity has become a major concern of the Chinese government and commands the attention of its most senior leaders. Yet by the same token it requires coordination across a vast and complex policymaking apparatus, a daunting task in the best of conditions. National cyber policy in any country must balance the competing goals of national security, law enforcement, and industrial regulation in an international market context of rapid technological change. China's attempt to police the content

---

Table 1.1 CYBERSECURITY AND INFORMATIZATION LEADING GROUP

Leadership

Chair: Xi Jinping (Central Military Commission Chairman, CCP general secretary, PRC president)

Vice-Chair: Li Keqiang (premier)

Vice-chair: Liu Yunshan (Standing Committee, Central Party School president)

Politburo and senior leaders

Ma Kai (vice-premier)

Wang Huning (Central Policy Research Office, director)

Liu Qibao (Central Propaganda Committee, director)

Fan Changlong (Central Military Commission, vice-director)

Meng Jianzhu (Central Political-Legal Committee, secretary)

Li Zhanshu (Central Committee General Office, director)

Yang Jing (Central Secretariat, secretary)

Zhou Xiaochuan (governor of the People's Bank of China)

Ministries involved in cybersecurity policy implementation

CILG office director: Lu Wei (SCIO vice-director and SIIO/CAC director)

Guo Shengkun (minister of public security)

Fang Fenghui (chief of the PLA General Staff)

Wang Yi (minister of foreign affairs)

Xu Shaoshi (National Development and Reform Commission, director)

Yuan Guiren (minister of education)

Wang Zhigang (Ministry of Science and Technology, secretary)

Lou Jiwei (minister of finance)

Miao Wei (minister of industry and information technology)

Cai Wu (minister of culture)

Cai Fuchao (State Administration of Press, Publications, Radio, Film, and Television director)

---

of the Internet while seeking to promote Internet-led growth makes this difficult balancing act even harder. Elite attention makes it more likely, ironically enough, that bureaucratic friction in the everyday administration of policy will continue, adding to the inefficiency of China's cyber defenses.

ORGANIZATION OF THE VOLUME

The chapters in this book are organized into four parts to explore different facets and implications of China's cybersecurity system. The first part examines Chinese network exploitation activity, including state intelligence gathering, economic espionage, internal political control, and economic cybercrime. The second part focuses on the PLA in particular, exploring Chinese strategy and doctrine, PLA cyber operations organizations, and PLA leverage of civilian militia. The third part presents Chinese and American perspectives on the challenges of developing and coordinating domestic and international cyber policy. The fourth includes chapters on US cyber policy in reaction to Chinese activity and on the general theoretical implications of this work.

Espionage and Cybercrime

Convincing evidence is now available that China is actively involved in cyber espionage against Western economic and diplomatic targets. The precise affiliation of espionage actors within the state is often less clear. Cyber exploitation can potentially be conducted by private for-hire organizations, the PLA, or by other Chinese intelligence services. The chapter by Nigel Inkster, a thirty-year veteran of the British Secret Intelligence Service, examines Chinese intelligence services and their adaptation to cyberspace, providing background on Chinese tradecraft and targeting prior to the cyber era. Inkster then examines how traditional Chinese intelligence tradecraft has adapted to the opportunities and challenges of the Internet. China's capacity to undertake large-scale cyber exploitation operations represents a step change in capabilities. Cyber collection eliminates much of the risk associated with traditional techniques, provides much greater reach, and has massively increased the quantities of information that can be collected. However, it remains to be seen what practical advantage China will be able to derive from the information it collects or how great its ambitions will be in terms of using it cyber collection as an adjunct to aggressive human intelligence (HUMINT) operations. The Ministry of State Security in particular has been adapting cyber means to work against the "three evils" of "separatism, terrorism, and extremism." Western groups and governments seen as supportive of dissident Chinese organizations can also expect to be targeted, as Sarah McKune details further in her chapter.

The chapter by Jon Lindsay and Tai Ming Cheung places industrial espionage in the broader context of the Chinese national innovation system. General Keith Alexander, former commander of US Cyber Command and director of the National Security Agency, has described the hemorrhage of economic secrets as the "greatest transfer of wealth in history."[51] However, the connection between espionage and state power in the international system is poorly understood. It is one thing to measure aggressive "advanced persistent threat" (APT) activity and to gather evidence of Chinese responsibility, but quite another to infer that this activity produces productivity gains of any consequence. Lindsay and Cheung present a model of the acquisition, absorption, and application of illicitly gathered foreign expertise and use it to examine Chinese APT trends, the ability of China's defense economy to digest foreign information, and the challenges China faces turning it into competitive advantage. Cyber espionage is not necessarily an easy shortcut to innovative excellence and may even lead China to become overly dependent on foreign expertise.

As Chinese commentators often and rightly point out, China is indeed a victim of cybercrime. The criminal online economy in China is unique in many aspects because of differences between Chinese economy, laws, and language, and those in other countries. National differences in patterns of cybercrime have not received enough attention in research on the economics of information security. The chapter by Zhuge Jianwei from Tsinghua University and coauthors Gu Lion, Duan Haixin, and Taylor Roberts provides the first empirical assessment of online underground markets on two popular social Chinese websites, Baidu and Tencent QQ. Their analysis covers eight years of data on black markets that have been built on the largest Chinese web forum and microblog chat groups. Drawing on familiarity with Chinese hacker jargon, they identify the primary profitable value chains, business model implementation techniques, and roles of different participants. Their study presents the first attempt to systematically estimate the overall damage rendered by the Chinese underground economy online, based on their own measurements and reports from security vendors and the Chinese government. According to the authors, authorities could improve their performance against the underground economy by monitoring black markets and enhancing cooperation between information security communities and law enforcement.

While crime and espionage account for the majority of actual threats detected in cyberspace, more dismal scenarios of cyberwarfare have captured more imaginations. Michael McConnell, former director of national intelligence under President George W. Bush, claims that "cyber-war mirrors the nuclear challenge in terms of the potential economic and psychological effects."[52] The chapter by PLA senior colonel (equivalent to the Western rank of brigadier general) Ye Zheng presents his perspective on the nature of cyberwarfare and how to avoid it. According to Ye, a strategist with the Chinese Academy of Military Science, the development of cyberwarfare has been driven by the United States and emulated by other countries. "As nuclear war was the strategic warfare of the industrial age," Ye writes, "cyberwarfare will be the strategic warfare of the information age." Therefore China must develop cyber capabilities in order to protect itself from the destabilization initiated by the United States. Ye describes five types of cyber combat operations and illustrates each of them with examples. He then articulates philosophical principles to help nations avoid cyberwarfare, arguing that most important thing is to extend the notion of sovereignty into the domain of cyberspace. Ye's normative prescriptions anticipate the discussion in the chapters by Li Yuxiao and Xu Lu and by Fred Cate of international Internet governance. The chapters by Cate and McKune both point out that there is some East-West controversy about how best to govern the cyber commons, in particular regarding how norms of "Internet sovereignty" might affect the legacy "multistakeholder" regime.

One interesting thing about kinetic cyber disruption is that there is little evidence of it in the historical record. Stuxnet and a few other reported instances of military cyber operations (mostly by the United States) might suggest the shape of things to come, or they may be outliers. In any case, visions of intense cyberwarfare remain unrealized for now. Without history as a guide, strategists must rely on assumptions about the nature of technology and future war to guide the development of military doctrine. The chapter by Kevin Pollpeter examines contemporary Chinese thinking about military cyber strategy and coercion. Drawing on extensive primary source material, Pollpeter reveals a strong consensus in China that cyberwarfare will play an important and potentially decisive role in any future conflict. Chinese thinkers emphasize the importance of integrating cyber operations into peacetime as well as wartime military operations, focusing on civilian as well as military targets. So far, known PLA operations have been limited to nonlethal cyber exploitation. However, the PLA's emphasis on the importance of striking first with cyberattacks and paralyzing enemy command and logistics systems could inadvertently provoke a rapid escalation during a militarized crisis. While Chinese authors are enthusiastic about the coercive and deterrent promise of cyber weapons, Pollpeter finds that they have not paid as much attention to the potential for destabilizing miscalculation.

Ideas about cyber or any other kind of warfare have to be implemented in an actual organization. Mark Stokes assesses what can be learned from openly available Chinese sources about the PLA's bureaucratic infrastructure for cyber operations. He identifies key PLA facilities and attempts to glean command-and-control arrangements for cyberwarfare, including the functional specializations of various units and their ability (or inability) to coordinate across bureaucratic lanes. There is far more information available about the PLA General Staff Third Department, which conducts cyber reconnaissance, than about parts of the PLA that may be responsible for more disruptive cyber operations, such as the Fourth Department. The PLA is an enormous and complicated organization with uneven levels of competency in its ranks. While Chinese ideas about cyberwarfare may be quite ambitious, the organizational ability of the PLA to plan, integrate, and adapt its cyber operations amid the uncertainty and tension of actual combat is another question entirely. If US experience with the limits of "network-centric warfare" doctrine in the quagmires of Iraq and Afghanistan offers any guide, there may be a considerable gap between ideas about future war and the reality of actual warfare.[53]

The specter of cyberwarfare remains far off, thankfully, but there are still lesser, yet more frequent, forms of disruption in Chinese cyberspace. There have been a number of episodes of nationalist outbursts or "hacker wars" featuring website defacements and temporary denial of service attacks (DDoS attacks are created by flooding a server with requests from thousands of human users or automated botnets). These online flare-ups have occurred during tensions between Taiwan and the mainland between 1996 and 2004 in the wake of Taiwanese elections; between the United States and China following the 1999 bombing of the Belgrade Chinese embassy and in 2001 after the US EP-3 spy plane collision; and between China and Japan throughout the past decade over controversy about Yasukuni shrine visits and the Senkaku/Diaoyu island disputes.[54] The prevalence of "hacktivism" leads some to worry that a vast network of PLA "cyber militias" might someday wage an Internet version of Maoist People's War. The chapter by Robert Sheldon and Joe McReynolds begins by highlighting the myriad ways in which the PLA interacts with civilian society, including industry and academia. They then identify a sample of network warfare militias referenced in Chinese-language sources and analyze their possible roles and missions, institutional associations and command-and-control relationships, geographic dispersion, and other characteristics. While civilians may be attractive recruits to the PLA if they have more technical expertise than soldiers, the lack of regular PLA chains of command appear to limit the usefulness of militias in wartime. Sheldon and McReynolds conclude that PLA cyber militias play a mostly defensive and peripheral role, yet the nationalist netizen factor in Chinese cyberspace remains a wild card in international politics.

National Cybersecurity Policy

The third part shifts back to China's cybersecurity system and more generally the national strategies and policies that states adopt to mitigate cyberthreats. The chapter by Li Yuxiao, director of the Internet Governance and Law Research Center at the Beijing University of Posts and Telecommunications, and his coauthor Xu Lu provides a Chinese perspective on the cyber challenges confronting the country, the inadequacy of Chinese policy responses to date, and the need for international cooperation to reduce the growing risks. While China has made some progress confronting the rising tide of cybercrime, to include massive outbreaks of "human flesh search" or cyber bullying where netizens collectively defame a victim, Li and Xu argue that serious deficiencies persist. Problems include a lack of consistent focus on cybersecurity by the government, an inadequate legal framework to both facilitate security coordination and protect user rights, imperfect alignment between fast-changing technology and slow-moving policy, and insufficient public education about the risks of cyberspace. Furthermore, Li and Xu argue, because cyberspace is international, international cooperation is essential for improving its safety and reliability. They highlight reasons for mistrust between the United States and China in this area, a situation only worsened by a continuous stream of media reports of systematic spying by each government on the other. Yet like many of the Chinese authors in this volume, they remain optimistic about the future and suggest explores potential ways to improve mutual trust.

Given the notoriety of Chinese Internet control, it is widely but incorrectly believed in the West that China has little meaningful concept of personal privacy or legal protections for it. Xu Jinghong shows that the Internet in China is indeed creating a growing demand for a right to privacy, and statutory support for privacy is slowly improving in response. Xu traces the evolution of the concept of privacy in Chinese discourse from a reference to shameful or embarrassing personal information to a broader concept of personal data, transactions, and opinions. He describes the relevant laws and explores reasons for their emergence and their effectiveness in practice. Privacy is critical for reliable e-commerce and the well-being of vulnerable users, but it is also strained by government imperatives to monitor the population. Xu concludes that the institutional foundations of Chinese cyberspace still have a way to go to catch up with technological progress.

Sarah McKune provides a perspective which contrasts starkly with the previous two chapters. Focusing on the cybersecurity implications of China's human rights record, McKune shows how cyber espionage and Internet policy have been employed as tools of Chinese internal security policy. Her chapter ventures onto controversial terrain insofar as China— like many other states—does not publicly acknowledge that offensive cyber operations have a role to play in its peacetime cybersecurity policy. Moreover, China's police actions against political dissidents and ethnic minorities have drawn criticism from human rights advocacy groups and Western governments, even as that criticism has in turn drawn sharp rebukes from China not to meddle in its sovereign affairs. McKune examines how China justifies cyber espionage through its propaganda on "foreign hostile forces," exemplified in cases of unrest in Xinjiang and protest in Tibet. While this activity has an internal security motivation, the global nature of the Internet has the effect of exporting China's domestic politics to other countries. McKune argues that China generates heightened insecurity in cyberspace by legitimizing politically motivated cyber espionage against Chinese expatriates abroad and foreign media outlets and other organizations. The internationalization of human rights concerns thus becomes problematic in China's calls for greater international respect for sovereignty in Internet governance, highlighting divergent visions of Internet governance.

Practical and Theoretical Implications

The final two chapters reflect on the implications of China's rise as a cyber power for US policy and for the study of international relations. The first of these also seeks to provide a comparative perspective on cybersecurity policy by examining how the other side of the Sino-American relationship has struggled with many of the same issues. Fred Cate describes the legal, political, and economic challenges of cybersecurity in the United States. If Chinese leaders often fail to focus adequately on cybersecurity given an agenda filled with other priorities, American policy on cybersecurity has been a similarly fraught affair. Cate describes the recurring dilemmas and impasses that have met successive attempts to better regulate America's sprawling information infrastructure and the industrial systems that depend upon it, while at the same time contending with idiosyncrasies of US government culture in the formulation and adoption of policy. Moreover, the rise of China is closely related to the emergence of cybersecurity as a pressing concern for US policymakers. Through the past decade, China has been an important factor motivating US cybersecurity policy, but one that pulls in two different ways as policymakers seek, on one hand, to protect American cyberspace from increasingly aggressive activity originating in China and, on the other hand, to maintain and enrich one of America's most important financial, commercial, and diplomatic relationships. Cate points out that in the American case personal privacy has proved to be a lightning rod of controversy for cybersecurity initiatives. The Snowden leaks have had the effect of exacerbating the domestic debate over civil liberties and the bilateral relationship with China.

The concluding chapter by Jon Lindsay and Derek Reveron reflects on the diversity of facts and opinions in these chapters and sketches out some of their strategic implications. They use the case of China to evaluate more general theoretical perspectives in international relations—technologist, liberalist, and realist—on the impact of cybersecurity on world politics. The problem of cybersecurity is wickedly complex, to be sure, abounding with incomplete and contradictory information and subject to change unpredictably as interdependencies develop.[55] The political and economic uncertainties regarding China's rise only complicate the analytical challenge. There is unlikely to be any simple logic leading from Chinese modernization and the technical potential for cyber harm to the profound international political consequences often feared (i.e., a "digital Pearl Harbor" or a "death by a thousand cuts"). The complexity of Chinese domestic politics and international relations is likely to exacerbate the complexity of cyber activity and domestic policy administration, with ambiguous international results. At the same time, the incentives of the anarchic structure of world politics, as well as the economic potential of interdependent networks, will continue to shape cybersecurity behavior.

CONCLUSION

By virtue of the ubiquity of computers throughout modern society, the policy challenges of cybersecurity in any country span problems in industrial regulation, law enforcement, military strategy, and civil society. China's rapid growth injects considerable energy into all of these tensions without providing easily predictable resolution to any of them. This complexity in turn may dull the strategic utility of the cyber instrument while at the same time intensifying the tussles involved in Internet governance. Cybersecurity is not just a technology problem but, more profoundly, a political-economic challenge. Economic incentives guide the buildout of the Internet while political incentives guide its exploitation by states and nonstate actors alike. The study of cybersecurity becomes a lens through which to understand the strategies, economies, and societies that shape it.

Our understanding of these issues has grown considerably since the early conferences that gave rise to this book, but there is still plenty to learn. Almost every month new reports of Chinese or Western cyber exploitation appear in the news or somebody proposes new remedies for cyber perils. Meanwhile Internet technology continues to evolve at breakneck speed because so many people find it so useful. There might seem to be a risk that anything written on this topic would soon become irrelevant. Yet while the details of any cyber policy debate are sure to change, the important structural and cultural influences change more slowly. The contributions in this volume describe how more enduring factors can affect cybersecurity institutions and activity in China. More fundamentally, political and economic incentives shape the invention and use of technology of any vintage. It is important to understand these deeper constraints and dynamics because future innovation is sure to create even more complex challenges and opportunities.

NOTES

1. Matthieu Pelissie du Rausas et al., *Internet Matters: The Net's Sweeping Impact on Growth, Jobs, and Prosperity*, McKinsey Global Institute, May 2011. See also David Dean and Paul Zwillenberg, *Turning Local: From Moscow to Madrid, the Internet is Going Native*, Boston Consulting Group, September 2011.
2. Dan Schiller, "Poles of Market Growth? Open Questions about China, Information and the World Economy," *Global Media and Communication* 1, no. 1 (April 1, 2005): 79–103; James W. Cortada, *The Digital Flood: Diffusion of Information Technology Across the United States, Europe, and Asia* (New York: Oxford University Press, 2012), 443–90; George R. G. Clarke and Scott J. Wallsten, "Has the Internet Increased Trade? Evidence from Industrial and Developing Countries," Policy Research Working Paper, World Bank, February 2004.
3. *Statistical Report on Internet Development in China*, China Internet Network Information Center, July 2013, 3.
4. Derived from the World Bank World Development Indicators, accessed May 2014.

5. Ross Anderson, Chris Barton, Rainer Böhme, Richard Clayton, Michel J. G. van Eeten, Michael Levi, Tyler Moore, and Stefan Savage, "Measuring the Cost of Cybercrime," in *The Economics of Information Security and Privacy*, ed. Rainer Böhme (Berlin: Springer-Verlag, 2013), 265–300.

6. Jon R. Lindsay, "Stuxnet and the Limits of Cyber Warfare," *Security Studies* 22, no. 3 (2013): 365–404.

7. Barack Obama, "Taking the Cyberattack Threat Seriously," *Wall Street Journal*, July 19, 2012.

8. Ellen Nakashima, "U.S. Said to Be Target of Massive Cyber-Espionage Campaign," *Washington Post*, February 10, 2013.

9. Rhys Blakely, Jonathan Richards, James Rossiter, and Richard Beeston, "MI5 Alert on China's Cyberspace Spy Threat," *Times* (London), December 1, 2007.

10. Maggie Lu Yueyang, "Australia Bars Huawei from Broadband Project," *New York Times*, March 26, 2012.

11. Mike Rogers and Charles Albert Ruppersberger III, *Investigative Report on the U.S. National Security Issues Posed by Chinese Telecommunications Companies Huawei and ZTE*, U.S. House of Representatives Permanent Select Intelligence Committee, October 8, 2012.

12. For example, US-China Economic and Security Review Commission, 2012 Report to Congress, November 2012, 147–69. The most thorough study of Chinese cyberwarfare and exploitation capability to date is Bryan Krekel, Patton Adams, and George Bakos, *Occupying the Information High Ground: Chinese Capabilities for Computer Network Operations and Cyber Espionage*, report prepared for the US-China Economic and Security Review Commission by Northrop Grumman Corporation, March 7, 2012.

13. "Xi Jinping Leads Internet Security Group," Xinhua, February 27, 2014, http://news.xinhuanet.com/english/china/2014-02/27/c_133148273.htm.

14. Hu Jintao, Beijing, November 8, 2012, transcript at http://news.xinhuanet.com/english/special/18cpcnc/2012-11/17/c_131981259_10.htm.

15. "China Has 'Mountains of Data' about U.S. Cyber Attacks: Official," Reuters, June 5, 2013.

16. Zhong Sheng, "The United States Bears Primary Responsibility for Stopping Cyber War," *Renmin Ribao Online*, February 7, 2013.

17. David E. Sanger and Nicole Perlroth, "N.S.A. Breached Chinese Servers Seen as Security Threat," *New York Times*, March 22, 2014.

18. Ellen Nakashima, Greg Miller, and Julie Tate, "U.S., Israel Developed Flame Computer Virus to Slow Iranian Nuclear Efforts, Officials Say," *Washington Post*, June 19, 2012.

19. Jiang Yong, "Cyberspace: An Invisible New Domain of Conflict," *Qiushi*, July 1, 2010.

20. Kenneth Lieberthal and Peter W. Singer, *Cybersecurity and U.S.-China Relations*, Brookings Institution, February 2012.

21. Erik Gartzke and Jon Lindsay, "Weaving Tangled Webs: Offense, Defense, and Deception in Cyberspace," *Security Studies* (forthcoming 2015).

22. An excellent textbook on technical cybersecurity is Ross J. Anderson, *Security Engineering: A Guide to Building Dependable Distributed Systems*, 2nd ed. (Indianapolis, IN: Wiley, 2008). Computer scientists and economists, loosely organized through the annual Workshop on the Economics of Information Security, have begun to produce formal models to describe interactions between "black hat" and "white hat" hackers and develop innovative measurement methods on the empirical dynamics and scope of cybercrime.

23. P. W. Singer and Allan Friedman, *Cybersecurity and Cyberwar: What Everyone Needs to Know* (New York: Oxford University Press, 2014); Gregory J. Rattray, *Strategic Warfare in Cyberspace* (Cambridge, MA: MIT Press, 2001); Martin C. Libicki, *Conquest in Cyberspace: National Security and Information Warfare* (New York: Cambridge University Press, 2007); Myriam Dunn Cavelty, *Cyber-Security and Threat Politics: U.S. Efforts to Secure the Information Age* (New York: Routledge, 2008); Chris C. Demchak, *Wars of Disruption and Resilience: Cybered Conflict, Power, and National Security* (Athens: University of Georgia Press, 2011); Derek S. Reveron, ed., *Cyberspace and National Security: Threats, Opportunities, and Power in a Virtual World* (Washington, DC: Georgetown University Press, 2012). Notable US government-funded books on cyber strategy and power include Franklin D. Kramer, Stuart H. Starr, and Larry K. Wentz, eds., *Cyberpower and National Security* (Washington, DC: National Defense University Press, 2009); Martin C. Libicki, *Cyberdeterrence and Cyberwar* (Santa Monica, CA: Rand, 2009); William A. Owens, Kenneth W. Dam, and Herbert S. Lin, eds., *Technology, Policy, Law, and Ethics Regarding U.S. Acquisition and Use of Cyberattack Capabilities* (Washington, DC: National Academies Press, 2009); National Research Council, *Proceedings of a Workshop on Deterring Cyberattacks* (Washington, DC: National Academies Press, 2010).

24. For example, Chinese cyber espionage—but not cyberwarfare or civilian information security—is examined as a component of China's overall technology transfer strategy in William C. Hannas, James Mulvenon, and Anna B. Puglisi, *Chinese Industrial Espionage: Technology Acquisition and Military Modernization* (New York: Routledge, 2013).

25. Evan A. Feigenbaum, *China's Techno-Warriors: National Security and Strategic Competition from the Nuclear to the Information Age* (Stanford, CA: Stanford University Press, 2003); Emily O. Goldman and Thomas G. Mahnken, eds., *The Information Revolution in Military Affairs in Asia* (New York: Palgrave Macmillan, 2004); Tai Ming Cheung, *Fortifying China: The Struggle to Build a Modern Defense Economy* (Ithaca, NY: Cornell University Press, 2009). US military-sponsored works that broach Chinese information warfare include Timothy L. Thomas, *The Dragon's Quantum Leap: Transforming from a Mechanized to an Informatized Force* (Fort Leavenworth, KS: Foreign Military Studies Office, 2009); Roy Kamphausen, David Lai, and Andrew Scobell, eds., *Beyond the Strait: PLA Missions Other Than Taiwan* (Carlisle Barracks, PA: U.S. Army War College Strategic Studies Institute, 2009); Jayson M. Spade and Jeffrey L. Caton, *Information as Power: China's Cyber Power and America's National Security* (Carlisle Barracks, PA: U.S. Army War College Information in Warfare Group, 2012).

26. Yuezhi Zhao, *Communication in China: Political Economy, Power, and Conflict* (Lanham, MD: Rowman and Littlefield, 2008); Guobin Yang, *The Power of the Internet in China: Citizen Activism Online* (New York: Columbia University Press, 2009); Susan L. Shirk, ed., *Changing Media, Changing China* (New York: Oxford University Press, 2010). China is often a focus of studies of government censorship of Internet content; see, for example, Ronald J. Deibert, John G. Palfrey, Rafal Rohozinski, and Jonathan Zittrain, eds., *Access Controlled: The Shaping of Power, Rights, and Rule in Cyberspace* (Cambridge, MA: MIT Press, 2010).

27. Adam Segal, *Digital Dragon: High-Technology Enterprises in China* (Ithaca, NY: Cornell University Press, 2003); Zhou Yu, *The Inside Story of China's High-Tech Industry: Making Silicon Valley in Beijing* (New York: Rowman and Littlefield, 2008); Dan Breznitz and Michael Murphree, *The Run of the Red Queen: Government,*

Innovation, Globalization, and Economic Growth in China (New Haven, CT: Yale University Press, 2011).

28. Johannes M. Bauer and Michel J. G. Van Eeten, "Cybersecurity: Stakeholder Incentives, Externalities, and Policy Options," *Telecommunications Policy* 33, no. 10 (2009): 706–19; Dieter Ernst, *Indigenous Innovation and Globalization: The Challenge for China's Standardization Strategy* (La Jolla, CA: IGCC; Honolulu, HI: East-West Center, 2011).

29. For an overview of intragovernmental politics in China see Shirk, *Fragile Superpower*. On the Politburo organization see Alice Miller, "The CCP Central Committee's Leading Small Groups," *China Leadership Monitor*, no. 26 (September 2, 2008); Alice Miller, "The New Party Politburo Leadership," *China Leadership Monitor*, no. 40 (January 14, 2013).

30. Document 27, "State Informatization Leading Group Opinion on Strengthening Information Security," is apparently classified, but it is frequently referenced in open sources; see "China's National Information Assurance Policy Framework: Ministry of Public Security Multi-Level Protection Scheme," USITO Issue Paper 626, United States Information Technology Office, 2009. Chinese informatization broadly, including but not limited to security, is described by Qu Weizhi, *China's Path to Informatization* (Singapore: Cengage Learning Asia, 2010), 185.

31. Wang Chuang, "Information Security: Policies in the Industry and Growth," China Electronics News, October 9, 2012, http://yjs.cena.com.cn/a/2012-10-09/134974719473439.shtml.

32. *Information Security (IS) Development in China*, Asian Technology Information Program (ATIP), September 18, 2013.

33. Wang Chuang, "信息安全：政策护航 产业壮" [Information Security: Policies in the Industry and Growth], 中国电子报 [*China Electronics News*], October 9, 2012.

34. This chart is a synthetic view drawn from the following sources: *China's Protection for Critical Information Infrastructure Blue Paper*, Information Security Law Research Center, Xi'an Jiaotong University, 2012; Wang, "信息安全"; USITO, *China's National Information Assurance Policy Framework*; "USITO Background and Position Paper—Commercial Encryption," United States Information Technology Office, 2011; *Information Security (IS) Development in China*. Asian Technology Information Program (ATIP), September 18, 2013; Jimmy Goodrich, "The Political Economy of Information Security in China," presentation at the Conference on the Political Economy of Information Security in China, UC San Diego, April 10, 2012; "China Sets Up State Internet Information Office," Xinhua, May 4, 2011; Ronald Deibert, John Palfrey, Rafal Rohozinski, and Jonathan Zittrain, eds., *Access Contested: Security, Identity, and Resistance in Asian Cyberspace* (Cambridge, MA: MIT Press, 2012); Qu, *China's Path to Informatization*; Mark Stokes, chapter 7 in this volume; Liang Fulong, ed., "中央网络安全和信息化领导小组成员名单 12正副国级兼职深改组" [The Central Cybersecurity and Information Leading Group Member List: 12 with National or Deputy National Rank and Also Members of the Deepening Reform Leadership Group], 观察者网 [Guancha.cn], February 28, 2014; Yang Ting, ed., "中央网络安全和信息化领导小组成立：从网络大国迈向网络强国" [The Central Cybersecurity and Information Leading Group Was Established: From a Power to a Leading Nation], 新华网 [Xinhua Net], February 27, 2014.

35. *Blue Paper*, Xi'an Jiaotong University; Goodrich, "The Political Economy of Information Security in China"; USITO, "Background and Position Paper."

36. "China closes 1.8 mln networking accounts in pornography crackdown," *Xinhua*, 20 September 2014.

37. CNCERT/CC homepage, http://www.cert.org.cn.

38. Michael Wines, "China Creates New Agency for Patrolling the Internet," *New York Times*, May 4, 2011; "China Sets Up State Internet Information Office," Deibert et al., *Access Contested*.

39. Qu, *China's Path to Informatization*.

40. *Blue Paper*, Xi'an Jiaotong University; Goodrich, "The Political Economy of Information Security in China"; USITO, *China's National Information Assurance Policy Framework*.

41. "China Information Technology Security Certification Center Source Code Review Lab Opened," Microsoft News Center Press Release, September 26, 2003.

42. *Blue Paper*, Xi'an Jiaotong University; ATIP, *Information Security (IS) Development in China*.

43. Personal communication with a delegate to CSIS-CICIR "Sino-U.S. Cybersecurity Dialogue," Beijing, June 2012.

44. U.S. Information Technology Office, "Written Comments to the U.S. Government Interagency Trade Policy Staff Committee in Response to Federal Register Notice Regarding China's Compliance with its Accession Commitments to the World Trade Organization (WTO)," September 22, 2009.

45. "国务院出台意见推进信息化发展切实保障信息安全" [State Council Opinions on Vigorously Promoting the Development of Information Technology and Effectively Protecting Information Security], 国发 [*Guofa*] 23, July 17, 2012.

46. Nicole Perlroth, "Chinese Hackers Infiltrate New York Times Computers," *New York Times*, January 30, 2013; Nicole Perlroth, "Washington Post Joins List of News Media Hacked by the Chinese," *New York Times*, February 1, 2013.

47. Mandiant, *APT1: Exposing One of China's Cyber Espionage Units*, White Paper, February 2013.

48. According to *M-Trends: Beyond the Breach, 2014 Threat Report*, Mandiant, April 2014, two major Chinese cyber collection teams (APT-1 and APT-12, based in Shanghai and Beijing respectively) took long operational pauses in 2013 and altered their collection infrastructure before resuming exploitation.

49. Kurt Eichenwald, "How Edward Snowden Escalated Cyber War with China," *Newsweek*, November 1, 2013.

50. Liang, "中央网络安全和信息化领导小组成员名单 12正副国级兼职深改组"; Yang, "中央网络安全和信息化领导小组成立: 从网络大国迈向网络强国."

51. General Keith Alexander, keynote address at the American Enterprise Institute, Washington, DC, July 9, 2012.

52. Mike McConnell, "Mike McConnell on How to Win the Cyber-War We're Losing," *Washington Post*, February 28, 2010.

53. Jon R. Lindsay, "Reinventing the Revolution: Technological Visions, Counterinsurgent Criticism, and the Rise of Special Operations," *Journal of Strategic Studies* 36, no. 3 (2013): 422–53.

54. On Chinese nationalist "hacker wars" see Desmond Ball, "China's Cyber Warfare Capabilities," *Security Challenges* 17, no. 2 (2011): 81–103; and Scott Henderson, *Dark Visitor: Inside the World of Chinese Hackers* (Fort Leavenworth, KS: Foreign Military Studies Office, 2007).

55. On "wicked" problems see Horst Rittel and Melvin Webber, "Dilemmas in a General Theory of Planning," *Policy Sciences* 4 (1973): 155–69.

PART I
Espionage and Cybercrime

CHAPTER 2

The Chinese Intelligence Agencies

Evolution and Empowerment in Cyberspace

NIGEL INKSTER

In comparison with other major powers, relatively little has been written about the modern capabilities of the Chinese intelligence agencies. The public consciousness of Western audiences is certainly not infused with dramatic episodes equivalent to the United Kingdom's code-breaking successes against Nazi Germany during World War II or the spy/counterspy narrative that characterized the Cold War. Within China itself there is such a narrative, but it is situated squarely within the context of the anti-Japanese war and the postwar struggle between the Chinese Communist Party (CCP) and the Guomindang (KMT), both campaigns where intelligence played a significant role. This era is amply covered in both academic writings and an increasing array of novels, films, and television series that form part of the CCP's ongoing Patriotic Education Campaign established in the aftermath of the 1989 June 4 Incident.[1] Much less coverage is devoted to China's contemporary intelligence capabilities, in particular in terms of successes in collecting against foreign targets. And there is nothing remotely comparable to the huge expansion in academic writings on all aspects of intelligence that has developed in the West since the end of the Cold War.

The concept of intelligence is, however, well entrenched in Chinese culture dating back to the time of the warring states (c. 475–221 B.C.), when Sunzi's *Art of War* (*Sunzi bingfa*), which deals at length with the subject of espionage, appeared. The role of espionage has also featured in classical literature such as the *Romance of Three Kingdoms* (*Sanguo yanyi*), which offers examples of classic espionage and of deception operations such as Zhuge Liang's empty city strategy. And intelligence undoubtedly played a role in the efforts of successive Chinese dynasties to manage relations with the so-called barbarian nomadic tribes, which throughout history constituted the major external source of threats. But successive Chinese dynasties have always been predominantly inward looking, and foreign intelligence collection as it has become understood in the West has not been a major feature of China's intelligence culture until comparatively recently.

LIMITED FOREIGN COLLECTION

As indicated above, intelligence did play an important part in the Sino-Japanese War and in the subsequent civil war between Mao Zedong's CCP and Chiang Kai-shek's KMT. The Communists in particular achieved some signal successes including the acquisition in 1941 of predictive intelligence on Hitler's invasion of the Soviet Union and Japan's military expansion into the Pacific. During China's civil war from 1945 to 1949, Communist intelligence operations achieved comprehensive penetration of the intelligence organs of a demoralized KMT.[2] But the overwhelming majority of such intelligence was generated from within China; Chinese capacity to collect useful intelligence overseas was limited.

Following the establishment of the People's Republic (PRC) in 1949, China's intelligence community was largely focused on combating perceived security threats from a variety of anticommunist groups and had little scope to engage in overseas collection on its own account. Excepting the then close relationship with the Soviet Union, China's external environment was largely hostile and the perceived threat from Chinese Communist subversion in Asia was a particular cause of international concern. Apart from formal diplomatic relations conducted through its Foreign Ministry, such external engagement as China had was in the form of liaison with fraternal communist parties, conducted via the CCP's International Liaison Department and the cultivation of links with Overseas Chinese diaspora communities and foreign sympathizers, a task undertaken by the CCP's United Front Work Department. Foreign intelligence collection capabilities were constrained by problems of access. China's intelligence officers had limited options for overseas deployments, were conspicuous, and hence easily kept under surveillance. Further, they were primarily reliant on ethnic Chinese sources, few of whom had high-level access in Western countries—and by a risk-averse bunker mentality that saw hostile threats everywhere.

At that juncture the organization primarily responsible for foreign intelligence collection was a Party rather than a state organ. Initially, this was done by the Social Affairs Department then, but since 1955, by the Investigation Department of the Central Committee of the Chinese Communist Party (ID/CCP) (in Chinese, *diaochabu*) while counterintelligence and counterespionage work were situated within a state entity, the Ministry of Public Security (MPS). Much of the ID/CCP's work was focused on dealing with ideological heterodoxy within the Party, and such foreign collection cases as were developed were in the main run by the MPS. These included Larry Wu-Tai Chin, a young interpreter who was infiltrated by the CCP into US government service in China before the establishment of the PRC. Chin went on to join the CIA-controlled Foreign Broadcast Information Service, from where he provided his MPS case officers with a stream of high-grade intelligence on Sino-US relations and related topics until his retirement in 1981. He was subsequently uncovered by a defector in 1985 and committed suicide before being brought to trial.[3] And the early 1960s witnessed the bizarre case of Bernard Boursicot, a young French diplomat serving in Beijing who was recruited through his transgender relationship with Chinese opera star Shi Beipu, a case that formed the basis of the opera *M. Butterfly*—though it should be emphasized that China regards this case, with its lurid sexual dimension and relatively limited intelligence product, as a source of embarrassment rather than a professional battle honor for its intelligence agencies. But these were exceptions during a period in which China became increasingly isolated and self-absorbed, culminating in the period of anarchy and institutional degradation that was the Cultural Revolution (1966–76), during which China's foreign intelligence activities all but ceased.

A slow restoration of normality after 1976 coincided with a gradual opening up to the outside world that had begun with US president Richard Nixon's 1972 visit to Beijing and the establishment of a Sino-US alliance against the Soviet Union. (One consequence of this opening up was the establishment in 1980 of two US-owned and Chinese-manned signals intelligence stations at Qitai and Korla in Xinjiang. The purpose of these stations, which continued operating until the end of the Cold War, was to collect telemetry on Soviet missile tests and space launches and to monitor antiballistic missile and nuclear weapons tests.)[4] The reform and opening-up program initiated by Deng Xiaoping saw the beginnings of a frantic race by China to make up for decades of Maoist obscurantism during which ideological conformity—"redness"—had been prized over any form of technical expertise. Selected foreign companies were invited to begin setting up assembly lines in China, and batches of students began to attend Western academic institutions—with China's minister of state security since 2007, Geng Huichang, one of the early beneficiaries of these programs. This period saw the beginnings of a major, broad-spectrum, overt, and covert collection effort aimed at bridging the gap between China and the developed world that has continued into the twenty-first century and which lies at the heart of, though does not encompass the totality of, China's foreign intelligence collection effort.

CHINA'S CURRENT INTELLIGENCE STRUCTURES

In 1983, a new Ministry of State Security (MSS—in Chinese *guojia anquanbu*, normally shortened to *guoanbu*) replaced the ID/CCP. The MSS combined the external collection functions of the ID/CCP with the counterintelligence and counterespionage functions of the MPS, which became a public order and police organization. The MSS served as both an internal security service and foreign collection organization, but its primary focus has always been on ensuring domestic stability. MSS defector Li Fengzhi has characterized its role as being to "control the Chinese people to maintain the power of the Chinese Communist Party,"[5] and much of the organization's effort both at home and abroad is focused on countering the "Three Evil Forces" of separatism, terrorism, and religious extremism, all seen as posing an existential challenge to the CCP.[6]

The MSS is organized on conventional lines: the First Bureau is responsible for the bulk of overseas collection using a wide range of nonofficial cover officers and casual sources such as students, academics, and businessmen engaged in short-term overseas travel. The Second Bureau is responsible for overseas collection via legal residencies—a relative innovation since the MSS had originally been banned by Deng Xiaoping from occupying cover posts in diplomatic missions—and officers using quasi-official cover as journalists for newspapers such as *Guangming Daily*. The MSS also has bureaus responsible for collection against domestic targets, counterintelligence and counterespionage, technical collection and surveillance, and intelligence analysis. In common with many Chinese ministries, the MSS has its own think tank, the Chinese Institute of Contemporary International Relations, an entity that long predates the formation of the MSS and which is well represented on the international conference circuit.

In addition to the MSS, China's military also has significant foreign intelligence collection capabilities situated in the Second and Third departments of the PLA General Staff (2/PLA and 3/PLA—in Chinese *zongcan erbu* and *zongcan sanbu*). 2/PLA is primarily visible through its global network of defense attachés, who are all cadre 2/PLA officers, selected largely on the basis of their analytical capabilities and language skills and with little if any conventional military training or experience. This global network has focused primarily on collecting and analyzing open-source information and does not appear to engage in covert collection operations out of legal residencies. It is, however, supplemented by a significant covert operational effort conducted via nonofficial cover officers, who have been responsible for some significant successes, particularly in the area of covert collection of high-grade US and Western weapons systems. These include the B-1 bomber, the B-2 stealth bomber, the Quiet Electric Drive submarine propulsion system, and the W-88 miniaturized nuclear warhead.[7]

3/PLA is China's signals intelligence (SIGINT) agency. Until the advent of the Internet 3/PLA operated as a conventional military signals intelligence agency with various collection platforms within China and, since the early 1990s, a gradually increasing overseas presence consisting of a chain of SIGINT stations along the coast of Myanmar, including a substantial facility at Great Coco Island in the Andaman Sea targeting Indian naval capabilities, in Laos, and in Cuba, where since 1998 China has operated SIGINT stations in Bejucal and Santiago de Cuba to collect US telecommunications and US military satellite communications.[8] These facilities have been supplemented by embassy-based SIGINT facilities in Ankara and Baghdad during the First Gulf War and Belgrade during the Kosovo conflict.[9]

3/PLA also has a variety of air- and ship-borne SIGINT collection capabilities. More recently there have been signs that 3/PLA has sought further to extend its reach through joint operations with selected states, a case in point being Indonesia, which has reportedly been using Chinese-supplied equipment to monitor Australian telecommunications and sharing the product with Beijing.[10] But overall very little is known about how 3/PLA operates or how it interfaces with other parts of the Chinese intelligence and policy communities. And, as is equally true of MSS and 2/PLA, there is no publicly available data regarding its budgets and staffing levels. The transformational impact for 3/PLA foreign collection capabilities that has been brought about by the development of cyber exploitation (i.e., cyber espionage and cyber sabotage) will be considered in detail in the sections that follow. Information and electronic warfare and computer network attack, subjects on which a great deal of open-source information is available within China, are the responsibilities of a separate entity, the Fourth Department of the PLA General Staff (4/PLA).

Most national intelligence apparatuses are organized on broadly similar lines, and simply looking at organizational charts offers few useful insights into the operational culture or effectiveness of any such agency, much less the policy impact it is able to exercise. In the case of China's intelligence agencies, operational effectiveness and policy relevance are a function of China's wider bureaucratic and political organization and culture. As previously indicated, the priorities of China's intelligence community strongly reflect the changing nature of China's wider engagement with the outside world.

As a general observation, it is safe to say that the modus operandi of China's intelligence agencies in respect of foreign collection has evolved from one of great caution and risk aversion to one of greater operational self-confidence commensurate with China's rising status and influence in the world. Observation of China's collection efforts in the United States and other Western states since the early 1980s may have taken insufficient account of this wider evolution to the point where counterintelligence services may have been slow to grasp the changing nature of the threat. In particular, it has become conventional wisdom that China's intelligence collection has been a wide-spectrum affair, much of which has not been conducted by the intelligence services—in the words of the Cox Commission, by no means is all Chinese intelligence collection carried out by China's intelligence agencies using traditional espionage techniques.[11] This conventional wisdom holds that Chinese intelligence officers have a strong preference for dealing with Chinese agents and are loath to make intelligence approaches to other nationalities; and Chinese intelligence officers tend to make oblique approaches in which their true affiliations and objectives are not spelled out. All of these observations are—or have been—to varying degrees true, but do not tell the whole story and need to be looked at as a phenomenon that is rapidly evolving rather than remaining static.

Science and Technology Collection

In 1986, China's foreign intelligence requirements in areas of science and technology determined to be key to China's economic development were brought together under Plan 863. This was originally a research and development program proposed to Deng Xiaoping by a group of nuclear weapons scientists that was at first military in focus but quickly morphed into a more general project designed to eliminate Chinese dependence on foreign technologies in areas deemed to be strategic.[12] The impetus to pursue the covert foreign collection element of Plan 863 was intensified following the First Gulf War of 1991 when the Chinese PLA were shocked by the scope and sophistication of US precision weaponry deployed against Saddam Hussein's forces. China quickly discovered that it had a number of assets it could deploy to help it bridge the technology gap. These included first-generation immigrant Chinese scientists such as Los Alamos physicist Wen-Ho Lee, who was accused of having passed to China the technology for the W-88 miniaturized nuclear warhead.[13] Such individuals were susceptible to the proposition that while their mainland compatriots had suffered, they had enjoyed comfortable lives and that this placed on them a moral obligation to assist China, a poor developing country, to catch up with the West.

A variant of the same argument was deployed against non-Chinese scientists and scholars judged to be sympathetic towards China and susceptible to the argument that science should know no boundaries. Apart from the high-profile cases such as that cited above, much Chinese science and technology collection was undertaken at a level just below the radar either by visiting academics and businessmen picking up individual items of information that were not in themselves especially sensitive or compromising, or by skillfully picking the brains of Western scientists visiting China, who could often be persuaded (following generous—and tiring—Chinese hospitality) to go the extra mile in revealing items of information. This was characterized by former FBI assistant director for counterintelligence Dave Szady as the "thousand grains of sand approach." This approach was described in a book written by two Chinese intelligence officers in 1991, the central thesis of which is that the majority of intelligence requirements can be met through an accumulation of open-source material.[14] China was also able to leverage the connections it established through engagement in defense sales undertaken by Chinese defense corporations like Norinco and Polytechnologies for collection purposes. But as time has gone by, it has become evident that at the top level, China's covert science and technology collection has become progressively more focused and professional even as the "noise" of low-grade acquisitions has continued.

Human Source Techniques

Western intelligence agencies aspire to create and nurture clear-cut relationships in which the agent is in no doubt for whom he is working. Financial remuneration generally plays an important part in the relationship irrespective of the agent's original motivation. In the Russian case there is almost a fetish made of "traditional" tradecraft options such as the use of dead letter boxes and dedicated covert communications systems. The ways China's intelligence agencies recruit and run sources differ markedly from the Western tradition and have been set out in detail in David Wise's book *Tiger Trap: America's Secret Spy War with China*, which draws heavily on court records and inputs from members of the US counterintelligence community specializing in China.

In the Chinese case, agent cultivations have often taken place over a prolonged period without explicit mention being made of "intelligence." The emphasis instead has tended to be on the development of friendly relations and discussions of mutual benefit, with Chinese case officers able to leverage a still largely state-run economy to provide business opportunities or assistance to family members as a quid pro quo for assistance. Prospective agents are asked by their case officers to help them achieve a better situational understanding—*liaojie yixie qingkuang*—and classified materials are referred to by the innocuous term *ziliao* (data or material).

The use of euphemism and analogy is, however, arguably no more than a reflection of a culture that lacks the West's Cartesian compulsion to have everything spelled out in exhaustive detail and of a language that lends itself to ambiguity and imprecision. When the need arises or when they are sure of their ground, Chinese intelligence officers can be very direct and explicit and capable of deploying sophisticated tradecraft in the form of cutouts and couriers. They have also proven particularly adept at exploiting the ambiguities in US legislation regarding espionage and the passage of classified materials—the latter not in and of itself a criminal offense—with the result that espionage investigations have often either not come to trial, as in the case of Wen-Ho Lee, or resulted in token sentences for charges not related to espionage, as was the case with MSS/FBI double agent Katrina Leung.[15]

China's intelligence agencies do not appear any longer to have reservations about recruiting non-Chinese assets, as evidenced by cases such as those of US nationals Noshir Gowadia and Glenn Duffy Shriver or the Russian Valentin Danilov, who in November 2012 was paroled after serving ten years of a fourteen-year sentence for selling Russian satellite technology to a Chinese corporation.[16] There has also been growing evidence of a readiness by China's intelligence services to initiate operations outside China. In 2008, an MSS officer was discovered to have recruited a Uighur émigré to report on the activities of Sweden's Uighur population. In 2009, a Chinese espionage network was identified in Munich, run by an MSS officer based in the Chinese consulate. And in 2011, the Taiwan army's director of telecommunications and electronic information was recruited in Bangkok.[17]

Within China, operations against foreign targets have become both more widespread and more blatant. In 2005, a diplomat serving in the Japanese consulate in Shanghai committed suicide following what was described as an attempt at blackmail involving a Shanghai State Security Bureau honey trap. In 2008, an aide to British prime minister Gordon Brown found that his mobile phone was missing after he had spent the night with a young Chinese girl he had met in a Shanghai discotheque.[18]

One area where China's intelligence community has always been relatively less risk-averse has been in terms of its engagement with Chinese diaspora communities with the aim of combating Taiwanese influence and the perceived threat from the "Three Evil Forces." In June 2010, Richard Fadden, the director of the Canadian Security Intelligence Organization (CSIS) made headlines with allegations that municipal officials and cabinet ministers in two Canadian provinces were being influenced by foreign governments, with the clear implication that China was one of these governments.[19] In fact, Fadden was commenting on a phenomenon that had been a subject of concern well before CSIS had come into being and which has been equally evident in other Commonwealth countries with large and well-integrated Chinese diasporas, such as in Australia. The issue of Chinese efforts to exercise influence in diaspora communities raises an important, and for some a dormant, question of how China perceives such communities. In 1955, at Bandung, Premier Zhou Enlai stated that overseas Chinese communities should consider themselves citizens of the countries in which they resided. But this was a statement made at a time when concern about the potential for such communities to serve as a fifth column for communist subversion was high. In fact China's position on nationality, though never clearly defined, has tended more towards *ius sanguinis* than *ius solis*, and is perhaps best exemplified by the widespread use of the term "descendants of the Yellow Emperor"—*yanhuang zisun*.

From a Chinese perspective, engagement in the politics of diaspora communities is seen instinctively as an internal affair. The nature of this instinctive response was apparent in the United Kingdom during the 2001 foot-and-mouth disease outbreak, which urban myth at one point attributed to untreated swill collected from Chinese restaurants. When the Chinese embassy expressed concern about the possible demonization of Chinese restaurateurs, British diplomats took mischievous delight in pointing out that the individuals concerned were almost exclusively British nationals and hence not within the purview of the Chinese Ministry of Foreign Affairs.

Any analysis of the role of intelligence in China's policy community will inevitably come up against the constraint that the workings of China's policy community have been and remain opaque, and this is particularly true when it comes to intelligence. In terms of formal structures, China has no central machinery for assessing intelligence and putting out analyses that reflects an agreed government position of the kind produced by the US National Intelligence Council, the Australian Office of National Assessments, or the UK's Joint Intelligence Committee. The nearest comparable institution is a Party organ, the Foreign Affairs Office of the Central Committee's Bureau of Policy Research. This office looks analytically at reporting received from government agencies and think tanks and offers commentary and requests for clarifications or supplementary information, but does not put out analyses of its own.[20] The General Office of the Chinese Communist Party Central Committee is responsible for distributing reporting to leaders and to government agencies but has no influence on content.

Likewise, until the conclusion of the Third Plenum of the Eighteenth Chinese Communist Party Central Committee in November 2013, China had no mechanism comparable to the US or UK National Security committees. Presidents Jiang Zemin and Hu Jintao reportedly made efforts to establish such a mechanism but were unable to overcome entrenched individual and departmental reluctance to cede or share power. The mechanism for coordinating top-level policy to date has been the Leading Small Group (LSG), which is used to address a range of strategic issues both foreign and domestic. There were eight LSGs in total as of mid-2013, three of which deal with foreign policy and national security. These are the Central Foreign Affairs Work Leading Small Group (*zhongguo zhongyang waishi gongzuo lingdao xiaozu*), the National Security Leading Small Group (*zhongguo zhongyang guojia anquan gongzuo lingdao xiaozu*), and the Taiwan Affairs Leading Small Group (*zhongguo zhongyang duitai gongzuo lingdao xiaozu*). The first two of these are to all intents and purposes the same organization with different titles (in Chinese *liangkui paizi yitao jigou*).

The role of the LSGs is to bring together senior policymakers to debate and provide advice and policy recommendations on major policy issues to China's ultimate decision-making body, the Politburo Standing Committee (formerly consisting of nine and, since 2012, seven members). The LSGs have little by way of executive capacity. In the words of one Chinese academic, "As an informal and ad hoc committee the National Security Leading

Small Group does not operate as the core national security team designated to follow, analyze, and coordinate daily national security. . . . In reality its role is more or less confined to the organization of research and coordination of policies."[21] The composition of Foreign Affairs and National Security Leading Small Groups has not formally been made public, but membership lists that appear in various open-source Chinese-language websites include the departments one might logically expect to find. These include the CCP secretary-general and president as chair, the head of the CCP Propaganda Department; the head of the CCP International Department (formerly International Liaison Department); the Foreign, Defense, Commerce, Public Security and State Security ministers; the state counselor, who is in practice China's most senior foreign policy representative and to all intents and purposes functions as China's national security adviser; the deputy chief of the PLA responsible for military intelligence; and the head of the State Council's Hong Kong and Macao Affairs Office. The LSGs have permanent offices—*bangongshi*—whose role is to provide administrative support, conduct research, prepare policy options for discussion, and play a coordinating role. In the case of foreign affairs and national security, the head of the office that serves both LSGs was until recently State Counselor Dai Bingguo and it is safe to assume that his replacement, State Counselor Yang Jiechi, China's former foreign minister, has assumed the same functions.[22]

Little is known about how the LSGs actually work, what sorts of intelligence feeds are provided to them, and what their policy impacts are. But there are some general underlying trends, which may to varying degrees influence the degree to which intelligence might affect the decision-making process in the foreign policy and national security domains. First, modern China has witnessed a significant growth and diversification of interest groups and centers of power to the point where it has become hard, if not impossible, for China's leadership to maintain full visibility across an ever-broader spectrum and for entities used to exercising control over foreign and security policy to continue doing so. It has become clear from some high-profile incidents such as the 2007 PLA destruction of a low-earth orbit weather satellite via a ballistic missile strike—causing substantial space debris—that the Ministry of Foreign Affairs is not always sighted on decisions taken by other departments that may have a foreign policy dimension.[23] The relative influence of other members of the LSGs is hard to assess, though it seems likely that the Ministry of State Security, whose budget has been significantly increased since the Beijing Olympics, may be on the rise due to the premium placed by Hu Jintao's government on internal stability and security.[24]

The role of the PLA is less clear, though there is little evidence to support contentions that it is either at odds with the Party or forcing it in the direction of a more muscular and assertive foreign policy. Indeed the PLA's role in Chinese politics and policymaking has been on a steady decline since the end of the Mao era. There are no longer any military leaders on the Politburo Standing Committee, and the institutional mechanisms available to the PLA—principally the Central Military Commission and its participation in the LSG process—do not obviously allow for the exercise of disproportionate influence over foreign policy.[25] To the extent that the PLA influences policy, this is largely the consequence of the high degree of operational autonomy it enjoys, which can translate into the creation of facts on the ground. As one Chinese academic has observed, "The challenge by the military to China's national security decision-making does not lie in the PLA's desire to dominate policy-making; nor is such desire evident. Rather it comes from the great autonomy the military has over its own professional and operational details."[26]

The interest of foreign observers was piqued by a brief reference in the record of proceedings of the Third Plenum of the Eighteenth Party Congress to a decision to establish a new entity variously translated as a National Security Committee or State Security Committee; the Chinese term, *guojia anquan weiyuan hui*, admits of both interpretations. Evidence of Chinese interest in the role and functions of the US National Security Council has led to assumptions that this new entity, about whose composition and functions nothing has been made public at the time of writing beyond the top-tier membership of President Xi Jinping, Premier Li Keqiang, and Politburo Standing Committee member Zhang Dejiang, would play a similar role. But as Samantha Hoffman and Peter Mattis have pointed out, there are strong grounds for believing that the primary role of this new entity will be to focus on internal security concerns, reflecting the reality that for China's leadership internal stability is a far more pressing preoccupation than foreign policy.[27] This analysis would seem to be supported by a quote attributed to President Xi Jinping that "ensuring [the Party's] political safety and political power will be the primary tasks facing the National Security Commission." In this context it is important to note that the new committee is a Party organization, and it remains to be seen whether a comparable state entity will be created.[28] PLA senior colonel Gong Fangbin has identified the priorities of the new committee as unconventional security threats including cultural contamination from Western nations, cybersecurity, separatist and extremist forces, ideological struggles, and intertwined traditional and nontraditional security threats. Gong described the role and functions (*zhineng*) of the new committee as somewhere between that of the US National Security Council and its Russian counterpart but tending more towards the latter with a focus on coordination of forces (*liliang xietiao*), deliberating important national security issues, and determining national security policies.[29]

Just as is true in the West, China's decision-makers do not rely exclusively on the intelligence produced by the appropriate national organs for their insights. As any intelligence officer knows, intelligence competes—not always successfully—with other material for the attention of policymakers. But Chinese leaders probably draw to a greater degree than is true of their Western counterparts on numerous alternative sources of advice and information in relationships characterized by varying degrees of formality. Former president Hu Jintao chaired an annual top-level meeting to assess the relative success of China's foreign policy attended by three top academics: Cui Liru, president of the Chinese Institutes of Contemporary International Relations; Wang Jisi of Peking University; and Jin Canrong of Renmin University.[30] It is as yet unclear whether Xi Jinping will follow suit. Every Chinese leader has his or her own preferred academic advisers—though some of those involved in providing foreign policy advice confess to finding it hard to secure adequate face time with a leadership overwhelmingly preoccupied with domestic issues.[31]

China's principal think tanks and some university departments also provide inputs to policymakers on both a pull and a push basis. Among the most influential think tanks are the China Institutes for Contemporary International Relations, which is affiliated to the Ministry of State Security; the China Institute of International Studies, which is affiliated to the Ministry of Foreign Affairs; the Chinese Academy of Social Science, affiliated to the State Council; the Central Party School; and the Chinese Institute for International Strategic Studies, linked to the PLA. Scholars in such think tanks routinely receive intelligence reports.[32] Information is also channeled to leaders from China's state-owned enterprises, some of which have their own private intelligence organizations, and from the burgeoning and ever more influential private sector, with each decision-maker needing to take account of the interests represented by these constituencies within a constantly shifting mosaic of relationships. In sum, it remains the case that, as Michael D. Swaine has observed, "Chinese national security leadership, structures, and processes do not function in a highly integrated, systematic, or formalized manner."[33] Indeed, since that judgment was made in 1998, the context within which China's leadership has to function has become ever more complex and diffuse.

China came relatively late to the Internet, but quickly made up for lost time.[34] Levels of Internet use have risen from just 2 million when the Internet first became publicly available in 1996 to 538 million in mid-2012, accounting for almost a quarter of all global users.[35] The wider strategic implications of information and communication technology (ICT) became equally quickly apparent to Chinese military and strategic thinkers. In 1998 Colonels Liang Qiao and Wang Xiangsui published the groundbreaking book *Unrestricted Warfare* in which inter alia they identified US military dependence on ICT-networked systems as a major vulnerability that China could exploit for asymmetric advantage.[36] That asymmetric advantage has since diminished as China's PLA has itself focused on developing increasingly sophisticated capabilities to meet its current mission of "fighting local wars under informationized conditions."

The PLA has undergone a doctrinal evolution that first linked electronic and cyberwarfare in a concept referred to as integrated network electronic warfare (*wangdian yitizhan*) and has subsequently incorporated information warfare in a concept referred to as "information confrontation"—*xinxi duikang*.[37] The PLA is pursuing a highly ambitious cyberwarfare agenda that aims to link all service branches via a common ICT platform capable of being accessed at multiple levels of command and has created three new departments—Informatization, Strategic Planning, and Training—to bring this agenda into being.

Much has been written within China on the subject of cyberwarfare. By contrast virtually nothing has appeared in print on the subject of cyber exploitation (i.e., cyber espionage) apart from a succession of denials that China is engaged in such activities, accompanied by assertions that China is itself a victim of such activities. But it is this phenomenon more than any other that constitutes a strategic concern for Western policymakers. The early years of the twenty-first century have witnessed a rapid and massive growth in cyber exploitation operations apparently emanating from China, which have targeted the classified systems of governments and major corporations as well as targeting opposition groups such as the Tibetan government in exile. The litany of such attacks is long. It arguably began in 2003 with a series of intrusions of US government and contractor networks collectively referred to by the code name Titan Rain.[38] During 2006–2007 the governments of the United Kingdom, Germany, and New Zealand all publicized details of cyberattacks alleged to have emanated from China, with the director-general of the UK Security Service taking the unprecedented step of writing a letter to three hundred chief executives and security advisers of private-sector corporations alerting them to the threat of cyber exploitation from China.[39] In 2009, the *Information Warfare Monitor* of the Citizen Lab at the University of Toronto's Munk School released a report on the so-called Ghost Net attack against the computer systems of the Dalai Lama, which ultimately infected 1,200 computers in 103 countries.[40] In 2010 Google suffered a sophisticated hacking operation designated with the code name "Aurora," which was apparently designed to access Google's source code as a prelude to accessing the systems of other US corporations. In August 2011, McAfee published the results of an investigation entitled "Shady RAT" into multiple cyber intrusions against the networks of governments, private-sector companies, and international organizations including the United Nations and the International Olympic Committee, which had taken place over the preceding five years.[41] In early 2012, NSA director and head of Cyber Command General Keith Alexander confirmed to the US Senate that China had been behind an attack the previous year on the RSA security system used by companies engaged in classified work for the Pentagon.[42]

A 2009 report prepared by Northrop Grumman for the US-China Economic and Security Review Commission describes in detail some of the more sophisticated operations emanating from China and targeted against US government agencies and private-sector networks. Such operations appear to be the product of detailed and careful reconnaissance aimed at understanding the workings of the network under attack and at undertaking social and professional network analysis to find the most appropriate entry point, normally a "spear-phishing" attack that may be directed against individuals several degrees of separation from the eventual target. (A "spear-phishing" attack involves sending to selected individuals e-mails with attachments containing Trojan viruses that, when activated, provide the attacker with remote access to the target network. In the best spear-phishing operations the e-mails are carefully designed to be consistent with those the intended target would expect to receive in order to maximize the likelihood of their being opened.) The Northrop Grumman team described a division of labor between the breach team, whose job is to gain covert entry to the system, and a separate exploitation team responsible for detecting and exfiltrating the data that is of interest. They observed that "the scale and complexity of targeting associated with this effort suggests that it is probably backed by a mature collection management bureaucracy able to collate and disseminate collection priorities to diverse teams of operators, intelligence analysts, and malware developers. These individuals are likely to be a mix of uniformed officers, military personnel, civilian intelligence operatives, and freelance high-end hackers."[43]

Both Western governments and entities involved in investigating episodes of cyber espionage have been cautious about unequivocally laying such activities at China's door on the grounds that in the cyber domain, where identities can be disguised and messages routed through multiple destinations to disguise their point of origin, it is difficult if not impossible to determine the origins of any particular activity. But while it is true that establishing facts to an evidential "beyond reasonable doubt" standard is hard to do, if one looks at this phenomenon in probabilistic terms the case for China's culpability becomes far more compelling. Many of these attacks, including some of the most sophisticated, have been traced back to servers located in China.[44] China, as indicated above, has a long track record of science and technology theft from the West and now has a powerful imperative to move up the economic value chain by whatever means if it is to avoid a middle-income trap. It is also hard to envisage many other states with both the capacity to conduct such attacks and the ability to withstand retaliatory pressure from the United States. And while many of the techniques used in such attacks are also used by, and are indeed often developed by, criminal gangs, such entities tend to deploy these techniques in a quick and opportunistic manner at variance with the patient, long-term approach described by Northrop Grumman.

This situation changed in February 2013 when the US-based IT security company Mandiant released a report detailing the activities of Shanghai-based PLA Unit 61398 as being responsible for conducting cyberattacks on the United States and other English-speaking countries dating back to 2006.[45] The Chinese government predictably denied the allegations in the Mandiant report, but shortly after its release the buildings identified by Mandiant appear to have been vacated. The Mandiant report was the catalyst for a more direct approach by the US government, and at the 2013 summit between US president Barack Obama and his Chinese counterpart Xi Jinping at Sunnylands the issue of cybersecurity was put at the top of the bilateral agenda—though without Xi giving any ground in terms of acknowledging Chinese culpability.[46] One month later the first meeting took place of a new Cybersecurity Working Group within the framework of the annual US-China Strategic and Economic Dialogue. This discussion was described by the official Chinese news agency Xinhua as having gone well, but there is little evidence that much progress had been made. By that point the revelations of rogue NSA contractor Edward Snowden had begun to emerge and the detail about the extent of the US and Five Eyes cyber espionage simply reinforced Chinese perceptions that the United States was using its privileged position within the cyber domain to perpetuate its hegemony and that its accusations against China reflected double standards.[47] There is no evidence that China was remotely responsive to US arguments that China's state-sponsored industrial espionage was qualitatively different from the espionage undertaken by the United States and its allies and that China's conduct put it in breach of international commitments made pursuant to joining the World Trade Organization.

Moreover, it is true that by no means all cyber activities emanating from China can be laid at the door of China's intelligence services. Many attacks have been and continue to be relatively unsophisticated in nature. Subjects of such attacks who know what to look for have logged multiple "noisy" attacks from separate entities, each apparently in pursuit of the same information. But the overall picture is reminiscent of China's earlier HUMINT-driven efforts to collect foreign science and technology. There is still a significant "Wild East" aspect characterized by an apparent absence of effective coordination and the involvement of a multiplicity of actors with different motivations. But all the indications point to a growing focus and professionalization as the collection of low-hanging fruit gives way to more refined requirements and collection techniques evident in the higher-end advanced persistent threats described above.

There are many aspects of China's cyber exploitation activities that remain unclear. Much of the technical capacity for operations directed against the Western defense and industrial sectors lies with 3/PLA or entities working in effect as contractors for the Chinese military. But it is not clear what mechanisms exist for triaging and processing the huge volumes of data that are being captured, nor is it apparent how 3/PLA interfaces with the rest of China's intelligence or customer communities. While much of the cyber exploitation activity that has preoccupied the West has focused on covert science and technology acquisition, it is evident that increasing effort has also gone into collecting more conventional political and economic intelligence on foreign governments and on NGOs and opposition groups located outside China. Logically, the latter in particular would be a focus for the MSS, and given that there exists little in the way of a collaborative culture between China's intelligence agencies, it is equally possible that MSS has developed independent capabilities to deal with these targets. It is in this context worth noting that China's efforts to monitor and filter domestic Internet content have evolved an export model. A case in point is the assistance reportedly being provided to Iran to implement its National Information Network or "clean Internet"—also known as the "halal Internet."[48] Such activity would be consistent with China's policy of asserting concepts of cyber sovereignty and enhanced government control of the Internet advance in forums such as the 2012 World Conference on International Telecommunications and the United Nations Group of Governmental Experts. But it is unclear whether such assistance is provided by China's intelligence community.

Nor is it yet apparent how much effective use China has been able to make of the data it has collected. Former NSA director Keith Alexander has characterized the industrial-scale cyber espionage directed against US government and private-sector networks as constituting "the greatest transfer of wealth in history."[49] But in the case of industrial espionage emanating from China it is probably too soon to gauge the true extent to which such activity poses an existential threat to Western economic capabilities. One case, which has been widely cited as illustrating the West's vulnerability, is that of US wind turbine manufacturer AMSC, which alleges that the Chinese company Sinovel, at one time AMSC's largest customer, had illicitly acquired the company's control software source code to use in its own products.[50] The resulting loss of business led to an almost 80% drop in the company's revenues, and it has since been engaged in extensive litigation with its erstwhile partner. An even more egregious example is that of the Canadian telecommunications company Nortel, which declared bankruptcy in 2009. According to Brian Shields, a former senior network security adviser at Nortel, the company had been the victim of large-scale industrial espionage from the emerging Chinese telecommunications giant Huawei, which over time had destroyed Nortel's competitive advantage (though Shields was compelled to admit that he had no direct evidence of Huawei's culpability).[51]

Whether in the long-term copying of existing Western technologies will offer China a reliable route to developing genuinely world-class corporations capable of significant technological innovation within an economically meaningful timescale needs to be considered in the light of a much wider nexus of issues determining China's corporate future. These include the future of the state capitalist model exemplified by China's state-owned enterprises, the nature of China's banking and financial systems, and the status of the rule of law. In this context it should also be noted that computer hacking and intellectual property theft are pervasive phenomena inside China, as is cyber criminality generally. The Chinese government's primary focus is on monitoring and filtering domestic ICT communications to eliminate threats and challenges to the rule of the CCP; there is by contrast relatively little capacity available to deal with hacking and intellectual property theft.

CONCLUSION

For China's intelligence community and corporate sector, cyber espionage has undoubtedly represented a step change in collection capabilities. It has eliminated much of the risk associated with covert collection using human sources, vastly enhanced the country's reach, and massively increased the volume of intelligence that can be collected. Cyber exploitation operations are at least deniable, if not always entirely plausibly. And Western policymakers confront the reality that effective retaliatory measures have so far proven elusive because China enjoys a significant asymmetry of vulnerability. Put bluntly, there is much that China wishes to steal from the West but relatively little that the West needs to steal from China—and much of the West's requirements are in the traditional areas of political and military secrets. It is unclear to what extent China's top leadership has an effective policy grip on what is being done by its intelligence agencies and by other relevant actors in the cyber domain or has undertaken any kind of systematic risk/benefit analysis of such activities. But to the extent that it may have done, it is likely that the imperatives of continued economic growth on the one hand, and the need to maintain domestic stability and avert challenges to the continued leadership of the CCP on the other, will have carried the day. A more relevant question might be to what extent China will make more extensive use of its cyber capabilities in promoting and projecting its growing power overseas, particularly in areas such as constraining and pressuring opponents who had previously been beyond its reach. Another relevant question might be to consider whether the vastly improved access China's leadership should in principle enjoy to the thinking and priorities of foreign governments and leaders will result in better-informed policy decisions by the Chinese state.

NOTES

1. See, for example, Zhao Suisheng, "A State-Led Nationalism: The Patriotic Education Campaign in Post-Tianamen China," *Communist and Post-Communist Studies* 31, no. 3 (1998): 287–302.
2. David Ian Chambers, "Edging in from the Cold: The Past and Present State of Chinese Intelligence Historiography," *Studies in Intelligence* 56 (2012), 32.
3. "Espionage: A Spy's Grisly Solution," *Time*, March 3, 1986. The defector in question was Yu Qiangsheng, a senior officer in the Ministry of State Security's counterespionage division and brother of Yu Zhengsheng, who was appointed a member of the Politburo Standing Committee at the Eighteenth Party Congress in November 2012. See Matthew Brazil, "Chinese Intelligence

Work, an Abbreviated History," 20, http://www.academia.edu/1250201/Chinese_Intelligence_Work_an_Abbreviated_History.

4. Philip Taubman, "US and Peking Join in Tracking Missiles in Soviet," *New York Times*, June 18, 1981.

5. Bill Gertz, "Chinese Spy Who Defected Tells All," *Washington Times*, March 19, 2009.

6. Sam DuPont, "China's War on the 'Three Evil Forces,'" *Foreign Policy*, July 25, 2007.

7. David Wise, "China's Spies Are Catching Up," *New York Times*, December 10, 2011.

8. On India, see "China Is Potential Threat Number One," *Indian Express*, May 4, 1998; on Cuba, Manuel Cereijo, "China and Cuba and Information Warfare (IW): Signals Intelligence (SIGINT), Electronic Warfare (EW), and Cyber-Warfare," http://camcocuba.org/html/ADDITIONAL%20PAGES/CEREIJO%20E/CEREIJO-ENGLISH/CEREIJO-16-E.html.

9. Bradley Martin, "China for Real: Embassy Bombing 'Part of Espionage War,'" *Asia Times Online*, July 23, 1999.

10. Ian McPhedran, "Indonesian Spies Are Using Chinese Electronic Equipment to Spy on Aussies," News.com.au, November 25, 2013.

11. US House of Representatives Select Committee on US National Security and Military, "Commercial Concerns with the People's Republic of China," January 3, 1999, 29.

12. For a detailed account of the genesis and evolution of Plan 863 see Evan A. Feigenbaum, *China's Techno-Warriors: National Security and Strategic Competition from the Nuclear to the Information Age* (Palo Alto, CA: Stanford University Press, 2000), 141–66.

13. David Wise, *Tiger Trap: America's Secret Spy War with China* (New York: Houghton Mifflin Harcourt, 2011), 81–98. Lee was arrested following a grand jury indictment but was subsequently released without charge.

14. Huo Zhongwen and Wang Zhongxiao, *Sources and Techniques of Obtaining National Defense Science and Technology Intelligence (guofang keji qingbao yuanji huoqu jishu)* (Beijing: Kexue Jushe Wenxuan Publishing, 1991). It appears that this book was never intended to be made public but somehow slipped through the cracks. It is available at http://www.fas.org/irp/world/china/docs/sources.html.

15. Wise, *Tiger Trap*, 1–5, 20–29, 109–21, 187–202.

16. "Russia Paroles Physicist Valentin Danilov Jailed for Spying," *Guardian*, November 13, 2012.

17. Peter Mattis, "Beyond Spy Versus Spy: The Analytical Challenge of Understanding Chinese Intelligence Services," *Studies in Intelligence* 56, no. 3 (2012), 52.

18. Andrew Porter, "Downing Street Aide in Chinese 'Honey Trap' Sting," *Daily Telegraph*, July 20, 2008.

19. "CSIS Comments Anger Chinese Community," CBC News, 24 June 24, 2010.

20. Sun Yun, "Chinese National Security Decision-Making: Processes and Challenges," Working Papers by CEAP Visiting Fellows No. 62, Brookings Institute, May 2013.

21. Ibid.

22. *Xianren zhongyang waishi gongzuo lingdao xiaozu lingdao chengyuan mingdan*, March 24, 2010. http://www.huayingya.com.cn/html/gonggao/21874.html (site now blocked).

23. For a detailed account of this incident, see Ashley J. Tellis, "China's Military Space Strategy," *Survival* 49, no. 3 (2007): 41–43.

24. In early 2011 China announced a 13.8% increase in spending on internal security, bringing that budget to RMB 624.4 billion, which compared with a military budget

of RMB 601 billion. It was not made clear what percentage of this increase would go to the MSS. See Chris Buckley, "China's Internal Security Spending Jumps Past Army Budget," *Reuters*, March 5, 2011.

25. Michael J. Swaine, "China's Assertive Behavior Part Three: The Role of the Military in Foreign Policy," *China Leadership Monitor*, no. 36 (winter 2012).

26. Sun Yun, "Chinese National Security Decision-Making."

27. Samantha Hoffman and Peter Mattis, "Inside China's New Security Council," *National Interest*, November 21, 2013.

28. Zhang Hong, "New Security Commission to Be Led by Top Three in Communist Party," *South China Morning Post*, January 24, 2014.

29. Study Times website, January 13, 2014, http://www.studytimes.com.cn/shtml/xxsb/20140113/3722.shtml.

30. Linda Jakobson and Dean Knox, "New Foreign Policy Actors in China," SIPRI Policy Paper 26, September 2010, 35.

31. Author's conversations with policy advisers.

32. Bonnie Glaser, "Chinese Foreign Policy Research Institutes and the Practice of Influence," in *China's Foreign Policy: Who Makes It and How Is It Made?* ed. Gilbert Rozman (London: Palgrave MacMillan, 2013), 87–124.

33. Michael D. Swaine, *The Role of the Chinese Military in National Security Policymaking* (Santa Monica, CA: Rand, 1998), ix.

34. For a general account of China's Internet evolution see Nigel Inkster, "China in Cyberspace," in *Cyberspace and National Security: Threats, Opportunities and Power in a Virtual World*, ed. Derek S. Reveron (Washington, DC: Georgetown University Press, 2012), 287–311.

35. http://www.internetworldstats.com/asia.htm.

36. Liang Qiao and Wang Xiangsui, *Unrestricted Warfare* (Beijing: PLA Literature and Arts Publishing House, 1999).

37. Bryan Krekel, Patton Adams, and George Bakos, *Occupying the Information High Ground: Chinese Capabilities for Computer Network Operations and Cyber Espionage*, report prepared by the Northrop-Grumman Corporation for the US-China Economic and Security Review Commission, March 7, 2012, 18–20.

38. Nathan Thornburgh, "Inside the Chinese Hack Attack," *Time*, August 25, 2005.

39. Sophie Borland, "MI5 Warns Firms over China's Internet 'Spying,'" *Daily Telegraph*, April 12, 2008.

40. *Tracking GhostNet: Investigating a Cyber Espionage Network*, Information Warfare Monitor, March 29, 2009.

41. Dmitri Alperovitch, *Revealed: Operation Shady Rat*, McAfee Corporation, August 2011.

42. Colin Clarke, "China Attacked Internet Security Company RSA, General Tells SASC," *AOL Defense*, March 27, 2012.

43. Bryan Krekel, George Bakos, and Christopher Barnett, *Capability of the People's Republic of China to Conduct Cyberwarfare and Computer Network Exploitation*, prepared for the US-China Economic and Security Review Commission, October 9, 2009.

44. Ken Dilanian, "U.S. Spy Agencies to Detail Cyber-Attacks from Abroad," *Los Angeles Times*, December 8, 2012. The articles cites an official involved in investigating cyber espionage as saying, "we have traced attacks back to a desk in a [People's Liberation Army] office building."

45. Mandiant, *APT1: Exposing One of China's Cyber Espionage Units*, White Paper, February 2013.

46. "Obama and Xi End 'Constructive' Summit," BBC News, June 9, 2013.

47. Michael D. Swaine, "Chinese Views on Cybersecurity in Foreign Relations," *China Leadership Monitor*, no. 42, September 20, 2013.

48. Mark C. Eades, "China's Newest Export: Internet Censorship," *U.S. News & World Report*, January 30, 2014.

49. Josh Rogin, "NSA Chief: Cybercrime Constitutes the 'Greatest Transfer of Wealth in History,'" *The Cable*, July 9, 2012.

50. Michael Riley and Ashley Vance, "Inside the Chinese Boom in Corporate Espionage," *Bloomberg Businessweek*, March 15, 2012.

51. Laura Payton, "Former Nortel Exec Warns Against Working with Huawei," CBC News, October 11, 2012.

CHAPTER 3

From Exploitation to Innovation

Acquisition, Absorption, and Application

JON R. LINDSAY AND TAI MING CHEUNG

The rising tide of Chinese cyber espionage has prompted deepening concern in the United States and around the world that, as a former head of US counterintelligence has pointed out, such espionage "is contributing significantly to the tidal flow of capital, intellectual and otherwise, from West to East."[1] The chairman of the US House Intelligence Committee similarly alleges, "There is a concerted effort by the government of China to get into the business of stealing economic secrets to put into use in China to compete against the U.S. economy."[2] Richard Clarke, special advisor on cybersecurity in the George W. Bush administration, claims that cyber espionage now poses a more pressing danger than cyberwarfare. His "Greatest fear is that rather than having a cyber–Pearl Harbor event, we will instead have this death of a thousand cuts" as "company after company in the United States spends millions, hundreds of millions, in some cases billions of dollars on R&D and that information goes free to China. . . . After a while you can't compete."[3] General Keith Alexander, former director of the National Security Agency and commander of US Cyber Command, describes cyber espionage dramatically as "the greatest transfer of wealth in history."[4]

These claims are hard to evaluate because espionage is by nature a self-hiding activity. It involves secret initiatives to steal classified information, and both the perpetrators and the victims want to protect their reputations. Espionage does not translate simply into innovation, however. Collected data must be processed by a complex network of government and industrial organizations and translated into successful performance against competitors. Inefficiencies throughout the entire intelligence-to-innovation process can erode the value of stolen data. This chapter provides a framework for understanding illicit acquisition, institutional absorption, and competitive application and then evaluates China's efforts to overcome obstacles in each step. While espionage inefficiency cannot be decisively demonstrated, there are real reasons to be skeptical that China's impressive cyber exploitation campaigns can deliver lasting strategic advantage. On the contrary, overreliance on economic espionage may become an impediment in China's quest to become a leading industrial superpower.

UNRELIABLE DAMAGE ASSESSMENTS

General Alexander claims, "Symantec placed the cost of IP theft to US companies at $250 billion per year, global cybercrime at $114 billion annually—$388 billion when you factor in downtime—and McAfee estimates that $1 trillion was spent globally on remediation . . . that's our future disappearing in front of us."[5] Unfortunately, numbers like these are the result of extrapolations from rare outliers, unrepresentative samples, and surveys with high nonresponse rates.[6] Most damage estimates originate from firms in the business of selling cybersecurity products, so there is reason to be wary of threat inflation. Ross Anderson and his colleagues have conducted the most rigorous academic attempt to date to measure financial cybercrime, but they stopped short of totaling UK and US losses across twenty-seven different categories because "it is entirely misleading to provide totals lest they be quoted out of context, without all the caveats and cautions that we have provided."[7] They did not even attempt to include industrial espionage in their analysis because of all the complex and intangible factors involved. The ultimate value of economic secrets, unlike directly monetizable assets like bank accounts, depends not only on the cost of producing them but also on a firm's ability to capitalize on the information in a competitive marketplace.[8] The net value of lost market share, lost jobs, and the overhead of technical and legal defense is a very complicated equation. As a recent US counterintelligence report concedes: "estimates from academic literature on the losses from economic espionage range so widely as to be meaningless—from $2 billion to $400 billion or more a year—reflecting the scarcity of data and the variety of methods used to calculate losses."[9]

Some evidence, moreover, points in ambiguous directions. Only twenty-seven of the one hundred largest American companies reported having suffered any cyberattacks in 2012 in required disclosures to the US Securities and Exchange Commission, and these attacks caused no significant financial losses.[10] James Lewis and Stewart Baker summarize loss estimates for all forms of cybercrime in the United States as ranging from $24 billion to $120 billion, equivalent to 0.4–1.4% of US GDP, which is comparable to losses from car crashes or traditional pilferage at, respectively 0.7–1.2% and 0.5–2% of US GDP.[11] The amount lost to cyber espionage alone would, presumably, only be a fraction of this, although it is hard to put a dollar figure on illicitly acquired political and military advantages. Lewis elsewhere calls US losses to espionage "a rounding error in our $15 trillion economy."[12]

The history of industrial espionage suggests further reasons for skepticism about its impact on competition. Cyber exploitation is only the most recent manifestation of a centuries-long tradition of economic theft practiced by major countries. Historian J. R. Harris observes that "the main method of taking technology from one European country to another in the eighteenth century seems unquestionably to have been industrial espionage."[13] Yet coal-fuel smelting and the refining of iron presented "the most obdurate technical problem" and "the new skills were not embodied in drawings and manuals." As late as 1824, "it was still not possible to make good machines abroad from drawings and models alone."[14] Even when France obtained entire pieces of machinery and foreign laborers to operate them, it still faced serious trouble assembling parts into a fully functional factory. Despite prodigious and deliberate French espionage, England maintained its industrial advantage.

Acquisitive countries have always faced challenges absorbing relevant foreign expertise and applying it. It would be surprising if computers changed any of this. On the contrary, the flood of digital data and the complexity of contemporary networked technology might make the intelligence-to-innovation problem even more complicated. Direct measurement of losses to espionage is probably futile, so we pursue an alternative approach here. We will examine the logical requirements for translating intelligence collection into competitive advantage in the marketplace. This enables us to identify assumptions about espionage effectiveness as well as potential obstacles states face in benefiting from it.

A MODEL OF ESPIONAGE EFFECTIVENESS

It is often assumed that the covert collection of valuable foreign data translates simply into industrial innovation, which in turn provides dramatic advantages in international competition. "The greatest transfer of wealth in history" thus leads to "death by a thousand cuts." This assumption gives rise to three widely held and interconnected beliefs about Chinese cyber espionage: (1) China is running an aggressive industrial espionage campaign to steal Western corporate secrets; (2) cyber espionage is a cheap and effective shortcut for improving industrial innovation; and (3) China is gaining an unfair competitive advantage through cyber espionage at Western expense.

Because Western organizations are directly exposed to Chinese intrusions and can collect data to support attribution, there is ample evidence to support proposition 1. There is less empirical evidence available about China's ability to absorb stolen data and apply it to improving innovation (propositions 2 and 3). Each of the links between these propositions in reality is embedded within a complex institutional context with potential to generate significant transaction costs, which in turn undermine the efficiency of intelligence collection and industrial digestion.

Figure 3.1 presents a more nuanced articulation of the intelligence-to-innovation process. It depicts institutional gaps across and within a country's boundaries that pose nontrivial obstacles to effective collection of, and profit from, intelligence. The actors in this model are ideal types in an acquisitive state rather than specific organizations in China. We further divide these actors into inputs and outputs in order to call attention to internal information processing (and pathologies) within bureaucratic entities. Connections from one actor's output to another actor's input depict the potential for data to get lost or misinterpreted in transactions

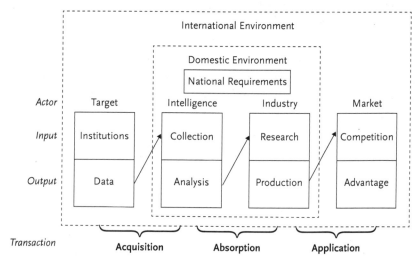

Figure 3.1 A Model of Espionage Effectiveness

between organizations as data is acquired from foreign targets, absorbed into the Chinese industrial system, and applied in international competition. The effectiveness of Chinese espionage is thus contingent, in part, on the absorptive capacity of the Chinese science and technology (S&T) system.[15]

In the acquisition phase, intelligence collectors must first gain physical access to the foreign target's valuable data and then recover it back to home base for analysis. As governments and corporations put more of their valuable data into digital form, there are more espionage targets available and more channels to access them at lower risk, as compared to human spies. At the same time, target networks are full of a lot of junk data that is meaningless to people outside the organization (and often inside it). Cyber spies confront a severe needle-in-the-haystack problem, and it is unclear whether the number and quality of valuable "needles" are increasing at the same rate as the size and messiness of digital "haystacks" as data storage capacity explodes. Moreover, a considerable amount of an organization's vital information is not in electronic format at all, but rather encoded in tacit knowledge, social relationships, physical layouts, and workplace routines.[16] Spies can steal digital text, but it is much harder to recover social context.

Intelligence collection also requires administrative infrastructure to identify lucrative targets, craft a covert intrusion, separate data wheat from chaff, analyze the valuable nuggets, and package the results into a format that is meaningful to the industrial or political consumer.

In our simple model of absorption, collection inputs come from interface with foreign targets in the international environment, while analysis outputs interface with domestic consumers of the stolen data. Yet incorporation of foreign data into industrial innovation involves further complications. The "hard" factor inputs to national innovation capacity are perhaps most easily measured, to include raw materials, research universities and human capital, factory capacity, research and development (R&D) laboratories and test facilities, and foreign expertise (obtained by whatever means). "Soft" factors are harder to measure but are just as critical for industrial performance, to include guidance and support from national leadership, industrial regulation policies, contract law and enforcement capacity, industrial organization and governance, technical standards and protocols, and other cultural properties. Hard and soft factors interact to shape the identification of needs and requirements, R&D, test and evaluation, factory production, material acquisition, development of marketing plans or doctrines for use, and finally, employment of a capability ready for the market (or battlefield).[17] In our stylistic model, hard and soft factors converge in research inputs, while functional products and processes emerge as production output. Because the absorption phase is complex and involves a lot of actors, national intelligence guidance and coordination overhead is necessary as well.

Only when the output of industrial innovation interacts and succeeds in a strategic arena can it be truly said to provide a competitive advantage relative to other actors in the market or in a political contest. Some promising products are never fielded or fail to work in practice. Others run afoul of legal and political obstacles. The ultimate fate of market interactions is usually unknowable in advance to the actors involved, not only because of scientific uncertainty but also because of the vagaries of interaction among strategic actors. At best, actors can make better or worse assessments of risk, and even then their most innovative outputs may fail in the crucible of application in the international environment.

This simple model does not definitively measure the efficiency or inefficiency of China's espionage contributions to innovation, but it does provide a qualitative feel for the significant challenges involved. In evaluating each phase, we can make some educated guesses based on what we do know from open sources about cyber exploitation attributed to China as well as China's ability to absorb foreign information from any source whatsoever. The remainder of this chapter will focus on the first two of the three gaps, acquisition and absorption. The broader problem of market application is beyond the scope of this chapter, but we will offer some comments.

ILLICIT ACQUISITION OF FOREIGN DATA

China uses espionage to support its interests in national security, maintenance of the Communist Party's rule on power, and economic development. Its cyber targets fall into all of these categories. The PLA is modernizing rapidly to meet its goal of "winning local wars under conditions of informatization." Chinese weapon designers and defense conglomerates strive to build an autonomous innovation system, and they are eager to exploit foreign technologies and expertise to do so.[18] Chinese authorities consider the notion of national security to broadly include social order and preventing challenges from political dissidents, human rights activists, and restive ethnic minorities. Cyber surveillance thus complements Internet censorship as a mode of political control.

The motivations for economic espionage, on which we focus here, are captured to some extent in China's "National Medium- and Long-Term Plan for Science and Technology Development (2006–2020) (MLP)." The MLP is a self-described "grand blueprint of science and technology development" for the "great renaissance of the Chinese nation." It promotes a policy of "indigenous innovation" (*zizhu chuangxin*) that involves "enhancing original innovation through co-innovation and re-innovation based on the assimilation of imported technologies." According to one business analyst, "the plan is considered by many international technology companies to be a blueprint for technology theft on a scale the world has never seen before."[19] It is striking that the chronicle of Chinese cyber espionage depicted in tables 3.1 and 3.2 begins to take off as the MLP is beginning to be implemented, and many targets of Chinese intrusions are in industries explicitly identified in the MLP.

Of particular importance in China's S&T modernization strategy is the National High Technology Research and Development Plan. Better known as the 863 Program (because it was launched in March 1986), it aims to close the gap between China and the global state of the art in a number of key areas, including information technology and telecommunications, in order to enhance military power and international competitiveness.[20] While 863 openly funds a number of military and civilian R&D initiatives, the US Counterintelligence Executive also assesses that it "provides funding and guidance for efforts to clandestinely acquire U.S. technology and sensitive economic information for PLA modernization."[21] Indeed, three of the nine foreign espionage cases prosecuted in the United States (from 1996 to 2011) have had some connection to 863.[22]

Of the nine foreign espionage cases prosecuted under the US Economic Espionage Act (EEA) of 1996, eight had some connection to China. In all but one of these, the defendant allegedly acted to benefit an entity associated with the Chinese government. Since 2008, moreover, 44% of all EEA cases (i.e., foreign espionage charges as well as the more widely prosecuted trade secrets provision of the law) had some sort of China connection.[23] The remarkably high level of EEA cases with a China connection is consistent with Verizon's finding that 96% of the espionage-related data breaches in 2012 originated from China, although this number is likely exaggerated.[24] The most serious EEA case to date resulted in the conviction of Dongfan Chung, an engineer at Boeing from 1979 until his arrest in 2006. Chung transferred hundreds of thousands of pages to the Chinese Ministry of Aviation and the Aviation Industry Corporation of China about the space shuttle program, Delta IV rocket, B-52 and B-1 bombers, F-15 fighter, and Chinook helicopters.[25] The physical volume of information Chung passed to his Chinese handlers could have filled four four-drawer filing cabinets, but the same amount of data could now be quickly exfiltrated by cyber means with less hassle and risk. Chinese human espionage persists in the cyber era, as Nigel Inkster points out in his chapter. Indeed, human and cyber intelligence collection operations have become complementary elements of a broad Chinese economic espionage campaign.

Table 3.1 PUBLICLY REPORTED INTRUSIONS ATTRIBUTED TO CHINA

Intrusion	Active	Report	Targets	Significance
Titan Rain[82]	2003.09	2005.08	US defense orgs and national labs	First public indication of methodical state-sponsored APT traced to PRC
State Dept[83]	2006.06	2006.07	US State Dept., US Embassy Beijing	Targeted Bureau of East Asian and Pacific Affairs; embassy lost connectivity for 2 weeks
US BIS[84]	2006.07	2006.10	US Commerce Dept.	Bureau of Industry and Security regulates US export licenses; attributed to PRC
US NWC[85]	2006.11	2006.11	US Naval War College	PRC APT prompts NWC to shut down network
US Sec Def[86]	2007.06	2007.09	Computers in the office of US sec. defense Gates	Cabinet-level CNE with confident attribution to PLA
Enfal[87]	2006	2007.12	US NGOs, defense, govt.	Linked to Byzantine Haydes
US Rep Frank Wolf[88]	2006.08	2008.06	Office of US congressman Frank Wolf	CNE targeted data on human rights activists and political dissidents; attributed to PRC
POTUS Campaign[89]	2008.07	2008.11	Obama and McCain campaigns	Targeted candidates' policy positions; intrusion linked to PRC
Ghost Net[90]	2007.05	2009.03	Govts., firms in 103 countries; Dalai Lama	First detailed public report on APT methods; interaction with cybercrime ecosystem
F-35 JSF[91]	2007.10	2009.04	BAE, Lockheed-Martin, Northrop-Grumman	APT compromised nonclassified data on F-35, monitored meetings and technical discussions
Aurora[92]	2009.07	2010.01	Google and 34 other firms; dissident Gmail accounts	Prompted Google's exit from PRC and Sec. State Clinton's Internet freedom speech
Shadows in the Cloud[93]	2009.01	2010.04	US, UK, India, SE Asian govts. and firms; UN	Exploits of cloud-hosted social media; classified information exfiltrated
Byzantine Haydes[94]	2002	2010.12	US Defense, State, Energy; IMF, World Bank; international firms, NGOs	US code name for PLA intrusions; subsets Byzantine Candor/ Foothold/Anchor cover particular PLA APT actors
Night Dragon[95]	2009.11	2011.02	Multinational firms in the oil/energy sector	Oil exploration, bidding, and control system data lost to technically unsophisticated attack

Table 3.1 (Continued)

Intrusion	Active	Report	Targets	Significance
RSA[96]	2010	2011.03	RSA, Lockheed	Compromise of industry standard RSA SecureID tokens enabled Lockheed intrusion
Shady RAT[97]	2006.07	2011.08	71 govt., corporate, NGO orgs. in 14 countries (mainly US); ASEAN	Targets of interest to PRC including Intl. Olympic Committee and WADA prior to 2008 Beijing Olympics; probably APT1
Lurid[98]	2011.06	2011.09	Russia, CIS, Tibetan targets	Related to previous Enfal Trojan campaigns
Nitro[99]	2011.04	2011.10	48 chemical and defense firms	Technically unsophisticated attack traced back to single hacker in Hebei province
Taidoor[100]	2008.03	2012.03	Think tanks involved in US-Taiwan policy	Activity peaks during 2011 US discussions of upgrading Taiwanese air force
Luckycat[101]	2011.06	2012.03	Defense and commercial firms, Tibetan activists	Linked to hacker working with students at Sichuan Univ. Information Security Institute
Ixeshe[102]	2009.07	2012.05	East Asian govts., IT firms, German telecoms	Highly targeted, leveraging internal C2 servers, attribution unclear but suggests PRC
VOHO[103]	2012.06	2012.07	Boston, Washington, DC, activists, defense, educational institutions	"Watering hole" and fake software patch attacks, conducted by Hidden Lynx APT
Elderwood, (Sneaky Panda)[104]	2009.07	2012.09	Defense, manufacturing, human rights NGOs	Sophisticated Beijing-based APT group; used at least 8 zero-day exploits; multiple attack vectors; includes Aurora/Google hack
Cyber-Sitter[105]	2009.06	2012.11	CA-based Solid Oak Software	CyberSitter software copied for PRC's Green Dam censorship software, then aggressive attacks against plaintiff in copyright suit
US News Media[106]	2012.10	2013.01	*NY Times, Washington Post, Wall Street Journal*	Targeted journalists covering PRC leaders, politics, and business (e.g., Huawei and ZTE)

(Continued)

Table 3.1 (*Continued*)

Intrusion	Active	Report	Targets	Significance
HeartBeat[107]	2009.11	2013.01	S. Korea govt., party, media, research, military	English and Chinese artifacts make attribution ambiguous, DPRK is possible
APT-1 (Comment Crew)[108]	2006	2013.02	141 English-speaking firms in 15 countries	Most detailed public attribution evidence to PRC to date, exposes Shanghai-based PLA GSD 3rd Dept., 2nd Bureau (Unit 61398)
Beebus, Mutter[109]	2011.04	2013.02	Aerospace, defense, telecom in US, India	Focus on drone technology and South Asia politics; linked to APT-1
Bit9[110]	2012.07	2013.02	MA-based cybersecurity firm	Stole digital certificate to sign malware used to attack follow on targets in VOHO campaign
Telvent[111]	2007	2013.05	Telvent/Schneider Electric	Prime evidence of Obama 2013 State of the Union claim of hackers in the power grid, likely PRC industrial espionage vice attack planning
QinetiQ[112]	2007	2013.05	CIA venture firm QinetiQ	Numerous advanced technology projects lost over 3 yrs.; inadequate network security
ASIO[113]	2013	2013.05	Australian Security Intelligence Organization	Obtained blueprints for new ASIO headquarters building
Safe[114]	2012.10	2013.05	Govt., NGOs, media, firms, academia	Author identified: professional engineer in PRC with access to ISP code repository
SCADA Honeypot[115]	2012.12	2013.08	Decoy water control systems in 8 countries	APT1 lured into exploiting mock-up plant controls; demos interest in US SCADA
G-20[116]	2013.05	2013.08	G-20 govt. and financial institutions	Traced to APT-12 (aka Calc Team) responsible for US news media intrusions
Hidden Lynx[117]	2009	2013.09	100s of firms, focusing on financial services and defense industry	Highly skilled APT, concurrent campaigns, regular zero-day usage, sizable infrastructure, linked to Aurora, potentially "hackers for hire"
Icefog[118]	2011.08	2013.09	S. Korea, Japan govt., industry, media	Espionage toolkit with Windows and Mac variants; infected Japanese Parliament in 2011

The term "advanced persistent threat" (APT) emerged within the US Air Force in 2006 as an unclassified reference to intrusion sets traced back to China.[26] It has since become a more general term of art for any computer network exploitation—including by the United States—targeting particular organizations on a chronic basis.[27] APTs require preparatory intelligence to penetrate target-specific defenses to discover and recover useful data. This focused effort sets APTs apart from retail cybercriminals who prey indiscriminately on millions of users in a one-shot interaction.[28] Most APTs achieve an initial compromise of the target's network through "social engineering" or confidence tricks that play upon the gullibility of human users. Once an initial foothold is gained, the attacker then escalates privileges in the system, reconnoiters the network, and exfiltrates data to command-and-control servers on the Internet.[29]

Table 3.1 summarizes thirty-seven cases of Chinese computer network exploitation (CNE, as distinguished from disruptive attack, or CNA) from 2005 through 2013. These intrusions have colorful names like "Shady RAT" or "Ghost Net" coined by the Western government agencies or cybersecurity experts that discovered or publicized them. The first significant public disclosure of sustained Chinese cyber espionage was the press reporting of "Titan Rain," a US intelligence code word for an intrusion into Department of Defense laboratories, NASA networks, and aerospace companies between 2003 and August 2005.[30] A great deal more has been learned since then through detailed technical reports such as Mandiant's exposé of "APT-1" (also known as "Comment Crew"), a reference to PLA Unit 61398, described by Mark Stokes in this volume (chapter 7). This data should be understood as English-language reporting on Chinese APTs, emphatically not of APTs themselves (which are in many respects not measurable insofar as they depend on deception). There is considerable ambiguity in these data. Some items refer to particular, identifiable groups who run many campaigns (e.g., APT-1), while others refer simply to related intrusion phenomenology or even just a particularly high-profile target (e.g., the F-35 Joint Strike Fighter). Multiple intrusion names may in reality be the work of the same group in China, but detected by different Western investigators. Since cybersecurity firms use expert technical analysis as a form of public marketing (security itself is hard to measure and advertise) and because reporters chase popular topics, this dataset tracks the appetite for APT reporting as much as APT activity itself. One should thus be very cautious about drawing any inferences. Nevertheless, this reporting does provide an open-source portrait, even if a sketchy one, of the targets and techniques exploited by

Table 3.2 APT TARGETS

Report year	Commercial targets		Government targets		Mixed targets		Total intrusions	Total average months
	Intrusions	Average months	Intrusions	Average months	Intrusions	Average months		
2005			1	23			1	23
2006			3	2			3	2
2007			1	3	1	23	2	13
2008			2	13			2	13
2009	1	18			1	22	2	20
2010	1	6			2	61	3	43
2011	3	12			2	32	5	20
2012	1	41			5	26	6	29
2013	8	42	2	4	3	23	13	32
Total	14	31	9	7	14	31	37	25

Chinese APTs as well as some evidentiary basis for claims by public officials and private firms about extensive Chinese espionage.[31]

APT targets include defense technology, foreign government policy regarding Chinese interests, positions of US presidential candidates, Chinese dissident activity, and a wide range of industries. Table 3.2 summarizes the number of APTs reported each year, divided into whether the APT emphasized mainly commercial or government targets or a mixture. The duration columns describe the average months elapsed between public reporting and the first reported evidence of infection (i.e., from the "report" to "active" dates in table 3.1), although this does not discriminate between cases where the intrusion remained hidden and those where it was detected but not publicly reported. For instance, APT-1 remained undetected in one organization's networks for almost five years,[32] but by contrast, the report date of "Byzantine Haydes" corresponds to the date of disclosure by WikiLeaks of US intelligence monitoring of Chinese APTs for eight years prior.[33] Bearing in mind all the caveats about data quality, it is striking to observe that the earliest public reporting on APTs involves government targets. There is a shift around 2010 or so toward greater reporting on economic espionage (exemplified by the Night Dragon and Shady RAT intrusions), as well APTs indiscriminately attacking government and commercial targets. It is possible that there was a shift in Chinese targeting priorities to increase collection on the industries detailed in China's MLP. Some support for this possibility can be found in the pattern of APT-1 penetrations against 141 firms reported by Mandiant. APT-1 starts out tentatively in 2006 but becomes highly active across twenty industrial sectors in 2011.[34]

Another possibility—not inconsistent with heightened Chinese activity—is that there has been an improvement in Western firms' awareness of and ability to respond to network intrusions. Better detection rates by victims or third-party investigators would result in heightened reporting rates. Conversely, heightened media reporting would also improve firms' awareness of the problem and, presumably, their detection posture. Google's announcement in 2010 that it had been hacked by mainland Chinese entities was followed by a major speech by secretary of state Hilary Clinton on Internet freedom. These events marked the turning point in public awareness of Chinese cyber espionage as a serious problem.[35] Before then, the APT threat was best known to intelligence experts, and thus government targets were more likely to be detected, whatever China was targeting. Throughout 2011 and 2012, there was an increase in public reporting about Chinese intrusions, which may or may not have corresponded with an uptick in Chinese APT campaigns. Additional, albeit tentative, evidence for improved corporate defenses is found in the increasing rate of detection of commercial APTs hidden for a long time as seen in the jump in average duration between activity and report date in 2012 and 2013. This increasing detection rate of long duration intrusions can be interpreted to suggest that cyber defenders are getting better at rooting out the toughest APTs.

Attribution to China

Attribution is often considered to be *the* hard problem of cybersecurity, and mistaken allegations by Western officials would be politically irresponsible. As Chinese authors often point out, "An IP address simply is not a valid proof for the source of a hacker."[36] Therefore, it is striking that US analysts and policymakers have been so willing to confidently attribute responsibility to the Chinese government recently. While each bit of evidence about Chinese involvement may be circumstantial by itself, a diverse mass of clues presents a more convincing picture of Chinese culpability. China has ample political and economic motives for industrial espionage, a documented history of spying in American court records, and the organizational capacity and technical expertise needed to run APTs. Moreover, Chinese APT operators themselves have left a number of clues through sloppy tradecraft. All this data in context enables forensic investigators to follow the attribution thread back to the Chinese government.

APT actors rely on standardized operating procedures, reusable technical infrastructure, a division of labor, and intelligence tradecraft to penetrate and operate undetected in target networks for extended periods of time. It is possible that private-sector corporate intelligence or cybersecurity firms might fit this profile.[37] The Ministry of State Security and Ministry of Public Security also fit the profile. Yet the PLA is an especially strong fit for the APT profile. It has doctrine for cyberwarfare as well as functionally and regionally specialized bureaus in the General Staff Department (GSD) Third Department and Military Region Technical Reconnaissance Bureaus (TRBs). The PLA can draw from a large talent pool of university-educated information security talent and a vibrant civilian hacker culture, and it can put them to work in a routinized, regimented, mission-focused institutional structure.[38]

Technical features of APTs provide much more specific evidence pointing to China and, in some cases, to the PLA. As the researcher who discovered the GhostNet and ShadowNet APTs explains, "The attackers can and do make mistakes. Careful monitoring of their command-and-control infrastructure can reveal the inner workings of their operations. The data obtained from the attacker's infrastructure often reveals the length of the operation, the number of individual attacks, the identity of the victims, additional tools used by the attackers and sometimes even the data that has been ex-filtrated."[39] The February 2013 Mandiant report describes a wide variety of data, including Internet addresses from the Shanghai neighborhood of PLA Unit 61398, simplified Chinese keyboard settings, domain names and phone numbers registered in the Shanghai locale, reliance on Chinese malware like Ghost RAT, characteristic Chinese grammar errors in English phishing emails, and routinely high levels of APT activity during weekday working hours in China Standard Time, complete with mealtime breaks.[40]

Furthermore, many human APT operators "have made poor operational security choices."[41] Some even check their personal Facebook and Twitter accounts, taking advantage of PLA attack infrastructure situated outside "Great Firewall" censorship restrictions for their personal use. Lax Chinese tradecraft could be the result of naïve operators or brazen indifference given the low risk of punishment for being caught. It is also possible that these easy clues may become harder to come by in the future after the announcement in early 2014 of a reorganization of Chinese cybersecurity policy with Xi Jinping assuming more direct control. One consequence of Xi's institutional shakeup could include greater enforcement of discipline and discretion in PLA cyber tradecraft.[42]

Gaping holes remain in our knowledge of who exactly in China is responsible and how APT operations are organized. However, attribution to China by corporate investigators has been corroborated by government analysts as well as academic and non-profit research outfits, notably by the University of Toronto's Citizen Lab. There is simply no credible alternative explanation for the individually circumstantial but collectively significant evidence for Chinese (and PLA) responsibility. It is commonly held that cyber attribution is very difficult, but in this case, Occam's razor points to a major institutionalized campaign of cyber espionage.

Needles in a Haystack

It is clear that Chinese APTs exfiltrate many terabytes from foreign networks. It is less clear how often their take includes valuable data. There is a vast and growing amount of information in cyberspace. According to one academic study, "In 2008, the world's servers processed 9.57 zettabytes [Zb] of information . . . or ten million million gigabytes." This translates into a per-company average of "63 terabytes of information annually."[43] A 2012 Symantec study of 4,506 organizations in 38 countries reported a total of 2.2 Zb of data on their networks, valued at $1.1 trillion. Of this vast amount, 42% was duplicate data, and 46% resided outside of protected data centers. Respondents reported that 69% had inadvertently exposed confidential information, and 30% said "information sprawl" was a factor in these mishaps.[44] Data fragmentation and spillage is thus a normal fact of life even in the absence of APTs. Moreover, the "live" portion of data on an organization's network—current, valid, meaningful, revisited, operational data—is usually small compared to the amount of data stored. Old versions of documents, working drafts, discarded plans, and normal data errors abound on corporate servers. This mess essentially functions as disinformation for the naïve spy who collects it. Understanding which bits are meaningful requires participation in meetings, ongoing conversations, laboratory interactions, and other embodied moments in the life of an organization.

As not everything valuable is digital and not everything digital is valuable, what is the probability that Chinese cyber intruders actually retrieve something of value from their targets? Do bureaucratic APT collectors even care about the answer, or are they simply rewarded for the number of targets infiltrated and the number of terabytes recovered? This latter possibility could produce a large collection effort with little effect on innovation.

SUBSTANTIAL INFRASTRUCTURE FOR THE ABSORPTION OF FOREIGN DATA

Determining how Chinese cyber-exploitation activities contribute to the country's advancement in S&T requires an understanding of how information obtained by illicit as well as legitimate means is disseminated, assimilated, and transformed into actual output. China's S&T development strategy of "indigenous innovation," described in the MLP, can be more precisely characterized as a four-part process known as "introduce, digest, assimilate, and re-innovate" (*yinjin, xiaohua, xishou, zai chuangxin*) or IDAR, which refers to the steps required to turn foreign technology into a remade domestic variant. The IDAR strategy is most clearly articulated in a supplementary document to the MLP that calls for encouraging the introduction of advanced foreign technology that can be digested and absorbed for re-innovation.[45]

A central Chinese goal is the building of a sophisticated apparatus that brings in foreign technology and allows for the effective absorption and re-innovation of products that China can effectively claim to be homegrown. The MLP highlights a number of industrial sectors that would benefit from this approach, including information and communications technology, biotechnology, civilian aviation and aerospace, advanced materials, and machinery manufacturing.[46] Key initiatives in the document include actively seeking bilateral and multilateral technical cooperation, expanding open-source international information services that can be disseminated to local actors, encouraging firms to go abroad to gain access to foreign R&D knowledge, and attracting more multinational firms to set up R&D institutes and facilities in China. Espionage, which is not mentioned, unsurprisingly, is thus only one small part of a much larger Chinese effort to acquire and absorb foreign expertise. This has two important implications for our topic: 1) China has many alibis for the legitimate acquisition of foreign technology to deflect charges of espionage; and 2) the contribution of espionage is only one small part of an ambitious foreign technology transfer effort, so spying cannot be given exclusive credit for Chinese advances.

Defense Research, Development, and Acquisition

A full study of Chinese absorptive capacity would consider defense and non-defense state-owned and private corporations. In the interest of brevity, we will look primarily at China's defense research, development, and acquisition (RDA) system. Many APTs focus on defense firms, and thus RDA is a useful starting point for understanding the more general challenges. The history of the Chinese defense economy has been a dueling tale of foreign imitation and autonomous innovation. Reliance on external sources has been a defining characteristic of the sprawling conventional weapons establishment from its origins in the early 1950s right up to the present day. By contrast, the smaller and more specialized strategic (nuclear, space, and ballistic missiles) arms complex forged a more independent development path because it was shut off from outside assistance. These two sectors were eventually consolidated in the 1980s, and the defense economy has sought to pursue a twin-tracked imitation-innovation approach ever since.[47]

An important turning point in China's industrial espionage efforts took place in the early 1990s with the collapse of the Soviet Union. This allowed China to take advantage of the economic chaos in Russia and former Soviet republics and gain access to their defense industrial facilities and scientific and engineering personnel. Hundreds of Russian defense scientists and engineers were recruited and brought over to China to provide expert advice.[48] The largest case of Chinese clandestine defense technological activity against Russia was the surreptitious non-authorized reverse engineering of the Sukhoi Su-27 combat jet to create the J-11B.[49] This led to a major rupture in the two countries' defense S&T cooperation, as Russia demanded that China halt intellectual property rights infringements and guarantee not to further engage in these practices.[50] Beijing and Moscow eventually settled their differences in the early 2010s, which allowed for the resumption of negotiations for major weapons packages. This access to former Soviet defense technology may have helped select portions of the Chinese defense industry to advance by at least one or more generations. The most significant contributions have been in fighter aircraft programs, air-to-air missiles, radars, fire-control systems, aircraft carrier and other naval systems, and manned space.

Nonetheless, foreign imitation remains the primary focus of Chinese RDA, notwithstanding a growing effort to promote original innovation, especially incremental and architectural innovation. Leadership and management are hierarchical and top-down in nature, and the insular system has restricted interactions with the outside world. The state plays a dominant role in setting priorities, providing strategic direction, and overseeing management of the system. These factors shape China's absorptive capacity in a number of important ways. First, there is heavy reliance on imitative techniques and processes such as copying and reverse engineering. Second, the Chinese defense innovation system is dependent on foreign technology and knowledge to make major advances in technological development. As much of this technology and know-how is off-limits to China, especially defense and dual-use capabilities from the West, the use of covert means to gain access to this information is a critical source for ensuring the country's continuing technological progress.

Table 3.3 provides a list of major Chinese weapons systems that have benefited from foreign technology. These data show foreign dependency across all of China's defense industrial sectors. To the extent that these systems improve China's relative advantage against its military rivals, this advantage is due in part to foreign assistance. While most acquisitions have been licitly obtained, it is striking that illicit gains are concentrated in sophisticated technology sectors, particularly fighter aircraft, where Chinese reliance on foreign content is considerable. These data can be interpreted to suggest that espionage is only a small part of China's overall foreign technology transfer strategy, but it is important for areas where China needs to catch up. We now turn to the actual process of foreign technology absorption in China.

Table 3.3 CHINESE WEAPONS SYSTEM DEPENDENCE
ON FOREIGN TECHNOLOGY

Platform	Sector	Country of origin	Foreign content	Illicitly obtained material
J-20	Aviation	Russia, United States?	5-High?	Unknown
Liaoning Aircraft Carrier	Maritime	Russia, Ukraine, United States	5-High	Unknown
J-11B	Aviation	Russia	5-High	Yes: Reverse-engineered Su-27SK
J-16	Aviation	Russia	5-High	Yes: Reverse-engineered Su-30MK2
J-15	Aviation	Russia, Ukraine	5-High	Yes: Reverse-engineered Su-33
Donghai-10 LACM	Space	Russia, Ukraine, United States	5-High	Yes: Reverse-engineered missiles
Y-20	Aviation	Ukraine, Russia	4-Medium-High	No
Zhi-10	Aviation	United States, Canada	4-Medium-High	No
KJ-2000 AEW	Electronics	Russia, Israel	4-Medium-High	No
Type 039A/B SS	Maritime	Russia, Germany	3-Medium	No
Type 039G	Maritime	Russia, Germany	3-Medium	No
Type 052B Luyang I destroyer	Maritime	Russia, Ukraine, France	3-Medium	No
Type 054A Jiangkai II frigate	Maritime	Russia, France	3-Medium	No
Type 053H3 Jiangwei II frigate	Maritime	Russia, Germany, France, Italy, United Kingdom	3-Medium	No
Nuclear reactors	Nuclear	United States, Japan, France, Russia, Finland, Germany	3-Medium	No
Hongqi 9 (HQ-9) SAM	Ordnance	United States, Russia, Israel?	3-Medium	No
Shenzhou-10	Space	Russia, United States	3-Medium	No
Chang'e 2	Space	Germany, United States	3-Medium	No

(Continued)

Table 3.3 (Continued)

Platform	Sector	Country of origin	Foreign content	Illicitly obtained material
DF-31	Space	United States, Russia?	2-Low-Medium	No
CBERS	Space	Brazil, United States	2-Low-Medium	No
Type 052C Luyang II destroyer	Maritime	Russia, Ukraine, Germany, France, United States	2-Low-Medium	Yes; German engine design
J-10 Fighter	Aviation	Russia, Israel	1-Low, Critical	No
FC-1	Aviation	Pakistan, Russia, Italy, United States	1-Low, Critical	No
JH-7	Aviation	United Kingdom	1-Low, Critical	No
H-6	Aviation	Russia	1-Low	No
J-8II	Aviation	Russia, Israel	1-Low	No
KJ-200 AEW	Electronics	Sweden, United States, Ukraine	1-Low	No
Type 94 SSBN	Maritime	Russia, Ukraine	1-Low	No
Type 93 SSN	Maritime	Russia, Ukraine	1-Low	No
Type 051C Luzhou destroyer	Maritime	Russia, United States	1-Low	No
Type 99 MBT	Ordnance	Russia, Germany, United States	1-Low	No
Type 96 MBT	Ordnance	Pakistan, Russia	1-Low	No
WZ752 AFV (Type 89)	Ordnance	Germany	1-Low	No
PTL02 Self-Propelled Arty	Ordnance	Germany, United Kingdom	1-Low	No
Julang-2	Space	United States, Russia?	1-Low	No
DF-15	Space	United States (potential)	1-Low	No
Beidou	Space	Switzerland	1-Low	No
Ziyuan	Space	Brazil	1-Low	No
Changzheng (LM-5)	Space	United States, Russia	1-Low	Yes: US engine designs

Source: Data compiled in Tai Ming Cheung, "'Standing on the Shoulders of Past Pioneers': The Role of Foreign Technology Transfers in China's Defense Research, Development, and Acquisition Process," presented at IGCC 2013 Annual Conference on the Chinese Defense Industry: Understanding the Structure, Process, and Performance of the Chinese Defense Research, Development, and Acquisition System, La Jolla, California.

Introduce

The initial role for defense S&T organizations in the IDAR process would be to provide technical targeting requirements to guide the work of intelligence collection units. Little is known about how this targeting process works, but the notoriously hierarchical and compartmentalized nature of the Chinese defense establishment would support an assumption that targeting requests by S&T organizations go up through their respective chains of command. Entities affiliated with the defense industry report to the State Administration for Science, Technology, and Industry for National Defense (SASTIND), while PLA units would go through their own departments and service arms. Requirements by military units belonging to the armaments system, for example, would go up through the hierarchy of the PLA General Armament Department (GAD).

Military targeting requests would eventually make their way to the PLA General Staff Department's Third Department in charge of signals intelligence. APT collectors and analysts would have to work together to discover potentially meaningful intelligence out of all the terabytes recovered. Then they would have to package it in a way that customers would be able to use. The effective management of these coordination and transmission channels is crucial to the performance of the acquisition process. Entities that are likely to play influential roles in providing targeting requirements include the Science and Technology Committees that belong to the GAD, SASTIND, each of the ten major defense industrial corporations, and S&T research organizations.[51]

Digest

A key mechanism that China has cultivated since its formative years has been an S&T information analysis and dissemination (IAD) apparatus. While the IAD system has close affiliations with the intelligence collection system, the two apparatuses are organized and operated separately. The historical rationale for the development of the IAD system was to provide information on global S&T developments to civilian and military S&T and academic organizations that were largely isolated from the outside world between the 1950s and 1970s. The output of this system consisted of the acquisition, collation, and translation of foreign S&T literature but also of specific technical information that was of direct utility to R&D organizations, especially for nuclear, space, and computational outfits.[52]

A number of major IAD entities were established within the S&T system, such as the Institute of Scientific and Technical Information of China, which belongs to the Ministry of Science and Technology, and the Electronics Science and Technology Intelligence Research Institute, affiliated with the Ministry of Industry and Information Technology (MIIT). The IAD system presently consists of around four hundred analysis and diffusion centers with around 50,000 personnel, according to a 2006 assessment.[53] However, only around thirty-five belong to central government agencies, and the rest are affiliated with provincial or lower-level institutions.[54] Each of the country's six defense industrial sectors also has its own IAD organization; these act as clearinghouses for specialized S&T information. These organizations, which range in size from two hundred to five hundred researchers, are attached to one of the principal conglomerates responsible for their sectors.[55]

The vast majority of the external information that IAD organizations analyze comes from open sources such as media, online, and academic outlets.[56] The classified intelligence collected by PLA intelligence agencies is likely to be available only for the military component of the IAD system, which is centralized under the China Defense Science and Technology Information Center (CDSTIC) affiliated with the GAD. CDSTIC has grown rapidly over the past few decades, especially since the end of the 1990s, to cope with intensive demand for its S&T information and analysis services from the defense innovation system, military organizations, and the country's leadership.[57] Concerted efforts have been made to improve the ability of the IAD system to assimilate and disseminate information in a timely and organized fashion. This includes the development of Internet-based and closed intranet S&T databases and information retrieval networks. CDSTIC, for example, operates an engineering technology information network, an all-army equipment S&T information network, a GAD-specific S&T intelligence network, and an online digital library.[58]

Assimilate

Chinese authorities are investing heavily in building up an extensive technology and engineering ecosystem to support efforts to combine digested foreign and local technologies. This includes the establishment of an extensive array of entities such as national engineering research centers, enterprise-based technology centers, state key laboratories, national technology transfer centers, high-technology service centers, and the recruitment of foreign technical experts through organizations such as the State

Administration of Foreign Expert Affairs. National engineering research centers are one of the most important types of institutions designated by the Chinese government for transforming the acquired and digested external technology into actual output.[59] There were nearly three hundred of these research centers in operation in 2013.

China's "combine and integrate" strategy figures prominently in the MLP and is being actively pursued by defense and high-technology-intensive industries that have major gaps in their technological capabilities that can best be addressed from external technology transfers. This strategy is carried out through collaborative joint ventures as well as through illicit transfers and unauthorized reverse engineering. The commercial and military aviation and high-speed rail sectors are at the forefront. For China's first narrow bodied jet airliner, the C919, the external technology absorptive process is occurring throughout the entire RDA cycle from initial design through to manufacturing.

Chinese expenditures on the acquisition of foreign technology and of the in-house assimilation of technology have grown strongly over the past past decades, as shown in table 3.4. Official Chinese statistics for spending on foreign technology acquisition (which almost certainly excludes defense-related acquisitions) shows a nearly fivefold increase between 1991 and 2011, from RMB 9.02 billion ($1.47 billion) to RMB 44.9 billion ($7.3 billion), although around half this total comes from acquisitions by foreign-owned firms based in China.[60] Strikingly, in the same period of time, expenditures for assimilation have grown faster relative to

Table 3.4 CHINESE EXPENDITURES FOR ACQUISITION AND ASSIMILATION OF FOREIGN TECHNOLOGY

Year	Expenditures for acquisition of foreign technology (RMB billion)	Expenditures for assimilation of technology (RMB billion)	Assimilation versus acquisition (%)
1991	9.02	0.41	5
2000	24.54	1.82	7
2007	45.25	10.66	24
2008	46.69	12.27	26
2009	42.2	18.2	43
2010	38.61	16.52	43
2011	44.9	20.22	45

Source: Data from State Statistics Bureau and Ministry of Science and Technology, *China Yearbooks on Science and Technology Statistics, 1991–2011* (Beijing: China Statistics Press).

expenditures for acquisition, from 5% to 45%. This suggests that assimilation is neither automatic nor easy and, in fact, is getting harder as China targets more sophisticated foreign technology. Whatever success China enjoys from licit and illicit transfer depends on a very expensive and extensive IDAR effort.

Re-innovate

One of the major challenges for the Chinese defense economy is how to turn all these efforts into actual output. While there is a growing list of advanced weapons projects from fifth-generation combat aircraft to turbofan jet engines at various stages of the RDA process, a major bottleneck is the underdeveloped state of advanced manufacturing capabilities that are critical for the precision production of high-technology products. In its five-year program in 2012 providing a detailed outline of the development of the country's high-end equipment manufacturing industry, MIIT noted that China's advanced manufacturing industry lagged well behind the global frontier, that its innovation ability was "weak," and "core technologies and core key components are in the hands of others."[61] Revenue from high-end equipment manufacturing accounted for only 8% of total revenues of the country's equipment manufacturing industry in 2012. While Chinese S&T development plans stress the importance of nurturing homegrown S&T capabilities, the reality is that China can only make major progress through gaining access to foreign technologies and know-how.

Industrial and cyber espionage activities and other illicit and gray acquisition strategies thus figure prominently in China's efforts to achieve its development goals in priority areas as well as sensitive defense and dual-use technologies. This approach has worked especially well in the building of its high-speed rail sector, which is one of the priorities in its high-end equipment manufacturing development plan. European and Japanese firms provided significant amounts of high-speed rail technology transfers to China during the 2000s that allowed the Chinese rail industry to replicate and improve upon these capabilities within five years and produce what they insisted were brand-new generations of "re-innovated" trains. Many of the foreign firms involved in these technology deals have been reluctant to publicly criticize the Chinese for reverse engineering their products, although Japanese firms have been more vocal in their protests.[62] The PRC's Twelfth Five-Year Development Program for the Rail Transportation Equipment Industry published in 2012 acknowledged that its high-speed rail sector was based on "secondary innovation of absorbed technology introduced from abroad."[63]

Foreign rail firms were surprised at how quickly their Chinese counterparts were able to absorb and reverse-engineer these advanced technologies. While the Chinese rail industry benefited greatly from the extensive level of technology transfers, it also invested heavily in building a robust absorptive capacity infrastructure that included the establishment of a state-of-the-art national rail transportation research laboratory, a state engineering technology research center, a state engineering research center, and more than a dozen national-level enterprise technology centers.[64] These research, development, and engineering bases are also being laid down in many other industrial sectors, and they are an essential component of China's growing absorptive capacity.

In sum, China has taken deliberate steps for decades to improve its capacity to absorb foreign technology and expertise. Intelligence collection, much less cyber espionage, is only one of many channels through which China accesses foreign technology, many of which are perfectly legitimate.[65] The secrecy of cyber espionage, moreover, surely complicates the bureaucratic problem of connecting APT collectors and intelligence analysts to the proper industrial customer in a way that open acquisition does not. When assessing the marginal effects of espionage on technological absorption, one must also consider these other important pathways that can contribute far more complete and detailed information and mentorship. There is no doubt that all of this ambitious activity—including espionage in some cases—has enabled China to catch up in many areas. However, it has also built a severe foreign dependency problem into the Chinese S&T system. By relentlessly seeking shortcuts to becoming a world-class innovator, China has actually become over-reliant on foreign imitation. We return to this theme in the chapter's conclusion.

THE UNCERTAINTY OF APPLICATION IN INTERNATIONAL COMPETITION

Even if China does manage to acquire secrets and absorb them efficiently, advantage cannot be guaranteed in a market where future interactions are uncertain. Western firms may be able to innovate new data faster than China can digest old data. Some scholars find evidence that the US advantage in S&T will endure despite China's rise.[66] Similarly, China may not be able to absorb very efficiently at the most lucrative end of the value chain. Studies of innovative regions like Silicon Valley or Cambridge, Massachusetts, suggest that social factors like personal relationships among entrepreneurs, open legal institutions, supportive research universities, the availability of local venture capital, expert knowledge in the labor force, and even recreational opportunities are key for promoting innovation.[67] Cyber spies might steal technical data, but without the social context to nurture it, the data could be useless for cutting-edge innovation. If data is easy to copy and products are easy to imitate, then the market is likely to price such products lower than goods that are better designed, marketed, and have greater appeal. Not all cyber theft has the same implications for all sectors.[68]

Figure 3.2 describes how different levels of acquisitive performance or absorptive capacity can affect a state's ability to apply espionage for market advantage. Acquisition is simple when an APT can easily access and exfiltrate data that can be readily understood out of context. Standardized databases, finished engineering blueprints, or negotiating positions on well-defined deals are examples of corporate secrets that could potentially be useful. If an acquirer has inefficient absorption institutions, then stolen secrets could potentially aid improvement if the utility of the secrets is straightforward. If the acquirer has advanced absorptive capacity, then there is a much better chance that simple secrets can be put to work to realize a competitive advantage. We assess that most of China's IDAR successes that leverage espionage are in this category.

However, acquisition will be more difficult if the critical target data is hard for an APT to identify or extract from its local social context. Gregory Treverton distinguishes between intelligence "puzzles" and "mysteries."[69] Puzzles are problems that can be solved by finding the missing pieces that are

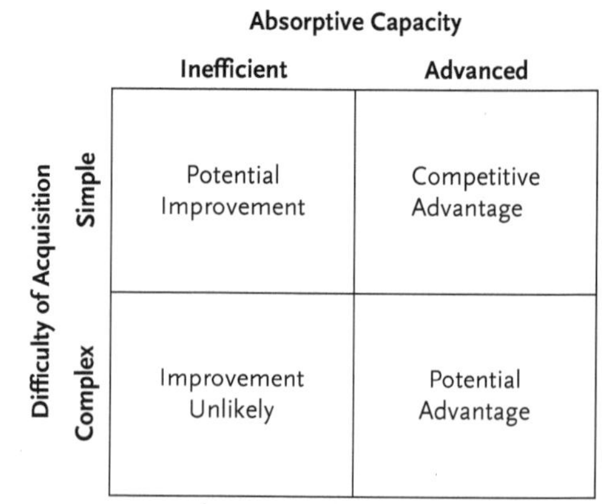

Absorptive Capacity

	Inefficient	Advanced
Simple	Potential Improvement	Competitive Advantage
Complex	Improvement Unlikely	Potential Advantage

Difficulty of Acquisition

Figure 3.2 Competitive Potential of Espionage

simply hidden from view because the target wants to keep them confidential. Mysteries, by contrast, turn on intangibles of context and intention that may even be poorly understood by the target itself. The acquisition of advanced technology trades in mysteries. An acquirer with weak absorptive institutions will most likely not be able to obtain and interpret complex target data. An acquirer with robust absorptive capacity has a better chance at understanding and adapting complex target data to productive ends, but it will still take a lot more work and the outcome will be uncertain. We assess that China will face continuing difficulties in this category no matter how much it spends on IDAR because the innovation targets are that much more sophisticated.

Further downstream factors could also affect the outcome of a strategic interaction, even if performance in acquisition and absorption does promote advantages. For instance, the victim state may take counteractions to blunt the utility of espionage. American officials have long insisted that the United States, unlike France or China, "does not, should not, and will not engage in industrial espionage."[70] Yet at the same time, "Economic intelligence has been a topic of concern to the CIA from the very beginning of its existence."[71] One former CIA director, Stansfield Turner, even argued that US agencies should directly assist US firms against foreign competitors: "Some argue that when it comes to specific data such as competitive bids, the government should not become a partner of business and distort the free enterprise system. The United States, however, would have no compunction about stealing military secrets to help it manufacture better weapons."[72] US intelligence has also provided special technical assistance to firms as, for example, when the National Security Agency reportedly aided Google in the wake of Chinese hacking.[73] Americans often attempt to take the moral high ground against China for economic espionage, but US intelligence support to industry is a more nuanced question of degree rather than an all-or-nothing relationship.[74] The important implication for espionage application is that robust two-sided intelligence competition—with US intelligence aiding US defense firms and monitoring Chinese S&T progress—should be expected to blunt whatever advantage for relative competitiveness that Chinese espionage might provide. This is to say nothing of fully above-board countermoves by firms and Western governments to compete with Chinese initiatives in the international marketplace.

CONCLUSION: SOVIET LESSONS FOR CHINA?

In early 2013 the US intelligence community reportedly produced a classified National Intelligence Estimate concluding that China, as part of its economic development strategy, is running a major espionage campaign to acquire American technology and gain competitive advantages.[75] A classified Defense Science Board report to the Pentagon allegedly concluded that "designs for many of the nation's most sensitive advanced weapons systems have been compromised by Chinese hackers."[76] Yet what do these compromises mean for China's quest to become a world-class science, technology, and military power?

As we have seen, there is very good evidence that China is indeed running an aggressive industrial espionage campaign to acquire corporate secrets from abroad. However, some secrets, and some of the most important ones, may be hard to extract from their localized context. There is also reason for cautious optimism that Western defenses are improving against Chinese intrusions, even as sloppy APT tradecraft is sure to improve in response. The belief that cyber espionage is a cheap and effective shortcut to improving industrial innovation is harder to substantiate. China has probably been able to use espionage to improve its S&T performance level, but this has happened in the context of an ambitious and expensive effort to absorb foreign expertise through any means possible. Absorption has not been cheap for China, and it has resulted in more imitation than true innovation. There are further reasons to be skeptical of the claim that espionage has given China a decisive competitive advantage at Western expense.

One of the most systematic and sustained campaigns of economic espionage in recent history was conducted by the Soviet Union against the United States throughout most of the twentieth century. Stalin relied heavily on illicit technology transfers prior to World War II. According to one historian, "the United States, as well as its wartime allies, became an important target for Soviet espionage of military industrial technology before the Cold War. This effort materially supported the industrial and technological development of the Soviet Union, particularly in the area of aircraft and weapons technology, and vitally assisted the war effort."[77] Soviet efforts continued and intensified during the Cold War. A 1985 assessment from the CIA, based on classified Soviet documents describing their technology transfer program, detailed "a massive, well-organized campaign by the Soviet Union to acquire Western technology illegally and legally for its weapons and military equipment projects. . . . Virtually every Soviet military research project—well over 4,000 each year in the late 1970s and over 5,000 in the early 1980s—benefits from these technical documents and hardware."[78] The implications of American losses for Soviet power were summarized with dramatic flair: "The assimilation of Western technology is so broad that the United States and other Western nations are subsidizing the Soviet military buildup."[79]

The Soviet effort was comparable in its scale and intensity to China's present cyber espionage campaign. The Soviets had thoroughly institutionalized industrial espionage by implementing a system of collection requirements, technical analysis, customer dissemination, and performance analysis. Given the central role that state, Party, and military institutions play in coordinating China's S&T development, it is reasonable that China has set up a similar program for systematic absorption of data from cyber operations as part of its IDAR system. The CIA judged that stolen Western technology had reduced Soviet weapons RDA by up to two years for research projects in an advanced stage of development. For projects in an earlier stage of research, the cycle could be lessened by as much as five years. The report concluded that espionage "considerably shrinks overall research time, reduces the amount of resources devoted to weapon systems research, and allows diversion of those resources to other Soviet military research projects."[80] China, likewise, appears to have been able to accelerate its RDA through cyber espionage, and certainly through broader foreign technology transfer.

However, the Soviet case also contains a cautionary tale for Chinese officials and Western analysts alike. Ironically, the Soviet Union's very success became a liability. It optimized its RDA system for imitation rather than innovation. Because the Soviets designed foreign dependence into the heart of their S&T apparatus, truly disruptive innovation was priced out of reach. The Soviets became trapped in a frantic game of catch-up with the West. The CIA thus concluded:

in spite of the several decades of massive investment in indigenous R&D, the prospects are small that the Soviets can reduce their dependence on a large variety of Western products and technology in this decade and the next without allowing the technological gap to widen. The main reasons for this continuing need are endemic to the Soviet system: the lack of adequate incentives, inflexible bureaucratic structures, excessive secrecy, and insularity from the West.[81]

The Soviet system required its Western competitors to be more technologically advanced than it was. It institutionalized second place. China is not the Soviet Union, and the Sino-American relationship is not the militarized hostility of the Cold War. The economies of both states are highly interdependent, and they have many reasons to seek mutual gains around the world. At the same time, however, the comparison between China and the Soviet Union with respect to systematic industrial espionage is suggestive. Espionage helped the Soviet Union to catch up, but it also contributed to its undoing. Chinese S&T leaders would do well to learn from this example. If China is to become the first-rate S&T power it aspires to be, it will have to perform on a level playing field without recourse to illicit technology. Whether China can actually give up its addiction to industrial espionage remains to be seen, but it certainly will not happen anytime soon.

NOTES

1. Economist Intelligence Unit, "Cyber Theft of Corporate Intellectual Property: The Nature of the Threat," 2012, 14.
2. Jennifer Schlesinger, "Chinese Espionage on the Rise in US, Experts Warn," CNBC Investigations, Inc., July 9, 2012.
3. Ron Rosenbaum, "Richard Clarke on Who Was behind the Stuxnet Attack," *Smithsonian Magazine*, April 2012.
4. General Keith Alexander, keynote address at the American Enterprise Institute, Washington, DC, July 9, 2012, http://www.aei.org/events/2012/07/09/cybersecurity-and-american-power/.
5. Ibid.
6. Dinei Florêncio and Cormac Herley, "Sex, Lies, and Cyber-Crime Surveys," Workshop on the Economics of Information Security, 2010; Peter Maass and Megha Rajagopalan, "Does Cybercrime Really Cost $1 Trillion?" *ProPublica*, August 1, 2012.
7. Ross Anderson, Chris Barton, Rainer Bohm, Richard Clayton, Michel J. G. Van Eeten, Michael Levi, Tyler Moore, and Stefan Savage, "Measuring the Cost of Cybercrime," Workshop on the Economics of Information Security, June 2012.
8. Even monetizing stolen digital assets, like compromised bank accounts and credit cards, turns out to be a difficult problem for cybercriminals because their crimes, if detected, are so easily reversible. See D. Florêncio and C. Herley, "Is Everything We Know about Password Stealing Wrong?" *IEEE Security & Privacy* 10, no. 6 (November 2012): 63–69.
9. Office of the National Counterintelligence Executive, *Foreign Spies Stealing US Economic Secrets in Cyberspace*, Report to Congress on Foreign Economic Collection and Industrial Espionage 2009–2011, October 2011, 4.
10. Chris Strohm, Eric Engleman, and Dave Michaels, "Cyberattacks Abound Yet Companies Tell SEC Losses are Few," *Bloomberg*, April 3, 2013.
11. James Lewis and Stewart Baker. "The Economic Impact of Cybercrime and Cyber Espionage," McAfee and the Center for Strategic and International Studies, July 2013.
12. James Lewis, "Five Myths about Chinese Hackers," *Washington Post*, March 22, 2013.
13. J. R. Harris, *Industrial Espionage and Technology Transfer: Britain and France in the Eighteenth Century* (London: Ashgate, 1998), 564.
14. Ibid., 559.
15. Absorptive capacity in the fields of business management and organizational economics refers to the ability of an organization to recognize, assimilate, and utilize new knowledge. The primary focus for economists and management experts has been on the role of firms in developed markets, but many of the same forces at play are also relevant for examining the Chinese defense S&T system. Wesley Cohen and Daniel Levinthal, "Absorptive Capacity: A New Perspective on Learning and Innovation," *Administrative Science Quarterly* 35, no. 1 (March 1990): 128–52. The

framework presented here is similar to that developed by Shaker Zahra and Gerard George, "Absorptive Capacity: A Review, Reconceptualization, and Extension," *Academy of Management Review* 27 (April 2002): 185–202, which distinguishes potential absorptive capacity (acquisition and assimilation) from realized absorptive capacity (transformation and exploitation). Our framework for espionage breaks out "acquisition" separately to focus on the intelligence problems, while we use "absorption" as a covering term for all the complex processes Zahra and George discuss as assimilation and realized absorptive capacity.

16. John Seely-Brown and Paul Duguid, *The Social Life of Information* (Cambridge, MA: Harvard Business School Press, 2000); Claudio Ciborra, *The Labyrinths of Information: Challenging the Wisdom of Systems* (New York: Oxford University Press, 2002).

17. Tai Ming Cheung, "The Chinese Defense Economy's Long March from Imitation to Innovation," *Journal of Strategic Studies* 34, no. 3 (2011): 325–54.

18. Ibid.

19. James McGregor, "China's Drive for 'Indigenous Innovation': A Web of Industrial Policies," U.S. Chamber of Commerce, Global Intellectual Property Center, 2010.

20. Evan A. Feigenbaum, *China's Techno-Warriors: National Security and Strategic Competition from the Nuclear to the Information Age* (Stanford, CA: Stanford University Press, 2003), 162–64.

21. Office of the National Counterintelligence Executive, *Foreign Spies Stealing US Economic Secrets in Cyberspace*, 7.

22. Rich Bell, J. Ethan Bennett, Jillian R. Boles, David M. Goodoien, Jeff W. Irving, Phillip B. Kuhlman, and Amanda K. White, "Estimating the Economic Costs of Espionage," paper prepared for CENTRA Technology by the George Bush School of Government and Public Service, Texas A&M University, May 3, 2010; BBC News, "Chinese Scientist Huang Kexue Jailed for Trade Theft," December 21, 2011, http://www.bbc.co.uk/news/business-16297237.

23. Peter Toren, "A Report on Prosecutions under the Economic Espionage Act," Trade Secret Law Summit, AIPLA Annual Meeting, Washington, DC, October 23, 2012, 6–7.

24. Verizon, *2013 Data Breach Investigations Report*, 21, www.verizonenterprise.com/DBIR/2013. It must be stressed that this high number may reflect a higher propensity for Chinese intrusions to get caught or reported, not an absence of other countries involved in cyber espionage. Indeed, Verizon (*2014 Data Breach Investigations Report*, 39, www.verizonenterprise.com/DBIR/2014) reports an increase in Eastern European cyber espionage, up to 21%, while East Asia (China and DPRK) account for 49%, and 25% was unattributed. Chinese tradecraft may be improving even as other actors are getting in on the game.

25. *United States v. Dongfan "Greg" Chung*, No. SACR 08-00024-CJC (2008).

26. Richard Bejtlich, testimony before the U.S.-China Economic and Security Review Commission Hearing "Developments in China's Cyber and Nuclear Capabilities," March 26, 2012. US Intelligence has tracked Chinese APTs in the classified domain at least since 2002 according to James Glanz and John Markoff, "Vast Hacking by a China Fearful of the Web," *New York Times*, December 4, 2010.

27. The Flame and Gauss intrusions discovered on computers in the Middle East, and assessed to be part of the US/Israeli Olympic Games family of malware that includes Stuxnet, can also be considered APTs. Ellen Nakashima, Greg Miller, and Julie Tate, "U.S., Israel Developed Flame Computer Virus to Slow Iranian Nuclear Efforts, Officials Say," *Washington Post*, June 19, 2012; Kaspersky Lab, "Gauss: Abnormal Distribution," Kaspersky Lab White Paper, August 2012.

28. Industrial-scale cybercriminals seek to be profitable at scale against thousands or millions of potential victims (or customers), and they are usually successful against only a tiny fraction of them; by contrast, APTs invest effort against each particular target to increase their odds of success. Low-grade, automated, scalable attacks—the majority of online crime—encounter a reasonably effective sum-of-effort defense, but high-end, customized, nonscalable APTs face a weakest-link defense that is much harder to defend against. Cormac Herley, "When Does Targeting Make Sense for an Attacker?" *IEEE Security & Privacy* 11, no. 2 (2013): 89–92.

29. Mandiant, *APT1: Exposing One of China's Cyber Espionage Units*, White Paper, January 2013, 27–38, provides an accessible description of one APT's "lifecycle."

30. Nathan Thornburgh, "The Invasion of the Chinese Cyberspies (and the Man Who Tried to Stop Them): An Exclusive Look at How the Hackers Called TITAN RAIN Are Stealing U.S. Secrets," *Time*, September 5, 2005.

31. This dataset has been cross-checked against other compiled lists of Chinese cyber activity such as Laura Saporito and James A. Lewis, "Cyber Incidents Attributed to China," Center for Strategic and International Studies, March 14, 2013. But there will inevitably be some Chinese intrusions reported in English and (more likely) non-English media that are not included here. This dataset does not include reports about Chinese cyber espionage aggregated across intrusion sets such as the 2011 report, Office of the National Counterintelligence Executive, *Foreign Spies Stealing US Economic Secrets in Cyberspace*; 2009 or 2012 Northrop Grumman reports for the U.S.-China Economic and Security Review Commission; or the many general alarms about widespread Chinese espionage that do not reveal new specific intrusions.

32. Mandiant, *APT1*, 3.

33. Glanz and Markoff, "Vast Hacking by a China Fearful of the Web."

34. For a timeline of APT1 intrusions by industry see Mandiant, *APT1*, 23.

35. Ariana Eunjung Cha and Ellen Nakashima, "Google China Cyberattack Part of Vast Espionage Campaign, Experts Say," *Washington Post*, January 14, 2010.

36. Zhang Yixuan, "US Finds an Excuse for Expanding Its 'Cyber Troop,'" *Renmin Ribao Online* (overseas edition), February 4, 2013.

37. A State Department cable commented on Chinese use of commercial firms: "TOPSEC Network Security Technology Company . . . China's largest provider of information security products and services . . . provides services and training for the PLA and has recruited hackers in the past. . . . While links between top Chinese companies and the PRC are not uncommon, it illustrates the PRC's use of its 'private sector' in support of governmental information warfare objectives, especially in its ability to gather, process, and exploit information." Secretary of State, "Diplomatic Security Daily," June 27–29, 2009, Wikileaks cable posted in *New York Times*, http://www.nytimes.com/interactive/2010/11/28/world/20101128-cables-viewer.html#report/china-09STATE67105.

38. Pollpeter, chapter 6 in this volume; Stokes, chapter 7 in this volume; Sheldon and McReynolds, chapter 8 in this volume.

39. Nart Villeneuve, testimony before the U.S.-China Economic and Security Review Commission Hearing "Developments in China's Cyber and Nuclear Capabilities," March 26, 2012.

40. Cyber exploitation has become such a matter of bureaucratic routine that one young Chinese hacker wrote on his blog, "If we're lucky enough we might be able to complete this year's target and earn a year-end bonus for everyone." He also despaired over long hours of hacking drudgery: "How can passionate young people like us handle a prison-like environment like this?" Barbara Demick, "China Hacker's Angst Opens a Window onto Cyber-Espionage," *Los Angeles Times*, March 12, 2013.

41. Mandiant, *APT1*, 51.
42. According to Mandiant (*M-Trends: Beyond the Breach, 2014 Threat Report*, April 2014), major APTs paused and altered their tradecraft after their compromise in early 2013.
43. James E. Short, Roger E. Bohn, and Chaitanya Baru, *How Much Information? 2010 Report on Enterprise Server Information*, Global Information Industry Center, School of International Relations and Pacific Studies, UC San Diego.
44. Symantec, State of Information Global Results (2012), http://www.symantec.com/content/en/us/about/media/pdfs/2012-state-of-information-global.en-us.pdf.
45. "Opinions to Encourage Technology Transfer and Innovation and Promote the Transformation of the Growth Mode in Foreign Trade" was issued by a group of eight powerful government economic, financial, and planning agencies that included the National Development and Reform Commission, Ministry of Finance, and Ministry of Commerce.
46. For an example of how one industry implemented this strategy, see "Railway Ministry: Our Country's Railway Is about How to Introduce, Absorb, and Re-innovate," Xinhua, April 29, 2007.
47. For detailed analysis of China's defense economy, see Tai Ming Cheung, *Fortifying China: The Struggle to Build a Modern Defense Economy* (Ithaca, NY: Cornell University Press, 2009).
48. Interview with senior Russian Defense Ministry official, Moscow, April 1993 and reported in Tai Ming Cheung, "China's Buying Spree," *Far Eastern Economic Review*, July 8, 1993, 24–26. See also Tai Ming Cheung, "Ties of Convenience: Sino-Russian Military Relations in the 1990s," in *China's Military: The PLA in 1992/1993,* ed. Richard H. Yang (Boulder, CO: Westview Press, 1993), 61–77.
49. "China's Imitation of Su-27SK and Its Impact," *Kanwa Asian Defense Review*, May 2008.
50. "China 'Cloning' Russian Weapons Despite Intellectual Property Agreement," *Nezavisimoye Voyennoye Obozreniye*, December 3, 2010.
51. On the role of the GAD S&T Committee, see Eric Hagt, "The Science and Technology Committee: PLA-Industry Relations and Implications for Defense Innovation," in *Forging China's Military Might: A New Framework for Assessing Innovation*, ed. Tai Ming Cheung (Baltimore, MD: John Hopkins University Press, 2013), chap. 3, 66–86.
52. See William C. Hannas, James Mulvenon, and Anna B. Puglisi, *Chinese Industrial Espionage: Technology Acquisition and Military Modernization* (London: Routledge, 2013), chap. 2.
53. Xu Guanghua, "The Development of the S&T Information Industry in the Building of an Innovation Country," speech at the Fiftieth Anniversary of the Institute of Scientific and Technical Information of China, October 16, 2006.
54. Hannas, Mulvenon, and Puglisi, *Chinese Industrial Espionage*, 22.
55. See http://www.dstpc.org for introductions to most of these entities.
56. One study suggests that 80% or more of S&T technical information requirements can be obtained from open-source publications, while the remainder needs to be collected from "special means." Huo Zhongwen and Wang Zongxiao, *Sources and Techniques of Obtaining National Defense Science and Technology Intelligence* (Beijing: Science and Technology Literature Press, 1991), 84–85.
57. "Science and Technology Vanguard, Think Tank for Decision-Making," *Zhongguo Jungong Bao*, November 17, 2012.
58. Ibid.

59. National Development and Reform Commission, "Administrative Measures on National Engineering Research Centers," National Development and Reform Commission website, March 2007.

60. "China Has over $10b Tech Trade Deficit," *China Daily*, December 6, 2012, and "China Signs More Technology Import Contracts in 2005," *People's Daily*, January 9, 2006.

61. MIIT, "12th Five-Year Program for Development of High-End Equipment Manufacturing Industry," July 9, 2012.

62. "Train Makers Rail Against China's High-Speed Designs," *Wall Street Journal*, November 17, 2010.

63. "12th Five-Year Development Program for the Rail Transportation Equipment Industry," which is contained in MIIT, "12th Five Year Program for Development of High-End Equipment Manufacturing Industry."

64. Ibid.

65. Only two of the ten chapters in Hannas, Mulvenon, and Puglisi, *Chinese Industrial Espionage*, are actually about espionage. The other chapters describe legitimate forms of technology transfer such as open-source analysis, students abroad, and joint ventures.

66. Michael Beckley, "China's Century? Why America's Edge Will Endure," *International Security* 36, no. 3 (2011): 41–78.

67. AnnaLee Saxenian, *Regional Advantage: Culture and Competition in Silicon Valley and Route 128* (Cambridge, MA: Harvard University Press, 1996); AnnaLee Saxenian, *The New Argonauts: Regional Advantage in a Global Economy* (Cambridge, MA: Harvard University Press, 2006).

68. Allan A. Friedman, Austen Mack-Crane, and Ross A. Hammond, "Cyber-Enabled Competitive Data Theft: A Framework for Modeling Long-Run Cybersecurity Consequences," Center for Technology Innovation Working Paper, Brookings Institute, December 2013.

69. Gregory F. Treverton, *Reshaping National Intelligence in an Age of Information* (New York: Cambridge University Press, 2001), 11.

70. George Lardner, "U.S. Demands for Economic Intelligence Up Sharply, Gates Says," *Washington Post*, April 14, 1992, A5.

71. Glenn Hastedt, "Seeking Economic Security through Intelligence," *International Journal of Intelligence and Counterintelligence* 11, no. 4 (1998): –387. For example, "the creation of economic profiles for such newly-independent states as Kazakhstan and Uzbekistan; predictions of the direction which Chinese macroeconomic policy would take; studies on the effectiveness of economic sanctions against Iraq; surveys of the scope of the Third World debt problem; predictions regarding the Mexican peso crisis of 1994; monitoring the operations of international financial institutions such as the Bank of Credit and Commerce International (BCCI); and recognizing and uncovering unfair business practices on the part of other nations and foreign companies" (388).

72. Stansfield Turner, "Intelligence for a New World Order," *Foreign Affairs* 70, no. 4 (Fall 1991): 152.

73. http://epic.org/foia/epic_v_nsa_google.html.

74. Joseph C. Evans, "U.S. Business Competitiveness and the Intelligence Community," *International Journal of Intelligence and Counterintelligence* 7, no. 3 (1994): 353–62; Kristen Michal, "Business Counterintelligence and the Role of the U.S. Intelligence Community," *International Journal of Intelligence and Counterintelligence* 7, no. 4 (1994): 413–27.

75. Ellen Nakashima, "U.S. Said to Be Target of Massive Cyber-Espionage Campaign," *Washington Post*, February 10, 2013.
76. Ellen Nakashima, "Confidential Report Lists U.S. Weapons System Designs Compromised by Chinese Cyberspies," *Washington Post*, May 27, 2013.
77. Katherine A. S. Sibley, "Soviet Industrial Espionage against American Military Technology and the U.S. Response, 1930–1945," *Intelligence and National Security* 14, no. 2 (1999): 94–123.
78. Central Intelligence Agency, *Soviet Acquisition of Militarily Significant Western Technology: An Update*, September, 1985, abstract.
79. Ibid.
80. Ibid., 8.
81. Ibid., 1.
82. Nathan Thornburgh, "The Invasion of the Chinese Cyberspies (and the Man Who Tried to Stop Them): An Exclusive Look at How the Hackers Called TITAN RAIN Are Stealing U.S. Secrets," *Time*, September 5, 2005.
83. Associated Press, "Computer Hackers Attack State Dept.," *New York Times*, July 12, 2006; Ted Bridis, "Agency Hacking Said to Originate in Asia," *Washington Post*, July 12, 2006.
84. Alan Sipress, "Computer System under Attack," *Washington Post*, October 6, 2006.
85. "Chinese Hackers Prompt Navy College Site Closure," *Washington Times*, November 30, 2006.
86. Demetri Sevastopulo, "Chinese Hacked into Pentagon," *Financial Times*, September 3, 2007.
87. Maarten Van Horenbeeck, "Crouching Powerpoint, Hidden Trojan," Twenty-Fourth Chaos Communications Congress, Berlin, December 27, 2007; Maarten Van Horenbeeck, "Is Troy Burning? An Overview of Targeted Trojan Attacks," SANSFire 2008, Washington, DC.
88. "Wolf Reveals House Computers Compromised by Outside Source," Congressman Frank Wolf, press release, June 11, 2008.
89. Demetri Sevastopulo, "Cyber-Attacks on McCain and Obama Teams 'Came from China,'" *Financial Times*, November 7, 2008.
90. Information Warfare Monitor, *Tracking Ghostnet: Investigating a Cyber Espionage Network*, Secdev Group and University of Toronto Citizen Lab, March 29, 2009.
91. Siobhan Gorman, August Cole, and Yochi Dreazen, "Computer Spies Breach Fighter-Jet Project," *Wall Street Journal*, April 21, 2009.
92. Ariana Eunjung Cha and Ellen Nakashima, "Google China Cyberattack Part of Vast Espionage Campaign, Experts Say," *Washington Post*, January 14, 2010; McAfee Labs, "Protecting Your Critical Assets: Lessons Learned from 'Operation Aurora,'" 2010.
93. Information Warfare Monitor, *Shadows in the Cloud: An Investigation into Cyber Espionage 2.0*, Joint Report of the Information Warfare Monitor and Shadowserver Foundation, April 6, 2010.
94. James Glanz and John Markoff, "Vast Hacking by a China Fearful of the Web," *New York Times*, December 4, 2010; Brian Grow and Mark Hosenball, "Special Report: In Cyberspy versus Cyberspy, China Has the Edge," Reuters, April 14, 2011; Michael Riley and Dune Lawrence, "China Hackers Hit EU Point Man and D.C. with Byzantine Candor," *Bloomberg*, July 26, 2012.
95. McAfee Labs, "Global Energy Cyberattacks: Night Dragon," February 2011.
96. Christopher Drew, "Stolen Data Is Tracked to Hacking at Lockheed," *New York Times*, June 3, 2011; Uri Rivner, "Anatomy of an Attack," RSA Blog, April 1, 2011.
97. Dmitri Alperovitch, "Revealed: Operation Shady RAT," McAfee Labs, 2011.

98. Nart Villeneuve and David Sancho, "The 'Lurid' Downloader," Trend Micro Inc. Research Paper, September 2011.

99. Eric Chien and Gavin O'Gorman, "The Nitro Attacks: Stealing Secrets from the Chemical Industry," Symantec, 2012.

100. Stephen Doherty and Piotr Krysiuk, "Trojan.Taidoor: Targeting Think Tanks," Symantec, March 2012.

101. "Inside an APT Campaign with Multiple Targets in India and Japan," Trend Micro Research Paper, 2012; "The Luckycat Hackers," Symantec, March 2012.

102. David Sancho, Jessa dela Torre, Matsukawa Bakuei, Nart Villeneuve, and Robert McArdle, "IXESHE: An APT Campaign," Trend Micro Inc. Research Paper, May 2012.

103. Alex Cox, Chris Elisan, Will Gragido, Chris Harrington, and Jon McNeill, "The VOHO Campaign: An in Depth Analysis," RSA FirstWatch White Paper, RSA, July 2012.

104. Mark Clayton, "Stealing US Business Secrets: Experts ID Two Huge Cyber 'Gangs' in China," *Christian Science Monitor*, September 14, 2012; Gavin O'Gorman and Geoff McDonald, "The Elderwood Project," Symantec, 2012.

105. Michael Riley, "China Mafia-Style Hack Attack Drives California Firm to Brink," *Bloomberg*, November 27, 2012.

106. Nicole Perlroth, "Hackers in China Attacked the Times for Last 4 Months," *New York Times*, January 31, 2013; Nicole Perlroth, "Washington Post Joins List of News Media Hacked by the Chinese," *New York Times*, February 1, 2013; Nicole Perlroth, "Wall Street Journal Announces That It, Too, Was Hacked By the Chinese," *New York Times*, January 31, 2013.

107. Roland Dela Paz, "The HeartBeat APT Campaign," Trend Micro Inc. Research Paper, January 2013.

108. Mandiant, *APT1*.

109. "Chinese Ties Suspected in APT Targeting Aerospace and Defense Industries," *Infosecurity Magazine*, February 4, 2013; "Fresh Operation Beebus Attack Targets Military Drone Technology," *Infosecurity Magazine*, April 22, 2013.

110. Harry Sverdlove, "Bit9 Security Incident Update," Bit9 Blog, February 25, 2013.

111. Nicole Perlroth, David E. Sanger and Michael S. Schmidt, "As Hacking against U.S. Rises, Experts Try to Pin Down Motive," *New York Times*, March 4, 2013.

112. Michael Riley and Ben Elgin, "China's Cyberspies Outwit Model for Bond's Q," *Bloomberg*, May 2, 2013.

113. John Kerin and Christopher Joye, "Chinese Hackers Steal ASIO Building Plans: Report," *Australian Financial Review*, May 28, 2013.

114. Nart Villeneuve and Kyle Wilhoit, "Safe: A Targeted Threat," Trend Micro Inc. Research Paper, May 2013.

115. Tom Simonite, "Chinese Hacking Team Caught Taking Over Decoy Water Plant," *MIT Technology Review*, August 2, 2013; Kyle Wilhoit, "The SCADA That Didn't Cry Wolf: Who's Really Attacking Your ICS Devices Part Deux!" presentation at Black Hat 2013, Las Vegas, Nevada, August 1, 2013.

116. Claudio Guarenieri, "Upcoming G20 Summit Fuels Espionage Operations," Rapid7 Security Street Blog, August 26, 2013.

117. Stephen Doherty, Jozsef Gegeny, Branko Spasojevic, and Jonell Baltazar, "Hidden Lynx: Professional Hackers for Hire. Security Response," Symantec, September 17, 2013.

118. Kaspersky Lab Global Research and Analysis Team, "The 'Icefog' APT: A Tale of Cloak and Three Daggers," Kaspersky Lab, September 2013.

CHAPTER 4

Investigating the Chinese Online Underground Economy

ZHUGE JIANWEI, GU LION, DUAN HAIXIN, AND
TAYLOR ROBERTS

The proliferation of Internet users in China has been accompanied by new security threats. These range from the theft of instant messaging and game accounts to compromised banking information.[1] Large-scale breaches of personal and private information have brought the security of personal information to the forefront of public attention. Behind most of these Internet security threats there exists an underground economy of online crime. Driven by the prospect of easy economic gain, cybercriminals use a variety of techniques to exploit vulnerabilities in network security and personal information protection. These criminals operate within a complicated economy with a clear division of labor and multiple value chains. These hidden markets link several components of the underground economy together to form a comprehensive platform for logistical and operational support, trading, and communications. In order to efficiently attract new participants, the markets are structured in order to remain accessible to potential entrants while eluding public scrutiny.

Criminals use idiosyncratic jargon and a variety of other methods to "hide in plain sight" within publicly available web platforms. Once the criminal argot and culture is deciphered, however, researchers can begin to investigate and measure the impact of these illegal markets. Previous analysis of the global underground online economy has been dominated by Western and Eastern European datasets. However, the online underground economy in China is unique in many ways. Given the differences in language, economies, legal systems, regulatory environments, and Internet cultures, the literature on Western underground online economies is not sufficient to explain underground markets in China. The work on Chinese markets which does exist relies on descriptive analysis and case studies, yet the literature lacks a comprehensive analysis of the structure, size, and characteristics of the Chinese online underground economy.[2] Given the increased influence of the Internet in China and the numerous differences between Chinese and Western markets, in-depth research and analysis on Chinese underground markets would positively contribute to a better understanding of the drivers of cybercrime in China, as well as efforts to combat these behaviors.

This chapter provides a detailed empirical and structural investigation of the Chinese online underground economy. Our estimation shows that the overall damage to China's economy in 2011 has exceed RMB 5.36 billion (USD 852 million), and the measured number of participants in underground markets was more than 90,000. First we review the existing literature on online underground economies both within China and globally. We then introduce a structural analysis of the Chinese online underground economy, highlighting four distinct value chains. The section following the structural analysis presents the methods and results of our empirical data analysis. The chapter closes with a discussion of the findings and suggests that improved monitoring of online underground markets could be used to support the investigation of cybercrime cases more effectively.

CHINESE VERSUS WESTERN CYBERCRIME

The existence of an underground economy in cyberspace is certainly not limited to China—it is a global phenomenon. Developed countries tend to be the targets of online criminals because of the prevalence of online shopping and payment mechanisms. As a result, the online underground economy in developed countries is not only more structured but has also been more readily researched and observed. Observing Chinese markets within the context of Western cybercrime provides a clear picture of the differences between these markets and the deficiencies in the literature on Chinese cybercrime. Prolific literature exists on the environment within which underground markets operate. Misaligned incentives, information asymmetries, and externalities allow online criminals to exploit network vulnerabilities and begin to establish marketplaces around these challenges to information security.[3] Within China, these challenges are intensified because laws prohibiting illegal online theft are poorly enforced and, in some cases, undefined (such as theft of virtual assets like video game accounts).

The structure and vehicles used in the underground market globally have also been explicitly researched. Various Internet relay chat protocols and online social networks not only serve as a means for online criminals to interact with each other in order to establish labor assignments, but also create an environment where distrusting parties exhibit certain behavioral characteristics in order to establish a relationship with one another.[4] Online web forums in China, specifically Baidu Post Bar and Tencent QQ chat groups, have provided a platform for these markets and interactions. Baidu Post Bar is a large online communication platform that consists of many forums indexed by keywords. Users can create and search a forum in Baidu Post Bar by typing a keyword. Tencent QQ is an instant messaging service that allows many people to chat at same time. However, the jargon used and the Internet culture in Chinese underground markets are different from their Western counterparts and thus require further exploration.

Several studies have been conducted on how commodities are being bought and sold in online underground markets, as well as the mechanisms used to illegally acquire them.[5] Sophisticated methodologies can be found in studies on botnets, phishing, spam, click fraud, and malware infection by pay-per-install service, all of which provide deeper and more comprehensive investigations into specific security threats driven by the underground economy.[6] While methods for using these tools are similar in both China and the West, the supply and demand for these tools differs between these economies. Finally, there has been a great deal of research conducted on the value chains within online underground markets. For example, Thomas Holtand and Danielle Graveshave created a typology, measured the distribution of goods traded on the market, and conducted price analyses, all based on the main goods within four different value chains.[7] Several other studies have attempted to measure the costs and prices of cybercrime.[8] The identification of value chains within the Chinese underground economy has been attempted, but the structure of the economy has not been systematically analyzed.[9] In addition, the only attempt to empirically measure the costs of trading in the Chinese underground economy did not publish the researchers' method of calculating this value.[10]

In the next sections, we comprehensively analyze the structure of the Chinese underground economy and methods of monetization. With the help of a variety of security monitoring systems developed by Chinese mainstream security vendors and government security departments, we estimate in detail the scale of underground markets online and the number of users affected. Finally, using an extensive long-term analysis of underground markets residing on Web forums and Tencent QQ chat groups, we map the evolution of the Chinese underground economy and give predictions for its future trends.

STRUCTURAL ANALYSIS OF THE ONLINE UNDERGROUND ECONOMY

Based on our investigation and analysis of the profit model and the relational structure of the Chinese online underground economy, we can delineate its overall structure. The economy includes four value chains, which are specialized economic functions and the transactions that connect them. Figure 4.1 depicts the relationship between these value chains:

1. Real assets theft: Stealing money from bank accounts or credit cards
2. Network virtual assets theft: Stealing virtual currency or equipment from online gaming accounts and selling them for real money
3. Internet resources and services abuse: Taking advantage of hacked Internet resources, including compromised hosts, hacked servers, and infected smartphones, with the intention of abusing these resources for profit
4. "Blackhat" techniques, tools, and training: Malicious hackers selling Trojan horses and attack tools to provide technical support for cybercriminals and training services to "newbies" (industry newcomers)

These four value chains are interdependent. The blackhat techniques, tools, and training value chain acts as the economic base, providing a technical foundation for the other three value chains. For example, the Internet resources and services abuse value chain builds off of the techniques, tools, and training industry to provide network resources for theft of real assets and network virtual assets. It is important to note that all participants in the underground economy could probably obtain profits in the real world, so they are not driven by necessity. All four industries are driven by the tremendous illegal profit to be made, although actual earnings are distributed quite heterogeneously across the population, which spurs the continuous development and expansion of the underground economy.

In the rest of this section, we provide in-depth analysis and interpretation of the four underground value chains shown in figure 4.1. We proceed

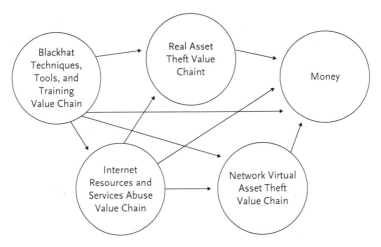

Figure 4.1 The Overall Structure of the Chinese Online Underground Economy

with a structural analysis of the value chains, participant roles, key industry terminology, and case studies.

The Real Assets Theft Value Chain

Stealing real assets is the primary driver for many cybercrimes in China. Cybercriminals can attempt to obtain direct profits by gaining illegal access to real assets and personal financial information. These criminals face greater potential for financial gain, but also greater risk of punishment. A major challenge for them is to monetize stolen assets, usually through money laundering. Real assets accessible on the Internet include online banking accounts, credit limits, online payment accounts, and investment accounts.[11] As most of these accounts use passwords as login credentials, account and password information (or envelopes) are the first targets of cybercriminals.

China's real assets theft value chain has evolved over the years. Its current form is reflected in figure 4.2.[12] There are two phases to this value chain, the theft phase and the money-laundering phase. In the theft phase, cybercriminals utilize a variety of techniques to acquire account and password information, such as phishing, Trojan horses, telephone fraud, and bank card copying.[13] The Chinese jargon used to refer to these techniques, the participants in the underground economy, and other tools can be found in table 4.1. This idiosyncratic jargon is important because it exposes nuances to the Chinese underground economy that differ from its Western

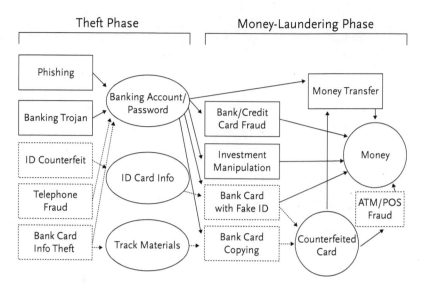

Figure 4.2 The Structure of the Real Assets Theft Value Chain

counterparts. "Material masters" (料主, *liaozhu*) and Trojan writers (木马 作者, *muma zuozhe*) are the central participants in this half of the value chain.

After cybercriminals harvest the account and password information, they proceed to the money-laundering phase. "Material-washing men" (洗料人, *xi liao ren*) may sell the information on the underground market, or hire a "car master" (车主, *che zhu*) or "car drivers" (车手, *che shou*) to impersonate the victim in order to obtain real assets. To evade detection by law enforcement, cybercriminals will apply for bank cards with fake or purchased ID information. Money-laundering strategies include transferring money from the victim's account to the criminal's by using a fake ID, withdrawing cash from an ATM, or performing bank or credit card fraud at the point of sale (POS).

Cybercriminals often perform several specialized roles in the real assets value chain and are involved in different transactions at the same time. In the 2009 "TopFox" cybercrime case, the individual "Jin X" performed dual roles: he served as the "material-washing man" for another cyber-criminal, as well as for his own credit card fraud operation. While performing these roles, Jin also cooperated with another "material-washing man," who sought the services of a blackhat named "ONaNa" in order to remove set payment limits on the accounts. The Internet provides a perfect environment for cybercriminals who have often never met in person to specialize in certain capabilities and gain illegal profits as a result.

Table 4.1 JARGON USED IN THEFT VALUE CHAINS

Chinese	Pinyin	English	Jargon (contextual meaning)
Real assets theft value chain			
料	*liao*	Material	Banking credentials
轨道料	*gui dao liao*	Track material	Stolen information
轨道	*gui dao*	Track	containing bank card encryption
料主	*liaozhu*	Material master	Criminal who steals and sells bank encryption information
洗料	*xi liao*	Material washing	Money-laundering phase
洗料人	*xi liao ren*	Material washing man	Criminal who performs money laundering
刷货	*shua huo*	Cargo unpacking	Procedure of counterfeit card copying and ATM/POS fraud
车主	*che zhu*	Car master	Group leader
车手	*che shou*	Car driver ("cowboy")	Criminal who visits the ATM
Network virtual assets theft value chain			
信封	*xin feng*	Envelope	Account and password
信	*xin*	Envelope	information of a variety
邮箱	*youxiang*	Mailbox	of online games and entertainment software
箱子	*xiangzi*	Box	Online Web applications that harvest the envelope
木马作者	*muma zuozhe*	Trojan writers	Trojan creators
木马代理	*muma daili*	Trojan agents	
包马人	*baoma ren*	Trojan buyout man	Criminal who performs envelope theft attacks
洗信人	*xixin ren*	Envelope-washing man	Criminal who buys the bundled envelopes and uses automated tools to steal network assets or gain control of valuable accounts
包销商	*baoxiao shang*	Channel trader	Person who buys stolen network assets through legal channels and sells the assets for real money

(Continued)

Table 4.1 (Continued)

Chinese	Pinyin	English	Jargon (contextual meaning)
Internet resources and services abuse, and blackhat techniques, tools, and training value chains			
黑客	*heike*	Hackers, crackers, or blackhats	Major source of network attacks driven by economic profits
黑客任务	*heike renwu*	Hacker jobs	Blackhat activities
收徒	*shoutu*	Seeking an apprentice	Advertisement for blackhat training services
拜师	*baishi*	Seeking a master	Advertisement for learning blackhat techniques
免杀	*miansha*	Detection evasion	Services to make Trojan products undetectable or resistant to antivirus software
0day攻击	*0day gongji*	Zero-day attack	A newly discovered software vulnerability with no released corresponding security patch

Labor specialization in illegal markets improves efficiency and expands the overall market size.

Network Virtual Assets Theft Value Chain

China's video game and online entertainment industries have been booming over the past decade. Most of the popular online game or entertainment systems have introduced virtual currency, equipment, and membership to enhance the gaming experience and earn more profits. Gamers must either pay real money for virtual assets or invest a great deal of time to earn them. Through online markets, these virtual assets can be sold to other players and converted into real-world money. In this sense, virtual assets have real value. Therefore, for gamers, virtual assets are a very close substitute for real assets in cyberspace.

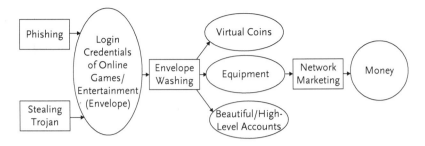

Figure 4.3 The Structure of the Network Virtual Assets Theft Value Chain

The network virtual asset theft value chain of the Chinese Internet is comprised of three phases, as shown in figure 4.3. In the first phase, cybercriminals steal account and password information for online gaming accounts using phishing or Trojan tools. In the second "envelope washing" (洗信, *xixin*) phase, they log into the online system with the stolen account credentials and steal assets such as virtual currency and game equipment. Alternatively, sometimes cybercriminals will modify the authentication password for all the accounts by replacing it with an easily remembered password or change the settings to allow for additional membership. In the last phase, cybercriminals sell the stolen virtual network assets to game players through the online market to earn real-world profits.

The 2007 "Panda burning incense" case exemplifies the relationships within the virtual assets theft value chain. Trojan writer Li, who had received training from Trojan master Lei, used the "Panda" virus to compromise several hosts and connect them to the website of the Trojan agent (木马代理, *muma daili*) Wang. The Trojan buyout man (包马人, *baoma ren*) Zhang then purchased compromised hosts from Wang and used the information to steal network virtual assets (envelopes) from these accounts. Zhang made profits of RMB 12,000 after paying more than RMB 225,000 to individuals identified as Li and Wang.[14]

Because the Chinese legal and regulatory environment surrounding the protection of virtual property is underdeveloped and poorly enforced, cybercriminals tend to exploit these legislative defects and make profits at a lower legal risk than if they stole real assets. With such a large online gaming market and little state regulation safeguarding virtual property, this value chain has become uniquely popular for Chinese cybercriminals.

Internet Resources and Services Abuse Value Chain

Today's Internet provides the means for illicit gains outside of direct profit. As long as an online resource or service can generate economic benefit, there will be someone aiming to exploit them for their own personal gain. Even nontradable resources and services can be abused to produce profits, through means such as blackmail or extortion. Abuse of Internet resources and services has developed in a piecemeal fashion due to the absence of comprehensive governance and industry regulation. The most popular and important resources on the Internet include computing capacity, storage, bandwidth, IP addresses, network traffic, and sensitive data. On the Internet, more resources provide more power for the owner. Cybercriminals abuse such resources and power to undermine existing Internet regulations for illegal economic gain and to support the hacking activities in the other value chains.

Blackhat Techniques, Tools, and Training Value Chain

"Blackhat" hacking techniques (as distinguished from "whitehat" hackers who create legitimate code in the software ecosystem) have a profound impact on the formation and development of the underground economy because they penetrate all aspects of the value chains. In this way, blackhat techniques provide the engine for the operation of the underground economy. The blackhat community provides its expertise to the underground

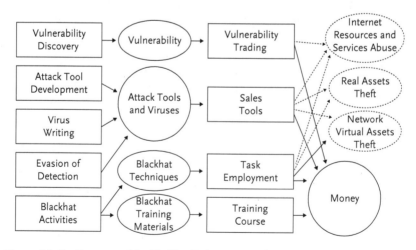

Figure 4.4 The Structure of the Blackhat Techniques, Tools, and Training Value Chain

Zhuge Jianwei, Gu Lion, Duan Haixin, and Taylor Roberts

economy in two different forms: products and services. As shown in figure 4.4, the blackhats discover software vulnerabilities, write a variety of malware or attack tools, and then sell the vulnerabilities or malicious programs to cybercriminals in the other three value chains. Without these products, low-skilled cybercriminals would have no capacity to engage in cybercrime activities. For example, a cybercriminal named Yan bought a Trojan called "blandness" from a blackhat named Zeng. He then had another blackhat, Lu, modify it for different online games. Thanks to the tools provided by these two blackhats, Yan sold the modified blackhat tools at a very large profit of RMB 950,000.[15] The blackhat community also provides various hardware tools to support cybercrime activities targeting mobile phone users. For example, GSM modems and SMS servers are two kinds of hardware sold in the underground market and are also used to send spam SMS to mobile phone users.[16]

In terms of services, blackhats also accept temporary employment to launch distributed denial of service (DDoS) attacks assigned by the employer. In addition, some blackhats provide paid training services to new entrants ("newbies") or will train them for free in exchange for labor. In this way, the blackhat community is the principal nexus for the endurance and development of the underground economy. With the expansion of the overall size of the underground online economy (explained further in the analysis below), the increasing number of blackhats will have a huge impact on the growth of this market, as these individuals provide the tools and training necessary for all other value chains.

EMPIRICAL ANALYSIS OF THE ONLINE UNDERGROUND ECONOMY

In order to perform a more in-depth investigation of the current state and trends of the Chinese underground online economy, we collected and analyzed information from a variety of sources. Our methodology estimates the overall damage of the cybercrime economy, the number of threatened users, and the distribution of participants and businesses. Finally, we monitored, tracked, and recorded messages posted on the web forum Baidu Post Bar and the chat group Tencent QQ in order to compile a dataset of criminal transactions. These two platforms are the primary means of communication in the Chinese underground markets, used by cybercriminals in order to both conceal their intentions from outsider scrutiny and to appeal to prospective participants.

We used several data sources to support our investigation of the current state and trends of the underground economy. Security threat monitoring reports and statistical information published by the leading Chinese security vendors and national security regulatory departments limited the need for independent research.[17] We also utilized records from court cases and media reports of certain cybercrime cases driven by the underground economy. We used a subscription database of legal cases to obtain the official case records and found media coverage of the cases for supplemental information. Observing advertisements and messages from the Chinese Internet underground markets provided a unique perspective on activity in the online underground economy. After conducting research to gain a thorough understanding of this underground economy, we were able to locate the majority of the black markets on the openly accessible Chinese Internet. The most prevalent of these platforms in China are Baidu Post Bar and Tencent QQ, and by tapping into these platforms we were able to continuously monitor advertisements and messages within these markets.

Baidu Post Bar is one of the largest Chinese web forums on the Internet. It provides a keyword-based forum organization, as well as a loose and convenient login and post mechanism. In our research we deciphered the meaning of a large number of hacker terms, and through exhaustive keyword searches on this slang we have monitored several underground markets built on Baidu Post Bar.[18] Since Baidu Post Bar is a public web forum, it retains historical entries for all post records. Not only did we use the search engine to continuously monitor and copy the posts in the underground black markets, we were able to retrieve historical records and add them to the database for further statistical analysis. As of March 15, 2012, we had trawled nearly 1.1 million posts from the 129 post bars dedicated to underground markets on Baidu Post Bar. Each post record includes the posting time, title, content, thread ID, sequence in a thread, author's nickname, author's member ID (for registered users), and author's C-class IP range (for anonymous users). After removing duplicate posts with identical titles and content, we built a dataset containing 753,806 posts and 255,544 threads from 2004 to 2011 for further empirical analysis. Each thread has an average of nearly three posts after removing duplicates, and about 248,970 nicknames or IP C-class ranges participate in the markets.

An even greater number of underground black markets are built on Tencent QQ chat groups; these groups also use advertisements in web forum-based black markets and jargon and group-specific search terms. Participants search and apply to join the groups, and the group operators

Zhuge Jianwei, Gu Lion, Duan Haixin, and Taylor Roberts

choose to accept or deny applications after verifying whether applicants are in the underground community. Because we have deciphered the jargon, we can use keywords to search the groups for black markets, taking advantage of the search function provided by Tencent QQ software.[19] We used a dataset from March to May 2012 of 130 Tencent QQ chat groups dedicated to underground markets. We adopted a simple strategy for thread identification: within one Tencent QQ chat group, messages sent within intervals of less than five minutes were considered to belong to a single thread; messages sent after an interval of more than five minutes were labeled as the first message of a new thread. We also removed duplicate messages that had identical content sent from the same sender's Tencent QQ number that were from the same thread. After processing the Tencent QQ messages in this manner we obtained a dataset of 76,516 messages in 23,720 threads sent by 7,996 Tencent QQ ID numbers in 130 Tencent QQ chat groups. Each record includes the timestamp, content, sender's nickname, sender's Tencent QQ number, thread ID, and the sequence of the thread.

We then wrote a variety of programs to parse the data, gather the IP range information of anonymous users, and eliminate extraneous data.[20] We then performed a detailed analysis of the size and trends of the underground markets, the number and distribution of participants, as well as the distribution of business types, in order to gain a better understanding of the underground economy.

In the following sections, we estimate the overall damage done by the underground economy, highlight characteristics and trends, and identify relationships between published information and our findings. While the empirical evidence only provides descriptive statistics, these previously unanalyzed findings can be the foundation for future research in this field. Through this analysis we also show how the measurement of underground markets can support cybercrime investigations.

ESTIMATED DAMAGES FROM THE ONLINE UNDERGROUND ECONOMY

Based on our structural analysis of the Chinese underground economy, we compiled descriptive statistics of the four different underground value chains and estimated the overall damage of these industries and the threat they pose to the Chinese population. The results are summarized in table 4.2 and discussed further below.

Table 4.2 AN ESTIMATE OF THE OVERALL DAMAGE FROM THE
UNDERGROUND ECONOMY IN CHINA, 2011

Value chain	Major profit approach	Threatened population (millions)	Population damaged	Estimated damage (millions of USD)
Real assets theft	Third-party payment theft and fraud	38.8	480,000	262
	Online banking theft and fraud		60,000	67
Network virtual assets theft	Game virtual assets theft	38.4	3,840,000	225
Resources and services abuse	Compromised hosts abuse	8.9	8,900,000	71
	Infected mobile phone abuse	24.71	49,420,000 (incidents)	157
	"Hacked" website abuse	1.1 (websites)	2,100,000 (incidents)	70
Totals		110.8 (users) 1.1 (websites)		852

Estimated Damages from the Real Assets Theft Value Chain

The real assets theft value chain presents a common threat to Internet users. According to a 2011 China Internet Network Information Center (CNNIC) report, 8% of Chinese Internet users encountered online shopping fraud or theft (that is, one in every twelve Internet users in China). This provides an estimated threatened population size of 38.8 million.[21] The security threats to online shopping and payment include phishing (89% of attacks), online fraud (8% of attacks), and account theft (3% of attacks).[22]

Third-party payment accounts are by far the most frequent target of phishing attacks.[23] Based on these estimates, we deduce that third-party payment account theft in 2011 caused direct economic losses of about RMB 1.65 billion (USD 262 million), and accounts for 7.6 ten-thousandths of the total market of third-party payments, totaling RMB 2.16 trillion.[24] Online banking accounts are also highly subject to real asset theft. We used the 2006 estimated losses from ICBC (the largest bank in China) as a base for determining the 2011 damage assessment in the banking sector.[25] After adjusting for the increased number of ICBC online banking customers and controlling for changes in network defense, the 2011 estimated overall damage involving ICBC alone reached RMB 153 million.[26] Considering that ICBC has 36.4% of China's online banking market share,[27] we can extrapolate the damage of real asset theft to ICBC's customers to the total population of online banking users—a total loss of RMB 420 million (USD 67 million) that affects approximately 60,000 victims.[28]

Estimated Damages from the Network Virtual Assets Theft Value Chain

Online games are one of the most popular applications on the Chinese Internet. In late 2011, the number of PC online game users (the largest user base) reached 120 million, while the market size grew to RMB 44.6 billion.[29] The majority of these games use virtual currency to purchase games, equipment, and other tools, nearly all of which are purchased with real currency. The ability to purchase online games and equipment creates a real value for virtual currency. Chinese law, however, has yet to sufficiently protect virtual assets, making them an easy target for fraud and assets theft.

The three major security threats present in the online game industry are phishing scams (58% of attacks), theft Trojans (38% of attacks), and general deception through social engineering attacks (9% of attacks).[30] In the first half of 2011, Qihoo 360 detected more than 30,000 phishing websites targeting online games that went beyond the 79 million traditional thieving Trojans, making them the most dangerous of all the threats to online gaming security.[31] By extrapolating from a 2012 Tencent QQ survey, we estimate that 3.84 million players suffered losses in 2011, causing direct economic losses of RMB 1.42 billion (USD 225 million).[32] This constitutes 3.18% of the online game market share in 2011.

Estimated Damages from the Internet Resources and Services Abuse Value Chain

The profit models in the Internet resources and services abuse value chain are even more diverse, rendering it more difficult to quantitatively estimate the overall market damage. Thus, in our analysis we only consider the three most important resource types: compromised hosts, infected smartphones, and "hacked" website servers. There were 8.9 million hosts compromised by botnets or Trojans, with an average loss of RMB 50 each.[33]

Smartphones were infected 49.42 million times throughout 2011, with an average loss of RMB 20 each.[34] Based on 57,000 drive-by download attacks, and 2.059 million hidden-link attacks, hacked servers at RMB 200 (search engine optimization) to RMB 500 (drive-by download) each, the total cost was RMB 440 million.[35] Although we present only three resource types in our estimate results in an incomplete picture of the total market damage, in 2011 the overall market damage brought by the Internet resources and services abuse value chain reached RMB 1,875 million ($298 million USD) with these types alone.

Estimated Damages from the Blackhat Techniques, Tools, and Training Value Chain

The blackhat techniques, tools, and training value chain does not directly bring market damage to Internet users. However, it is the foundation of the other three underground value chains. Due to the sophistication and sensitivity of the blackhat business, we are not aware of any methodology to measure the estimated damage presented by this value chain. For example, zero-day vulnerabilities are likely sold at a very high price, but are transacted in a more secretive and secure marketplace.[36] We also lack the necessary data sources to perform even a rough quantitative estimate.

Damages from the Underground Economy Summarized

Utilizing the aforementioned conservative estimates, we believe that the current overall damage attributable to the Chinese online underground economy exceeds RMB 5.36 billion (USD 852 million). Even when taking into account the full range of protections security vendors provide to Internet users, the underground economy still threatens more than 110.8 million Internet users today, which accounts for 21.6% of the total 513 million Chinese Internet users.[37] In addition, the underground economy jeopardizes 1.1 million websites, which constitute 20% of all monitored Chinese websites.[38] Taking into account the upstream phases of the three estimated chains, feedback to the blackhat techniques, tools, and training value chain, as well as the profit chain of "service fraud" that employs a large number of participants, we estimate that the overall market size of the Chinese online underground economy is greater than RMB 10 billion—equivalent to a year's revenue of one of the largest Internet companies in China, such as Baidu or the Alibaba Group.

ANALYSIS OF THE UNDERGROUND MARKETS

Our empirical model and dataset were built through careful observation of Baidu Post Bar and Tencent QQ chat groups. These web forums are the primary platforms for underground market transactions and are publicly available. By using the search function and our list of key jargon phrases, we were able to observe important trends in market behavior and participation, as well as conduct a business analysis of the market, all of which demonstrate the unique environment of the Chinese underground economy. In this section we describe several notable features of the structure and dynamics of these markets.

Market Behavior

Clear trends in the Chinese online underground economy can be charted from annual statistics of Baidu Post Bar and Tencent QQ posts, threads, and participants (see figure 4.5). It is evident from the trajectory observed that the Chinese underground economy is expanding at an alarming rate.[39] Any effort to halt the expansion of this market, like the criminal law amendment to combat cybercrime in February 2009, has met with only short-term and minimal success. While the number of threads did decrease from 2008 to 2009, this change was only temporary, and all three measures of participation increased the following year. Without effective and long-term countermeasures, we expect the Chinese online underground economy to sustain its rapid growth.

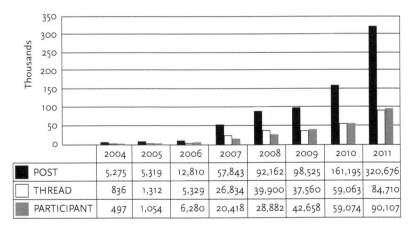

	2004	2005	2006	2007	2008	2009	2010	2011
POST	5,275	5,319	12,810	57,843	92,162	98,525	161,195	320,676
THREAD	836	1,312	5,329	26,834	39,900	37,560	59,063	84,710
PARTICIPANT	497	1,054	6,280	20,418	28,882	42,658	59,074	90,107

Figure 4.5 Annual Posts, Threads, and Participants in Underground Markets

If we look at monthly statistics for posts and threads, a clear annual cycle emerges: January and February exhibit low activity, while June to August is the peak period of activity. We believe that the winter lull in activity relates to the observation of the Chinese New Year holiday, while the summer spike coincides with the education system's summer holiday, when online shopping and gaming increase. The daily statistics of the total number of Tencent QQ messages, threads, and ID numbers indicate that the peak traffic time is on the weekends, reaching nearly eight hundred messages within the monitored period.

Market Participation

Figure 4.6 portrays the types of participants in the underground market. The number of "new participants" in the economy is indicative of the growth potential of this underground economy. A policy change made by Baidu requiring all members to hold a valid account if they wish to post resulted in a reduction of new anonymous participants in the market. The steady increase in the "old registered" participants shows that these backbone members still hold a strong influence within the market. Finally, it is worthwhile to point out that even though the number of total threads decreased during the implementation of the 2009 efforts to combat cybercrime, the underground community continued to grow at a rate of 47.7%. This trend reflects the holding power of the underground economy in that participants are continually motivated by the potential for high profits,

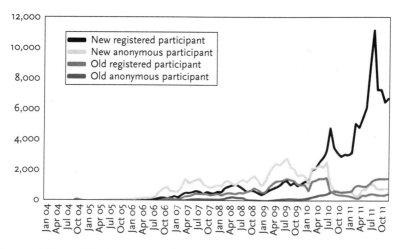

Figure 4.6 Types of Participants in Baidu Post Bar Underground Markets, by Month

Zhuge Jianwei, Gu Lion, Duan Haixin, and Taylor Roberts

incentivized to participate on a long-term basis, and are not deterred by short-term law enforcement campaigns.

In addition, according to our dataset, 55.8% of Baidu posts contain Tencent QQ contact information and 67.6% of participants have advertised their Tencent QQ number in underground markets. This statistical data supports our hypothesis that Tencent QQ is the contact method of choice for further communication between participants.[40]

Geographical Distribution of Participants

By comparing the IP ranges of anonymous participants against an existing location library of provinces, cities, and the specific address, we generated a geographical distribution of participants in the underground economy in China.[41] Figure 4.7 shows the geographical distribution of the 86,337 distinct C-class IP ranges used by anonymous participants in the underground markets on Baidu Post Bar, by province. The top ten are all either coastal provinces with prevalent Internet access and large economies or slightly less economically developed central provinces with large populations. Given this geographical distribution, it is clear that cybercrime prevention

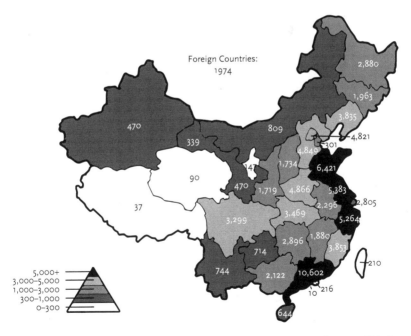

Figure 4.7 Geographical Distribution of Anonymous Participants in Underground Markets, by Province

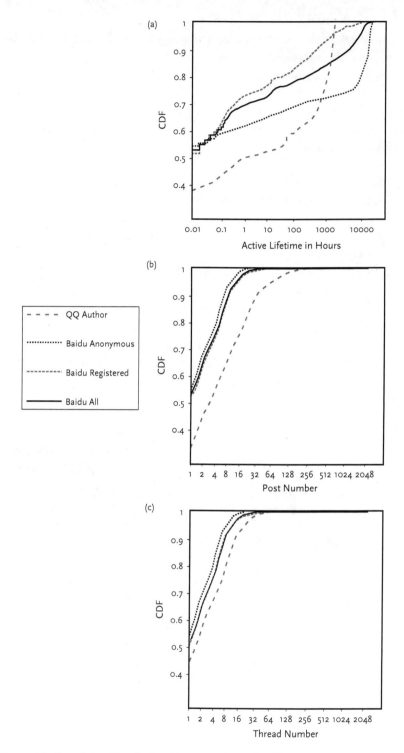

Figure 4.8 Cumulative Distribution Functions for Behavior of Underground Market Participants

efforts must be focused on coastal regions. Further investigation of the geospatial relationship between cybercrime and particular industries may yield more insight into participant characteristics and behaviors.

Participant Behavior

We performed further statistical clustering applying cumulative distribution function (CDF) curves to the identification information in our datasets such as nickname, IP range, and Tencent QQ number. Our goal was to analyze participants' behavior including characteristics such as initial presence, latest presence, duration of active lifetime, number of posts/messages, number of involved threads, and number of involved post bars / Tencent QQ chat groups.[42] With this data, we conducted behavioral analysis of different types of participants in different underground markets in order to map various characteristics of the underground economy. Figure 4.8 displays three cumulative distribution functions (CDF) depicting, on the vertical axis, the percentage of values (the hours a transaction is active, the number of posts, and the number of threads, respectively) which have less than a given amount on the horizontal axis.

When interpreting the results of the CDF curves, certain behavioral characteristics can be identified. Part of the figure shows that more than 80% of participants have a "short" active lifetime of less than one hundred hours (4.2 days), while nearly 15% of the participants who have what can be considered a "long" active lifetime of over one thousand hours (41.7 days). The difference between "long" active lifetimes of registered and anonymous participants can be explained by the ability of registered participants to change nicknames to avoid detection. The long-active lifetime participants are important to observe because the experience and tools they accrue over this time constitute the backbone of the market. Also, the change in slope of the CDF curve of Tencent QQ chat groups at around twelve hours may reflect the maximum number of work hours in a day.

The CDFs of participants' posts and threads are shown in parts b and c respectively. These graphs indicate that participants seem to rely on Baidu Post Bar for advertising and then utilize Tencent QQ private messages for communication in order to protect their anonymity.[43]

Distribution of Goods and Services Behavior

To analyze the business distribution of the datasets, we labeled posts with tags related to illicit goods and services accordingly. We also created labels for

Table 4.3 ADVERTISEMENTS FOR THE FOUR VALUE CHAINS IN THE UNDERGROUND MARKETS

Value chain	Ads selling illicit material	Ads seeking illicit material	Ratio	Ads selling illicit material	Ads seeking illicit material	Ratio
	Baidu			Tencent QQ		
Real assets theft	31,980	17,270	1.85	1,481	86	17.22
Network virtual assets theft	121,191	29,105	4.16	2,087	128	16.3
Internet resources and service abuse	119,233	70,872	1.68	5,417	328	16.52
Blackhat techniques, tools, and training	61,183	44,781	1.37	3,898	217	17.96
Total (with duplicates)	333,587	162,028	2.06	12,883	759	16.97
Total (duplicates deleted)	265,980	118,710	2.24	10,816	608	17.79

business behaviors including ads selling illicit material and want ads seeking such material.[44] The results of this analysis can be found in table 4.3.

After tagging posts with these different classifications on the Baidu Post Bar dataset, we discovered that total want ads outnumbered ads selling materials by more than two to one (four to one in the popular virtual assets theft value chain). This imbalance shows that the supply in the market still significantly lags behind demand. The real assets theft industry chain had fewer ads than the other three industry chains, perhaps because participants involved in this chain experience a higher degree of risk due to the severity of the crime.

When comparing the Baidu dataset with the Tencent QQ dataset, we find that the percentage of ads in the Tencent QQ dataset is much lower than in the Baidu dataset, further supporting our hypothesis that the instant messaging feature of Tencent QQ chat groups encourages interaction within the underground markets. The reason behind this is that Tencent QQ chat groups allow real-time online conversation between many users, which lowers the number of messages irrelevant to ads, such as greeting messages in Baidu Post Bar. In addition, the ratio of sales to want ads in the Tencent QQ dataset is higher than that in the Baidu dataset. Figure 4.9 shows the distribution of ads for goods and services from the processed Baidu Post Bar dataset for the four underground market value chains.

The advertisement distribution in each value chain reflects several noteworthy attributes. In the real assets chain, banking information is requested

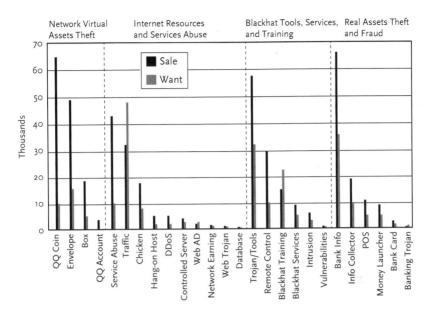

Figure 4.9 The Distribution of Goods and Services Advertisements in the Baidu Post Bar Underground Markets

Table 4.4 FOREIGN AND DOMESTIC GOODS

Goods	Goods as a percentage of all advertisements	Domestic goods advertisements (percentage)	Foreign goods advertisements (percentage)
Banking materials	0.1	62.5	37.5
Compromised hosts	0.3	72.5	27.5
Controlled servers	2.1	58.5	41.5
Website traffic	0.4	69.5	30.5

most often. When observing the virtual assets chain, the sales-to-want ratio is more than three to one, reflecting the high vulnerability for theft in online games in China. A noteworthy point for the Internet resources and services abuse value chain is that website traffic want ads outnumber sale ads by about 47%, showing the inability of supply to meet demand for this specific type of resource. In blackhat training, supply also falls short of demand, as want ads (i.e., "seeking a master") outnumber sale ads (i.e., "seeking an apprentice") by nearly 25%. This result suggests that the underground economy will continue to maintain rapid growth with constant infusion of new blood unless effective and persistent countermeasures are implemented.

Table 4.4 shows the domestic or foreign origin of popular goods in the dataset. Few advertisements were obviously labeled "domestic" (内, *nei*), "foreign" (外, *wai*), or with a unique country name. According to our observations, the majority of both labeled and unlabeled advertisements are related to domestic goods and services. These results contribute to our hypothesis that the online underground economy in China is still a very internally oriented economy, unlike the Russian or Nigerian online underground economies, which are export-driven.[45]

Roles of Participants

We also analyzed the distribution of roles in the underground economy based on the type of ads posted by participants.[46] The business distribution among these participants is shown in table 4.5. The role with the most participants is "envelope-washing man" with 29,916 participants, because this job does not involve blackhat techniques—thus it serves more as a "gateway" role to bring new participants into in the underground.

Table 4.5 BUSINESS DISTRIBUTION OF PARTICIPANTS IN THE BAIDU POST BAR UNDERGROUND MARKETS

Chain	Participants	Percentage	Major role	Participants	Percentage
Real assets theft	21,460	16.5	"Material master"	14,524	11.1
			"Material washing Man"	8,345	6.4
Network virtual assets theft	58,963	45.5	"Trojan buyout man"	20,486	15.8
			"Envelope-washing man"	29,916	23
Internet resources and services abuse	67,003	51.6	"Computer hacker"	16,078	12.4
			"Website hacker"	14,259	11
Blackhat techniques, tools, and training	39,605	30.5	"Trojan author/ agent"	18,945	14.6
			"zero-day trader"	421	0.3
			"blackhat master"	8,140	6.3
			"blackhat apprentice"	11,439	8.8

Zhuge Jianwei, Gu Lion, Duan Haixin, and Taylor Roberts

Price Extraction and Analysis

Another aspect of our analysis utilized the five most popular and important types of goods in order to perform a price extraction: banking information, "envelopes,"compromised hosts, website traffic, and Trojans/tools. Although most goods advertised did not have a listed price, a small portion of posts did. We used common Chinese sentence models and regular expressions to extract price information from the ads, and then calculated the monthly average price for sales and purchases; we left months without any price information blank. Table 4.6 summarizes these results.

This tracking and analysis of prices for major goods and services sold in the underground markets can help the security community quantify the costs of certain attacks. For example, the cost of a DDoS attack with 1,000 compromised hosts in November 2011 was approximately RMB 200 (about USD 30), using an average selling price of compromised hosts as low as RMB 0.1 (about USD 0.15) and DDoS tools that averaged RMB 100 (about USD 15). This approach of quantifying attack costs provides valuable reference information for deploying targeted security precautions.

Cheating in the Underground

Apart from advertisements, there are many posts revealing fraudulent behavior from other participants in the underground markets. A considerable number of advertisements also contained warnings of fraud. Although

Table 4.6 AVERAGE PRICE OF GOODS IN THE MARKET

Type of good	Cost per good	Relative supply
Banking information	Revenue sharing model[a]	Varies
Envelope	RMB 1–3 (USD 0.2–.5)[b]	Steady supply
Website traffic	RMB 330 (USD 50) per 10,000 visits	Undersupplied
Compromised hosts	RMB 0.1–0.5 (USD 0.01–0.1)	Oversupplied
Trojans/tools	RMB 100–1,000 (USD 15–150)[c]	Varies

[a] For banking information, there is no specific pricing. Rather, a revenue sharing model is used to divide up illegal profits. In the few ads that did mention the specific method of revenue-sharing, the ratios used were typically "split equally" or "you sixty and me forty [percent]."
[b] Low-price dumping occurred over a span of several months, with a sale price of lower than RMB 0.5 (about USD 0.1).
[c] The majority of the ads are posted by sellers rather than buyers. Typically Trojan or virus program want ads are seeking a particular type of Trojan or virus, and in this case purchase prices are generally higher than sale prices (up to RMB 2,000 or USD 300).

underground markets function as online exchange platforms for collaboration on cybercrimes, they still exhibit bad-faith transactions and criminals
who try to cheat one another. By tabulating mentions of cheating activity,
our results suggest that 2.1% of posts describe incidents of cheating, while
one in every twenty-five participants who suffered serious cheating behavior revealed the offender.

These statistics indicate the disorder and uncertainty present in the
underground markets. Nonetheless, participants are still able to use other
communication and payment channels to follow up with deals advertised
in the open on an underground market, including Tencent QQ private
messages and Alipay guaranteed payment. Due to the private nature of the
follow-up on an initial post, we are unable to perform detailed measurement of the prevalence of cheating in the underground economy.

The Relationship between Cybercrime Cases and Underground Market Activity

In order to verify the applicability of our findings to actual cybercrime
cases, we analyzed the relationship between our measured dataset of
underground markets and four Chinese cybercrime cases. Through careful investigation of court profiles and media reports of these cases, we
matched the offenders' profile information with posts in the underground
markets dataset that matched this information for every case before the
public exposure date of the case in question.[47] This method uncovered
posts mentioning goods and services, related posts, and traceable clues fit-
ting the information collected from each case, thus identifying the historical trail of these four cybercrimes in the underground markets.

The matched results are shown in table 4.7. In the "Topfox" case, posts
relating to the nickname Topfox and sale ads for the malicious programs
utilized in the attack were referenced up to four years before the offender's
arrest in 2008. Further exhaustive review of related posts in the dataset
revealed some critical tracing clues such as IP range, Tencent QQ number, and payment banking account, which would have been of use to law
enforcement agencies in tracing the offender or his accomplices, had they
been actively investigating the underground in real time.

Based on the above results, we are confident that monitoring underground markets can help to identify, track, and perhaps prevent a portion
of ongoing cybercrime activities, and can also provide critical evidence for
criminal investigations.

Table 4.7 HISTORICAL EVIDENCE OF KNOWN CYBERCRIME CASES FOUND IN UNDERGROUND MARKETS

Case/public exposure date	Case information	Matched posts	First appearance	Latest appearance	Clues
Topfox, April 14, 2008	Topfox	98	July 8, 2005	February 26, 2008	
	Topfox Downloader	3	November 11, 2006	August 15, 2007	IP
	Password Stammer	290	January 1, 2004	April 1, 2008	Tencent QQ number
	Password Extractor	346	February 26, 2004	April 1, 2008	Bank account
	Fox King Virus	6	June 30, 2005	July 5, 2007	
Panda burning incense, February 12, 2007	689565	1	January 23, 20073	January 23, 2007	
	www.krvkr.com	155	January 14, 2007	February 2, 2007	Whois
	Wuhan Boy 2005	42	December 12, 2004	February 10, 2007	website, IP
Swordsman DDoS, November 27, 2009	Swordsman stress test	6	December 29, 2008	September 24, 2009	website, IP
Blandness Horse, August 6, 2008	Blandness horse	128	January 26, 2008	August 3, 2008	website, Tencent QQ

DISCUSSION AND CONCLUSION

In this chapter, we have carried out a comprehensive, multi-method investigation of the Chinese underground economy in cyberspace. Through the measurement of cybercrime markets, we were able to observe typical advertisements and communication behaviors, and present a detailed empirical exploration of underground activities.

Participants in the online underground economy engage in illegal activities while simultaneously attempting to remain undetected. Thus, underground markets are primarily advertising venues, and further illicit activities including communication, bargaining, transaction, and payment are most likely to occur via private messages and peer-to-peer transmission. Some high-tier aspects of the underground economy, such as trading of zero-day vulnerabilities, selling business intelligence, and advanced persistent threat (APT) tasks, are likely to occur in even more hidden and secure communication channels between small groups with mutual trust. As researchers outside of law enforcement agencies, we have no means to conduct a more comprehensive survey of the phases further down the transaction chain or the high-tier aspects of the underground economy.

Although our estimate remains in many ways incomplete and conservative, we find that the Chinese online underground economy has developed a complicated yet well-organized structure, with dozens of profit models deriving from four different value chains. We estimate the overall damage in 2011 to have exceeded RMB 5.36 billion (USD 852 million), endangering 110.8 million Internet users and 1.1 million websites. It is important to emphasize that these numbers are inherently imperfect since criminals go out of their way to hide their activity; however, we have been as transparent as possible with our methodology and have provided the first systematic quantification of damages to the Chinese economy. We welcome others to improve on this foundation.

Our measurements also indicate that online underground markets have experienced rapid growth in both the number of posts and the number of participants: in 2011, there were at least 90,000 participants involved in the underground markets, posting more than 320,000 messages belonging to 80,000 threads. Without intervention, growth is not likely to diminish. Our long-term empirical analysis of the underground markets dataset reveals the structural and quantitative characteristics of this underground economy, including market behavior, participant distribution, market business, and fraudulent behavior. In addition, we correlated four major cybercrime cases with activity in our underground markets dataset and found potential evidence to support the criminal cases. This analysis suggests that monitoring underground markets can play a significant supporting role in cybercrime countermeasures.

It would be useful for Chinese cybersecurity authorities and law enforcement agencies to build a more comprehensive monitoring system of online underground markets and establish both standard procedures of investigation and digital forensics of suspicious cybercriminals, within the scope of the law. They should also collaborate more with other countries and international organizations to respond effectively to transnational cybercrime cases. Effective legal countermeasures will contribute to the fight against cybercrime and deter participants in the underground economy, thereby protecting the privacy and property of Chinese Internet users. Although the monitoring of underground markets by law enforcement agencies may lead to more concealment in the underground markets, it will also weaken their activities. Any monitoring of the underground economy and cybercrime countermeasures must be continuous and long term to achieve the best results. To our knowledge, some law enforcement units have built monitoring systems against specific cybercrimes, for example, phishing and phone fraud, but the scope and effectiveness of their systems still need to be improved.

Previous versions of this study have gained public attention, to such an extent that the vice-minister of MIIT issued written instructions for the notification of a Special Action Plan for Governance of the underground economy in August 2013. However, the strategy lacks the necessary nuanced understanding of the online underground economy; for example, simply shutting down the discovered underground black markets may drive the underground economy to evolve and escape from the monitoring scope of law enforcement agencies.[48]

Lastly, a word on the "gray" value chains that threaten Internet infrastructure and Internet users: network virtual assets theft, theft of private information, and Internet services abuse do not yet violate existing legal provisions in China. The priority of law enforcement agencies should be to establish legal protection of individuals' private information and network assets by means of legislation. In China, the "Citizens' Personal Information Protection Law" has been gaining support for six years, yet to this day it has not officially begun the legislative process. During the "Two Sessions" in 2012 (the annual meetings of the National People's Congress and the Chinese People's Political Consultative Congress), the law reemerged as a focus of social concern. In terms of protecting network virtual assets, some courts have cited the property features of network virtual assets to convict cybercriminals involved in virtual assets theft. However, there are still no clearly defined legal protections for these assets.

It is desirable to abate the rapid growth of the Chinese underground economy. Only under a framework of well-formed laws and regulations, more effective measurement and tracking techniques by law enforcement agencies, and a variety of threat protection measures from commercial security vendors, can the risks and hazards of cybercrime suffered by Chinese Internet users be reduced. Yet all these measures must be based on clear understanding of the economic incentives that structure the cybercriminal economy.

NOTES

1. According to a Tencent QQ survey of 2,000 Internet users, 45.5% have experienced theft of instant messaging accounts and 32% have had their game accounts hacked. Increases of false-phishing scams have resulted in hijacked payments or stolen online banking accounts in 5.8% and 5.6% of users, respectively. See Tencent QQ and IResearch, "2011年下半年个人网络安全报告" [Personal Internet Security Report of the Second Half of 2011], http://guanjia.qq.com/security/report2011.

2. M. Q. Chen, "Research of Internet Dark Industry Chain in China," *Modern Science and Technology of Telecommunications* 11 (2006): 8–11 [in Chinese]; "黑客产业攻击网络愈演愈烈国家四部委协同作战联手反黑" [Network Attacks Driven by Underground Economy Growth, Four National Ministries Jointly Perform Coordinated Operations against Cybercrime], *21st Century Business Herald*, January 2007, http://www.bigsea.com.cn/archives/386/; J. Zhuge, T. Holz, C. Song, J. Guo, X. Han, and W. Zou, "Studying Malicious Websites and the Underground Economy on the Chinese Web," paper presented at the Seventh Workshop on the Economics of Information Security (WEIS 2008), Hanover, NH, June 2008; J. Zhuge, Y. Zhou, J. Guo et al., "Malicious Websites on the Chinese Web: Overview and Case Study," paper presented at the Twentieth Annual FIRST Conference (FIRST'08), British Columbia, Canada, June 2008.

3. Tyler Moore and Ross Anderson, "Economics and Internet Security: A Survey of Recent Analytical, Empirical, and Behavioral Research," Computer Science Group, Cambridge, MA, March 2011.

4. Rob Thomas and Jerry Martin, "The Underground Economy: Priceless," *;login:* 31, no. 6 (2006); Marti Motoyama, Damon McCoy, Kirill Levchenko, Stefan Savage, and Geoffrey M Voelker, "An Analysis of Underground Forums," in *IMC'11 Internet Measurement Conference, Berlin, Germany, November 2–4, 2011* (New York: ACM, 2011).

5. J. Franklin, V. Paxson, A. Perrig, and S. Savage, "An Inquiry into the Nature and Causes of the Wealth of Internet Miscreants," Conference on Computer and Communications Security, 2007.

6. On botnets, see Brett Stone-Gross, Marco Cova, et al., "Your Botnet Is My Botnet: Analysis of a Botnet Takeover," in *Proceedings of the 16th ACM Conference on Computer and Communications Security (CCS '09)* (New York: ACM, 2009), 635–47; Zhen Li, Qi Liao, and Aaron Striegel, "Botnet Economics: Uncertainty Matters," in *Managing Information Risk and the Economics of Security*, ed. M. Eric Johnson (New York: Springer Science, 2009), 245–67. On phishing, Marco Cova, Christopher Kruegel, and Giovanni Vigna, "There Is No Free Phish: An Analysis of 'Free' and Live Phishing Kits," in *Proceedings of the 2nd USENIX Workshop on*

Offensive Technologies (WOOT'08) (Berkeley, CA: USENIX Association, 2008). https://www.usenix.org/legacy/events/woot08/tech/full_papers/cova/cova.pdf. On spam, see C. Kreibich, C. Kanich, K. Levchenko, B. Enright, G. M. Voelker, V. Paxson, and S. Savage, "Spamcraft: An Inside Look at Spam Campaign Orchestration," in *Proceedings of the 2nd USENIX Conference on Large-scale Exploits and Emergent Threats: Botnets, Spyware, Worms, and More* (Berkeley, CA: USENIX Association, 2009); C. Kanich, C. Kreibich, K. Levchenko, B. Enright, G. M. Voelker, V. Paxson, and S. Savage, "Spamalytics: An Empirical Analysis of Spam Marketing Conversion," in *Proceedings of the 15th ACM Conference on Computer and Communications Security* (New York: ACM, 2008), 3–14; Kirill Levchenko, Andreas Pitsillidis, Neha Chachra, et al., "Click Trajectories: End-to-End Analysis of the Spam Value Chain," in *Proceedings of the 2011 IEEE Symposium and Security and Privacy* (Oakland, CA: IEEE, 2011), 431–46. On clickbots, Neil Daswani and Michael Stoppelman, "The Anatomy of Clickbot.A," in *Proceedings of the First Workshop on Hot Topics in Understanding Botnets (HotBots'07)* (Berkeley, CA: USENIX Association, 2007); Nicolas Christin, Sally S. Yanagihara, and Keisuke Kamataki, "Dissecting One Click Frauds," in *Proceedings of the 17th ACM Conference on Computer and Communications Security (CCS '10)* (New York: ACM, 2010), 15–26. On pay per install, Juan Caballero, Chris Grier, Christian Kreibich, and Vern Paxson, "Measuring Pay-per-Install: The Commoditization of Malware Distribution," in *Proceedings of the 20th USENIX Security Symposium (Security '11)* (Berkeley, CA: USENIX Association, 2011).

7. Thomas J. Holt and Danielle C. Graves, "A Qualitative Analysis of Advanced Fee Fraud Schemes," *International Journal of Cyber-Criminology* 1, no. 1 (2007): 137–54.

8. Ross Anderson, Chris Barton, Rainer Böhme, Richard Clayton, Michel J. G. van Eeten, Michael Levi, Tyler Moore, and Stefan Savage, "Measuring the Cost of Cybercrime," in *The Economics of Information Security and Privacy*, ed. Rainer Böhme (Berlin: Springer Verlag, 2013), 265–300.

9. Chen, "Research of Internet Dark Industry Chain."

10. "Network Attacks Driven by Underground Economy Growth."

11. By late 2011, the number of online shoppers reached 194 million, comprising 37.8% of all Internet users. Online payment and online banking users also rose to 167 million and 166 million, respectively. See CNNIC, 第29次中国互联网络发展状况统计报告 [The Twenty-Ninth China Internet Development Statistics], January 2012, http://www.cnnic.cn/research/bgxz/tjbg/201201/P020120116330880247967.pdf.

12. Certain offline mechanisms are often utilized by cybercriminals, illustrated in figure 4.2 with dotted lines.

13. Phishing uses both social engineering and technical means—usually a fraudulent email designed to dupe the user into voluntarily loading malicious software—to steal personal identity data and financial account credentials. Trojan horses are a kind of malicious code that can be used to steal users' online banking, credit card, online payment, investment, and other account information.

14. "熊猫烧香"案解密网络病毒产业链 [Uncover the Network Virus Industry Chain from "Panda" Case], Xinhua Net, February 2007, http://news.xinhuanet.com/legal/2007-02/16/content_5745932.htm.

15. "全国最大制售木马案宣判 案犯涉16省市百余人" [Sentencing of Criminals in Country's Largest Case of Manufacturing and Selling Trojans Involved More Than 100 People from 16 Provinces and Cities], Xinhua Net, December 2009, http://news.xinhuanet.com/legal/2009-12/16/content_12656680.htm.

16. Gu Lion, "The Mobile Cybercriminal Underground Market in China," Trend Micro, 2014.

17. We collected the annual security reports for 2011 and other special reports on related subjects published by Antiy Lab, Kingsoft, Qihoo 360, Rising, Tencent QQ, NetQin, and Knownsec. The statistical information on different types of security threats were published by the Anti-Phishing Alliance of China (APAC), the National Computer Network Emergency Response Technical Team Coordination Center, and other national network security regulatory departments.

18. In searching a total of eighty-four terms from the four industrial chains explained previously (alongside the terms for targets, such as online games and online banking), we discovered 129 post bars dedicated to the underground market. We also found 23 post bars with the most common terms of the industry banned by Baidu operators.

19. We searched for a total of eighty-four jargon keywords, and we discovered 2,738 QQ chat groups dedicated to underground markets. Due to workload and time constraints, we selectively joined the 130 largest groups (others were too small), and continuously monitored them from March to May 2012.

20. We used MySQL database, ChunZhen ip2location database, and other programs when collecting this information.

21. CNNIC, "第28次中国互联网络发展状况统计报告" [The Twenty-Eighth China Development Internet Statistics], July 2011, http://www.cnnic.cn/research/bgxz/tjbg/201107/P020110721502208383670.pdf.

22. Due to the heavy influence of phishing in the market, we utilized data of eradicated phishing sites published by APAC and found that third-party payment and banking/stock-market account for over 90% of all the target industries. See APAC, "钓鱼网站处理简报月刊" [Monthly Reports of Phishing Website Dealings], 2011, http://www.apac.org.cn/gzdt/. When comparing the number of phishing sites intercepted by endpoint security vendors like Rising Anti-Virus Software and Qihoo 360 (more than 500,000) with the number of phishing sites eradicated by APAC (approximately 40,000), we find that only a small proportion of phishing sites have been effectively eradicated, mainly because of their short lifespans (phishing sites typically use foreign domains and server hosting, leading to high costs and other difficulties).

23. YeePay received 169 user complaints on account theft from January to October 2011. See Qihoo 360 Security Center, "360联合易宝发布2011网购支付安全报告" [360 and Yeepay Released the 2011 Payment Security Report], January 2012, http://bbs.360.cn/5473016/252581925.html?recommend=1.

24. Assuming that the user complaint rate is 10%, the number of users that encountered account theft in 2011 can be estimated to be about 2,000 users. As of December 2011, third-party payment accounts exceeded 1 billion. See "2011年中国第三方支付市场规模翻番" [Third-Party Payment Market Doubled], *Beijing News*, February 2012, http://tech.ifeng.com/internet/detail_2012_02/23/12715156_0.shtml?_from_ralated. Estimates show that account theft has occurred with more than 480,000 accounts. In addition, according to Kingsoft's security report on online shopping, the average loss per victim is RMB 3,437 (approximately USD 500). See Kingsoft Security, "2011上半年中国网络购物安全报告" [First Half of 2011: China's Online Shopping Security Report], August 2011, http://www.ijinshan.com/download/2011zgwlgwaqbg.pdf. These results are further described in Yiguan, "2011年中国第三方支付连续4季高速发展" [Third-Party Payment Market Quarterly Monitoring for Year 2011], February 2012, http://tech.qq.com/a/20120220/000392.htm.

25. In 2006, after totaling the number of registered victims and announced losses and estimating that about 10% of the victims who suffered account theft or fraud registered at the victim compensation website, we found that nearly 5,000 customers encountered online banking theft, with total losses estimated at RMB 35 million.

26. "工商银行个人网银客户数过亿" [The Number of ICBC Personal Internet Banking Customers Now over 100 Million], *Securities Times*, April 2011, http://www.p5w.net/today/201104/t3572526.htm.

27. DynamiCode, "艾瑞咨询：2010–2011年中国网上银行年度监测报告" [IResearch Consulting: 2010–2011 Online Banking Annual Monitoring Report], September 2011, http://www.dynamicode.com.cn/Chinese/NewsInfo.Asp?ID=850&ClassID=45.

28. This is just a conservative estimate. The Ministry of Public Security uncovered more than 24,000 cases of real assets theft in 2011 during a special mission to combat bank card crime. This crime-fighting mission purportedly prevented economic losses of over RMB 400 million. See "公安部公布"天网—2011行动十大案例" [Ministry of Public Security Announces 10 Cases of "Skynet-2011" Action], December 2011, http://www.gov.cn/fwxx/sh/2011-12/30/content_2033631.htm. Based on this information we can deduce that the online banking theft and fraud value chain could potentially have caused the loss of several hundred million renminbi to RMB 1 billion.

29. Tencent, Netease, and SNDA, the three most popular companies, have market shares of 35.4%, 13.9%, and 11%, respectively. See iResearch, "2011年网络游戏核心数据发布" [2011 Online Game Market Core Data Release], 2011, http://www.iresearch.com.cn/coredata/2011q4_4.shtml; "2011年度中国游戏产业调查报告" [2011 Chinese Online Games Industry Report], http://games.qq.com/a/20120109/000095.htm.

30. Qihoo 360 Security Center, "2011年上半年网络游戏产业安全报告" [Online Game Industry Security Report of the First Half of 2011], http://bbs.360.cn/3229787/250724377.html?recommend=1.

31. This number is a decrease of 19.8% compared to the same period in the previous year. The decline of the traditional Trojan theft threat is notable, leaving room for speculation regarding up and coming threats. APAC's 2011 report cites that Tencent, Netease, and SNDA are the main targets of phishing websites, accounting for 7%, 0.62%, and 0.62% of all targets, respectively. APAC, "钓鱼网站处理简报月刊."

32. This survey of 2,000 Internet users revealed that 32% of those polled encountered online game account theft during the second half of 2011. See Tencent QQ and IResearch, "2011年下半年个人网络安全报告" [Personal Internet Security Report of the Second Half of 2011], http://guanjia.qq.com/security/report2011. If we conservatively estimate that 10% of those polled actually suffered economic losses due to account theft, average losses are assumed relative to the average annual cost on the online games, RMB 371 RMB (about USD 57). See iResearch, "2011年网络游戏核心数据发布."

33. Derived from a variety of profit models including spam, click fraud, PPI fraud, DDoS, and blackmail, various types of online service abuse behavior, and theft of private information. CNCERT/CC, "CNCERT/CC Annual Security Report of 2011" [in Chinese], March 2012, http://www.cert.org.cn/UserFiles/File/201203192011annualreport(1).pdf.

34. Kingsoft, "Chinese Internet Security Report for 2011" [in Chinese], February 2012, http://www.ijinshan.com/news/20120217001.shtml; Qihoo 360 Security Center, "Chinese Network Security Report of Year 2011" [in Chinese], February 2012, http://w.qhimg.com/images/v2/site/360/2011report/2012.pdf; NetQin

Mobile, "2011 Mainland China Mobile Security Report" [in Chinese], January 2012, http://www.netqin.com/upLoad/File/baogao/20120112.pdf.

35. KnownSec, "Chinese Internet Website Security Reports of 2011 to 2012" [in Chinese], March 2012, http://preview.tinyurl.com/877fqwb.

36. Zero-day vulnerabilities are vulnerabilities that are unknown to the developers. These vulnerabilities are highly valued because there no existing patch for this exposure.

37. CNNI, "第29次中国互联网络发展状况统计报告."

38. Knownsec, "2011–2012中国互联网网站安全报告" [2011–2012 China Website Security Report], http://blog.knownsec.com/wp-content/uploads/2012/03/%E7%9F%A5%E9%81%93%E5%88%9B%E5%AE%872011-2012%E5%B9%B4%E4%B8%AD%E5%9B%BD%E4%BA%92%E8%81%94%E7%BD%91%E7%BD%91%E7%AB%99%E5%AE%89%E5%85%A8%E6%8A%A5%E5%91%8A.pdf.

39. The underground market reached its peak growth rate of 352% in 2007. From 2010 to 2011, these markets once again experienced rapid growth, reaching 90,000 participants and nearly doubling the number of posts.

40. References often include QQ numbers in the title, content, or nickname of the posts.

41. We used the C-class IP range information to query the ChunZhen ip2location library. Only 2.79% of anonymous participants use foreign IP ranges to conceal themselves from tracing, implying that most market participants use their real IP addresses. We believe most of these IP ranges are accessed via proxy or VPN in order to evade law enforcement agencies.

42. Attempting to compare the distributions of the number of post bars / QQ chat groups led to biased results due to the potential for several anonymous partici- pants in the same C-class IP range, frequently changing nicknames, or using more than one user account. Also, results from QQ underground chat groups produced skewed results due to the limited scope of monitoring time.

43. The disparity between QQ chat groups and Baidu Post Bar (about 10%–15% more posts in QQ) and since more than 90% of the participants were involved in less than eight threads, it seems clear that these two platforms play different roles in the underground economy.

44. Because the jargon used in the underground economy obscures the information from unintended users, we wrote SQL stored procedures based on our understand- ings in table 4.1. Using this system, we were able to add tags to delineate types of goods and services as well as business behaviors. We also introduced exclusionary keywords to remove commonly used words whose definitions do not pertain to our intended meaning and inclusionary keywords to improve the precision of our search.

45. Group-IB, "State and Trends of the Russian Digital Crime Market 2011," http://group-ib.com/images/media/Group-IB_Report_2011_ENG.pdf;   Cormac Herley, "Why Do Nigerian Scammers Say They Are from Nigeria?" Economics of Information Security and Privacy, June 2012, Berlin, Germany.

46. We monitored 129,968 participants (52% of the total) who posted at least one advertisement. Because it is common for participants to be involved in more than one value chain, the sum of percentages exceeds 100%.

47. Criminal profile information includes nicknames and QQ numbers as well as the names of the malicious code or tools developed or used in the case.

48. And the final effect of the short-time Action Plan is unclear since the results were not published as of March 2014, when this chapter last underwent revision.

PART II
Military Strategy and Institutions

CHAPTER 5

From Cyberwarfare to Cybersecurity in the Asia-Pacific and Beyond

YE ZHENG

TRANSLATED BY YANG FAN

The Asia-Pacific region, which has experienced sustained and rapid growth, has become a vibrant market and a most important engine for economic recovery and growth, and it has acquired an increasingly strategic position in the pattern of global interaction in the twenty-first century. This not only enhances the welfare of the Asia-Pacific but is also a contribution to overall world prosperity.

A comparatively stable security environment has played an important role in the development of the Asia-Pacific in recent years, which is also essential to future development. As an important regional player, China upholds principles such as communicating actively, seeking common ground while minimizing differences, and realizing mutual development. With these principles in mind, China seeks to work with other peaceful countries to address new security challenges in the Asia-Pacific and the world.

Much attention has been paid to security in the physical spaces of land, sea, and air, but not yet enough to security in the virtual world of cyberspace. Born in a US university laboratory in the 1960s, the Internet is one of the most successful inventions in human history.[1] These days, cyberspace, like the air we breathe, is a ubiquitous carrier of information in every field of society, politics, economy, military, culture, foreign affairs, and science and technology. Yet like many advanced technologies, it is a double-edged sword—benefiting mankind but also bringing new security issues. Ironically, the United States, the birthplace of the Internet, is suffering from daily hacking attacks from all over the world. The ability to freely use the Internet is becoming considered a basic human right that deserves respect and maintenance. However, it could also bring new threats to world security if these rights are abused.

Peace and development are still the main melody of the times, but the phantom of cyberwarfare is already hovering at the edges. Cyberwarfare is still in its early stages, yet most countries and armies are quickening their preparations of cyber arms to avoid being the losers in this competition. Under these circumstances, China has also turned more attention to cyberspace security.

National security now depends on cyberspace, and cyberspace is global. Securing the cyberspace will require international cooperation; however, the threats emanating from cyberspace and cyberwarfare are still poorly understood. Without a clear understanding of cyberwarfare, it will be impossible to improve cybersecurity. This chapter first explains the different types of cyberwarfare threats. It then suggests a number of cybersecurity principles all countries advocating peaceful use of the Internet should observe in order to reduce the risk of cyberwarfare.

THE FORMS OF CYBERWARFARE

A tornado of cyberspace conflict has been sweeping across the globe in recent years. The Suter attack on Syria, the Stuxnet virus and "Flame" attack on Iran, Wikileaks disclosures, the Arab Spring events in the Middle East and North Africa, and the PRISM case have come one after the other, bringing cyber conflict to the forefront on the world stage.[2] Not surprisingly, superpowers are behind the curtain of most of these episodes. On May 17, 2011, the White House announced its "International Strategy for Cyberspace," for the first time clearly establishing a comprehensive US policy on cyberspace.[3] The strategy put cybersecurity at the same level of importance as economic and military security and claimed the right to enforce cybersecurity by armed force when necessary, all of which seemed to express a heavy attention to cyberspace warfare. Today the United States has established the world's first dedicated Cyber Command and fully functional cyberwarfare units in order to establish a controlling position over cyber power.[4] Following this example, other countries are developing their own cyber power in competition with one another.

That countries are paying close attention to cyberwarfare reflects their concerns about cyberspace security as well as the latest development in warfare. Looking ahead, cyberwarfare is likely to become a form of combat at the highest levels. It has become a new way for actors to achieve political and military goals through independent activity, and it can be combined with conventional military activities to enhance fighting power. Just as nuclear warfare was the strategic choice of the industrial age, cyberwarfare is becoming the strategic go-to of the information age and an important factor of national security and survival.

Differing from traditional modes of heavy-fire warfare, cyberwarfare is a hidden and quiet type of combat. It is not only active in wars and violent conflict, but also in normal political, economic, military, cultural, and science and technology activities. However, cyberwarfare, as a deterrent and destructive military means, has been behind a veil for a long time. Its mysteries can be unveiled through the example of a few recent skirmishes. Cyberwarfare can be broken down into five categories of combat: the four offensive categories are cyber intelligence, cyber paralysis, cyber and electronic integration, and cyber psychology; the defensive category is aptly named cyber defense.

Cyber Intelligence

People usually think of James Bond and the KGB when talking about the intelligence wars. However, in reality, the war is conducted in silence and is not that exciting. "Cyber warriors" use viruses, Trojan horses, hacker software, and other tools to steal valuable information without leaving their computer screens. Intelligence operations over the Internet have been pervasive and very hard to detect, yet the data they can obtain are rich in timely, sometimes highly classified military information, and at a low cost. Private citizens can become the target of hackers easily and unnoticeably when surfing on the Internet or chatting with friends.

Recent examples abound. In May 2011, one of the world's top military suppliers, Lockheed Martin, and several other US defense enterprises were hacked, even though these enterprises are protected by advanced security technologies and have strict management measures.[5] Lockheed Martin was invaded through the network by unidentified users copying its internal authentication tokens. The company's network stores large amounts of sensitive data on future weapons development and the US military technologies used in Afghanistan and Iraq, which are highly classified.

In a 2006 incident, the Social Security numbers and personal information of more than 100,000 US naval officers and Marine Corps members were leaked on the Internet, and viewed and downloaded more than 10,000 times, causing significant panic among the troops. It was not until the end of June that year that the US Navy was able to detect and stop the leak.[6]

On June 6, 2013, former contractor Edward Snowden disclosed the National Security Agency's (NSA) PRISM information-monitoring program to the *Guardian* and the *Washington Post*, sparking a public uproar and intense instability. On January 14, 2014, the *New York Times* revealed National Security Agency's "Quantum" program, which was an even bigger surprise to the world. The NSA can secretly implant software into computers not connected to the Internet through radio waves that are sent by preinstalled circuit boards and USB cards. According to the report, since 2008, the United States has carried out nearly 100,000 "computer network exploits." American experts said that the White House has strongly criticized Chinese hackers for trying to steal US military and commercial secrets, but it turns out that the United States has been doing the same thing to China. That is the same as building a "digital highway for launching cyberattacks," and if true, the enormous threats and risks presented to other countries by the "Quantum" program are obvious.[7]

According to statistics revealed by the US intelligence community, 80% of the information that their offices obtain comes from publicly available sources, and approximately half of that 80% comes from the Internet.[8] Learning from the American experience, the intelligence agencies of various countries have started to use Internet technologies to either decipher or attack the websites of targeted objects in order to obtain vital intelligence data.

While it is common, even expected, that countries carry out intelligence activities, taking advantage of information and network technology to openly implement a wide range of monitoring, such as PRISM and the "Quantum" program, is very rare. The United States sets a bad example.

Cyber Paralysis

The Internet is becoming the controlling "nerve center" everywhere and the new space of human activity in this information society. Once parts of the Internet are paralyzed, the consequences are disastrous. Cyber paralysis warfare seeks to target the "Achilles heel" of the network to cause paralysis.

The paralysis attack focuses on the network trunks and key nodes and is able to win big through small investments. From the attacks mounted by some countries, it is clear that a common method is to use a botnet to attack the network portals and key nodes through "swarm tactics," also known as Distributed Denial of Service (DDoS) attacks, where a target becomes overwhelmed with more signals than it can process. Another method is to attack local nodes with a potent virus. Either technique will paralyze the networks of the target.

A botnet implants malware in a large number of computers through various methods. The attackers can obtain centralized control over these machines and send attacking commands directly to them. Russia successfully attacked Estonia and Georgia in 2007 and 2008 through this method.[9] On August 8, 2008, Russia launched a comprehensive "swarm" attack against Georgia's network while Russian troops were crossing the Georgian border. The attack paralyzed networks in the Georgian television, financial, and transportation systems. Georgian government operations were in chaos and their airport, logistics, and communication networks collapsed. As a result, urgently needed war materials could not be delivered on time, war efforts were severely affected, and the social order, combat commands, and logistics were damaged significantly. This instance of cyber combat was also supported by a large number of Internet users in Russia. They could simply download hacker software, install it, and launch a "swarm" attack by clicking a button to join. This cyberwar became a Russian netizen's war on Georgia and a vivid example of the application of a network paralysis attack.

Numerous computer viruses have spread throughout the Internet, many of which have become a trump card in cyberwarfare. For example, a virus-infected chip was installed in the printers of the air defense weapon system the United States imported to Iraq before the 1991 Gulf War. During the Gulf War, the "back door" was remotely activated, causing the Iraqi air defense system to go haywire, which led to the defeat of Iraq in combat.[10]

It is worth mentioning that such attacks, once limited to computer software systems, are now expanding to the hardware side. For instance, Iran's nuclear progress has become a big worry of the United States and Israel. In July 2010, there was a computer worm attack on the Siemens industrial control system used in Iranian nuclear stations.[11] The "Stuxnet" attack, suspected to have been launched by Israel, disabled one-fifth of Iran's centrifuges and caused an approximately two-year delay in its nuclear development plan.[12] Stuxnet is the first reported virus targeting industrial control systems,[13] and demonstrates a new stage of cyberwarfare dedicated to hardware damage as well as marking the transformation of global computer network security into a problem for national infrastructure protection as well. The Stuxnet case also provides a warning that physically isolated area networks are not impregnable anymore, and dedicated software and hardware systems can also be attacked.

Cyber and Electronic Integration

Cyberwarfare used to be limited to wired transmissions. However, the development of wireless networking is breaking these limits, and cyberspace and electromagnetic space are becoming gradually integrated.

"Cyber and electronic integration" refers to the war against the enemy's network systems using various means, including energy suppression of the signals, attacks on network components, information deception, and many other activities. Without special means and support of integrated advanced technology, cyber and electronic integration is difficult to carry out. For instance, the US Suter system is a typical measure for cyber and electronic integration. Until now, there has been very little understanding of the Suter system by the external world. With limited information from scattered reports, all we know is that it is a set of wireless reconnaissance, attack, and control combat systems. Through upgrades and integration, the Suter system has been tested on the RC-135 electronic warfare reconnaissance aircraft, EC-130H electronic jamming aircraft, and the F-16CJ fighter (with electronic warfare pods), and is now able to achieve a high level of integration of electronic warfare, cyberwarfare, kinetic destruction, and many other attacking techniques.[14] The US Army tested Suter 1, Suter 2, and Suter 3 in its "Joint Expeditionary Force Experiment" (JEFX) in 2000, 2002, and 2004 respectively.[15] In 2006, the US Army did not exercise Suter 4, probably because they used it directly in the Iraq war and the war in Afghanistan. In 2008, Suter 5 was tested in the JEFX again.[16]

On September 6, 2007, the Israeli Air Force successfully invaded Syrian airspace and bombed intended targets. The Israeli Air Force first attacked a radar station at Tall al-Abyad, near the Turkish border, which led to the collapse of the Syrian radar system for a time. Eighteen F-16I fighters from the Israeli Air Force Sixty-Ninth Fighter Squadron flew across the border and along the Syrian coastline at a low altitude to a large building located 100 kilometers west of the Syrian-Israeli border, about 400 kilometers northeast of Damascus. Then the fighters bombed the precise location and flew back the same way. That the entire process was completely unnoticed shocked the world. It has been speculated that the main reason the airstrike was successful was that Israel used a technology similar to the US Suter system to invade the enemy's radar defense network and to take control, disabling the air defense system.[17]

Cyber Psychology

Cyber psychological warfare is the psychological game launched in cyberspace, also known as "psychological politics." It is the extension and development of traditional psychological warfare in cyberspace.

The target of cyber psychological warfare has been extended from the military to the public domain in order to trigger a "butterfly effect" to reach political and military goals. Mathematician Edward Lorenz's "butterfly effect" describes scenarios where minor changes at the early stage can result in long-term and significant chain reactions, and the Internet, where a piece of information can set off a huge storm of public opinion, often seems to be a test bed for this theory. In March 2011, the *Guardian* broke the news that US Central Command, which is responsible for the Middle East and important military operations there, sought to build what might be called a "water army." Through a contract with the firm Ntrepid, the Americans allegedly developed "online personal management service" to support soldiers from their psychological warfare task force, enabling each soldier to have ten fake identities with IP addresses shown in different countries at the same time. Furthermore, they can manipulate a variety of network platforms in secret to post comments and opinions that support the United States and undermine other governments on the major microblogging social network sites, and forums in their imagined enemy's country. The result would be to generate, incite, and lead public opinion.[18] The recently published "War 2.0" by the United States illustrates that the final tool of information and cyberwarfare is shaping public opinion and popular support.[19]

Cyberspace today has greatly expanded its previous bounds, especially with the integration of television, telephone, and data networks, mobile phones, blogs, and podcasts, all of which have formed a new, larger, and more powerful medium. The Internet has become the index of social psychology, the main transmission medium of focal events, the main battlefield of public opinion, the competitive arena of multiple cultures, and the testing base of the "Color Revolution" theory (i.e., the Orange Revolution in Ukraine, the Rose Revolution in Georgia, and the Pink Revolution in Kyrgystan). All information can be reflected in cyberspace, and any small actions in this virtual world can deeply affect the real world. The instabilities in the Middle East and North Africa have been dubbed the "revolutions caused by a basket of fruit," a phrase that encapsulates the evolution of events in the region: the self-immolation of a street vendor in Tunisia and the corruption of the Tunisian president revealed by Wikileaks leads to fermentation of public opinion, diffusion of information through social network platforms, protestors in the streets, loss of control of the security situation, overflow of insecurity to neighboring countries, the involvement of Western powers, the domino effect, and, eventually, the sword drawn on Libya.

Cyber Defense

Attack necessitates defense, and where there is action, there is typically reaction. Protecting information infrastructure and systems and preventing cyberattacks have become the focus of most nations' cybersecurity.

Throughout each country's cyberspace operations, several capacities have become important prerequisites for winning cyber combat. A defense system must be established that can evaluate safety levels, monitor and send out early warnings, conduct defensive invasions, and perform self-recovery under emergencies. The system should combine active defense with in-depth defense. It is necessary to prevent leakage of classified information onto the Internet. It is especially important to prevent attacks from hackers or intelligence agencies from other countries.

According to what was reported by the US naval intelligence experts to the media, top-level classified devices or internal information regarding military facilities could possibly be revealed from a working photo of a soldier.[20] Thus, since 2002, the personal web pages of US military personnel on active duty and National Guard soldiers have been under surveillance. After the start of the Iraq war in 2003, although the US military allowed the soldiers to use video chat and e-mail to contact their families, the content of e-mails and chats was strictly screened. Meanwhile, Internet blogs were forbidden in the US military, especially for those who were on duty. Other military personnel, although allowed to blog, must not discuss any military weapons or usage of troops, and must not comment on daily military operations.

In order to have an effective response to cyberattacks and to ensure national security, the United States has carried out "Cyber Storm" exercises every two years since 2006, to fully test national cybersecurity and actual combat ability. "Cyber Storm I" in 2006 and "Cyber Storm II" in 2008 were mainly to test network security and emergency response capabilities.[21] "Cyber Storm III" in 2010 simulated network attacks on the key basic infrastructures in the United States in order to test the coordination and response capabilities of important departments facing large-scale network attacks.[22] Thousands of people participated, and seven US cabinet-level government departments took part in the exercise: the Department of Homeland

Security, Department of Commerce, Department of Defense, Department of Energy, Department of Justice, Department of Transportation, and Department of the Treasury. Participating industrial sectors included finance, chemistry, communications, water dams, defense, information technology, nuclear power, transportation, and water resources from sixty companies in eleven states. Also involved were twelve international partners, including Australia, Canada, France, Germany, Hungary, Italy, Japan, and Britain.

PRINCIPLES OF CYBERSECURITY

Facing the threat of cyberattacks and cyberwarfare, we could accept that this mode of combat is inevitable. An alternative is for peace-loving people and governments to act together to avoid cyber conflicts and a "virtual arms" race. It is possible that some cyber arms control agreements will be formulated akin to nuclear arms control and that they will lock up the "Pandora's box" of cyberwarfare. Such a goal requires a common understanding of the principles of cybersecurity. Some core concepts that could form the basis of a common understanding are building better "cyber borders," establishing "cyber defense," defending "cyber sovereignty," and maintaining "cyber freedom."

From Cyber Freedom to Cyber Sovereignty

We first need to define and clarify the relationship among cyber freedom, cybersecurity, and cyber order. The term "cyber freedom" usually refers to the freedom to use cyber resources to meet the demands of one's life and work. It is beginning to be considered a basic right of human beings. But there is another kind of cyber freedom, which attempts to justify committing crimes and terrorism through cyberspace. This kind of cyber freedom poses a threat to social stability and the life of common citizens. The former is the real cyber freedom, while the latter is pseudo cyber freedom. To paraphrase John Stuart Mills, real freedom is limited to not invading the freedom of others.[23] To achieve real cyber freedom, we need to limit pseudo cyber freedom.

To achieve cybersecurity requires "cyber rules." Rules are the basis of order, and order is the basis of security. The core of cybersecurity is to establish cyber rules and implement them. Without cyber rules, activities in cyberspace will be out of control, cybercrimes will be rampant, and cybersecurity will be harmed. Cyberspace is now in a disordered state because no actions have been taken to develop cyber rules and there is no international consensus about how to work out the rules.

To set cyber rules requires respect for "cyber sovereignty." Cyber rules are essentially a reflection of the rules of the physical world that apply in cyberspace, and they cannot be divorced entirely from human and social development processes. The spirit contained in most of these rules can also apply to cyber activities. International law's spirit of nonaggression and peaceful coexistence, for example, should also be reflected in cyberspace. Rules in the physical world are set on many grounds, among which sovereignty is crucial. Just as one has no autonomy to set rules without sovereignty, one has no autonomy to set cyber rules without cyber sovereignty. International rules in cyberspace should respect but not reject sovereignty, just as in international law. In sum, one should set cyber rules on the ground of respecting cyber sovereignty, not only that of one's own country but also that of other countries.

From Cyber Sovereignty to Cyber Defense

We need also to clarify the relationship among cyber sovereignty, the "cyber frontier," and cyber defense. Cyber sovereignty is a new constituent part of sovereignty, which will need to be defended. Cyber sovereignty, the independent exercise of a nation's authority over activities in cyberspace, including political, economic, cultural, and technological activities, is a new development in the information age. If we look back into history, alongside the expansion of the spaces in which people live and work, we can see that the boundary of sovereignty has expanded from land only, to the sea and oceans, and then the sky. This expansion of boundaries is acknowledged and respected by international society. It is very natural for sovereignty to expand further, into this new cyberspace, to include the entirely new component of cyber sovereignty.

As cyberspace plays a greater role in the traditional physical world, cyber sovereignty becomes the new dominating issue. In recent years, almost all countries have experienced some invasion in cyberspace. Yet people are not paying enough attention to cyber sovereignty violations and their wider implications. I would argue that invading a country in cyberspace is in essence the same as invading its lands, seas and oceans, skies and space, which are all considered violations of national sovereignty.

Sovereignty over land, sea, and sky has physical boundaries, and so does cyber sovereignty. The cyber frontier, although lacking fixed geographical borders, has clear-cut boundaries, and is characterized by a combination of the tangible and intangible, the virtual and physical. The cyber frontier is becoming the new frontier of national security, combining the physical world with its clear-cut borders and the virtual world.

Where is the cyber frontier of one country? First, the cyber infrastructures of a country, including all kinds of network equipment and ports located on its geographical territory, are tangible components of its cyber frontier. Second, the exclusive domain names of a country on the Internet and the sphere under them are the intangible components. In addition, the key network systems that provide critical services such as government, finance, telecommunications, traffic, and energy are also important components of a country's cyber frontier. A country has its right to establish information gateways for its cyber frontier and to monitor the information that flows into and out of its cyber boundaries.

To defend cyber frontiers, it is necessary to establish cyber defenses. Cyber defenses are becoming the new defensive walls. These need to be led by the state and implemented mainly by the military, with combined efforts from civil society. Up to now, many countries' national cyber defenses have lagged behind and are vulnerable, with boundaries but no defense. In the world today, the United States takes the lead in cybersecurity and defense. The armed forces of the United Kingdom, Japan, South Korea, India, Russia, and Israel have also set up cybersecurity forces and command organizations. China is now aware of the urgency to establish its own national cyber defense.

To sum up, cyber freedom, cyber sovereignty, cyber frontiers, and national cyber defense are closely interrelated factors. Cyberspace freedom calls for cyber sovereignty; cyber sovereignty requires defining cyber frontiers; and cyber frontiers depend on a national cyber defense. The same logic could be argued in reverse: cyber frontiers cannot be established without cyber defense; sovereignty means nothing without frontiers; and there is no need to talk about security and freedom without sovereignty. Defending cyber sovereignty is the basis of setting common rules, which are very important to safeguard cybersecurity. In addition, it is in most people's interests in cyberspace to safeguard freedom through achieving security.

SAFEGUARDING SECURITY IN THE ASIA-PACIFIC

Cybersecurity has become one of top issues in the Asia-Pacific just as it has in the whole world. China seeks to coordinate with all other progressive forces to ensure the peaceful use of networks and to help establish a healthy, orderly cyber environment. Agreement on the general principles of security in the Asia-Pacific will also improve cybersecurity in the region and help to lower communication barriers. Based on Asia-Pacific's reality, three propositions may be accepted. First, security in the Asia-Pacific involves every country in the region. No one should be totally neglected, and no single power should have the final say. Second, the security of each country in this region should be respected while respecting the security in the whole Asia-Pacific. Third, Cold War–era thinking should be rejected, and a confrontational security system targeting any single country should not be established. Asia-Pacific security requires continuous communication and consultation on the basis of peaceful coexistence. Based on these propositions, there are three main points that are needed to understand Asia-Pacific security.

Asia-Pacific Security Needs China

China is a big regional power undergoing rapid development. China always pursues friendly cooperation with other countries in the region and is now a crucial power in stimulating regional development. In 2011, eight of the ten biggest trading partners of China were Asia-Pacific countries. In recent years, China has been the largest import market in Asia and has become the largest trading partner of Japan, South Korea, India, Vietnam, and Mongolia. China accounts for more than 58% of the economic growth in Asia.[24] China also plays a crucial role in the security of the Asia-Pacific and cooperates with many countries on such security issues as counterterrorism, nuclear nonproliferation, transnational crime, and environmental protection. China also provided aid for natural disaster relief during the Indian Ocean tsunamis, Pakistan's flood, and Japan's earthquake. China and the Asia-Pacific are interdependent. Security in the Asia-Pacific cannot be realized without the participation of China.

Asia-Pacific Security Requires Attention to China's Security

China and the other parts of the world are now interrelated as the result of globalization. With the rapid development of its economy, China faces greater and greater security challenges. Many global issues, such as the potential impact of the global financial crisis on Chinese economic development; the intensification of disputes with neighboring countries, especially over the South China Sea and the East China Sea; climate change; disaster prevention and mitigation; overseas investment; cybercrime; and counterterrorism, to name a few, have become more prominent in China. If China—with a population of more than 1 billion—were in trouble, it would harm the stability of political patterns in the Asia-Pacific and the world, and the economic relations and national interests of foreign countries in China. Therefore, China's security cannot be ignored in addressing the Asia-Pacific security and world security.

Asia-Pacific Security Concerns Should Not Focus Exclusively on China

To maintain security in the Asia-Pacific, we have to reject the logic that there must be fierce hostilities between the traditional, established superpowers and rising powers. Although relations between China and the United States have been characterized as a war between a dragon and an eagle, there is an entire Pacific Ocean between them and no need for these two creatures to fight to the death. China's president, Xi Jinping, and former US Secretary of State Hillary Clinton both said in 2012 that the Pacific is big enough for both China and the United States.[25] The era in Sino-US relations ushered in by Mao Zedong and Richard Nixon is worthy of emulation by future generations. China's rapid development is in the interest of the Asia-Pacific and does not pose a threat to other countries.

CONCLUSION

In this chapter, I have discussed different forms of cyberwarfare and ways to maintain cyberspace security with the aim of promoting peace and common prosperity in the Asia-Pacific region. I hope that my point of view can have a positive effect on understandings of this issue.

All nations are concerned about security and development, which have become two persistent themes in the global psyche. I would count security as more important. However, people's understanding of security can be quite different due to differences in values. I believe there is little need to worry about those differences. We will be able to withstand all sorts of challenges and find a way to resolve our differences as long as we can look forward, cherish peace, and respect all countries' security demands without exception. The thing that we need to worry about is loss of communication. If everyone "sees with one eye," or even deliberately misinterprets, cracks will expand little by little, and potential security issues will be blown out of proportion. Therefore, mutual respect, mutual understanding, and cooperation between nations should be the foundation of Asia-Pacific and world security, including cybersecurity.

NOTES

1. Li Xiao, Chen Chengfeng, and Guo Taowen, 键与屏的搏杀—网络战扫描 [Fight between Keyboard and Screen: A Look at Cyberwarfare] (WuHan: Hubei Science and Technology Press, 2001), 1.
2. On Suter, see Department of Defense Report to Congress, "Network Centric Warfare (Appendix)," July 27, 2001, E-135. On Stuxnet, see Robert McMillan, "Siemens: Stuxnet Worm Hit Industrial Systems," *Computerworld*, September 16, 2010; Laboratory of Cryptography and System Security (CrySyS Lab), sKy-WIper: A Complex Malware for Targeted Attacks (v1.05), May 28, 2012; Liu Yu, "世界大事综览" [Overview of World's Events], 国际资料信息 [*International Information*], 2010, 3.; Chen Zhou, "西亚北非动荡对国际战略格局的影响" [The Influence of Turbulence in West Asia and North Africa on International Strategic Patterns], 外国军事学术 [*World Military Review*], 2011, 10; and on PRISM, see Charlie Savage, Edward Wyatt, and Peter Baker, " U.S. Confirms That It Gathers Online Data Overseas," *New York Times*, June 6, 2013.
3. "International Strategy for Cyberspace: Prosperity, Security, and Openness in a Networked World," May 2011, http://www.whitehouse.gov/sites/default/files/rss_viewer/international_strategy_for_cyberspace.pdf.
4. "Cyberwar: War in the Fifth Domain," *Economist*, July 1, 2010; Jianshi, "美国网络战队三成来自陆军" [Thirty Percent of Cyberwarfare Unit Comes from Army], 参考消息网 [*Cankao Xiaoxi*], October 26, 2013, http://mil.cankaoxiaoxi.com/2013/1026/292210.shtml.
5. "美国头号军火商回应：确遭黑客入侵，数据未受损" [American Top Military Supplier Responded: Did Get Hacked, but No Damage to Data], *Global Times Online*, May 29, 2011, http://news.xinhuanet.com/world/2011-05/29/c_121471203.htm.
6. Li Dongfeng, "美国海军10万人信息外流，网络军事泄密危害大" [Information of More Than 100,000 Naval Officer Was Leaked: Huge Damage of Cyber Military Leakage], 人民网 [*People's Daily Online*], July 13, 2006, http://military.people.com.cn/GB/4586000.html.
7. David E. Sanger and Thom Shanker, "N.S.A. Devises Radio Pathway into Computers," *New York Times*, January 14, 2014; Liao Zhengjun, Yang Shasha, Du Tianqi, and Liu Yupeng, "美被爆秘密监控中国军方 能攻击不联网电脑" [The US Was Reported to Secretly Monitor Chinese Military and Can Attack Nonconnected Computers], *Global Times*, February 17, 2014.
8. "美国十万军人信息外流　军事网络安全引人关注" [Leakage of Hundred Thousand US Soldiers Brought People's Attention to Military Cybersecurity], *Global Times*, July 13, 2006, http://news.qq.com/a/20060713/001491.htm.
9. Yang Jiahua and Xia Wencheng, "美空军网络空间司令部简介" [Introduction to the US Air Force Cyberspace Command], 外军信息战 [*Foreign Military Information Warfare*], 2008, 3; Duan Haozhi, "俄军在俄格战争中的信息化作战运用及启示"

[Application of Information Warfare and Enlightenment of Russian Troops in the War with Georgia], 海军学术研究 [*Navy Academic Research*], 2009, 3.

10. Yu Kailiang and Zhang Bing, 骇世黑客 [*Hackers Startle the World*] (Beijing: Chinese Overseas Publishing House, 2000). [Editors' note: No corroboration of this event is available in English-language sources.]

11. Jonathan Fildes, "Stuxnet Worm 'Targeted High-Value Iranian Assets,'" *BBC News* (Technology), September 23, 2010.

12. Zhang Hong, "美大肆渲染网络战另有所图" [The US Has Other Reasons to Render Cyberwarfare], *People's Daily* (international edition), June 8, 2013, 3.

13. "Stuxnet Worm Hits Iran Nuclear Plant Staff Computers," *BBC News* (Middle East), September 26, 2010.

14. Department of Defense Report to Congress, "Network Centric Warfare (Appendix)," July 27, 2001, E-135.

15. CRS Report for Congress, "Information Operations, Electronic Warfare, and Cyberwar: Capabilities and Related Policy Issues," June 5, 2007, CRS8; Jim Garamone, Air Force Experiment Tests Future Concepts, American Forces Press Service, July 29, 2004.

16. Larry van der Oord, "Experiment Identifies Timely Solutions to Warfighter," Global Cyberspace Integration Center Public Affairs, March 21, 2008.

17. Richard A. Clarke and Robert K. Knake, *Cyberwar: What It Is and How to Fight* (New York: HarperCollins, 2010).

18. Yu Saisai, "2011年外军网络战发展动态与分析" [Analysis of 2011 Foreign Military Cyberwarfare Development Trends], 军事学术 [*Military Academic*] 3 (2012): 17.

19. Thomas Rid and Marc Hecker, "战争2.0 信息时代的非常规战" [War 2.0: Irregular Warfare in the Information Age], trans. Jin Miao (Beijing: PLA Publishing House, May 2011).

20. "'不能说的秘密被曝光' 聚焦美军泄密事件" [Secret Was Exposed—Focusing on US Military Leakage], Xinhua Net, January 20, 2011, http://news.xinhuanet.com/mil/2011-01/20/c_121002182_2.htm.

21. "Fact Sheet. Cyber Storm Exercise (Department of Homeland Security)," February 1, 2008; Ian Grant, "Cyber Storm 2 Exercise Reveals Security Preparedness," Computerweekly.com, March 21, 2008.

22. Bipartisan Policy Center, "Cyber ShockWave," February 24, 2010, http://bipartisanpolicy.org/events/2010/02/cyber-shockwave.

23. Sun Yet-sen, 孙中山文集 [*Collected Works of Sun Yet-sen*] (Beijing: Unity Press, 1997).

24. Liu Juntao, ed., "杨洁篪：中国对亚洲经济增长的贡献率超过58%" [Yang Jiechi: China Accounts for More Than 58% of the Economic Growth in Asia], *People's Daily Online*, July 12, 2012, http://world.people.com.cn/n/2012/0712/c1002-18506529.html.

25. "习进平：太平洋够大 容得下中美两国" [Xi Jinping: The Pacific Is Big Enough for Both China and United States], *Phoenix Online*, February 2, 2012, http://v.ifeng.com/news/world/201202/0f72021e-137f-44a6-ab28-1548d2176583.shtml?_from_ralated; "希拉里发表告别演说 称太平洋足够大容得下中美两国" [Hillary Clinton Gave Her Farewell Speech and Said That the Pacific Is Large Enough to Accommodate Both China and the United States], *Phoenix News*, February 1, 2013, http://news.ifeng.com/world/detail_2013_02/01/21839821_0.shtml.

CHAPTER 6

Chinese Writings on Cyberwarfare and Coercion

KEVIN POLLPETER

The well-publicized cyber operations being conducted by the People's Republic of China against foreign entities have raised many questions about China's use of computer network operations in peacetime, the role that cyber may play in a future Chinese conflict, and how China may use its growing cyber capabilities in a coercive role. Although no official Chinese military document defining its cyberwarfare doctrine is available, and it may be that no such document exists, this chapter relies on a variety of reputable Chinese primary sources to address these questions. These include works by authoritative sources such as the Chinese Academy of Military Science, the Chinese National Defense University and books by Dai Qingmin, former head of the General Staff Department's (GSD) Fourth Department, and Xu Xiaoyan, former head of the GSD Third Department.

Although a great number of sources were consulted for this study, Chinese strategists offer largely consistent assessments of cyberwarfare. They conclude that information warfare plays a critical role in modern warfare and that cyberwarfare, called network warfare by Chinese analysts, is a main form of information warfare. Chinese analysts assess that cyberwarfare draws its strength from the central role that computers play in information systems and the susceptibility of computer systems to attack. Specifically, cyberwarfare provides China with three capabilities. First, it allows China to identify vulnerabilities in targeted computer networks that can be exploited to exfiltrate data. Second, cyber operations can target logistical, communication, and commercial networks to constrain an adversary's actions or slow its response time. Third, cyber operations "can serve as a force multiplier when coupled with kinetic attacks during times of crisis or conflict."[1] Chinese researchers also see cyberwarfare as having a coercive role. Chinese analysts assess that the United States has an established and capable cyber force and that China must develop its own cyber force to deter the United States from conducting strikes against China. In addition, computer network attacks can be conducted against adversaries to force an action.

To date, Chinese computer network operations have been limited to political and economic espionage, but analysis of Chinese writings reveals several doctrinal and cultural factors conducive to the use of network warfare as a warfighting and coercive tool that could lead to misunderstanding and instability in times of crisis. These include a firm belief in the legitimacy of Chinese interests, a strong emphasis on offensive action and striking first, a search for asymmetric weapons to compensate for the relative inferiority of the Chinese military in relation to the US military, and the characterization of cyberwarfare as possessing nearly unlimited destructive potential. As a result, Chinese leaders may view cyberwarfare as an attractive low-risk/high-reward option that can succeed where kinetic attacks may fail or as a more attractive tool of coercion to support economic development.

COMPUTER NETWORK OPERATIONS

Chinese writers describe computer network operations as an important new form of warfare and an "asymmetric assassin's mace weapon" that has the potential to change traditional operational concepts, thinking, and methods.[2] Computer network operations have both coercive and warfighting applications and can have a large effect on an adversary's political, economic, and military capabilities. It is also regarded as an important method for a military equipped with inferior weapons to effectively counter a high-technology opponent.[3] This belief is striking in light of Chinese perceptions that the United States has important advantages in the cyber domain.

Computer network operations, called network warfare (网络战) or network countermeasures (网络对抗) by the Chinese military, is defined by the *Chinese People's Liberation Army Military Terminology* volume as "within the information network space, destroying an enemy's network systems and information and degrading its operational effectiveness; and protecting one's network systems and network information and the conduct of operational activities."[4] Another authoritative source defines computer network warfare (计算机网络战) as "a contest between two opposing operational command systems conducted within the computer network domain over network supremacy by degrading or destroying an enemy's computer network information and secure use and its ability to conduct information operations."[5]

The interest in computer network warfare results from two overarching factors. First is the nature of computer network warfare itself, which can be described as relatively low cost, covert, and massive. Because of the interconnectedness of the Internet, even if computer systems are not directly connected, a malware issue can still spread to seemingly separated systems.[6] Computer network attack is said to possess the capability for large destructive capability, including that equal to nuclear weapons, and also possesses the ability for China to achieve its aims without fighting or by fighting a small war.[7] Finally, because computers are so commonplace, civilians and government personnel can conduct computer network attacks, thus facilitating larger operations.[8]

The second factor increasing interest in computer network attack is the ubiquitous presence of computers.[9] As one researcher writes:

> In future wars, computers will be the core of automatized command and control systems, integrating command, control, telecommunications, and intelligence to gain battlefield situational awareness, high-speed analysis, and top quality leadership for making estimates and selecting the best solutions. Thus strikes of this type can seek to achieve partial or large-scale paralysis of enemy systems. As soon as a virus enters the enemy's command and control system, it will have tremendous destructive impact. . . . Therefore computer network war is an important means for paralyzing the enemy in wars of the future.[10]

Another author, referring to "network-electronic operations" (a combination of cyber and electronic warfare), writes:

> the degree of reliance on networks and electromagnetism is increasing. Some experts predict that wars in the 21st Century will be integrated network electronic warfare with computer networks as the core. Whoever possesses superiority in integrated network electronic operations will then control the high point of future wars and will win future wars.[11]

The rise of network-centric warfare and its emphasis on the use of computer networks to link organizations and people both horizontally and vertically and provide them with common situational awareness has led countries to devise countermeasures against it.[12] Given the prominence of cyberspace in US national security, networks have become important targets. According to Chinese analysts, Serbian and Russian hacker attacks against NATO computer systems during the 1999 Operation Allied Force are said to have produced tangible results. These attacks are said to have shut down the White House website, disabled some military computer systems, and disabled the command-and-control systems of the USS *Nimitz*, which halted flight operations for several hours.[13] These reports lead contemporary thinkers to add network warfare to future conflict plans.

Doctrinal Context

To best understand how the People's Liberation Army (PLA) may conduct computer network warfare, it is first useful to understand Chinese doctrine and how it conceives of information warfare. Information operations are described as the most important operational method of modern war with electronic warfare and computer network warfare considered the main types of information operations.[14] Chinese writings regard information collection, processing, and transmission, and the denial of those capabilities to an adversary, as vital to the successful prosecution of a modern high-tech war. According to Chinese writings, information supremacy, defined as achieving information control within a specific time and place, is the precondition for achieving supremacy in the air, at sea, and on the ground and it is critical to achieving and maintaining battlefield supremacy.[15]

Pursuant to this, Chinese military strategy is strongly weighted towards offensive action as embodied by the PLA's military strategic guideline of active defense (积极防御). Active defense is best thought of as a politically defensive, but operationally offensive strategy in which China will rhetorically maintain a defensive posture up until the time it decides to attack.[16] According to the 2006 work *The Science of Campaigns*, the PLA "strategically continues with active defense, but at the campaign level it stresses active strikes to seize the initiative (积极主动的进攻)."[17] The authors of the 2006 *Science of Campaigns* also state that no matter what kind of operation is conducted, the PLA should be flexible, attack first, and be offensively oriented.[18] In fact, within the context of protecting China's interests, Chinese writers make clear that the full range of offensive actions, including preemptive strikes, is permissible.[19]

This emphasis on offensive action is also rooted in the PLA's strategy for information warfare: active offense. The strategy of active offense is based on the assertion that, unlike traditional defensive operations that can reduce an enemy's combat power, defensive information operations merely fend off attacks without weakening the opposing side's forces. Consequently, offensive information operations are the only way information superiority can be achieved.[20] In fact, information operations facilitate offensive action, which are easier to conduct covertly and over longer distances than kinetic attacks, require fewer personnel and resources than traditional operations, and can be sustained for longer periods of time.[21]

An emphasis on striking first is also a main component of PLA doctrine. In fact, striking first is stressed to such an extent in Chinese writings on computer network warfare that the beginning of a war is said to determine the outcome: "whoever strikes first prevails."[22] Consequently, offensive operations should involve the strongest first strikes possible against key targets.[23] The primary reason for striking first is to counter a future enemy that is predicted to be stronger than the PLA. If the PLA allows the enemy to strike first, it may be unable to recover from the enemy's initial onslaught.[24] The focus on seizing the initiative at the beginning of a conflict has led to an emphasis in Chinese writings on the concept of "gaining mastery by striking first," which covers several types of strategies, including preemption, surprise attacks, and general aggressiveness. Indeed, numerous Chinese strategists emphasize achieving victory through surprise by striking at an unexpected time and place.[25]

This goal is particularly important to the PLA, which would prefer to fight "quick wars with quick resolutions." Chinese analysts have indicated that bringing a war to a quick resolution benefits the PLA due to the ability of a more strongly armed opponent such as the United States to eventually bring the full might of its military to bear.[26] In the words of one Chinese analyst, "If [the PLA] just sits there and waits for the enemy to complete assembling its full array of troops, China's fighting potential will certainly be more severely jeopardized because the enemy will then be in a position to put its overall combat superiority to good use, making it more difficult for China to win the war."[27]

The focus of Chinese attacks is on an adversary's center of gravity in which the PLA would determine a target or target set so critical that its destruction would gravely affect operations and bring about victory.[28] Attacking an enemy's center of gravity is closely related to the PLA's concept of "key point strikes." According to the year 2000 edition of *Science of Campaigns*, "key points" are defined as targets "that could have a direct impact on the overall situation of the campaign or produce an overall effect."[29] The 2006 *Science of Campaigns* takes a slightly different approach and instead refers to "vital targets" as those targets that directly influence military operations at the campaign or strategic level and that when struck will destroy or paralyze the enemy's operational structure and weaken its operational capabilities.[30]

PLA writings overwhelmingly assert that the key points of a high-tech adversary are its information systems. Modern militaries have highly capable, long-range precision strike platforms supported by reconnaissance assets that can conduct strikes against an enemy while remaining beyond the reach of an adversary's weapon systems. By striking enemy information systems, the PLA can take out the "eyes, ears, brain, and nervous system" of weapons systems, thereby causing paralysis and achieving victory with lower costs and in a shorter amount of time.[31] Chinese analysts make clear that attacking C4ISR (command, control, communication, computers, intelligence, surveillance, and reconnaissance) systems and command nodes can paralyze an enemy and have a decisive influence on the campaign.[32] These centers of gravity can exist at the strategic, campaign, and tactical levels and it is through the destruction or debilitation of these targets that Chinese analysts assert that a weaker military can defeat a stronger military.[33] Pursuant to this, computer network forces are to be concentrated against centers of gravity with the ultimate goal being to destroy and control an adversary's information infrastructure. Targets can include C4ISR systems, communication nodes, financial centers, and transportation nodes. Attacking these targets can directly affect the enemy's strategic decision-making and overall strategic situation, and completely weaken and paralyze the enemy's political system, economy, and military.[34] Strategic C4ISR systems are emphasized as particularly important targets with space systems being singled out as targets that, if successfully struck, can critically affect the outcome of a war.[35]

Computer network warfare also follows the principle of active offense. While network defense is stressed, it cannot win wars. Only offensive measures can seize the initiative, and it is only through active offense that enemy information systems can be weakened. Offensive operations are facilitated by the inherent tendency of information systems to possess weak points, even for militaries that have superior information systems. As a result, even though the PLA is weaker than the US military, it is still possible to achieve relative information superiority through the use of asymmetric operations.[36]

The PLA divides computer network warfare into three components: computer network reconnaissance, computer network strike, and computer network defense.[37]

Computer Reconnaissance

Computer reconnaissance refers to the use of computers to identify, seize, monitor, and analyze enemy computer networks and systems.[38] The goal of computer reconnaissance is to collect and assess the structure of the enemy's network and the disposition of its hardware; to discover weak points, security holes, and clients, and is conducted, in part, through the use of password crackers, network scanning, typology mapping, and monitoring technologies.[39]

Computer reconnaissance is considered the foundation of computer network strikes because the basis for successful strikes is good intelligence. Indeed, intelligence gathering is stressed in writings on network warfare not only for use throughout a conflict, but also during peacetime. During peacetime, the main mission of computer reconnaissance is to collect and analyze the information systems of possible adversaries to identify weaknesses in order to facilitate first strikes.[40] The goal is to paralyze enemy systems through quick strikes with operations at the beginning of a conflict forming the basis for victory.[41]

Computer Network Strike

A network strike is defined as jamming or destroying an enemy's information network systems and network information technologies through the use of denial of service attacks, malware, and deception.[42] Chinese analysts describe a variety of roles for computer network strikes.[43] These include computer network exploit, conduct strikes, network protocol deception, false network deception, integrated network electronic warfare.[44] "Computer network exploit" is defined as the compromise of enemy information networks to steal information or to insert false information.[45] A "conduct strikes" is the penetration of enemy networks to disrupt or disable computer systems with an emphasis on paralyzing C4ISR systems. These strikes can use logic bombs, back doors, and Trojan horses.[46] Chinese writers describe a number of systems that could come under attack, including command-and-control, air defense, and space systems.[47] Offensive systems are also discussed as targets, as their disabling can enable the PLA to better defend itself. In addition, computer strikes can also be targeted at financial, commercial, transportation, and civilian communication networks.[48]

"Network protocol deception" (网络协议欺骗) refers to using altered network protocols to deceive enemy information systems by altering information or entering false information. This can include changing a network's URL and designing a source routing so that the attacker can impersonate a trusted machine. "False network deception" (虚假网络欺骗), called honey-potting in the West, refers to establishing a fake website to entice the enemy into accessing it so that malware can be uploaded. False network deception is also used to entice enemy attacks so that attack methods can be analyzed.[49]

A final method of computer network strike is known in Chinese writings as "integrated network electronic warfare" (网电一体战, INEW). INEW is defined as "a highly fused combination of electronic warfare and network warfare that uses information strikes and information operation forms against enemy networked information systems."[50] It was first conceived in 1999 by Dai Qingmin, who later became the head of the GSD's Fourth Department, responsible for electronic warfare. At that time Dai observed that the PLA faced a daunting task in defeating the US military and proposed a joint force made up of electronic and cyberwarfare forces as a way to overcome PLA deficiencies.[51] As technology has advanced, INEW now also includes the insertion of malicious algorithms into wireless networks. The efficacy of these types of attacks have been recognized by Chinese analysts, with one source suggesting that "research on INEW should draw lessons from the INEW tenants of foreign militaries and research the use of electronic and network war in integrated operations."[52] By using wireless network viruses to paralyze enemy C4ISR systems, this tactic can cause aircraft, cruise missiles, and helicopters to lose control.[53] According to another author:

> A military satellite cannot connect with the Internet. Therefore some people think "hackers" cannot attack a satellite's command and control [system]. But in actuality, the microwave antenna of the satellite control is open, so one can intercept satellite information through technological means and seize the satellite's command and control [system]. Using this as a springboard to invade the enemy's independent network systems is entirely possible.[54]

Network Defense

Network defense refers to defending the operation of one's information networks in order to maintain the security of information and data. This can include firewalls, access control, data encryption, passwords, antivirus software, technologies to reduce electromagnetic signatures, and fixing security holes.[55] China's network defense capabilities are apparently in a low state of development. According to one military officer speaking in 2014, China's Internet is "effectively undefended" with China only just beginning to research how to protect critical information technology facilities.[56] China, however, is beginning to place more emphasis on cybersecurity with the February 2014 announcement of the establishment of the Internet Security and Informatization Leading Small Group (网络安全和信息化领导小组) "to support Internet security, protect the national interest, and promote the development of informatization in China."[57] According to the group's head, President Xi Jinping, "No Internet safety means no national security," indicating that one of its major focuses will be improving the security of China's computer networks.[58]

In the midst of this weakness, China views itself as facing a severe cyberthreat, especially from the United States. According to Chinese sources, China's Ministry of National Defense and military networks were attacked 144,000 times per month in 2012 with 62.9% of the attacks originating from US IP addresses.[59] According to a 2013 report by China's National Computer Network Emergency Response Technical Team Coordination Center (CNCERT/CC), 16,388 web pages in China, including 1,802 government websites, were attacked over a twelve-month period. Additionally, "in 2012, around 73,000 overseas Internet Protocol (IP) addresses were involved in hijacking nearly 14.2 million mainframes in China via Trojans or botnets, with the United States being the largest source of such hacking activities." CNCERT also reported 22,308 phishing websites targeting Chinese Internet users, with 96.2% of them being run on foreign severs. Of those, US-based sites accounted for 83.2% of the total phishing websites.[60]

Indeed, Chinese analysts assess that the United States holds the advantage in cyber capabilities in terms of overall IT industry dominance, malware design, training of cyber forces, and control of Internet infrastructure. A critical vulnerability for China is its reliance on foreign technologies. US companies like Apple, Microsoft, and Google dominate the IT industry, and US processor, chip, network switch, and other core technologies are said to be far ahead of other countries. The dominance of these companies is said to give the United States de facto access to the critical infrastructure of other countries that could be exploited during wartime. Chinese writers point to the apocryphal example of the United States placing malware on air defense system technologies for import to Iraq before the 1991 Gulf War as an example of the threats that China faces.[61] In fact, one source calls this "a great threat that cannot be ignored" and "a threat that is very possibly fatal," while another calls for the use of domestically manufactured information technology as the only solution to the problem.[62]

The United States is also considered to be far ahead of other countries in the development of malware, theoretical research on cyberwar, and in the training of cyber personnel. In fact, Chinese analysts point to Stuxnet as evidence that Western powers have more advanced cyberwarfare capabilities and that they possess an advantage in cyberspace.[63] According to a 2013 article, more than 80% of the industrial control systems in China use foreign technologies, and this use is increasing. According to data compiled by the China National Vulnerability Database, there was a tenfold increase in the security vulnerabilities of industrial control systems from 2010 to 2011, making China especially susceptible to attack from a Stuxnet-like cyber weapon.[64] Additionally, the US control of ten of the world's thirteen root nameservers is seen as giving the United States control over the infrastructure used to govern the Internet, which could be used to restrict access to the Internet in times of conflict.[65]

CYBER COERCION

This section examines Chinese ideas about the coercive, as distinguished from warfighting, applications of computer network operations. The Chinese term *weishe* (威慑), commonly translated as "deterrence," is defined in similar ways by Chinese scholars and military researchers. According to one source, "It is the use of momentum or force to create submission."[66] *The Science of Strategy*, published by the Chinese Academy of Military Science, defines *weishe* as "a country or a political organization using the display of the intent to use force or the display of the intent to prepare to use force to force an opponent to yield to its will so that it does not dare conduct operations or escalate its military posture."[67] *Weishe* has two basic uses: to prevent the enemy from taking an action and to force an enemy to take an action.[68] These actions include taking measures to prevent military action and forcing another side to engage in cooperative agreements, preventing an adversary from entering into an alliance or treaty, or forcing a country to sever diplomatic or trade relations with other countries.[69] From these writings, it is apparent that *weishe* includes the Western concepts of both deterrence and compellence. Deterrence employs threats to prevent the target from taking an action, while compellence is intended to force an action. Taken together, deterrence and compellence are more broadly defined as elements of coercion, and it is this term that is best translated as the Chinese term *weishe*.[70]

Chinese writers state that in practice the Chinese approach to coercion is more principled than the Western approach. Apparently based on the Sun Zi precept to subdue the enemy without fighting, Chinese writers assert that coercion is geared to finding a way to avoid war while maintaining China's interests by focusing on nonmilitary methods of resolving disputes. This is in contrast to the Western method of accepting force as a legitimate way to reach political goals.[71] For example, the authors of *The Science of Strategy* discuss two kinds of coercion: offensive coercion and defensive coercion. Offensive coercion is said to be conducted by expansionist countries, whereas defensive coercion is said to be conducted by strategically defensive countries. The authors then describe China as following a strategy of deterrence characterized by self-defense. The goals of this strategy are to prevent foreign invasion, protect China's rights and interests, and prevent foreign and domestic separatist and subversive activities in order to maintain the country's stability and territorial integrity.[72] Another researcher takes this point even further, stating that one should replace coercion with a strategy of influence, which seeks to both deter an enemy and dispel its concerns by convincing other countries that China does not plan to violate their major interests. This strategy seeks to establish mutual benefit for all parties concerned through political mutual trust, economic cooperation, dialogue, and military exchanges.[73] Underpinning this understanding is an explicit belief that China uses coercion to defend its legitimate interests, whereas the West uses coercion in the pursuit of illegitimate gain. As former president Jiang Zemin pointed out, "China never invades other countries, it also never allows other nations to invade its sovereign territory and sea interests."[74]

Chinese analysts write that coercion possesses three elements: capability, will, and signaling.[75] Of these three, capability and will are the most important and are described as the two "wings" of coercion.[76] Capability is considered the foundation of coercion and refers to having the means to carry out threats.[77] Although bluffing is considered an element of coercion, Chinese analysts write that China must possess some form of actual coercive capability; otherwise the threat will be viewed as empty.[78] Will, on the other hand, refers to a clear willingness to carry out threats with action.[79] Effective coercion not only requires a strong capability and the will to carry out threats, those threats must be communicated effectively so that the target of the coercion is cognizant of the full costs of coming into conflict with China.[80] It is recognized, however, that not every form of coercion is perceived, understood, received, or known by the enemy. As a result, an ability to carry out threats must be complemented by an effective means of communication.[81] In effect, the object of coercion must be made to believe that the coercer has both the capability and the will to use it.[82]

Development of Assassin's Mace Weapons

One important factor in the development of an effective coercive military capability is the requirement for so-called assassin's mace weapons (杀手锏). Although Western analysts frequently discount the identification of specific assassin's mace weapons due to its liberal use by Chinese writers, the impetus to build such weapons is the result of policy guidance from the highest levels of the Chinese government and military.[83] According to the biography of Chinese general and former vice chairman of the Central Military Commission Zhang Wannian, the roots of the assassin's mace weapons program lie in the accidental US bombing of the Chinese embassy in Belgrade. On the day of the bombing an emergency meeting was held to discuss the event, which was followed by an expanded meeting of the Central Military Commission, in which the PLA was ordered to develop strategic capabilities that could deter the United States.[84]

Although no details are given as to which specific weapons were approved under the assassin's mace program, according to guidance given by Jiang Zemin, "what the enemy is most fearful of is what we should be developing." Furthermore, Zhang instructed the PLA to look at the requirements of future war and solve the problems of "seeing far, striking far, and striking accurately."[85] Cyberwarfare is a capability that allows the PLA to do all three and, as a result, may be a strategic weapons system that is intended to deter the United States from coming into military conflict with China.

Coercive Network Warfare

The Chinese interest in cyberwar raises the question of if and how it may be used in a coercive context. Chinese writings on computer network coercion are premised on the assumption that computer network attack will be a main form of warfare with an unprecedented destructive capacity. According to Chinese analysts, the disabling of military and civilian networks not only affects a military outcome, but also a nation's economy and societal order. In fact, Chinese analysts assert that as countries become more reliant on computer networks, computer network coercion will be equal in importance to nuclear deterrence due to its immense destructive potential.[86] As a result, as "hegemonic countries" develop cyber capabilities, China must also develop its own network strike capabilities.[87] Such thinking indicates that Chinese analysts emphasize deterrence in kind, in which its cyber forces are used to deter cyberattacks, rather than the use of cross-domain deterrence, in which other capabilities may be used to deter cyberattacks. Such distinctions are lost, however, during actual warfighting when cyber operations could be employed against a range of targets.

A number of Chinese analysts, however, appear to be suspicious of the deterrent effect of cyber operations.[88] The ambiguous nature of cyber-attacks can make it difficult to determine their source and motivation and thus serves as a negative influence on the third condition of deterrence: signaling. If a country does not know why it is being attacked and by whom, then it cannot be expected to take the actions expected of it by the attacking country. Moreover, retaliating with cyberattacks can also be more complicated than other types of coercion. The response to a cyberattack can depend on whether the attack was conducted by an individual, group, or organization and whether the attack was criminal in nature or conducted for national security purposes. Criminal activities, for example, may require a legal response. National security-related attacks, on the other hand, may require a military response.[89] As countries become more reliant on information technology, attacks on information nodes such as financial centers can not only affect the target country, but can also have spillover effects on other countries, including the attacking country.[90]

If deterrence fails, however, China could also use computer network attack for compellence. For example, if an enemy believes China lacks credibility, the PLA might conduct attacks "to strike fear into the enemy."[91] The suggestion that China can use "strong information strikes" to force an enemy to submit to its will suggests that China may attempt to use cyber capabilities to force an opponent to take an action desired by China.[92] Based on this, Chinese leaders could be advised by PLA strategists that attacking computer systems in the United States, for example, would raise the cost of conflict for the United States and could make apparent the costs of war to the American populace and serve as a useful measure to force the United States to deescalate or to more severely limit its actions against China. There is no discussion about whether such a strategy might backfire or result in inadvertent escalation.

Psychological Warfare

Another aspect of network warfare that appears to be closely associated with coercion is "network psychological warfare." According to Guo Shengwei, network psychological warfare is defined as the use of computer networks to influence the enemy. Network psychological warfare is conducted on the Internet and is described as capable of having a large effect on people's psychology. It can decrease morale, lower popular sentiment, and collapse the enemy's will. According to this author, strikes against the "soft" targets of the psychology of armed forces personnel and civilians will have a better result than striking "hard" targets.[93]

The ultimate goal of network psychological warfare is to achieve a country's goals without going to war. Network psychological warfare is considered more effective than other types of psychological warfare and includes the use of audio, video, and written information over computer networks to mislead people in order to influence their decision-making and actions.[94]

Network psychological warfare has four advantages. The first is that it has no limits in regard to geography or time. As Guo states, "wherever a network exists network psychological warfare can be conducted."[95] The second is that it can be used to distribute information, including fictitious or misleading information that can be detrimental to an enemy's warfighting effort. The third is that it can be conducted in many forums, including websites and mass e-mails directed at groups of people or individuals. The fourth characteristic is that it is flexible and can be changed or updated rapidly.[96]

CONCLUSIONS

Chinese writings on computer network warfare suggest that Chinese network warfare operations will play an important role in future Chinese military operations.[97] Many of these writings describe computer network warfare as a new type of warfare that holds the potential to change the face of war as we know it. These assertions are premised on the belief that because of the prevalence of computers in government, military, and commercial information systems, cyber operations have the potential play a decisive role in future conflicts by debilitating information systems critical to military operations and the civilian economy. What is apparent in Chinese writings on information warfare in general, and computer network warfare in particular, is that China aims to take an asymmetric approach to fighting the United States and has identified C4ISR systems as the primary target for these attacks. Certainly, identification of cyberwar as an "assassin's mace" weapon and its ability to fulfill Zhang Wannian's request to develop systems that allow the PLA to "shoot far, see far, and shoot accurately" suggest that cyber may be a strategic capability identified for development after the 1999 bombing of the Chinese embassy in Belgrade.

The large amount of resources apparently being devoted to computer network operations by the PLA also suggests that computer network operations may play an important role in future Chinese military operations.

As discussed in Mark Stokes's chapter in this volume (chapter 7), China has a sophisticated program dedicated to computer network operations, and Nigel Inkster's chapter (chapter 2) explains the importance of China's intelligence services. The massive Chinese cyber espionage effort currently underway is also a reflection of the emphasis in Chinese writings on network reconnaissance. Although analysis of the Chinese advanced persistent threat focuses on the theft of intellectual property, the knowledge acquired by infiltrating computer networks could also provide knowledge of security vulnerabilities that could be exploited during wartime. In addition, the apparent large effort spent on developing malware to infiltrate and pilfer foreign intellectual property suggests that China has the capability and willingness to develop malware that can degrade or debilitate critical systems in wartime and that China may already have deployed such malware. These attacks could also be facilitated by the use of "backdoors" placed in components manufactured in China.

Targeting Preferences

Chinese writings discuss a wide range of targets at the strategic, operational, and tactical levels. These include all types of C4ISR systems, such as communication, radar, space-based systems, and command-and-control nodes. These attacks do not necessarily have to be conducted through landlines. Attacks against wireless systems, including air defense radar, aircraft radar, and any system with an antenna widens the scope of computer network warfare in a way that merges cyberattack with electronic warfare. Therefore, computer network attack will be an ever-present danger to a broad spectrum of technologies, especially as military technology becomes more software based.

Moreover, Chinese writings do not limit their discussion to military targets. Civilian infrastructure such as power grids, transportation, and commercial centers are also identified as potential targets. Although such discussions could be an acknowledgment that China is also vulnerable to these types of attacks, the emphasis in Chinese writings on network reconnaissance and network attack suggests that these could be targets of Chinese attack. The cyberattack against Iran's nuclear weapons facilities and spread of the Stuxnet worm to countries beyond Iran, including China, may provide Chinese cyberwarfare units with the opportunity to examine and learn valuable lessons from the structure of a sophisticated piece of malware that could be applied to Chinese malware. The discussion of attacking civilian targets also suggests that the Chinese could use computer network attack as a means to extend its military reach at a time when much of its conventional and nonmissile forces lack potent power projection capabilities, especially against the United States. As a result, China could attack civilian targets with cyber capabilities, especially if an adversary were to conduct kinetic strikes against targets on Chinese territory.

Moreover, the emphasis in Chinese doctrine and writings on computer network warfare on "gaining mastery by striking first" suggests that the Chinese could strike first in cyberspace against mission-critical C4ISR systems or important civilian information systems. These strikes could be facilitated by the massive Chinese intelligence operation being conducted against foreign government and military entities, which could identify security weaknesses and permit the deployment of backdoors, Trojan horses, or logic bombs.

Indeed, Chinese strikes at the beginning of an operation may be intense. Based on historical evidence since 1949, the PLA has in a majority of cases used overwhelming force at the beginning of operations.[98] This historical propensity, coupled with a doctrinal emphasis and backed up by a strong belief that China only fights just wars in defense of its sovereignty and territorial integrity, suggests that cyberattacks at the beginning of a military operation may be widespread and strong. Despite this, Chinese writings on computer network warfare have not reached the level of sophistication that is present in US writings. For example, there is no discussion of collateral damage or unintended consequences that may be incurred by conducting a computer network attack.[99]

Coercive Dynamics

It is difficult to determine whether China's current cyber operations have an intended deterrent element to them. Indeed, the assessment by some Chinese analysts that deterrence through cyber means is fraught with difficulty due to the ambiguous nature of cyberattacks as well as the secretive nature of these operations and the strident denials by the Chinese government that it conducts any sort of offensive computer network operations despite overwhelming evidence suggest that China is not conducting these operations for a deterrent effect. Nevertheless, the raw display of cyber capabilities by China in recent years demonstrates a capability and a will to conduct offensive computer network operations and implies an ability to inflict losses against an opponent using cyber means. The statements by the head of the General Staff Department Fang Fenghui during a April 2013 visit by the US chairman of the Joint Chiefs of Staff Martin E. Dempsey that a major cyberattack "may be as serious as a nuclear bomb" and that "anyone can launch the attacks—from the place where he lives, from his own country, or from another country" indicate that the top leadership is not only influenced by Chinese writings on computer network operations but also suggests that the Chinese leader may have been stressing the power of cyberattacks to remind the United States that China thinks it can inflict serious harm on the United States.[100]

This raises the question of whether cyber deterrence could follow the principles of mutually assured destruction, in which the immense destructive effects of cyberattacks keep two opponents from engaging in cyberattack. Although some Chinese strategists predict this outcome at some point in the future, including those from the influential Academy of Military Sciences, the current demonstrated capabilities of cyberattack indicates that this is unlikely.[101] In addition, the ample discussion in Chinese writings on the use of offensive cyber capabilities during wartime suggest that equating nuclear deterrence with cyber deterrence may be an inexact comparison. In addition, there is no discussion of escalation control in Chinese writings and how to prevent lower-level cyberattacks from escalating into the more destructive type of attacks described by Chinese analysts.

The emphasis in Chinese writings on striking first, perhaps in cyberspace, appears to lend an element of uncertainty to Chinese coercive and warfighting efforts. Schelling points out that "when speed is critical the victim of an accident or a false alarm is under terrible pressure to get on with the war if in fact it is war or if the enemy seems likely, even in 'self-defense,' to anticipate war by starting it. If each side imputes similar urgency to the other the urgency is aggravated."[102] The vulnerability of computer systems to attack would also seem to present a potential attacker with a low-risk/high-reward outcome that could facilitate striking first. However, unlike in nuclear deterrence, where retaliatory forces are at risk, cyberattacks do not appear to be able to eliminate or greatly reduce the cyberattack capabilities of an adversary. The covert nature of cyber operations, the secrecy surrounding organizations conducting cyber operations, and the ease with which malware can be transferred from one location to another suggest that debilitating an adversary's cyber retaliatory capability would be difficult. This is a situation where the Chinese might perceive a first-move advantage where one does not actually exist, which contributes to crisis instability and miscalculation.

Although an overwhelming number of Chinese writings indicate that China will use computer network operations during an armed conflict, determining whether China will use its cyber power in a compellence role is much more difficult. Discussions over the necessity at certain times to fight small wars to prevent large wars suggest that cyber methods could be employed to punish an opponent. Russia's cyberattack against Estonia in 2007 went unpunished, and China would likely receive little or no effective retribution were it to do the same to a weaker nation. The inability of Western countries to deal with the massive amount of Chinese cyber espionage also suggests that finding an appropriate response to cyberthreats remains elusive. As a result, the lack of an adequate response to cyberattacks, along with their purported effects, may make their use more attractive to a state that has invested considerable resources in the development of such capabilities.

In addition, the Chinese belief that their coercive measures are fundamentally different from the coercive measures of Western countries due to the legitimacy of their interests and the pursuit of illegitimate interests by the West may also facilitate the use of cyber coercion. Although every country views its interests as legitimate and those of others less so, the Chinese propensity to raise its growing list of disputes with other countries in the context of sovereignty makes it difficult to resolve disputes without the use of coercive measures. As a result, coercive cyber measures could play a role in China's demonstrations of force, especially with countries that lack an effective means of cyber retaliation.

Cyberattacks: Unrealized Potential or Less Than Meets Eye?

The uncertainty over the true potential of cyberattacks also raises the question of their efficacy. Although cyber espionage has been proven to be very effective, its coercive and warfighting potential have yet to be fully realized. Certainly some level of discomfort can be visited upon an enemy through cyber means, but whether those effects can be decisive remains questionable. Russian cyber operations against Estonia in 2007 and Georgia in 2008 achieved some effects, but in no way caused a decisive level of societal disruption. Even the Stuxnet worm only managed to delay Iran's nuclear weapons ambitions. As a result, the full potential of cyber remains uncertain.

There is a propensity in Chinese writings to overemphasize the efficaciousness of computer network attack, and the reference to apocryphal events to support the use of cyber measures may lead the PLA to conduct cyberwar on the mistaken belief that these attacks may inflict widespread paralysis on the US military or inflict massive damage on the US economy that will force the United States to capitulate. For example, the numerous references to attacks against the flight control systems of the USS *Nimitz* that caused a halt to flight operations are false. The USS *Theodore Roosevelt* actually took part in the Kosovo operation and it did so without the interruption of flight operations described in Chinese sources. In addition, equating the effects of cyberwar with nuclear war disregards the immense and permanent destructive power of nuclear weapons. Similarly, the conclusion by one researcher that cyberwar can be conducted without resorting to military means or that cyberwar can limit the scope of war disregards the widespread belief that cyberwar is military action. Interestingly, most of these writings asserting the immense destructive power of computer network operations occur well before the advent of Stuxnet.

But achieving decisive effects may be too high a bar to judge the effectiveness of Chinese computer network operations. Simply by disrupting an adversary, especially one like the United States that must flow forces over long distances, cyberwarfare, in conjunction with other measures, may play a role in enabling China to achieve its goals. The August 15, 2012, cyberattack on the Saudi Arabian oil giant Saudi Aramco damaged 30,000 computers and took more than a week to repair, though failed to stop oil production.[103] A similar type of attack against US logistical systems could delay the arrival of reinforcements or critical enabling technologies and much-needed supplies. These types of strikes, even those that disable a system for a short time, may open a window of opportunity that could be exploited by the PLA. Consequently, even if cyber operations do not live up to the potential ascribed to them by Chinese strategists, their use in conjunction with other types of information warfare such as electronic warfare and space warfare may provide the desired effects of debilitating an adversary's critical C4ISR systems.

Offensive or Defensive: In the Eye of the Beholder

Finally, although this chapter has described a Chinese concept of cyberwarfare that is operationally offensive, at a strategic level China views its cyber activities as inherently defensive. China has long insisted that it is the target of cyberattacks, many of them originating from the United States. This has led many in China to conclude that not only does the United States pursue a double standard when it comes to cyber but also considers China an enemy.[104] According to a Chinese Foreign Ministry spokesperson referring to the United States, "For some time, the relevant country has on one hand played up the cyberthreats from other countries, and on the other hand used various methods to implement cyber surveillance endangering the sovereignty, security, and public privacy of other countries."[105]

As a result, because China sees itself as the United States' identified cyber enemy and views US offensive cyber capabilities as more impressive and ubiquitous than its own, it is doubtful that China will discontinue its cyber espionage campaigns. China has too much to gain through these efforts in terms of acquiring intellectual property and intelligence. Moreover, President Xi Jinping's call to make China a "strong informatization power" indicates that China's cyber efforts will only improve. This has resulted in some calls for China to reduce or eliminate its dependence on foreign technology by improving its domestic IT industry and human capital base for IT.[106] Nor can it be expected that China will officially acknowledge its increasing cyberwarfare capabilities, especially when it views itself as the lesser cyber power when compared to the United States. In this regard, the Chinese view transparency at their stage of development as a tool used by the strong against the weak.

China's current posture of not officially acknowledging its own cyber capabilities thus gives China an opportunity to hide its capabilities while at the same time building them up without having to commit to measures that may restrict their development or use. It also lends a degree of uncertainty to any retaliatory efforts undertaken by a foreign power since assigning attribution remains difficult. Chinese analysts, for example, assess US efforts to implement a strategy of cyber deterrence as problematic.[107] (By the same token, in hiding its capabilities it is difficult for China to use them to make clear coercive threats.) As a result, China can be expected to improve its offensive and defensive cyber capabilities and to engage in efforts to build up its IT industry to reduce its reliance on foreign powers, and will continue to regard cyberwar as an integral and perhaps increasingly important part of military operations.

NOTES

1. Office of the Secretary of Defense, *Annual Report to Congress: Military and Security Developments Involving the People's Republic of China 2013*, 36.
2. Lu Yunsheng and Liu Haifeng, "计算机网络攻击体系构想" [A Vision for Computer Network Attack], 计算机网络攻击体系构想 [*Network Security Technology and Application*], December 2009, 43.
3. Academy of Military Science Operational Theory and Regulations Research Department Information Operations Theory Laboratory, 信息化作战理论学习指南-信息化作战400题 [*Information Operations Theory Study Guide: 400 Questions on Information Operations*] (Beijing: Military Science Press, 2005), 97.
4. Academy of Military Science, 中国人民解放军军语 [*Chinese People's Liberation Army Military Terminology*] (Beijing: Military Science Press, 2011), 286.

5. Academy of Military Science Information Operations Theory Laboratory, *Information Operations Theory Study Guide*, 97.

6. Xiao Wenguang and Li Yuanlei, "计算机网络于未来战争" [Computer Networks in Future Wars], 江苏航空 [*Jiangsu Aviation*] 1 (2007): 31.

7. Guo Shengwei, 信息化战争与网电部队 [*Informationized War and Network Electronic Units*] (Beijing: National Defense University Press, 2008), 257–59, 265–66, 275; Shang Liang, Yang Guoxin, Shi Jianlai, and Sui Shilong, "网络战部队—各国军中新宠" [Network Warfare Troops: The New Favorite of Armies in Various Countries], 国防科技 [*National Defense Science and Technology*] 30, no. 4 (2009): 89.

8. Guo, *Informationized War and Network Electronic Units*, 364.

9. Xu Xiaoyan, ed., 信息作战学 [*The Science of Information Operations*] (Beijing: Liberation Army Press, 2002), 157–58; Xiao and Li, "Computer Networks in Future Wars," 31.

10. Xu, *The Science of Information Operations*, 167.

11. Guo, *Informationized War and Network Electronic Units*, 1.

12. Dai Qingmin, 网电一体战 [*Integrated Network Electronic Warfare*] (Beijing: Liberation Army Press, 2002), 57.

13. Ibid., 7–8, 28; Guo, *Informationized War and Network Electronic Units*, 26; Li Kai, "'网电一体战'中网络防御体系研究" ["Net Electric Integrated War": Network Defense System Research], 航天电子对抗 [*Aerospace Electronic Warfare*] 2 (2002): 31.

14. Peng Guangqian and Yao Youzhi, 战略学 [*The Science of Strategy*] (Beijing: Military Sciences Press, 2001), 358; Dai, *Integrated Network Electronic Warfare*, 1, 258.

15. Academy of Military Science, *Chinese People's Liberation Army Military Terminology*, 79; Peng and Yao, *The Science of Strategy*, 358.

16. Liu Zhenwu, "论国家安全与积极防御战略" [National Security and the Active Defense Strategy], 军事学术 [*Military Art Journal*] 4 (2004): 9.

17. Zhang Yuliang, ed., 战役学 [*The Science of Campaigns*] (Beijing: National Defense University Press, 2006), 82.

18. Ibid.

19. Liu Zhenwu, "National Security and the Active Defense Strategy," 9.

20. Zhang, *The Science of Campaigns*, 159.

21. Ibid., 163.

22. Ibid.

23. Dai, *Integrated Network Electronic Warfare*, 153.

24. Ibid., 115.

25. Peng Guangqian and Yao Youzhi, *The Science of Strategy*, 307; Wang Houqing and Zhang Xingye, eds., 战役学 [*The Science of Campaigns*] (Beijing: National Defense University Press, 2000), 108–10.

26. Pan Youmu, 非接触战争研究 [*Noncontact Warfare Research*] (Beijing: National Defense University Press, 2003), 118.

27. Lu Linzhi, "Preemptive Strikes Are Crucial in Limited High-Tech Wars," *Liberation Army Daily*, February 7, 1996.

28. He Dingqing, 战役学教程 [*A Course on the Science of Campaigns*] (Beijing: Military Science Press, 2001), 244.

29. Wang Houqing and Zhang Xingye, *The Science of Campaigns*, 96.

30. Zhang Yuliang, *The Science of Campaigns*, 90.

31. Ibid., 157.
32. Guo, *Informationized War and Network Electronic Units*, 223, 280, 281; Liu, "Joint Campaigns under Informationized War Conditions Operational Guidance," 4.
33. Dai, *Integrated Network Electronic Warfare*, 113–14.
34. Ibid., 38, 160.
35. Ibid., 114.
36. Ibid., 107–8.
37. Academy of Military Science Information Operations Theory Laboratory, *Information Operations Theory Study Guide*, 97.
38. Dai, *Integrated Network Electronic Warfare*, 146.
39. Lu and Liu, "A Vision for Computer Network Attack," 43; Academy of Military Science, *Chinese People's Liberation Army Military Terminology*, 592.
40. Dai, *Integrated Network Electronic Warfare*, 154, 115, 146, 33; Guo, *Informationized War and Network Electronic Units*, 218.
41. Guo, *Informationized War and Network Electronic Units*, 216, 218.
42. Academy of Military Science, *Chinese People's Liberation Army Military Terminology*, 597.
43. Guo, *Informationized War and Network Electronic Units*, 267–68, 274.
44. Ibid.
45. Guo, *Informationized War and Network Electronic Units*, 311; Dai, *Integrated Network Electronic Warfare*, 33.
46. Guo, *Informationized War and Network Electronic Units*, 255–56.
47. Dai, *Integrated Network Electronic Warfare*, 114; Guo, *Informationized War and Network Electronic Units*, 255.
48. Guo, *Informationized War and Network Electronic Units*, 255–56.
49. Ibid., 312.
50. Academy of Military Science, *Chinese People's Liberation Army Military Terminology*, 597.
51. Dai, *Integrated Network Electronic Warfare*, 116.
52. Wu Tianhao, Li Ningning, and Jin Dong, "大型舰艇编队防空作战电子对抗情报体系分析" [An Analysis of Electronic Warfare Confrontation Intelligence Systems for Large Naval Formation Air Defense], 情报杂志 [*Journal of Intelligence*] S2 (2010): 110; quote from Wang Kehai, Wang Bing, and Cao Zhengcai, 一体化联合作战研究 [*Research on Integrated Joint Operations*] (Beijing: PLA Publishers, 2005), 92–93.
53. Wang, Wang, and Cao, *Research on Integrated Joint Operations*, 93.
54. Xiao and Li, "Computer Networks in Future Wars," 31. The threat posed by the insertion of malicious algorithms through antennas appears to be increasing. Aircraft equipped with active electronically scanned array (AESA) radar, such as the US F-35, F-22, and F-16, appear to be more susceptible to this type of attack due to the radar's ability to conduct wide searches for unknown signals. This susceptibility increases as modern aircraft become more software oriented. For example, according to the US Air Force's chief scientist, "90 percent of the F-35's, 70 percent of the F-22's, 60 percent of the B-2's, and 20 percent of the F-15's functionalities are cyber-based." See David A. Fulghum, "Cyberwar Strategy," *Aviation Week*, April 9, 2012, 51.
55. Guo, *Informationized War and Network Electronic Units*, 312–31; Academy of Military Science, *Chinese People's Liberation Army Military Terminology*, 597.

56. Liang Jun and Gao Yinan, "Expert Calls for Network Warfare Unit in China," *People's Daily Online*, January 10, 2014.

57. Jiang Wei, "中央网络安全和信息化领导小组成立:从网络大国迈向网络强国" [The Central Internet Security and Informatization Leading Small Group Established], Xinhua, February 27, 2014.

58. Zhu Ningzhu, "Xi Jinping Leads Internet Security Group," Xinhua, February 27, 2014.

59. Yin Siming, "国防部网和军网月均遭受境外攻击14.4万余次" [Ministry of Defense Networks and Military Networks Subjected to 14.4 Million Outside Attacks], 国防部网 [*Ministry of National Defense Network*], February 28, 2013.

60. Tang Danlu, "China's Cyber Security under Severe Threat: Report," Xinhua, March 19, 2013.

61. George Smith, "One Printer, One Virus, One Disabled Iraqi Air Defense: You Can't Keep a Good April Fool's Down," *The Register*, March 10, 2003.

62. Quotes from Academy of Military Science Information Operations Theory Laboratory, *Information Operations Theory Study Guide*, 159; see also Wu, Li, and Jin, "An Analysis of Warfare Electronic Confrontation Intelligence Systems," 110.

63. Li Shan, "揭开 Stuxnet 病毒神秘的面纱" [Lifting the Veil of the Stuxnet Mystery], 科学与文化 [*Science and Culture*] 4 (2011): 25.

64. Wei Qinzhi, "工业控制系统安全现状及安全策略分析" [Industrial Control System Security Situation and Safety Strategy Analysis], 信息安全与技术 [*Information Security and Technology*] 2 (2013): 23–24.

65. See, for example, Yang Yanbo, "聚焦美 军'网络威慑'战略" [Focusing on the US Military's 'Network Deterrence' Strategy], 中国国防报 [*China National Defense Daily*], January 9, 2012; and Guo Ji, "网络不应成为美国霸权新工具" [The Internet Should Not Become a New Tool of American Hegemony], 求是 [*Seek Truth*], August 1, 2013.

66. Chen Jie, "论威慑在军事斗争准备中的运用" [Discussions of the Use of Deterrence in Preparation for Military Struggle], 电子科技大学学报(社科版) [*University of Electronic Science and Technology of China (Social Science Edition)*] 4 (2006): 75.

67. Peng and Yao, *The Science of Strategy*, 230.

68. Ibid., 232.

69. Zhan, *Coercive Warfare*, 2.

70. Ibid., 71.

71. Ibid., 2, 3.

72. Peng and Yao, *The Science of Strategy*, 234.

73. Zhao Juan, "Research on the Strategic Deterrence of Target Nation Policymaker Rationality," 南京政治学院学报 [*Journal of PLA Nanjing Institute of Politics*] 26, no. 6 (2010): 4.

74. Feng Yongjun, "新中国国防威慑力量的构建与运用" [The Construction and Use of New China's Defense Deterrent Force], 南京政治院学报 [*Journal of PLA Nanjing Institute of Politics*] 2 (2000): 104.

75. See Peng and Yao, *The Science of Strategy*, 230–32, for a more extensive discussion of these three factors.

76. Ibid., 231.

77. Chen, "Discussions of the Use of Deterrence in Preparation for Military Struggle," 76; Zhan, *Coercive Warfare*, 6; Wu, "A Preliminary Exploration of Our Army's Military Deterrent Thinking," 14.

78. Zhan, *Coercive Warfare*, 11.

79. Chen, "Discussions of the Use of Deterrence in Preparation for Military Struggle," 76; Zhan, *Coercive Warfare*, 6; Wu Qiong, "我国新时期军事威慑思想浅探" [A Preliminary Exploration of Our Army's Military Deterrent Thinking], 军事历史研究 [*Military Historical Research*] 2 (2002): 14.

80. Ibid.

81. Chen Jie, "Discussions of the Use of Deterrence in Preparation for Military Struggle," 76.

82. Zhan, *Coercive Warfare*, 5.

83. Dennis Blasko, "'Technology Determines Tactics': The Relationship between Technology and Doctrine in Chinese Military Thinking," *Journal of Strategic Studies* 34 (2011): 369–71.

84. Wu, "A Preliminary Exploration of Our Army's Military Deterrent Thinking," 16.

85. Zhang Wannian Biography Group, 张万年传 [*The Biography of Zhang Wannian*] (Beijing: PLA Press, 2011), 163.

86. Dai, *Integrated Network Electronic Warfare*, 32.

87. Ibid.

88. See, for example, Dong Qingling and Dai Changzheng, "网络空间威慑: 报复是否可行?" [Deterrence in the Network Space: Is Retaliation Feasible?], 世界经济与政治 [*World Economics and Politics*] 7 (2012): 101–2; and Yu Xiaoqiu, "网络威慑力"是个危险的游戏" [Network Deterrence Power Is a Dangerous Game], *People's Daily*, July 25, 2011.

89. See for example, Yang Xiaobo, "网络空间威慑的实现与应用" [Realization and Application of Deterrence in the Network Domain], 轻兵器 [*Small Arms*] 10 (2013): 12; Dong and Dai, "Deterrence in the Network Space," 101–2; and Peng and Yao, *The Science of Strategy*, 237–38.

90. Peng and Yao, *The Science of Strategy*, 237–38.

91. Ibid., 117–18.

92. Ibid., 180–81.

93. Guo, *Informationized War and Network Electronic Units*, 299.

94. Ibid., 310.

95. Ibid., 302.

96. Ibid.

97. Xiao and Li, "Computer Networks in Future Wars," 31.

98. Forrest E. Morgan, Karl P. Mueller, Evan S. Medeiros, Kevin L. Pollpeter, and Roger Cliff, *Dangerous Thresholds: Managing Escalation in the 21st Century* (Santa Monica, CA: Rand, 2008), 177–95.

99. John Markoff and Thom Shanker, "U.S. Weighs Risks of Civilian Harm in Cyberwarfare," *New York Times*, August 2, 2009.

100. Jane Perlez, "U.S. and China Put Focus on Cybersecurity," *New York Times*, April 22, 2013.

101. AMS Strategic Studies Group, "论战略威慑" [Strategic Deterrence], 中国军事科学 [*China Military Science*], 2004–5, 238.

102. Thomas C. Schelling, *Arms and Influence* (New Haven, CT: Yale University Press, 1966), 227.

103. "Saudi Aramco Says Cyber Attack Targeted Kingdom's Economy," *Al Arabiya News*, December 9, 2012.

104. See, for example, Yang Jian, "美国推动全球网络军备竞赛 刻意将中国当敌人" [The United States Promotes Global Cyber Arms Race While Making China the Enemy], Sina.com, March 8, 2013; and Cai Cuihong,

"美国网络空间先发制人战略的构建及其影响" [The Origin and Influence of the US Preemptive Strike Cyber Strategy], February 27, 2014, accessed at http://www.wyzxwk.com/Article/guofang/2014/02/314821.html.

105. Li Xiaokun and Zhao Yanrong, "U.S. Double Standards Threaten Other Nations," *People's Daily Online*, January 17, 2014.

106. Zhang Yongfu, "全球网络军备竞赛激烈" [The Global Network Arms Race Intensifies], Chinanews.com, February 3, 2012.

107. Lu Jinghua, "奥巴马政府网络空间安全政策述评" [The Obama Administration's Cyberspace Security Policy], GlobalView, http://www.globalview.cn/ReadNews.asp?NewsID=29587.

CHAPTER 7

The Chinese People's Liberation Army Computer Network Operations Infrastructure

MARK A. STOKES

Computer networks are the main arteries of cyber operations. Information and communications technology enable and enhance the capabilities of actors to engage in the cyber realm. Modern societies and governments increasingly rely on cyber-based information systems in order to process, coordinate, and manage critical processes necessary to function. Yet due to the highly automated and interconnected nature of economic transactions and the protection of critical infrastructure, the cyber domain is emerging as a new dimension in conflicts of the future. Therefore, the capability inherent in the exploitation of computer network operations (CNO) represents a significant evolutionary stage in both civil and military affairs. In the case of the People's Republic of China (PRC), driven by political insecurities and a quest for total information awareness, the Chinese Communist Party (CCP), state authorities, and the Chinese People's Liberation Army (PLA) are allegedly waging a coordinated CNO campaign against a broad range of international targets.

Chinese cyber espionage constitutes an advanced persistent threat (APT)—an intrusion above and beyond traditional cybercrime—to US national and economic security. Groups operating from PRC territory are believed to be waging a coordinated cyber espionage campaign targeting US government, industrial, media, and think tank computer networks.

A dozen of these groups have been identified and linked with the PLA, and others are connected with universities and information security enterprises. The largest and most active of these groups may operate from Beijing and Shanghai.[1]

The PRC government views *informatization* of Chinese society as a means to ensure sustained economic growth, enable China to compete globally in the information technology realm, and to ensure national security against domestic and international threats.[2] Informatization relies on information security systems that can support economic restructuring and national security. In the information age, information security can be viewed within the broadest context as ensuring CCP legitimacy, enhancing the Party-state's ability to consolidate power, defending national networks against internal and external threats, and supporting economic development. Therefore, security of the Party and state requires mastery of the global cybersphere.[3]

Party and state leaders oversee an expansive, but fragmented cyber operations policy infrastructure. In the past, the State Informatization Leading Group (SILG), consisting of senior representatives from Party, state, and military organizations, established national informatization policies. A subordinate working group advised senior leaders on network and information security.[4] In February 2014, however, Chinese media reported the establishment of a new organization responsible for developing policies related to CNO and Internet security. The leading group is to be directed by the chairman of the CCP Central Military Commission (CMC), Xi Jinping, and includes PLA chief of the General Staff General Fang Fenghui among its members[5]

Few, if any, US entities that work on China issues have escaped intrusions. Attributing responsibility to a specific Chinese entity is a difficult task. However, this assessment posits that the General Staff Department (GSD/总参某部/总参), Third Department (3/PLA) manages a complex cyber reconnaissance infrastructure that exploits vulnerable computer networks around the world, while also ensuring the integrity of classified networks within China. Also referred to as the Technical Reconnaissance Department, 3/PLA enjoys a traditional core competency in signals intelligence (SIGINT), advanced high-performance computing and encryption/decryption technical capabilities, and a status as China's largest employer of well-trained linguists.[6]

The GSD, one of four departments that report to the CMC, is the heart of the PLA and a driver of its future. The GSD develops policies, plans, and programs, establishes requirements, and allocates resources to support the PLA mission to defend the interests of the CCP. The GSD is responsible for day-to-day joint operations, intelligence, strategic planning and operational requirements, training, mobilization, military diplomacy, and security of senior Party and state leadership. GSD leadership includes the chief of the GSD (Gen. Fang), deputy chiefs of the General Staff, the general office director, and assistants to the chief of staff.

The GSD encompasses a large, complex bureaucracy consisting of a general office and at least twelve second-level departments and subordinate bureaus. Roughly analogous to the US National Security Agency (NSA), 3/PLA today manages one of the largest intelligence collection and information security infrastructures in the world. With modest origins in the 1930s, 3/PLA was previously known as the CMC Second Bureau and consisted of three entities responsible for collection, translation, and deciphering/encryption.[7] Faced with its own challenges to communication systems and computer networks, 3/PLA has responsibility for assuring the security of PLA computer systems in order to prevent foreign adversaries from gaining access to sensitive national security information. These functions are encompassed within the euphemism of "technical reconnaissance," which is the foundation of "informatized" warfare.[8]

Like its American counterpart, the NSA, 3/PLA appears to be diversifying its traditional SIGINT mission. Computer network operations in China often are referred to as "network attack and defense," based on the premise that "without understanding how to attack, one will not know how to defend."[9] In the US lexicon, CNO includes computer network attack (CNA), computer network exploitation (CNE), and computer network defense (CND).[10] CNE represents the cutting edge of SIGINT, and indications exist that 3/PLA may serve as the national executive agent for CNE.[11] Previous studies have outlined 3/PLA organizational structure, but only tentative links have been drawn between 3/PLA and CNE.[12] This assessment posits that the PLA's CNO infrastructure also relies on an advanced computing center and a handful of 3/PLA-managed information security bases that serve as a platform for cooperation with academia and cybersecurity companies. Operational 3/PLA entities also appear to play a prominent role within a broader CNO network, alongside technical reconnaissance bureaus under military regions. While unclear, entities engaged in CNO likely are fragmented and stovepiped. Among the most important bureau-level entities that appear to be dedicated to technical aspects of CNO include 3/PLA's First Bureau, possibly the Ninth Bureau, the Beijing North Computing Center, and the GSD Fifty-Eighth Research Institute.

Which organization within the PLA has responsibility for CNA remains an open question. Most assessments point toward the GSD Electronic Countermeasures and Radar Department (also known as the GSD Fourth

Department), which traditionally has been the principal staff organization responsible for radar-related planning and electronic countermeasure (ECM) operations. A preliminary survey reveals few clues about a Fourth Department strategic cyberattack mission. GSD 3/PLA itself and the PLA Second Artillery Force, China's answer to US Strategic Command, are alternate candidates. In general, the organizational structure for strategic cyberattack requires greater attention.

This chapter first examines 3/PLA's command structure and subordinate research institutes. It then offers an overview of 3/PLA's twelve operational bureaus. The discussion then turns to technical reconnaissance assets under each of the PLA's seven military regions, navy, air force, and Second Artillery Force. A final section examines candidates within the PLA possibly responsible for CNA.

LEADERSHIP AND TECHNICAL SUPPORT

Headquartered in the northwestern hills of Beijing's Haidian District, 3/PLA manages a large SIGINT and cyber reconnaissance system targeting foreign diplomatic communications, military activity, economic entities, public education institutions, and individuals of interest. Leadership, staff, technical personnel, and linguists in 3/PLA are distributed in general headquarters staff positions, twelve operational bureaus, a computing center, and three research institutes. Directors of GSD second-level departments, such as 3/PLA and Fourth Department (4/PLA), have grades equivalent to a corps leader. Bureau directors under second-level departments have grades equivalent to division leader. The 3/PLA bureau, office, and section facilities and sites, located throughout China, report directly to Beijing, and are not under administrative jurisdiction of military region commanders or political commissars.

Major General (MG) Liu Xiaobei (刘晓北; b. 1956) has directed 3/PLA since 2012, with MG Meng Xuezheng (孟学政; b. 1956) serving as 3/PLA political commissar. Liu formerly served as 3/PLA deputy director and filled in temporarily as political commissar for a brief period.[13] He appears to have replaced Lieutenant General Wu Guohua, who directed 3/PLA between 2005 and December 2010, when he was assigned as Second Artillery deputy commander.[14]

The 3/PLA command oversees headquarters, political, and logistics departments, as well as a Science and Technology (S&T) Intelligence Bureau (科技情报局), and S&T Equipment Bureau (科技装备局). The S&T Equipment Bureau oversees three research institutes responsible for computing, sensor technology, and cryptography. The Fifty-Sixth Research Institute, also known as the Jiangnan Computer Technology Research Institute, is the PLA's oldest and largest computer science research and development (R&D) organization. Located in Wuxi, the institute is heavily invested in high-performance computing, and supports 3/PLA and other national-level computer centers. The director of the Fifty-Sixth Institute is a member of the 863 Program Expert Working Group on Computing and Software.[15] The Fifty-Seventh Research Institute appears to be responsible for development of communications intercept and signal-processing systems.[16] Formerly collocated with the First Bureau complex in the Dujiangyan area, the institute is based in the Chengdu area and also known as the Southwest Institute of Electronics and Telecommunications Technology.[17] Among the institute's key focus areas is satellite communications technology, and it has been noted working with China Academy of Space Technology on satellite R&D.[18] The Fifty-Eighth Research Institute is probably responsible for R&D on cryptology and information security technology. The institute appears to have a close relationship with 3/PLA First Bureau.[19]

The 3/PLA S&T Equipment Bureau likely has administrative oversight of at least three information security engineering bases/centers located in Shanghai, Beijing, and Tianjin.[20] The National Information Security Engineering Technology Center (NISEC) within 3/PLA was established in Shanghai in 2001 and is directed by Senior Colonel Wen Zhonghui (文仲慧; b. 1954). Senior Colonel Wen is a cryptologic specialist who rose through the ranks of the GSD Fifty-Eighth Research Institute. He sits on the 863 Program Information Security Expert Working Group (863-917 Program), which funded establishment of the Great Firewall of China security system, and two information security standardization committees (WG-3 and WG-7).[21] Established in 2005, the National Research Center for Information Security Technology serves as the national authority on risk assessment for China's network security.[22] Director Major General Yuan Jianjun (袁建军) was formerly head of the PLA Information Security Evaluation and Certification Center (a 3/PLA Third Bureau–affiliated entity).[23] Also referred to as the Information Security Research Institute (信息安全研究所) or National Information Center (国家信息中心), the organization maintains a close affiliation with 3/PLA S&T Equipment Bureau.[24] Central authorities approved the establishment of a third information technology security base in Tianjin in 2009, which specializes in cryptographic keying material, systems integration, and computer network attack technology.[25] Collocated with these engineering centers are National Information Security Industrial

Bases (国家信息安全产业基地), with additional industrial bases located in Wuhan and Chengdu.[26]

Beijing North Computing Center

The 3/PLA Beijing North Computing Center (BNCC) appears to be responsible for cyber reconnaissance architecture design, technology development, systems engineering, and acquisition. At least ten subordinate divisions appear responsible for design and development of computer network defense, attack, and exploitation systems. One of China's earliest organizations engaged in high-performance computing, BNCC is run by leaders equivalent in grade to an army division commander or 3/PLA bureau director. Senior representatives from BNCC, which is also referred to as the GSD 418th Research Institute, have served as senior advisors to the State Council Informatization Office's Information Security Working Group, and are also committee members of national-level computing associations.

A thick veil of secrecy shrouds specific BNCC responsibilities. Initial indications of a role in cyber operations emerged in 2000, when Falun Gong authorities accused BNCC of launching denial of service attacks against the organization's mail servers.[27] Facility construction projects underway since 2006 indicate a significant growth in its scope of operations.[28] China's leading cybersecurity experts have highlighted the need for active defense involving intrusions of and attacks against enemy systems.[29] BNCC likely plays a leading role in command-and-control network management, code breaking, advanced malware development and acquisition, data storage, and vulnerability assessment. BNCC officers have experience in computer network attack and defense, network intrusion monitoring and control, and information collection. BNCC software source code has been made available to enterprises for commercialization. In addition to developing one of China's first stealthy remote access tools (RATs), BNCC fielded China's most advanced network intrusion detection system for analyzing threats and assessing vulnerabilities, including those associated with operating systems such as Android.[30]

BNCC's active defense software was certified in tests involving attacks against target networks.[31] Its risk assessment function includes analysis of command-and-control systems. Supercomputing is required to crack advanced encryption systems. BNCC's advanced computing networks servers appear sufficient to handle vast databases containing collected electronic communications and files, including recorded phone calls, radio chatter, private e-mails, Internet search records, passwords, password-protected computer files, as well as an abundance of personal data on individuals of interest.

BNCC maintains a close relationship with a number of organizations within China's broader CNO community. In addition to formal positions within China's parallel and high-performance computing community, BNCC senior engineers have served as advisors to the State Council Informatization Office, specifically the Information Security Working Group. Basic and developmental research support on high-performance computing is carried out by 3/PLA Fifty-Sixth Research Institute in Wuxi and National University of Defense Technology in Changsha. BNCC divisions rely on at least a dozen cybersecurity companies for day-to-day work. BNCC-affiliated companies also support information security engineering bases in Beijing, Shanghai, and Tianjin.[32]

Training and Education

Training and education for 3/PLA personnel is generally conducted at one of two institutions. Most linguists assigned to 3/PLA bureaus and technical reconnaissance bureaus (TRBs) receive language training at the PLA University of Foreign Languages in Luoyang, the rough counterpart of the Defense Language Institute in Monterey, California.[33] Upon graduation, they are assigned to a bureau for mission-specific technical training. Technical training for electrical engineers, communications specialists, computer scientists, and network security personnel is conducted at the PLA Information Engineering University in Zhengzhou, Henan Province.[34] Personnel for regular duties, such as drivers, administration, facility security, and so forth, are recruited in the normal annual conscription. Personnel security requirements are likely more stringent than in other parts of the PLA, which gives the political commissar system increased stature.

OPERATIONAL 3/PLA BUREAUS

The Third Department has direct authority over twelve operational bureaus. Eight of the twelve bureau headquarters are clustered in Beijing. Two others are based in Shanghai, one in Qingdao, and one in Wuhan.[35] The department's twelve operational bureaus mostly likely report to the Headquarters Department. The operational bureaus are separate and distinct from TRBs under the PLA's seven military regions, and the three services: air force, navy, and Second Artillery. TRB directors likely report to military region and armed services chiefs of staff. However, 3/PLA likely provides TRBs with policy guidance and tasking for collection and analysis.

Bureau-level directors and political commissars have grades equivalent to that of a division leader, and oversee between six and fourteen subordinate sites or offices (*chu*; 处). Office directors have a grade equivalent to a deputy division and regiment leader.[36] Sites/offices under bureaus are further divided into sections (*ke*; 科), although some sections report directly to bureau headquarters. In addition to a liaison office in Shanghai, 3/PLA manages a Hong Kong and Macao Liaison Bureau (总参三部港澳联络局) in Shenzhen.[37]

The First Bureau (61786 Unit) headquarters is collocated with 3/PLA command complex in northwestern Beijing. As one of China's foremost authorities on CNO and information security, and overseeing at least twelve offices operating in various parts of China, the bureau appears to have a functional rather than regional mission. Formerly centered in the Chengdu suburb of Dujiangyan, the bureau's mission appears to include decryption, encryption, and other information security tasks.[38] The First Bureau, for example, is the only military representative on the national 863 Program Information Assurance Expert Working Group.[39] At least one First Bureau element, possibly the Seventh Office, is based south of Dujiangyan. The bureau also oversees an Information Security Research Center.[40]

The Second Bureau (61398 Unit) appears to function as a key 3/PLA entity targeting the United States and Canada, most likely focusing on political, economic, and military-related intelligence. Most Second Bureau elements are situated in Shanghai City. The Second Bureau command compound is located in Shanghai's northeastern Gaoqiao district. The First Division is collocated with Second Bureau headquarters, and appears responsible for analysis. Four of the eight identified divisions under the Second Bureau are located in Shanghai's northern Baoshan District.[41] The Second Bureau maintains relationships with a range of entities in the greater Shanghai area and leverages access to the Shanghai City's Internet monitoring center (dubbed the Shanghai 005 Center), which is managed by China Telecom.[42] It maintains facilities in the vicinity of submarine cable landing stations on Chongming Island and in Shanghai's southern Nanhui District.[43] Senior officers, both retired and active, maintain academic affiliations with the Shanghai Association of International Strategic Studies and the Shanghai Strategy Association.[44] The Second Bureau managed the establishment of 3/PLA's information security engineering base in Shanghai.[45] Based on the number of technical studies jointly produced by representatives from both organizations, the Second Bureau also enjoys a cooperative working relationship with Shanghai Jiaotong University's School of Information Security Engineering.[46]

Headquartered in the southern Beijing suburb of Daxing, the Third Bureau (61785 Unit) appears to have a functional mission.[47] Given the dispersed nature of subordinate offices, the mission of the Third Bureau may be front-end collection of line-of-sight radio communications, including border control networks, as well as direction finding, and emission control and security. The bureau has at least thirteen subordinate units, including offices based in Harbin, Dalian, Beijing, Hangzhou, Ningdu County (Jiangxi), Shanghai, Xiamen, Shenzhen, Kunming, Xian, and Wulumuqi.[48] Members of the Third Bureau's Third Division have conducted studies on cyberwarfare, including analysis of weaknesses in Android operating systems and NTLM (Windows NT Local Area Network Manager) authentication protocols. Members also have carried out joint studies with Shanghai Jiaotong University's Department of Computer Science and Engineering.[49]

Headquartered in Qingdao, the Fourth Bureau (61419 Unit) appears to be focused on Japan and Korea.[50] Many of the Fourth Bureau offices, including the First, appear to be located in the Qingdao area. The Second Office incorporates Korean linguists. The Fourth Bureau's Seventh Office is located in Hangzhou.[51] Another office is located in Jimo City Wenlongzhen. Other subordinate offices appear to be located in the Qingdao area, Dalian, Beijing, and Shanghai. The bureau was formerly based in the Shanxi provincial city of Xinzhou, specifically Huanglong Wanggou village. While its headquarters moved to Qingdao, the Fourth Bureau may still maintain its training base in Xinzhou.[52]

Headquartered in Beijing's Daxing District Huangcun Village, the Fifth Bureau (61565 Unit) appears to have a Russia-related mission. Fifth Bureau offices are located in Heilongjiang's Suihua City, Jiuquan, and Xinjiang.[53] The Sixth Bureau (61726 Unit) is headquartered in Wuhan's Wuchang District.[54] Bureau headquarters were centered in the area of Jingmen, Hubei province, until moving to Wuhan more than a decade ago.[55] Sixth Bureau offices stretch across central China from the eastern coastal city of Xiamen to the Yunnan city of Kunming, indicating a Taiwan and South Asia mission.[56]

The mission of the Seventh Bureau (61580 Unit), headquartered in Shucun area of Beijing's northwest Haidian District, is unclear. Selected bureau engineers specialize in computer network defense and attack, and have conducted joint studies with the PLA Information Engineering Academy Computer Network Attack and Defense section.[57] Divided into at least ten offices, the Seventh Bureau employs English translators.[58] One

Seventh Bureau study examined support vector machine (SVM) applications for detecting intrusion patterns.[59] Two senior engineers outlined US network-centric warfare, while another published an assessment of the future of the Internet and dense wavelength division multiplexing.[60] Another study focused on psychological and technical aspects of reading and interpreting written foreign language.[61] Another addressed legal aspects of the global economy.[62]

Nestled in Hanjiachuan, the Eighth Bureau (61046 Unit) is adjacent to 3/PLA headquarters in Beijing's northwest suburbs.[63] It also appears to have a presence in Wenquanzhen in far northwestern Beijing.[64] Based on language capabilities of members assigned, the Eighth Bureau appears to focus on Western and Eastern Europe and perhaps rest of world (e.g., Middle East, Africa, and Latin America).[65] Western reporting has speculated that the Eighth Bureau has a Russia mission. Among its ten offices, at least one major office is located in the Hainan Island city of Haikou.[66] The Seventh Office is based in Hubei Province's Xiangfan City.[67] The Eighth Bureau satellite receiving station is in northwestern Beijing suburb of Xibeiwang.[68]

Among all the bureaus, the Ninth (61221 Unit) is the most opaque. Headquartered near the Summer Palace in Beijing, the Ninth Bureau appears responsible for computing, strategic intelligence analysis, database management, and audiovisual technology.[69] At least one office is responsible for computing equipment.[70] The Tenth Bureau (61886 Unit), sometimes referred to as the "7911 Unit," is headquartered in Beijing's northwest suburb of Shangdi on Xinxi Road.[71] The Tenth Bureau appears to have a Central Asia- or Russia-related mission, perhaps focused specifically on telemetry and missile tracking and/or nuclear testing.[72] The Eleventh Bureau (61672 Unit), also known as the "2020 Unit," is headquartered in the Malianwa community, just east of the 3/PLA headquarters compound.[73] The bureau headquarters was previously based in Jiamusi City in Heilongjiang province until its move to Beijing in 2011.[74] The distribution of offices throughout northern China and assignment of Russian linguists indicate a Russia-related mission. With Russian linguists assigned to both entities, differences between the Eleventh and Fifth Bureau missions is unknown.[75]

Headquartered in Shanghai's Zhabei District, the Twelfth Bureau (61486 Unit) appears to have a functional mission involving satellites, likely inclusive of intercept of satellite communications, support for space surveillance, and possibly space-based SIGINT collection. Subordinate offices and sites are in the Shanghai area, and in southeast, northeast, southwest, and northwestern China. More specifically, Twelfth Bureau offices are situated in Taicang, just outside of Shanghai, Fuzhou, Hangzhou, Kunming, Changchun, Guangzhou, Gansu, and Xinjiang.[76] One site appears to host a large phased array radar system.[77]

MILITARY REGION AND SERVICE/BRANCH TECHNICAL RECONNAISSANCE BUREAUS

The Third Department's twelve operational bureaus are separate and distinct from technical reconnaissance bureaus under the seven military region headquarters in Beijing, Chengdu, Guangzhou, Jinan, Lanzhou, Nanjing, and Shenyang. Each Military Region Headquarters Department chief of staff exercises authority over at least one TRB.[78] However, senior 3/PLA authorities in Beijing likely issue policy guidance and general tasking for TRB collection, analysis, and reporting.[79] TRB missions may parallel those of 3/PLA, and include communications intelligence, direction finding, traffic analysis, translation, cryptology, computer network defense, and computer network exploitation. However, their primary role is to support the military region command. Military region TRBs also likely support border security forces.[80]

Service/branch TRBs appear to specialize in monitoring communications networks related to their specific areas of interest. Although unconfirmed, it appears that the PLA air force (PLAAF) and navy technical reconnaissance units had formerly been under Military Region Air Force headquarters and PLA navy North, East, and South Sea fleets. Over the last several years, technical reconnaissance assets may have been consolidated under Air Force and Navy Headquarters Departments in Beijing. The PLAAF Headquarters Department oversees three TRBs with regional responsibility (north, south, and west) for monitoring of neighboring air forces and air activity around China's periphery. PLAAF TRBs likely conduct airborne SIGINT missions as well. As an aside, PLAAF representatives have implied adoption of independent computer network operations as an air force mission.[81]

The PLA Navy (PLAN) oversees two TRB bureaus that appear to be organized geographically. Indications exist of a reorganization that removed PLAN TRBs from the fleets and subordinated them to Navy Headquarters Department. The PLAN's First TRB is headquartered in Beijing and appears to oversee at least ten subordinate offices in northern China, including sites in Hunchun, Qingdao, and Yantai. The PLAN's Second TRB is headquartered in Xiamen's Si'men District. Subordinate offices are located in Ningbo, Wenzhou, Xiamen, Shantou, and Haikou. While this focus is unconfirmed, the PLAN's First and Second TRBs likely oversee ship-based SIGINT collection assets.[82] The Second Artillery Headquarters Department Technical Reconnaissance Bureau appears to be based in Beijing's Huilongguan suburb. Locations of subordinate elements have yet to be identified. The bureau's political department director formerly served as political commissar of the Second Artillery's communications command.[83]

COMPUTER NETWORK ATTACK

Beyond the intrinsic value of cyber reconnaissance, computer network exploitation is the foundation for computer network attack. GSD 3/PLA appears to play a primary role in CNE and CND operations. However, the PLA organization responsible for CNA remains an open question. Most assessments point toward the GSD Electronic Countermeasures and Radar Department, also referred to as the GSD Fourth Department (4/PLA). Conclusions often are based upon the writings of a former 4/PLA director, Dai Qingmin, who advocated integrating electronic warfare with computer network operations in a widely cited book published in 2002.[84] While a 4/PLA CNA mission is certainly possible, particularly at the operational and tactical level, a preliminary order of battle and organizational survey offer few clues.

The Fourth Department is responsible for radar-related joint operational requirements development and electronic countermeasures (ECM).[85] Priorities appear to include satellite jamming and counterstealth radar systems. With regard to the former, GSD appears capable of disrupting adversary use of communications, navigation, synthetic aperture radar, and other satellites.

In addition to an advisory group and the GSD Fifty-Fourth Research Institute, 4/PLA consists of at least four bureaus. The Radar Bureau may specialize in counterstealth force modernization, among other responsibilities. The ECM Bureau is responsible for planning, programming, and budgeting for ECM systems. The Technical Equipment Bureau appears to be responsible for acquisition. The PLA Electronic Engineering Academy in Hefei, Anhui province, is the department's institution for cadet education and technical training as well as officer PME.[86] Operational units include at least one ECM brigade (61906 Unit) that appears to be have been headquartered in the Miyun area north of Beijing. Another unit, possibly an ECM brigade (61251 Unit), is headquartered in the Qinhuangdao area of Hebei province. The Fourth Department may operate electronic reconnaissance satellite ground receiving stations to support joint targeting, and one or possibly two satellite jamming regiments, including the 61764 Unit on Hainan Island.

The Third Department itself and PLA Second Artillery Force, China's answer to US Strategic Command, are alternate candidates for the CNA mission. The Second Artillery Force is the CCP's and CMC's principal instrument for achieving strategic effects through direct targeting of enemy centers of gravity. The Second Artillery's core mission has been nuclear deterrence. For more than thirty years, however, it has assessed first-, second-, and third-order effects of neutralizing single points of failure in a foreign adversary's critical infrastructure. A former director of the 3/PLA, Lieutenant General Wu Guohua, was promoted to serve as Second Artillery Force deputy commander. The Fourth Department's traditional core competency has been interference of radar and communications system within a given theater of operations.

CONCLUSION

In short, 3/PLA manages a complex infrastructure that exploits vulnerable computer networks around the world. While appearing to exercise executive authority, 3/PLA does not enjoy a monopoly over cyber espionage. Technical reconnaissance bureaus subordinate to military regions, the PLAAF, PLAN, and Second Artillery also may collect against foreign targets of interest. For example, one source with a record of reliable reporting on cyber issues has highlighted operations traced back to the Shenyang Military Region Technical Reconnaissance Bureau. Public security bureaus at city and provincial levels also have computer-monitoring groups, as does the Ministry of State Security. The Third Department's First Bureau manages an information security research center that is most likely focused on cryptography, and the Seventh Bureau has published a number of studies on cyber operations. The Third Bureau of 3/PLA oversees several cybersecurity functions, such as certification of public keying material.[87]

Cyber espionage and potential disruption of critical US computer networks have emerged as a significant national security challenge. In his May 2011 "International Strategy for Cyberspace," President Obama declared that the United States will work with partners to "encourage responsible behavior and oppose those who would seek to disrupt networks and systems, dissuading and deterring malicious actors, and reserving the right to defend these vital national assets as necessary and appropriate." In response, the US national security community is adopting a multifaceted approach to address the cybersecurity challenge, including through strengthened awareness, deterrence, greater investment in counterintelligence, and international partnerships. Defenses require a combination of measures. Counterintelligence tools include both disruption and deception, which offset the inherent asymmetric advantages that the attacking side enjoys.[88]

Passive or defensive network operations alone are inadequate to defend sensitive data. Offensive operations are core to counter-cyber espionage doctrine.[89] An initial approach to defending against Chinese cyber surveillance is deception and perception management. Cyber deception likely would be effective due to a PLA tendency for stovepiping and an ingrained cognitive bias regarding the United States and its intentions. Deception as a defense complicates an attacker's ability to plan and execute operations.[90]

Another approach to cyber defense is engaging PRC civilian and military authorities on the International Code of Conduct for Information Security, an initiative that Chinese and Russian representatives proposed in September 2011.[91] While Chinese expression of interest in an international code of conduct is a positive move, the proposal fails to strengthen international cross-border law enforcement. While challenges exist in developing a common set of interests, most important would be a focus on managing nonstate actors engaged in cyber-related criminal activities. Worth noting is Beijing's claim that nonstate actors are responsible for cyber reconnaissance activities launched from Chinese territory.[92]

While developing an international code of conduct presents challenges, greater collaboration with allies and coalition partners in the Asia-Pacific region may be warranted. The Republic of China (Taiwan) is the most obvious candidate for co-development of techniques best suited for the challenges emanating from the PRC.[93] Taiwan was the first and most intense target of CCP-sponsored cyber espionage.[94] According to Chuang Ming-Hsiung, section chief at the Taiwan Criminal Investigation Bureau's High-Technology Crime Prevention Center: "Before China releases a virus to the United States, it will test it on Taiwan. That's why Taiwan has a faster response rate than the United States."[95] Furthermore, cyber defenders on Taiwan are assisted by a shared cultural heritage with China, helping them to better decipher a Chinese attacker's strategic culture and way of thinking.[96]

The PLA's ambitious cyber operations also warrant consideration of appropriate responses to hostile cyber network attacks intended to neutralize US command-and-control and critical infrastructure. Most important would be the determination of what types of computer network attacks would constitute an act of war, and whether or not kinetic responses would be appropriate.[97]

To mitigate the challenges posed by Chinese cyber espionage and counter a coordinated cyber reconnaissance campaign requires reducing the value of information through thoughtful deception, enhanced counterintelligence, greater cooperation with international partners such as Taiwan, and imposing costs through effective deterrence. The United States appears to be taking the Chinese cyber challenge seriously and dedicating resources to countermeasures. As noted earlier, deception and technological defenses are two viable investments that could be augmented with an expanded dialogue on a cyber code of conduct. Greater consideration of appropriate and measured deterrent options and potential forceful responses are warranted as well.

NOTES

1. David Barboza, "Hacking Inquiry Puts China's Elite in New Light," *New York Times*, February 21, 2010; Michael Riley and Dune Lawrence, "Hackers Linked to China's Army Seen from EU to D.C.," *Bloomberg*, July 26, 2012; Siobhan Gorman, "U.S. Homes in on China Spying," *Wall Street Journal*, December 13, 2011; and Bill Gertz, "White House Hack Attack," *Washington Free Beacon*, September 30, 2012.
2. "China Maps Out Informatization Development Strategy," May 11, 2006, PRC Embassy in Washington, DC, http://www.china-embassy.org/eng/xw/t251756.htm.
3. See Bryan Krekel, Patton Adams, and George Bakos, "Occupying the Information High Ground: Chinese Capabilities for Computer Network Operations and Cyber Espionage," Northrop Grumman Report Prepared for the U.S.-China Economic and Security Review Commission, March 7, 2012.
4. Among various sources, see Jimmy Goodrich, "Chinese Civilian Cybersecurity: Stakeholders, Strategies, and Policy," in *China and Cybersecurity: Political, Economic, and Strategic Dimensions*, ed. Jon Lindsay (Institute on Global Conflict and Cooperation Workshop Report, April 2012). The working group has included Li Keqiang, Zhang Dejiang, Liu Yunshan, Ling Jihua, Meng Jianzhu, and Chen Bingde. Members of the State Informatization Leading Group included Wen Jiabao, Li Keqiang, Liu Yunshan, Zeng Peiyan, Zhou Yongkang, and Guo Boxiong. The leading group was assisted by an Advisory Committee for State Informatization (ACSI). The State Council Informatization Office (SCITO; 国务院信息化工作办公室) was responsible for day-to-day tasks. Among various sources, see the ACSI website, http://www.acsi.gov.cn/en/. The 863-917 Program has served as an extrabudgetary source of funding for cyber technology development, and is best known for the developing the National Information Security Management System (国家信息安全管理系统), also known as the 005 Engineering project (aka, the Great Firewall of China).
5. See "Xi Jinping Leads Internet Security Group," Xinhua, February 27, 2014. CMC chairman Xi Jinping is dual hatted as CCP Central Committee general secretary and PRC president. Premier Li Keqiang and Politburo Standing Committee member Liu Yunshan reportedly will serve as deputy directors.

6. See James Mulvenon, "PLA Computer Network Operations: Scenarios, Doctrine, Organizations, and Capability," in *Beyond the Strait: PLA Missions Other Than Taiwan*, ed. Roy Kamphausen, David Lai, and Andrew Scobell (Strategic Studies Institute, US Army War College, 2009), 274; and Bryan Krekel, *Capability of the People's Republic of China to Conduct Cyber Warfare and Computer Network Exploitation*, Northrop Grumman Corporation Information Systems Sector Report for the U.S.-China Economic and Security Review Commission, October 2009. For an excellent review of Chinese cyber operations, see Desmond Ball, "China's Cyber Warfare Capabilities," *Security Challenges* (Australia) 7, no. 2 (2011): 81–103.

7. The Third Department is also known as the Technical Reconnaissance Department (技术侦察部). See "走夜路的灯笼":军委二局" [Lantern through the Night], Xinhua, July 4, 2011.

8. For one report on challenges to Chinese networks, see "瑞星发布2010企业安全报告 九成国内企业曾被入侵" [Rising Releases 2010 Report on Threats to Corporate Security], *China Rising*, March 11, 2011.

9. For the concept "Without understanding how to attack, one will not know how to defend" (不懂进攻就不会防守), see Qiu Junbo and Hu Zewen, "'黑客MM'实力不俗 成都高校举办网络攻防大赛" [The Incredible Abilities of Hacker MM: Chengdu Area Universities' Cyber Defense and Attack Competition], *Sichuan Morning News*, April 25, 2005. Also see You Ming and Zhou Xiyuan, "信息网络对抗机制的攻防分析" [Analysis of Attack and Defense Mechanisms in Information Network War], *Network Security Technology and Application*, December 6, 2004.

10. See Joint Chiefs of Staff, "Information Operations," Joint Publication 3-13, February 13, 2006.

11. See, for example, *Tracking GhostNet: Investigating a Cyber Espionage Network*, Information Warfare Monitor, March 29, 2009. SIGINT consists of communications intelligence (COMINT) and electronic intelligence (ELINT). The latter involves collection, analysis, and storing of radar emissions. While Third Department has the COMINT portfolio, the GSD Fourth Department likely is responsible for ELINT. See Ian Easton and Mark Stokes, *China's Electronic Intelligence Satellite Developments: Implications for U.S. Air and Naval Operations* (Arlington, VA: Project 2049 Institute, 2011).

12. Among various sources, see David E. Sanger, David Barboza, and Nicole Perlroth, "Chinese Army Unit Is Seen as Tied to Hacking against U.S.," *New York Times*, February 28, 2013; Mandiant, *APT1: Exposing One of China's Cyber Espionage Units*, February 18, 2013; Mark A. Stokes and L. C. Russell Hsiao, "Countering Chinese Cyber Operations: Opportunities and Challenges for U.S. Interests," Project 2049 Occasional Paper, October 29, 2012; Mark A. Stokes, Jenny Lin, and L.C. Russell Hsiao, "The Chinese People's Liberation Army Signals Intelligence and Cyber Reconnaissance Infrastructure," Project 2049 Institute, 2011, 8; and David Finkelstein, "The General Staff Department of the Chinese People's Liberation Army: Organization, Roles, and Missions," in *The People's Liberation Army as Organization: Reference Volume v1.0*, ed. James C. Mulvenon and Andrew N. D. Yang (Santa Monica, CA: RAND, 2002), 122–24.

13. See "总参援建疏勒县 '八一爱民学校' 竣工投入使用" [General Staff Department Investment into Construction of Bayi Aimin School Put into Use], Shule Government website, September 26, 2010, http://www.shule.gov.cn/ShowNews_Content4457.shtml. Liu replaced Wang Yongsheng (王永生) as political commissar. See "延安:总参三部政委王永生视察军委二局旧址修复工程"

[Yan'an: Wang Yongsheng, General Staff Department Third Department Political Commissar, Inspects Restoration Site of Central Military Commission Second Bureau], *Yan'an Daily*, October 19, 2009.

14. "喀什地区疏勒县总参援建疏勒县'八一爱民学校'竣工投入使用," Shule County website, September 26, 2010, http://klmy.xjkunlun.cn/10019/10026/10028/100 31/2010/1344505.htm. The deputy directors include MG Zheng Junjie, MG Ju Qiansheng, and MG Zhang Qinchen. Zheng Junjie (郑俊杰) previously directed the Third Department's S&T Equipment Bureau; Ju Qiansheng (巨乾生) previously directed the Twelfth Bureau; and Zhang Qinchen (张钦贞) previously directed the Ninth Bureau.

15. For example, the Fifty-Sixth Research Institute may be linked with the National Information Assurance Engineering Technology Research Center (国家信息安全工程技术研究中心). "SSL　VPN密码机通过国家密码局鉴定" [SSL VPN Password Generator Passes National Cryptological Bureau Certification], Sanjiang Space Group Communications Company website, May 14, 2011, http://www.ssnc.com.cn/Item/37.aspx; "(国家'十五'863计划（民口）第一届领域专家委员会和主题专家组成员名单" [China 15th 863 Program First Area Expert Working Group and Focus Area Expert Working Group Member List], undated, http://www.kjc.dicp.ac.cn/meeting/committee-list.htm. As of early 2013, Huang Yongqin (黄永勤; b. 1955) directed the institute. The institute's chief engineer, Chen Zuoning (陈左宁), is one of China's most prominent computing engineers. She is dual hatted as chief engineer of the State Parallel Computing Engineering Technology Center (国家并行计算机工程技术研究中心).

16. The Fifty-Seventh Research Institute may also host a Signal Processing Key Defense Laboratory (信号盲处理国防科技重点实验室).

17. See "成都市西南电子电信技术研究所招聘（实习生）" [Chengdu City Southwest Electronics and Telecommunications Research Institutes Recruitment for Interns], Sichuan University State Software Demonstration College, December 29, 2009, http://sw.scu.edu.cn/new_sw/infoDetail.jsp?id=1714. Also see "我校与总参第五十七研究所签署战略合作协议" [Our School and General Staff Department's Fifty-Seventh Research Institute Sign Strategic Cooperative Agreement], Xdnice.com, March 15, 2011, http://www.xdnice.com/news/2011-03/90181.html. The specific location in Dujiangyan is 崇州市, 青城山.

18. Key researchers at the Fifty-Seventh Research Institute (西南电子电信技术研究所) include Ye Shangfu (叶尚福) and Zhu Zhongliang (朱中梁). See "朱中梁" [Zhu Zhongliang], Baidu Baike, http://baike.baidu.com/view/238698.htm.

19. See "企业简介" [Introduction to the Company], SWAI website, undated, http://www.58suo.com/index/about.asp?id=2; "'信息安全技术'技术科学论坛在京举行" [Information Security S&T Seminar Begins in Beijing], China Academy of Sciences Academic Divisions website, November 27, 2005, http://www.casad.cas.cn/gzdt/200511/t20051128_43265.html. As of early 2010, the Fifty-Eighth Research Institute director was Zuo Yanmin (左艳民).

20. The Third Department likely supports the State Council's Ministry of Science and Technology, National Crypto Management Center, State Secrecy Bureau, Ministry of Public Security, and Ministry of State Security.

21. See "国家信息安全工程技术中心网站完工" [Construction Completed on National Information Security Engineering Technology Center Network Station], Beijing Lan Bo Synergy Technology Co. Ltd. (北京蓝博融智科技有限 公司), September 22, 2008. The Beijing Guowei Xin'an Network Technology Company (北京国卫信安网络技术有限公司) works closely with Third Department First

Bureau in supporting the project. See Yin Chuan-xi (尹传喜), http://www.ushi.cn/p/2991; and "Cooperation Partners," China Cuslink Co., Ltd. (北京中海通科技有限公司), http://www.cuslink.cn/Partners.aspx. Among various sources, see "Wen Zhonghui," Nanjing University of Science and Technology website, http://web2.nuist.edu.cn:8081/JRY/toArticle.action?id=1153. For an official NISEC overview, see the National Information Security Engineering Technology Center website (国家信息安全工程技术研究中心), http://www.nisec.cn/.

22. The National Research Center for Information Technology Security (国家信息技术安全研究中心) has also been referred to as the PLA Information Security Center (解放军信息安全中心). See "国家信息技术安全研究中心" [National Information Technology and Security Research Center], ISRA website, undated, http://www.isra.org.cn/about/index.htm; and "中国期货业协会信息部主任刘铁斌：IT系统安全体系设计思路" [China Futures Association Information Director Liu Tiebin: Ideas for IT System Security Design], China Information Network, September 4, 2009, http://www.cio360.net/Page/1802/InfoID/307354/SourceId/11300/PubDate/2009-09-04/Default.aspx.

23. The National Research Center for Information Technology Security is located adjacent to GSD Third Department Seventh Bureau command headquarters on Nongda Road in northern Beijing suburb of Shangdi. Li Jingchun (李京春) is the center's chief engineer and has spoken publicly on cyberwarfare issues (see "网络特攻"，谁主沉浮？). Gong Yafeng (宫亚峰), who has been linked with the Third Department's 61062 Unit, serves as deputy chief engineer. For further background, see the National Research Center for Information Technology Security website at http://www.isra.org.cn/.

24. See "国家信息中心专家委员会主任宁家骏简介" [Profile of National Information Center Expert Ning Jiajun], DoSTOR, December 8, 2008, http://www.dostor.com/article/2008/1208/4538078.shtml. Also see "国家电子政务外网安全保障体系方案通过专家评审国家电子政务外网安全保障体系方案通过专家评审" [National Electronic Political Affairs Network Security System Program Approved by Experts Review], Hainan Province Industry and Informatization Office Network, May 29, 2006, http://iitb.hainan.gov.cn/hnsgxt/zwgk_7771/2/200606/t20060602_336833.html.

25. "天津国家信息安全工程技术研究中心" [Tianjin National Information Security Engineering Center] website, http://www.nisib.cn/News_4.aspx.

26. Among various sources, see "Construction Completed on National Information Security Engineering Technology Center Website." Sichuan University houses an Information Security and Network Attack/Defense Research Lab (四川大学信息安全及网络攻防研究室).

27. See "Falun Gong Mailboxes Attacked," Minghui.org, April 28, 2000, http://en.minghui.org/html/articles/2000/4/28/8378.html#.UI6ApMXEZ_Q. The attacks started on April 24. Most of the attackers used the servers of 263.net, 163.net, and 371.net. The article notes that the organizations involved in the attacks included the "Internet Security System Lab of the Beijing North Computing Center (seal.bncc.edu.cn)," "Department of Computer Science of Beijing North Commercial College," "Shangdu information center," and "Zhengzhou data communication branch bureau of Zhengzhou city, Henan Province 450052." "Shangdu" may be a misspelling of Shangdi, where BNCC registers its IP addresses.

28. One source asserts that BNCC is expanding to a corps leader-level institute (军职). Another source claims that BNCC is no longer subordinate to the GSD Third Department.

29. Inter alia, Gao Lihua, "Information Security: The Solution Lies in the 'Core'?" (信息安全：出路在于"中国芯"？), *Computer World*, November 22, 2002.

30. See Stokes and Hsiao, "Countering Chinese Cyber Operations."

31. "杀毒软件'杀'气渐微 微点主动防御强者自强," Xinhua, September 27, 2008.

32. Sources can be made available upon request.

33. In addition to the Third Department's Luoyang language center (解放军外国语学院), the GSD Second Department may also have a foreign language training center in Nanjing.

34. See Stokes and Hsiao, "Countering Chinese Cyber Operations."

35. For reference to the First, Eighth, and S&T Intelligence Bureaus in Dujiachuan (韩家川), see "韩家川军休所介绍" [Introduction to the Dujiachuan Military Retiree Institute], Haidian District Military Retiree Network, http://hdjxb.bjhd.gov.cn/znjg/jxs/jxs12/.

36. Units that are regiment level and above are assigned a military unit cover designator (MUCD). The PLA MUCD system was most recently changed in 2002. Before 2002, Third Department units were assigned an MUCD block between 57301 and 57425. A new system was implemented in 2002. GSD units were assigned MUCDs numbered from 61001 to 61999. The old system had some logic in its numbering system. Now, MUCDs appear to be randomly assigned to all GSD units, including the Operations Department, Second Department, Third Department, Fourth Department, and so forth.

37. K'an Chung-kuo: "Intelligence Agencies Exist in Great Numbers, Spies Are Present Everywhere; China's Major Intelligence Departments Fully Exposed," *Chien Shao*, January 1, 2006, no. 179, 21–27. Also see http://www.rand.org/pubs/conf_proceedings/CF182/CF182.ch4.pdf.

38. For references to GSD Third Department First Bureau, see "韩以明" [Han Yiming], Qinhuangdao Government website, June 23, 2008, http://121.22.8.170:81/content.jsp?code=188/2008-00006&name=. Dujiangyan was formerly known as Guanxian (灌县).

39. Huang Minqiang (黄民强), who also has been affiliated with the GSD Fifty-Eighth Research Institute, is referenced in a membership list as a member of the Information Assurance Expert Working Group. See "国家'十五'863计划（民口）第一届领域专家委员会和主题专家组成员名单" [China Fifteenth 863 Program First Area Expert Working Group and Focus Area Expert Working Group Member List], undated, http://www.kjc.dicp.ac.cn/meeting/committee-list.htm.

40. For reference to the Dujiangyan site (61480 Unit) in the area, see "驻军61480部队及时参加抗震救灾" [Resident 61480 Unit Troops Join Earthquake Rescue in Timely Manner], China Shuangyong Network, May 29, 2008, http://sy.mca.gov.cn/article/kzjz/200805/20080500015675.shtml. For reference to the First Bureau's Information Security Research Center, see "刘向军副主任主持信息中心2013年基建项目申报专家评审会" [Deputy Director Liu Xiangjun Presides over Information Center's 2013 Expert Review of Infrastructure Projects], China Light Industry Information Center website, http://cnliic.clii.com.cn/zxyw/201205/t20120515_380874.html.

41. At least two of these divisions appear to operate from a Third Department Second Bureau satellite ground station in Baoshan District's Caijiaying village. Other elements probably under command of the Second Bureau are located in Sichuan Province and on Hainan Island. More specifically, the Sichuan site has a military cover designation of Unit 61357 and is located in Minzhu City's Zundao Village. The facility was damaged during the Sichuan earthquake in 2008. The old MUCD was 57332.

42. See "关于总参三部二局需使用我公司通信管道的请示" [Regarding GSD Third Department Requirements for Our Company's Communication Channels], China Telecom Marketing Department announcement, March 20, 2009.

43. These landing sites are high-volume entry points for Internet traffic to and from China. The Chongming facility may be subordinate to the 61161 Unit (possibly the Second Bureau's Third Office). As a side note, a GSD Fourth Department brigade (61251 Unit) oversees an element in the Nichangzhen area, and possibly on Chongming Island.

44. The former is not to be confused with its affiliate, the Shanghai Institute of International Strategic Studies (SIIS; 上海国际问题研究院). Zhou Jianping is a senior officer from the Second Bureau's First Office who has an affiliation the Shanghai Association of International Strategic Studies (SAISS; 上海国际战略问题研究会) and the Shanghai Strategy Association (上海战略研究会). Former Second Bureau leader Lu Peng (吕蓬) serves as SAISS deputy director.

45. A construction company listed the Second Bureau as the contracting organization for construction of the Engineering Center's six-story building in Pudong. The same company also won the bid for construction of the Second Bureau's new general headquarters building in 2007. See "报名单位及项目经理信息." [Notice of Unit and Project Management], Changzhou Project Bidding Center website, http://www.czzbb.net/czzb/YW_Info/YW_ZiGeYS/BaoMingInfo.aspx?YW_RowID=41726&BiaoDuanBH=CZS20091202901&enterprise_id=70362377-3. A Shanghai company refers to the Information Security Engineering Technology Center as a Third Department window for international cooperation, and was awarded a contract for a malicious network attack behavior lab (网络恶意攻击行为研究实验室).

46. The school is collocated with the Third Department's National Information Security Engineering Technology Research Center. See "School of Information Security Engineering at Shanghai Jiao Tong University," School of Information Security Engineering website, http://infosec.sjtu.edu.cn/infosec/en/introduction/intro1.html. For an example of joint research, see Jiang Weixin, Xue Zhi, and Chen Yiqun, "协同式入侵监视系统的体系结构设计" [Design of a Collaborative Intrusion Monitoring System Architecture], *Computer Applications and Software*, June 2007. Other Third Department elements in the Shanghai area include the Third Department Twelfth Bureau command (61486 Unit); and the Third Bureau's Third Division (61587 Unit).

47. See "区民政局领导走访驻区部队" [District Administration Bureau Leaders Visit Local Military Units], Dongcheng District website, February 23, 2011, http://www.beijing.gov.cn/zfzx/qxrd/dcq/t1150643.htm.

48. Dalian (61120 Unit) is the Third Bureau's First Office. Formerly designated the 57346 Unit, the Sixth Office (61542 Unit; 121 Institute) appears to be situated in Xian, and functions as a networking center (网络中心). For reference to Ningdu, see "总参三部军官在宁都县进行革命传统教育" [GSD Third Department Officers Conduct Revolutionary Education in Ningdu County], Red Star News, September 9, 2009, http://www.zg1929.com/news/yaowen/20090909/919.html. Possible office cover designators are Harbin (61401 Unit), Dalian (61120 Unit), Hangzhou (61791 Unit), Xiamen (61816 Unit), Shenzhen (either the 61377 or 61508 Unit), and Xian (61542 Unit).

49. See Chen Yiqiang, "简析Android系统的安全性能" [Brief Analysis of Android System Security], *Information Systems Engineering*, 2011 (9), http://d.wanfangdata.com.cn/periodical_xxxtgc201109035.aspx.

50. The Fourth Bureau may have previously carried a cover designation of the 57324 Unit.

51. See "2009年受表彰资深翻译家" [Recognizing Top Translators for 2009], China Translators Association website, http://www.tac-online.org.cn/ch/tran/2010-12/09/content_3888394.htm; "以更优质的服务态度做好军休工作" [To Provide Better Quality Services to Military Retirees], Hangzhou Civil Affairs Bureau website, undated, http://www.hzmz.gov.cn/files/20110328/c988dc99-1d7a-4868-b6e6-8d06cc1087f8.shtml.The Fourth Bureau's Seventh Office (probably the 61085 Unit) may have formerly been the 57367 Unit. The Eighth Office is the former 57368 Unit.

52. "Recognizing Top Translators for 2009."

53. "Recognizing Top Translators for 2009"; and "市人大常委会副主任" [Deputy Directors of the City People's Congress], December 6, 2005, http://www.jzsrd.gov.cn/news_view.asp?newsid=234. For linkage between the Fifth Bureau and the 61565 Unit, see "就业信息浏览" [Employment Information], Chongqing University website, undated, http://graduate.cqu.edu.cn/mis/student/wantad/edit.jsp?wantAdId=130.

54. Zhang Yunju (张运炬) serves as the Sixth Bureau political commissar. The Sixth Bureau was formerly assigned an MUCD of the 57316 Unit.

55. Jingmen Zone B (荆门乙区) has been associated with Sixth Bureau Second Office, and possibly located in Luoji Village, southeast of Jingmen. Reference to a Third Department–affiliated Jingmen Zone A (荆门甲区) has also been noted. The Sixth Bureau also had a presence in the village of Ziling, possibly the Sixth Office.

56. More specifically, offices are located in Xiamen, Nanchang (Seventh Office), Xiangfan; Ningdu County's Xiaobu Village, Wuhan, Jingmen, and Kunming's Panlong District (Fourth Office). For reference to the Kunming office, see "寻甸县雷锋希望小学举办'回顾过去，展望未来'建校十周年庆祝活动" [Xundian County Lei Feng Hope School Recalls the Past: Looking Toward the Tenth Anniversary of School Building], *Yunnan Province Youth Network*, July 19, 2007, http://www.ynyouth.cn/city/HTML/26873.htm. For reference to a 61815 study on satellite communications, see Fu Di and Gao Yong, "非对称PCMA卫星信号的截获方法" [Asymmetric PCMA Satellite Signal Interception Method], *Modern Electronic Technology* 30 (2007): 28–34.

57. See, for example, "一种基于多元组鉴别文本語种的 方法" [Diverse Language Identification Method], *Journal of Computer Applications*, 2005 (25), http://d.wanfangdata.com.cn/periodical_jsjyy2005z1172.aspx.

58. For example, Li Hongqiang (李宏强) has been associated with the Seventh Bureau and has published translated volumes written by prominent US and British writers.

59. Li Jian, Jiang Chengshun, and Dong Liying, "基于選擇性集成SVM的數據類型識別" [Data Type Recognition Based on Selective Integration of SVM], *Computer Engineering* 36 (2010), http://d.wanfangdata.com.cn/Periodical_jsjgc201013064.aspx. Dong Liying is from the 61580 Unit.

60. See Wang Qi and Dan Jun, "'网络中心战'网络建设和技术策略" [Network-Centric Warfare Development and Technology Strategy], 信息安全与通信保密 [Information Assurance and Communications Security] December 2005, 82–84, http://www.lw23.com/pdf_90d61a36-6c45-48bc-b6c2-4e2ddc8edbb8/lunwen.pdf. The authors are senior engineers within the bureau who specialize in computer network attack and defense. For the Internet study, see Yu Hongbo, "新世纪的Internet网" [Internet Networks of the New Century],

全国信息技术高级研讨会 [National Senior Conference on Information Technology], 2001, http://scholar.ilib.cn/A-%E4%BC%9A%E8%AE%AE%E8%AE%B0%E5%BD%95ID~6061126.html. The author has been a member of a national level encryption working group. See http://blog.sina.com.cn/s/blog_5dd035dc0100egjq.html.

61. Zhang Ya'nan and Chen Tao, "浅析外语阅读心理机制" [Psychological Mechanism of Analyzing Foreign Language Reading], *Sciences and Wealth* 2011 (3), http://d.wanfangdata.com.cn/periodical_kxycf201103095.aspx.

62. Zhang Lidong, "經濟全球化視角下國際經濟法的新發展" [New Developments in Economic Globalization and International Economic Law], *Law and Society* 2009 (33), http://d.wanfangdata.com.cn/periodical_fzysh200933235.aspx.

63. "GSD Eighth Bureau Satellite Receiving System" (总参三部八局卫星电视接收系统), Beijing Blue Satellite Company website, undated, at http://www.chinabsc.com/html/265.html. The Eighth Bureau was formerly assigned a 57318 Unit designation. Former Eighth Bureau PC in the 2005 timeframe was Senior Colonel Hu Dengqiang (胡登强). However, he appears to have been recently transferred to serve as Eleventh Bureau political commissar. See 履行神圣职责争做合格纪检干部 [*Military Party Life*], 2011 (4), http://oldweb.cqvip.com/qk/60743A/201104/37100809.html.

64. See "Branch Construction" (分馆建设), Beijing Haidian District Library website, undated, at http://www.hdlib.net/hdlib/opencms/hdlib/htgk/fgjs.html. The Wenquanzhen site is collocated with an air force communication unit.

65. "Recognizing Top Translators for 2009."

66. One of ten major generals serving as senior engineers within the Eighth Bureau Second Office is Ran Chongwei (冉崇伟; b. 1962). Born in Chongqing, Ran is a graduate of the PLA Information Engineering Academy. See "Ran Chongwei Visits Alma Mater to See Teachers and Students," Chongqing Wuxi County website, April 23, 2010, http://www.cqwxzx.com/Article_Print.asp?ArticleID=580. For a general introduction, see "中国人民解放军六一〇四六部队" [PLA 61046 Unit], *Baike Zhige*, undated, http://baike.zhige.net/doc-view-4276. Also see "优化环境聚人气, 强健身心凝军魂—记61046部队" [Strengthening the Military Soul through Improvement in Physical and Mental Conditioning—Commemorating the 61046 Unit], *China Sports News*, September 13, 2005, http://sports.sina.com.cn/s/2005-09-13/1105660025s.shtml. The Haikou unit (61708 Unit) is said to be near the village of Yunnei Village (云内村).

67. See "中国共产党襄樊市委员会）（通知）" [Notice of the Xiangfan City Committee of the Chinese Communist Party], Xiangfan City website, August 13, 2010, http://www.xf.gov.cn/contents/2575/355663.html. The address of the Xiangfan office (61245 Unit) main compound is 43 Zhongyuan Road. The Eighth Bureau is known to have a relationship with Xiangfan University. See http://xtu.cuepa.cn/show_more.php?doc_id=199537; and http://www.xiangyangnews.com/news/xiangyangxinwen/xiangzhouqu/2012/0829/52836.html.

68. The downlink site (61449 Unit) is visible on Google Earth along Xibeiwang East and Houchangcun roads. More specifically, the site is located at 西北旺镇六里屯村.

69. Among various references, see "公安情报学系与总参某部建立情报研究合作机制" [Gong'An Intelligence Department and GSD Establish an Intelligence Analysis Cooperative Mechanism], Chinese People's Public Security University website, June 28, 2010, http://www.cppsu.edu.cn/cfm_data/shownews_dw.cfm?newsid=1656&fyear=2010; "公安情报学系与总参某部建立情报研究合作机制" [Public Security Intelligence Section and General Staff Department Establish Seminar Cooperation Mechanism],

Public Security website, June 28, 2010, http://www.cppsu.edu.cn/cfm_data/shownews_dw.cfm?newsid=1656&fyear=2010. The Ninth Bureau may have formerly had a MUCD of 57319.

70. Zhang Qing (张清) has been affiliated with both the GSD Third Department Ninth Bureau and the 61221 Unit. See, for example, "恩施利川在北京优秀同乡人才名录," China Merchants Network Information Center website, July 31, 2012, http://www.cnzsyz.com/hubei/Print.asp?ArticleID=148903. Gao Jizhong (高吉中) served as Ninth Bureau director in the 2008 timeframe.

71. One reference asserts that the unit is headquartered in Jiamusi. See "Post 8684," undated, at http://post.8684.cn/o4985030_1645.htm. One office under the Tenth Bureau may be the old 57398 Unit. Ma Lanzhu (麻兰柱) was political commissar. The unit appears to maintain a Beijing post office box address of 2651 (北京市2651信箱), and address of 33 Xinxi Road in Shangdi.

72. A China Academy of Social Sciences study notes cooperation along these lines after establishment of relations with the United States in 1979 (thus a 7911 Unit designation for subordinate offices). For a China Academy of Social Sciences assessment of the western sites, see Tao Wenzhao, "中美关系史'下卷（1972–2000）之第五章：平稳发展" [History of US-China Relations, vol. 2 (1972–2000)] (Shanghai: People's Publishing, 2004), chap. 5, http://ias.cass.cn/show/show_project_ls.asp?id=733.

73. See "61762部队邮编" [Zip Code for 61762 Unit], 邮编网 [Zip Code Net], undated, http://post.8684.cn/o4985030_1645.htm. The Eleventh Bureau's previous MUCD may have been 57321 (or 总字791部队). The commander or political commissar of the Eleventh Bureau may be Yang Keqiao (杨可巧).

74. "高新区就2020部队搬迁事宜赴京进行磋商会谈" [New High-Tech Zone and 2020 Unit Discuss Relocation in Beijing], Jiamusi City government website, March 22, 2011, http://www.jmsgx.gov.cn/Article/gaoxindongtai/177.html. Also see "每周通报" [Weekly Bulletin], Jiamusi New High Tech Zone Weekly Bulletin (Issue 9), July 25, 2011.

75. "市人大常委会副主任" [Deputy Directors of the City People's Congress], December 6, 2005, http://www.jzsrd.gov.cn/news_view.asp?newsid=234. Also see "Director Overview," China Economic Network, undated, http://hn.ccngov.cn/hn/jiaozuo/rd.html.

76. For linkage of the Twelfth Bureau with the MUCD, see http://www.kshr.cn/ksasp/unit/SHOWEMPL.ASP?employee_id=660550. Also see "区领导周平、曹立强会见 61486部队领导" [District Leaders Zhou Ping, Cao Liqiang Meet with Unit 61486 Leadership], Shanghai Chabei Civil Affairs Bureau, July 14, 2011, http://mzj.sh.gov.cn/gb/mzzbq/mzxw/zxxw/userobject1ai637.html. Also see http://www.hzsouth.com/nanfang-News-25813/. The Jiangnan Institute of Remote Sensing Applications shares the same address.

77. The large phased array radar site may be affiliated with the Twelfth Bureau's 61232 Unit, located near Lin'an City's Tianchi scenic area, west of Hangzhou.

78. Despite the Nanjing Military Region's absorption of the Fuzhou Military Region, Chengdu Military Region's absorption of the Kunming Military Region, and Lanzhou Military Region absorption of the Xinjiang Military Regions, the TRBs in the absorbed regions remained independent and active. Therefore, Nanjing, Chengdu, and Lanzhou military regions each have two TRBs.

79. K'an Chung-kuo, "Intelligence Agencies Exist in Great Numbers, Spies Are Present Everywhere." Also see http://www.rand.org/pubs/conf_proceedings/CF182/CF182.ch4.pdf.

80. For background on the PLA's role in border defense, see Dennis J. Blasko, *The Chinese Army Today: Tradition and Transformation for the 21st Century*, 2nd ed. (New York: Routledge, 2012), 86–87.

81. The three PLAAF TRBs are headquartered in Beijing (95830 Unit), Nanjing (95851 Unit), and Chengdu (95879 Unit). Among various sources discussing PLAAF technical reconnaissance, see Jiang Mingyuan, Ning Bo, and Yong Jing, "信息化空军武器装备的五大特征" [Five Characteristics of Air Force Equipment Informatization], *Aeronautical Science and Technology* 2004 (6), http://d.wanfang-data.com.cn/Periodical_hkkxjs200406009.aspx.

82. The Navy's First TRB likely carries a cover designator of the 91746 Unit. The Navy Second TRB likely has a cover designator of the 92762 Unit. For one reference to the Xiamen office, see "厦门市好和惠商贸有限公司" [Xiamen City Haohe Trading Company], Xiamen City Simen District business portal, undated, http://www.smgsxh.org/honorBusiness/detail.asp?id=356. For reference to the Eighth Office in Wenzhou, see "八一拥军 军地深情" [Affectionately Support the Military on Army Day], Wenzhou Kuaile Corporation website, July 28, 2010, http://www.wzkuailu.com/Newsmain.asp?id=214.

83. References available upon request.

84. See Dai Qingmin, 网电一体战 [*Integrated Network Electronic Warfare*] (Beijing: PLA Press, 2002).

85. The Fourth Department director is former GSD Fifty-Fourth Research Institute director Hao Yeli (郝叶力).

86. The Technical Equipment Bureau may also be known as the GSD ECM and Radar Department Third Bureau. Its PO box is (北京市8315信箱三局).

87. The PLA Secrecy Committee Technical Security Research Institute (解放军保密委员会技术安全研究所) is the 61600 Unit, which is most likely Third Department.

88. Office of the National Counterintelligence Executive, *Foreign Spies Stealing U.S. Economic Secrets in Cyberspace: Annual Report to Congress on Foreign Economic Collection and Industrial Espionage, 2009–2011*, October 2011, http://www.ncix.gov/publications/reports/fecie_all/Foreign_Economic_Collection_2011.pdf.

89. Among various references, see James M. Olson, "Ten Commandments of Cyber Counterintelligence: A Never-Ending Necessity," *Studies in Intelligence* (Central Intelligence Agency Center for the Study of Intelligence), June 27, 2008.

90. For an excellent overview on deception in cyber defense operations, see Neil C. Rowe, Deception in Defense of Computer Systems from Cyber-Attack," in *Cyber Warfare and Cyber Terrorism*, ed. L. Janczewski and A. Colarik (Hershey, PA: Information Science Reference, 2008), 97–104.

91. "China, Russia and Other Countries Submit the Document of International Code of Conduct for Information Security to the United Nations," Chinese Ministry of Foreign Affairs, September 13, 2011, http://nz.chineseembassy.org/eng/zgyw/t858978.htm.

92. Camino Kavanagh with Matthew Carrieri, "Cyber Dialogue 2012 Briefs: Thinking Strategically about Cyber Security," Second Annual Cyber Dialogue Forum, March 18–19, 2012, Toronto, Canada, http://www.cyberdialogue.citizenlab.org/wp-content/uploads/2012/2012briefs/brief-4.pdf.

93. Chung Chen-fang, "專家說台灣是中國網絡攻擊優先目標" [Experts Say Taiwan Is China's Primary Target], Voice of America, May 15, 2012, http://www.voacan-tonese.com/articleprintview/1149438.html.

94. Mark Stokes and L. C. Russell Hsiao, "Taiwan's Role in Air-Sea Battle," *AsiaEye*, April 16, 2012, http://blog.project2049.net/2012/04/taiwans-role-in-air-sea-battle.html.

95. Tsen-Hsi Wu, "Taiwan's Cyber Defense Honed by Frequent Attacks," *Epoch Times*, May 21, 2012, http://www.theepochtimes.com/n2/china-news/taiwans-cyber-defense-honed-by-frequent-attacks-240544.html.

96. Ibid.

97. Zachary Fryer-Biggs, "U.S. Military Goes on Cyber Offensive," *Defense News*, March 24, 2012, http://www.defensenews.com/article/20120324/DEFREG02/303240001/U-S-Military-Goes-Cyber-Offensive.

CHAPTER 8

Civil-Military Integration and Cybersecurity

A Study of Chinese Information Warfare Militias

ROBERT SHELDON AND JOE MCREYNOLDS

INTRODUCTION

This chapter seeks to assess Chinese civil-military integration in the context of operations in the cyber domain, focusing particularly on the development of cyberwarfare capabilities in China's militia forces. As Chinese industries become more competitive across most sectors of the economy, civil-military integration issues have become an increasingly important area of PLA studies. As the PLA has sought to wean itself from foreign military technologies over the past several decades, the strength and trajectory of China's defense-industrial base—particularly the large, state-owned defense conglomerates—has been a central consideration for outsiders gauging China's military capabilities. This will remain true in the future. But increasingly, and to the extent that China's leaders are successful in their quest to leverage military ends through capabilities that exist outside of their defense-industrial base, outside observers will need to make judgments that account for broader Chinese civilian capabilities.

The concept of civil-military integration in China manifests in various ways. According to Tai Ming Cheung, it encompasses a diverse range of activities based on the notion of harnessing the technological and industrial capabilities of the civilian economy to advance defense capabilities. Instead of relying on its own resources, the defense economy seeks to make use of commercially available technologies and manufacturing processes as a suitable substitute.[1] In popular usage, the term is characteristically holistic, potentially including issues like organizational and management culture.[2]

Chinese literature identifies information warfare systems as a promising civil-military integration candidate.[3] This is an intuitive finding. China's next-generation bomber, for example, is unlikely to be developed by a small start-up in Changsha. China's next great cyber tool, on the other hand, might very well be. The Internet is ubiquitous; some of the most sophisticated technical equipment (as well as applications and users, as Sarah McKune argues in chapter 11 in this volume) exist in the public sphere. This trend is apparently consistent in relatively developed to highly developed countries, regardless of levels of militarization. In that sense, in China as elsewhere, there is a special imperative to draw on civilian resources and capabilities to pursue military ends.

As a result, the information technology sector has the potential to be an area of deep civil-military integration. However, in network warfare operations, people are generally an order of magnitude more critical than tools. Since analyses of civil-military integration are traditionally more focused on products than operations, they may not be the most appropriate lens for assessing China's evolving network operations capabilities. Nevertheless, China's military clearly draws on civilian capabilities to conduct operations. Beyond civil-military integration proper, this could be carried out on the basis of any number of different initiatives, such as "Locating Military Potential in Civilian Capabilities" (于军于民), announced in the Tenth Five-Year Plan, or its later iteration, "Civil-Military Fusion" (军民融合), announced during the Eleventh Five-Year Plan.[4] For the purposes of this study, we use the term "civil-military integration" broadly, as shorthand for any processes, programs, and initiatives by which the PLA leverages civilian capabilities. We focus in particular on operational capabilities and workforce sharing.

This chapter advances as follows: the next section briefly surveys the major categories of civil-military integration in the network domain, focusing on China's operational, rather than technical, capabilities. In order to manage the scope of the chapter, we focus in the third section on Chinese information warfare militia units and network warfare subunits as a component of China's efforts to utilize civilian capabilities in developing its computer network operations capacity. We describe the characteristics of information warfare militia units and their role in civil-military integration. Then, we discuss and analyze a fifty-unit sample of information warfare militia units and network warfare subunits throughout China and present two case studies. The remainder of the chapter offers some areas for additional research, identifies some conclusions, and offers several policy implications.

Chinese network warfare militia subunits' precise functions—and indeed, conclusive data about their significance in China's overall computer network operations infrastructure—remain somewhat ambiguous. We did not find that network warfare militias represent a core component of China's large and active intelligence apparatus, well documented in Nigel Inkster's chapter in this volume (chapter 2), or the "pointy end" of China's cyberwarfare spear. Based on descriptions of these militias' training and activities, as well as their place within the context of China's militia system, we believe their responsibilities tend toward defensive operations.

Nevertheless, we argue that network warfare militia forces do merit consideration from foreign cyberwarfare analysts. Although we do not have compelling evidence to suggest that network warfare militia members are involved in the routine conduct of peacetime intelligence operations, the organizational grouping of these subunits within overarching information warfare militia units that also sometimes contain intelligence-oriented militia subunits is potentially a cause for concern. The fact that civilian organizations hosting network warfare militia units sometimes interact with foreign businesses and educational institutions, possibly without any knowledge of the militia unit's existence, is also potentially problematic.

RESEARCH APPROACH

With regard to computer network operations, civil and military entities have numerous points of potential intersection (see figure 8.1). For the purposes of this chapter, these junctures can be loosely (and imperfectly) grouped into four categories: formal procurement relationships, formal outsourcing, transactional and coerced outsourcing, and operational "insourcing." Although each of these categories might be considered forms of civil-military integration, if the term is defined broadly, not all fall within the boundaries of the archetypical notion of civil-military integration we utilize here. This analysis considers "durability" an essential characteristic of civil-military integration. Civil-military interactions that are informal, incidental, or episodic may illustrate coordination and

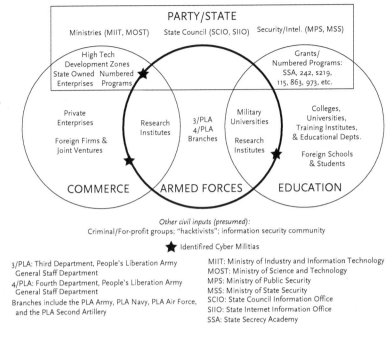

Figure 8.1 Civil-Military Integration and Chinese Computer Network Operations

are interesting and important in their own right, but represent a somewhat lesser achievement. "Integration" implies a higher threshold where interactions are not only deliberate, responsive, and scalable, but also fully institutionalized, with all of the attendant benefits such as subordination and political reliability.

Formal Procurement Relationships

The PLA procures information technology-related equipment and services from vendors to yield "spin-on" benefits, as well as funding cyber-related research and development (R&D) activities within state-owned, state-associated, and certain private Chinese enterprises. Some of these relationships are more robust than others, with the apparently close ties between the PLA and Datang Telecom, Zhongxing Telecommunication Equipment Corporation (ZTE), and Huawei best typifying the more enduring end of the spectrum.[5] Relationships with other companies run the gamut from short to long term, casual to regimented, and tangential to mission critical.

Formal Outsourcing

Separate, but related to procurement, is PLA funding of university centers and research institutes. The main distinction here is whether transactions are commercial in nature (through formal procurement mechanisms) or essentially directed transfer payments or government payrolls (considered here). In the case of transfer payments, with respect to universities, a US-China Economic and Security Review Commission study reported that at least forty-six Chinese universities receive funds for information warfare-related research from one or more of China's major "numbered" research programs.[6] With respect to direct or indirect payrolls, certain government- or military-funded research institutes likely engage in cyber capabilities-related R&D, but a comprehensive open-source study of these entities and their activities has yet to appear.[7]

Transactional and Coerced Outsourcing

China has a vibrant "hacking scene" with figures that range from career criminals to ostensibly professional "information security" groups with varying degrees of legitimacy. Evidence recovered from hacking forums suggests that various arms of the Chinese government have looked to elements of this community in the past to help identify personnel with cyber-related expertise.[8] It stands to reason that the PLA has done the same, particularly in the late 1990s and early 2000s as the military sought to aggressively capitalize on vulnerabilities in foreign systems and struggled to close gaps in domestic networks. Cooperation between the PLA and illicit hacking groups could have been purchased, compelled, or bartered for protection or other ends. These relationships remain one of the most interesting unanswered questions about PLA cyber operations, but a paucity of data presents challenges to any comprehensive study.

Operational "Insourcing"

Skilled operators are the central imperative for cyber operations and thus a primary consideration for civil-military integration. Still, not all PLA-civilian interactions and relationships constitute civil-military integration. For example, PLA recruitment of talented young student-hackers and others will not be considered in any level of detail in this chapter. That process more closely resembles absorption than integration. One point of civil-military integration is to leverage civilian capabilities without the burden of bearing the full cost and without isolating the individuals from the arguably more dynamic private sector. As one means toward that end, the PLA formed permanent and formal information warfare militia units. Although frequently referenced in literature about PLA cyber operations, little is known about these groups as an institution. Their exact function is somewhat opaque, and (like the militia system generally) no reasonably comprehensive "order of battle" is available.[9] The remainder of this chapter seeks to fill some of those gaps.

THE MILITIA SYSTEM

Information warfare militia units serve as a useful evaluative case of civil-military integration in cyberspace for several reasons. First, they seek to bring about operational integration—an important distinction from the more straightforward types of civil-military integration related to procurement and transfer payments. Second, as an institution, information warfare militia units meet the durability criteria highlighted above: they are formal, ongoing groups that operate partially at the behest of the PLA through a dual civil-military command structure. Third, from a practical standpoint, information warfare militia units are more observable than whatever interactions the PLA maintains with China's hacking underground. Although not necessarily well-publicized in media intended for foreign consumption, references to information warfare militia units appear in Chinese-language press reports and regional, provincial, military, or local government websites and publications.

Militias are an enduring feature of Chinese military planning. Their modern form dates back to at least the late Qing Dynasty, when they were employed primarily to fight bandits in the countryside. In the Nationalist era, they were employed to engineer infrastructure projects and, later, fight the Japanese military.[10] In the early history of the People's Republic of China (PRC), they were viewed as an "essential part of the "people's war" strategy of drowning any invader in a "sea of humanity," particularly vis-à-vis the Soviet threat. Throughout this history, militias have been a tool to economize local defense.[11]

As China's threat environment evolved, so too did militia functions. With the decline in the prospects for a Soviet land invasion, China placed greater emphasis on "People's Air Defense," "People's Maritime Defense," and other functions. (Indeed, People's Air Defense units, drawn from urban *danwei*, or work units, are probably the most frequently discussed, prolific, and extensively organized of all militias.)[12] A recurring theme throughout these reorientations has been militias' persistent focus on helping China cover a soft flank. Particularly in the PRC, official sources characterize militias as a form of mobilization of civil resources for military ends.

Today, China has an eight-million-strong militia system that supplements the PLA. Officially defined as "an armed organization composed of the masses not released from their regular work,"[13] militias fulfill a variety of supporting military missions in wartime and, in peacetime, contribute to disaster relief operations, strengthen border security, and may even help contain demonstrations or other incidents.[14] Though historically associated with "rural towns and townships, administrative villages, urban sub-districts, and enterprises and institutions of a certain scale,"[15] militia units are increasingly formed in urban areas and in firms with a skilled workforce. They may even be established within foreign-owned companies.[16] Units are designated as either "ordinary" or "primary" militia units, with technically specialized groups such as information and network warfare units falling into the latter category.[17] As of 2004, there were roughly 10 million primary militia unit members across China.[18]

In 2009, militias accounted for just 2.74% of the official budget of China's armed forces. While the budget provided money for militia "training and maintenance" and "equipment," it did not fund militia "personnel" costs,[19] a line item that includes "salaries, allowances, food, bedding and clothing, insurance and welfare benefits for officers, NCOs [noncommissioned officers], enlisted men and contracted civilians, as well as pension for the disabled or the family of the deceased."[20] The extent to which militiamen receive compensation and benefits is unclear, but the expense is borne by local governments.[21]

Notwithstanding their humble origins, militias increasingly purport to carry out advanced functions, such as information warfare. According to Bryan Krekel and coauthors:

> Since approximately 2002, the PLA has been creating [information warfare] militia units comprised of personnel from the commercial IT sector and academia, and which represents [sic] an operational nexus between PLA [computer network operations] and Chinese civilian information security . . . professionals. The PLA has established militia units directly within commercial firms throughout China to take advantage of access to staff with advanced education, modern commercial-grade infrastructure, sophisticated software design capabilities, and the greater likelihood of finding "politically reliable" operators.[22]

With the PLA's continuous evolution into a more professionalized military, the future of the militia system as a whole appears to rest on the success of militias' transformation into a force equipped to operate under modern conditions. In many respects, information-focused militia units have an advantage over those focused other advanced functions, such as air defense, which have no direct civilian analog. However, this advantage (as discussed below) does not necessarily translate into a viable military capability.

Militias are administered jointly through the Central Military Commission (under the auspices of the PLA General Staff Department,[23] via a military region, provincial military command, and prefectural military command) and the state council (via a provincial government, prefectural government, and local Party committee) in the form of the People's Armed Forces Departments.[24] Joint administration is a function of all local headquarters offices up to the provincial military command level serving concurrently as departments of local civilian Party committees and local government organizations.[25] This style of administration is a key illustration of militias' dual civil-military nature.

INFORMATION WARFARE MILITIA UNITS

For the purposes of this study, the term "information warfare militias" is used as an umbrella term for both information warfare militia units and a number of subunits related to network attack and defense as well as other forms of information warfare that are generally situated within information warfare militia units. Our research identified information warfare militia units dating back to 1999, although they appear to have operated on an experimental basis until the early-2000s. Several factors converged in the mid-2000s to promote the expansion of information warfare militia programs. The first reference to "information-specialized" militia detachments in China's defense white papers occurred in the 2004 edition, which describes them as having recently been "reinforced." Around the same time, the PLA Academy of Military Sciences, "the PLA's highest-level research institute and center of military science," first publicly described information and network warfare militia units in 2003 and had fully endorsed the concept by 2006.[26] Another reference to information militia units occurs in the 2006 defense white paper, but the topic is not explicitly referenced in the 2008 and 2010 editions. The 2008 white paper does, however, mention that "importance has been attached to establishing militia organizations in emerging enterprises and high-tech industries to increase the technology content of the militia force."

China's "Medium- and Long-Term National Science and Technology Development Program (2006–2020)," a high-level policy-planning mechanism, potentially provided some of the strategic impetus for the expansion of information warfare militia units in the mid-2000s. Promulgated by the State Council, the MLP provides a road map for science and technology (S&T) development that includes defense and national security issues as central priorities.[27] Implementation guidelines for the plan explain that

> [China] must establish a defense-related S&T innovative system that combines military and civilian production and embeds military capabilities in civilian capabilities. We must promote the close integration of military and civilian S&T in terms of overall management, development strategy and planning, R&D activities, and S&T industrialization; step up efforts to develop technologies for both military and civilian uses; and foster a good pattern in which outstanding S&T forces across the nation serve defense-related S&T innovation, and defense-related S&T achievements are swiftly converted for civilian purposes.[28]

The Commission for Science, Technology and Industry for National Defense passed a defense-specific supplement to the MLP that likely contains more detailed direction. A description of that supplement identifies as priorities the creation of "key scientific and technological laboratories, state laboratories and major-discipline laboratories for national defense," "centers for research and application of industrial technologies," and "comprehensive scientific research facilities and bases." Finally, the plan orders that research on "defense and related resources will be shared by military and civilian institutions and businesses," which could potentially include the prioritization of information warfare militia development.[29] We identified two instances of provincial MLP implementation plans (Shanghai and Hunan) that explicitly referenced strengthening high-tech militia programs.

STRUCTURE OF INFORMATION WARFARE MILITIA UNITS

In order to understand the organizational structure of China's information warfare militias, it is important to first understand how Chinese military theorists in institutions such as National Defense University and the Academy of Military Sciences understand the battlespace in which these militias are expected to operate.[30]

The Chinese do not have a singular conception of cyberspace directly analogous to that employed by military theorists in the United States. The term "cyberspace," which is itself borrowed from Western science fiction and has traditionally lacked clearly defined boundaries, is transliterated into Chinese as *saibo* for the purposes of analyzing Western writing on network warfare but is otherwise absent in Chinese writings. The foundational concept used by Chinese analysts in its stead is the existence of an "information domain" alongside the traditional battlefield domains of air, sea, land, and space. Although the information domain is defined broadly and maximally in classic Chinese works such as the Academy of Military Sciences' seminal *Science of Military Strategy* and others, the domain is seen as containing a number of discrete, clearly defined subdomains, such as the computer network domain, the electromagnetic domain, the psychological domain, and the intelligence domain (see figure 8.2). Warfare in the information domain, or "information warfare," is thus not merely a synonym for computer network warfare or "cyberwar," but rather an umbrella term that encompasses warfare in each of these distinct subdomains.

This conception of the information domain is not simply a theoretical construct; it directly shapes the organizational structures of China's armed forces. Based on our compiled dataset, China's information warfare militia units (generally represented as subunits, or *fendui*, of larger organizations, but referred to here as "units" for ease of explanation) appear primarily to be umbrella organizations that can contain combinations of network warfare, electromagnetic warfare, psychological warfare, and even intelligence warfare units as appropriate. One early article on information warfare militias in the periodical *National Defense* (国防) lays out a typical organizational division within such a unit, including subunits devoted to both network warfare and electronic (electromagnetic)

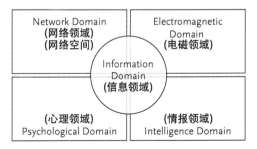

Figure 8.2 Chinese Military Theorists' Conception of the Information Domain

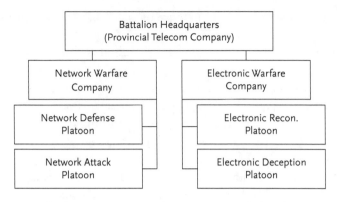

Figure 8.3 Typical Information Warfare Militia Organizational Chart (c. 2003)

warfare, as seen in figure 8.3.[31] Although this archetypal arrangement remains accurate, some recent sources describe these units' network and electromagnetic warfare subunits as being at the battalion (营) rather than company level. Insufficient information exists in open sources to resolve this discrepancy; it could potentially indicate a restructuring of the information warfare militia system at some time after 2003, the existence of a range of possible unit structures, or simply a factual error on the part of one of the authors.

Not every information warfare militia has every possible type of subunit. The specific composition of any given unit appears to be determined by both the needs of the local militia leadership and the civilian human and technical assets available. Militia leaders have detailed local knowledge of their local information technology industries' human capital availabilities, including local census data listing postgraduate students with relevant educational backgrounds, overseas returnees, and others who could be of use.[32] Different responsibilities could also be a function of the missions of PLA units linked to the militia system; the balance of power in organizational development matters between local militia commanders and the PLA's oversight remains unknown.

Command and Control

Although we did not discover open-source information explaining militia command and control in the specific context of information warfare militia units, it appears that they are commanded in the same way as traditional militias, with all the attendant layers of administration.[33] It is unclear whether highly regimented administration translates into good operational oversight and accountability in practice (perhaps not only to the authors, but to the PLA as well). We identified one interesting reference to a 2006 civil air defense exercise in Guizhou province, involving information warfare militia units and the PLA, which posed the key question: "Modern airstrike weaponry is rapid, stealth has increased, coordination against an airstrike is now a greater requirement. . . . How do you create top to bottom unified communication between hundreds of militias in many institutions?"[34] Unfortunately, the source did not address the extent to which the exercise in question successfully addressed this problem.

More directly, there are at least some indications that China's leadership understands the delicacy of command and control in the network domain, and the implications of its fracture. Most persuasive, if true, are unsubstantiated reports that Wu Guohua, commander from 2005 to 2010 of the PLA General Staff Department Third Department (3/PLA), which reportedly has responsibility for China's computer network exploitation missions, was transferred out of this role for conducting unauthorized computer network operations (CNO).[35] One of the main imperatives of retaining command and control (both in the network domain and in warfare more generally) is to maintain levers for escalation and de-escalation. Examining the prevalent Chinese views on these issues can offer additional—albeit indirect—insight into the seriousness with which command and control is taken. Consider, for example, a *China Daily* editorial, which states:

> Washington's excessive emphasis on absolute cybersecurity and concerns about China's growing cyber threat might lead to misjudgments and hostilities. With both state actors and non-state actors joining the cyber game, the risks of miscalculation between states will increase, especially if a non-state hacker can infiltrate a country's military networks and launch an attack against another country.[36]

Although ostensibly a call for diplomacy (and an attempt to play up the "attribution problem" in order to introduce doubt about the extent of China's malicious network espionage activities), the statement suggests some level of sensitivity to the uncertainty of signals, intentions, and motivations associated with computer network attacks.

Functions, Roles, and Missions

Information warfare militia units' functions, particularly those of network warfare militia subunits, are varied and not always entirely clear.

Complicating matters, Chinese analysts have advanced different types of missions, including:

- Preparing to operate in the network domain[37]
- Recruiting talented computer network attack and defense operators
- Serving as "reserve strength in network warfare"[38]
- Conducting network defense activities (e.g., network management, intrusion detection and monitoring, and systems defense implementation)
- Executing network attacks against enemy systems
- Researching and analyzing network security and network warfare issues[39]
- Raising military awareness of network security issues (e.g., training)[40]
- Conducting espionage in wartime[41]

Some of these missions may be aspirational in nature. However, given the range of network and information warfare militia subunits described in open sources, some of which explicitly mention attack and defense missions, it is possible that at least some quantity focus on even the most complex of these different missions.

We found no evidence concretely linking information warfare militia units to involvement in peacetime espionage activities, although various information warfare units were described as containing "intelligence warfare" and "information collection and processing" subunits. Although open-source information regarding the institutional affiliations of Chinese APT (advanced persistent threat) actors involved in computer network espionage is very limited, nothing disclosed to date by information security firms analyzing these actors has indicated any involvement by network militia subunits. This is in keeping with the Chinese literature on these units, which tends to emphasize defensive missions such as infrastructure hardening and network protection. However, certain facets of the militia system, such as the aforementioned ability of militia recruiters to specifically target and select returned overseas Chinese for recruitment into information warfare militia units (including network warfare and intelligence warfare subunits), remain causes for concern. Even if the bulk of information warfare militia units were found to be defensive in nature, it would remain plausible that a specialized minority may be involved in network warfare or espionage activities.

Mobilization

In the context of militias, PLA authors often reference the importance of being able to mobilize the populace for assistance in a war effort. But for information warfare militia units specifically, little has been written to differentiate between peacetime and wartime activities. This is symptomatic of a general lack of information about the concepts of operations and operational plans developed by China's armed forces for the network domain. At the risk of mirror-imaging US preferences upon a state with its own unique institutions and history that are very different from our own, several different possible scenarios bear examination.

Peacetime Operations

From the perspective of a commander, central oversight of—and deconfliction between—scores of different groups and thousands of different operators conducting peacetime computer network exploitation would prove a nightmarish task.[42] For example, consider a hypothetical scenario where a professional group like 3/PLA used sophisticated means to compromise a critical network and had been able to maintain persistent access to that network over a long period, perhaps months or years. If a part-time network warfare militiaman subsequently sent an unsophisticated spear-phishing message to a user on the compromised network that, when executed, came to the attention of a network defender, actions to remediate the more recent breach could easily disrupt the theretofore unnoticed and presumably bountiful original operation. The result would be a form of "electronic fratricide."[43]

From the perspective of the operator, computer network operations probably require a higher level of responsiveness than network militias could hope to offer (unless mobilized in wartime). Successful compromises can be fleeting, which is why in the early phases of an attack, operators appear to place almost as much emphasis on moving laterally across a compromised network, installing backdoors as they go, as they do on escalating privileges within the network to gain access to the most prized data.[44] Assuming network militia members are working part time, that could complicate efforts to exploit successful breaches in a time-sensitive manner. Although the PLA might be able to alleviate the problem to some degree by maintaining twenty-four-hour watch officers or queuing operators, this would create a thoroughly disorienting operational environment. There are certainly indications that Chinese hackers work in separate teams, but by most accounts the latter team acts on the basis of detailed knowledge of the victim network.[45]

Wartime Operations

The use of information warfare militia units (particularly their network warfare subunits) to conduct computer network operations during wartime is more fathomable. Even though defensive operations would be the least controversial application, a wartime attack mission cannot be ruled out, as wartime mobilization of the PLA would probably strengthen oversight capabilities. Also, the PLA would likely have a greater tolerance for risk in some areas, "taking the good with the bad" if unable to deconflict operations in real time. The PLA, moreover, could employ a "swarming" strategy that actually encourages both PLA and militia units attacking the same target, if not for increased "lethality," then perhaps to dilute defenders' attentions and obfuscate the most potent threats.

ANALYZING INFORMATION WARFARE MILITIA ACTIVITY

For this chapter, we sought to identify a broad range of information warfare militia units and subunits in the hope of gleaning insights about their roles, missions, operational prospects, and the attendant implications for civil-military integration. We gathered a dataset of eighty different units across China, characterized below and listed in detail in the appendix, using open-source Chinese materials. The sample included numerous different types of militia units with information warfare functions. Although all subunits attached to a given information warfare militia unit have been recorded in the appendix, only those units that are either described as information warfare militia units (which typically contain some network warfare subunits) or explicitly labeled as network warfare subunits were analyzed in the section that follows; this narrowed our dataset from eighty to fifty militia units. For the sake of simplicity, in this section we use the overarching term "information warfare militia units" to refer to both these umbrella units housing multiple functions and also their network warfare subunits (as discussed alongside figure 8.3).

We do not, unfortunately, know the extent to which our sample is representative. Several factors could have influenced our dataset and, as a corollary, our findings. Perhaps most importantly, in addition to references on Chinese government (including local and provincial) websites, we relied heavily upon media references to information and particularly network militias. As best we can tell, keeping in mind both the wide range of militia affiliations found in the dataset and the extremely large size of the "primary" militia force (10 million members), it is quite plausible that there are thousands or tens of thousands of information warfare militia units and subunits within China, in which case this dataset would represent less than 1% of that total. These data should thus be taken not as a fully representative sampling of the distribution of Chinese militia unit types and

Table 8.1 INFORMATION WARFARE MILITIA UNITS BY CITED NAME

Cited Name	Number of Militia Units in Sample
Network Warfare Militia Subunit	13
Information Warfare Militia Subunit	9
Network Militia Subunit	6
Network Attack and Defense Militia Subunit	5
Information Network Militia Subunit	4
Computer Network Attack and Defense Militia Subunit	2
Computer Network Militia Battalion	1
Information Warfare Militia Group, Network Warfare Battalion	1
Information Warfare Militia Training Base	1
Informatized Network Militia Subunit	1
Network Attack and Defense High-Tech Specialized Militia Subunit	1
Network Defense Militia Detachment	1
Network Mobilization Militia Subunit	1
Network Security Militia Subunit	1
Network Warfare Militia Detachment	1
Network Warfare Militia Special Subunit	1
Special Network Attack Militia Subunit	1
Total	50

characteristics, but rather as a tentative attempt to chart the breadth and variety of this organizational ecosystem (see table 8.1).[46]

Associations

With respect to information warfare militia unit affiliations, our data yielded an interesting finding. Of the fifty units, fully eighteen units were associated with educational institutions. There was no outwardly apparent trend linking the schools we identified: some are prestigious, others relatively undistinguished. Many of these, unsurprisingly, were housed in institutions that also receive grant money for information warfare-related research through China's large numbered research funding programs (e.g., 863, 973). We did not identify militias operating out of some of the schools we expected to see, either because of their notability on cyber issues (e.g., Beijing University of Posts and Telecommunications) or because of their infamy (e.g., Shanghai Jiao Tong University of "Operation Aurora" fame). This should not necessarily be taken as an indication that information warfare militia units at these schools do not exist; it is more likely to reflect the incomplete nature of open sources in this regard. Finally, we discovered that some universities host information warfare militias that include both students and faculty of the university and professionals from the surrounding community's information technology industries.

Rate of Creation

We observed the largest uptick in militia creation from 2004 to 2006. In that period alone, 36% of militias in our sample were formed or first documented (see table 8.2).

Here again, however, the nonrepresentative nature of our dataset is relevant. Short of excluding media-reported militias from our sample, which we chose not to do, we cannot control for the possibility that information warfare militia units were simply a "sexy story" in the mid-2000s but are no longer of great interest to the Chinese mainstream press. This could explain the apparent decrease in militia unit creation in recent years. On the other hand, as many militia units in our sample were created in the first quarter of 2012 as were created in the whole of 2011. This fluctuation merits further observation.

Table 8.2 INFORMATION WARFARE MILITIA UNIT
RATE OF CREATION

Year of Creation	Number of Militia Units Created
2000	3
2001	1
2002	2
2003	1
2004	5
2005	5
2006	3
2007	2
2008	5
2009	2
2010	2
2011	1
2012	4
Year Unknown	14
Total	50

Table 8.3 INFORMATION WARFARE MILITIA UNITS BY
PROVINCIAL-LEVEL ADMINISTRATIVE DIVISION

Province	Number of Identified Militia Units
Jiangsu	7
Hebei	4
Guangdong	3
Guizhou	3
Hunan	3
Shanghai	3
Sichuan	3
Tianjin	3
Zhejiang	3
Beijing	2
Chongqing	2
Henan	2
Ningxia	2
Shandong	2
Fujian	1
Gansu	1
Hainan	1
Hubei	1
Liaoning	1
Shaanxi	1
Shanxi	1
Yunnan	1
Total	50

Geographic Dispersion

Since we are working with a small, publicly identifiable subset of a much larger, more secretive whole, our data precludes a simple analysis of weighting in the assignment of militia units between provinces and military regions. However, we made a conscious effort to seek out information warfare militia units from all across China, and when viewed through the lens of China's military regions, our sample appears more evenly distributed (with the exception of Shenyang Military Region) than when viewed geographically along provincial lines (see table 8.3 and figure 8.4). There appears to be some bias toward information/network militia units being located in the more populous Eastern and Southeastern provinces of China. If our data sample is representative in this regard, one possible

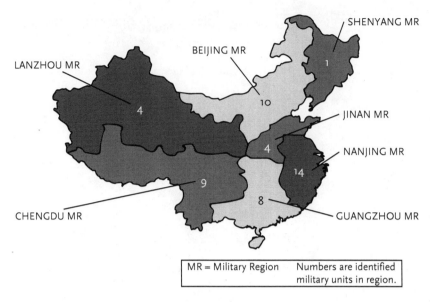

Figure 8.4 Information Warfare Militia Units by Military Region

explanation for the discrepancy would be that the Lanzhou and Chengdu Military Regions sprawl into central China, and militia units within these large regions appear to be disproportionately weighted toward a few cities that serve as high-tech hubs.

CASE STUDIES

To better understand the trends in our data, we relied on case studies of specific militias to provide insights into their roles and purpose (both within their host organizations and within the larger PLA). A comparison of network militias hosted in a specific enterprise in China's state-owned sector and within China's university system is particularly revealing.

The Case of China Mobile

One of the three state-owned enterprises that dominate China's domestic telecommunications industry, China Mobile has over 175,000 staff serving over 680 million customers.[47] In recent years, several of the organization's provincial- and local-level branch companies have established information warfare militia units. For example, China Mobile's Guangyuan, Sichuan, office established a network warfare militia subunit in 2010. According to contemporaneous media coverage, the militia's goal was to assist with national network and communications security, explicitly for the purposes of maintaining domestic security. Company executives appeared to leverage the militia to interface with the military and prove their patriotic bona fides. The militia's earthquake preparedness-related activities, for example, have provided China Mobile with favorable publicity.[48]

China Mobile's militia in Hubei, established in 2012, also appears to be part public relations tool, part mechanism for company officials to interface with their military counterparts. Although its functions are not explicitly articulated, it appears to fulfill general government goals of building cooperative relationships between commercial entities and the military.[49] A Hebei-based China Mobile militia unit, however, is explicitly described as being tasked with supporting the maintenance of military information systems.[50]

These information warfare militia units share several important commonalities. The first is their function as an interface between the state sector and the military. The second is their utility as a public relations tool. In Hubei and Sichuan, for example, China Mobile executives attended militia-related events and posed for photographs with regional military leaders. A third commonality is the presence of vague references to the militias as fulfilling government program requirements, suggesting the existence of high-level guidance regarding which enterprises should house information warfare militia units. Specific operational details are scarce, however, since published materials on the groups provide essentially anodyne mission descriptions that aim to present the groups as patriotic yet innocuous public servants.

University-Based Information Warfare Militia Units

Information militias based in Chinese universities offer an interesting counterpoint to those at China Mobile. Although no one university militia offered enough information to merit exclusive treatment, a review of several university militias provides some insight into differences between how corporate and educational-based units are regarded (though not sufficient detail to determine differences in their actual activities). For example, Tianjin Polytechnic University documents use the phrase "improving and training students in national security awareness" to describe the militia's central goal. Materials on the militia indicate another aim is hacking into and destroying enemy military systems.[51] Likewise, Hainan University's information warfare and network attack militia units emphasize the impact that such units have on "national security consciousness."[52] South China Normal University's information warfare militia emphasizes network attack explicitly, as does the militia at the North China Institute of Aerospace Engineering.[53]

University-sponsored militias are similar to the corporate militias described earlier in several respects. Like those based in the private sector, university-based information warfare militias tend to be based within a single institution rather than containing personnel from multiple institutions in a single grouping. They present an opportunity for university officials, like corporate executives, to build relationships with military and civil officialdom, and may offer public relations benefits.

However, there appear to be some important differences. A central aim of university militia units appears to be instilling a patriotic ethos in students. University militias emphasize the transfer of technology and know-how to the military. Finally, universities' militia-related public relations strategies diverge sharply from the understated language used by their corporate counterparts, instead offering sometimes-colorful descriptions of the units' responsibilities to engage in offensive operations against enemy military systems.

CONCLUSIONS, AREAS FOR FURTHER RESEARCH, AND POLICY IMPLICATIONS

Their potentially impressive end strength notwithstanding, nothing we saw places information warfare militia units at the core of China's operational network warfare forces or shows that they operate differently from China's other traditional militia units that are similarly designated as "primary" militia units.[54] Placing information warfare militia units in the civil-military context, we have assessed that several types of missions are most likely, in part because they sidestep some of the operational constraints (e.g., command-and-control issues) described above. There are reports of information warfare militia members training PLA operators, a seemingly straightforward application of militiamen's expertise. Defensive operations—both in peacetime and wartime—also seem to be an especially promising application for information warfare militias, largely because, at least at the most base level, such missions can be somewhat pro forma. Even in wartime, defensive functions could include such mundane tasks as updating firewalls, replacing systems, and "rolling back" corrupted systems to their last known clean configurations. Interestingly, network defense operations are strikingly analogous to traditional militia missions. As characterized by Dennis Blasko:

> Much of their work focuses on providing rear area security . . . for PLA active duty units as well as the civilian population; logistics support; and repair of infrastructure damaged from long-range strikes on China. . . . [T]he majority of them do not add to the PLA's power projection capabilities.[55]

Defensive missions in the network domain, therefore, are both operationally and strategically sensible and rooted in traditional militia norms.

Civil-Military Integration in the Network Domain: A Nonconclusion

For a decade or more, China's defense authorities have sought to increase civil-military integration, with some noticeable success. The extent to which this trend applies to operations, rather than staying in the domain of procurement, is difficult or impossible to quantify. However, the PLA does appear to be attempting to centralize and streamline its computer network operations infrastructure, as evidenced by such reforms as the 2010 creation of the PLA Information Assurance Base.[56] The implications of this movement for operational civil-military integration are not yet clear.

The general maturation of China's computer network operations capabilities is a trend that may also affect the trajectory of civil-military integration in the network domain. As the PLA's core information warfare operators—the PLA GSD Third and Fourth Departments—presumably evolve and improve on the basis of experience, whatever value may have once accrued from drawing upon, for example, militiamen a few days each month from a local business' technical support team, may decline in kind. On the other hand, the prevalence of information warfare militia units at educational institutions, likely conducting research and development, could increasingly serve as a pipeline of new tools, tactics, techniques, and procedures, even if not a basis for operations themselves.

Areas for Further Research

The professional PLA-watching community in Western countries—even those focused on cyber issues—has seemed somewhat uninterested in information warfare militia units. In the community's (by all accounts accurate) assessment that these militias are not the PLA's central actors in the network domain, PLA watchers also discount the possibility that militias could even serve as a PLA force enabler in network domain. This seems premature given the absence of open-source information about information warfare militia units' wartime roles.

Most intriguing would be associations to organizations without inherent network operations missions, which would validate some of the PRC's traditional talking points about civil-military integration generally and information warfare militia units specifically. For example, we saw some indication that a Kunming, Yunnan province, network warfare militia subunit drilled with the Second Artillery (China's "Strategic Rocket Forces"). It appeared that the militia unit acted as technological support.[57] We were surprised to find little other evidence of this sort of arrangement. Consider the following examples of organizations that have critical technical functions but may not necessarily have the network operations-related institutional capacity resident in organizations like 3/PLA and 4/PLA:

- *First (Operations) Department of the GSD (1/PLA)*: Among other things, the 1/PLA "mans and operates the PLA's national command and control center," which "functions as the C3I [command, control, communications, and intelligence] nerve center for all PLA units 24 hours a day" according to one Western description.[58]
- *Second (Intelligence) Department of the GSD (2/PLA)*: In addition to traditional human intelligence missions, 2/PLA maintains a Tactical Reconnaissance Bureau and Technology and Equipment Bureau, which suggest functions that may require enhanced network defense in wartime.[59]
- *General Logistics Department (GLD)*: The PLA reportedly uses a "secure" (i.e., buried, hardened, and presumably segmented or air-gapped) fiber optic network for military communications.[60] However, it stands to reason that the PLA, like the US military, entrusts at least some sensitive logistics functions to public or otherwise vulnerable networks.[61] If so, skilled cyber operators would be crucial to GLD functions. Moreover, protection of "strategic logistic depots" and "transport hubs" is a traditional militia mission that has obvious analogues in cyberspace.[62]
- *Various air defense units*: Air defense systems—particularly the modern, integrated variety—are at least in theory a quintessential network attack target.[63] Though network defense is not a traditional competency of air defense, wartime attacks on enabling information systems could require the appropriation of people skilled in network operations. Militias, for their part, played an important historical role in Chinese air defense missions and this apparently remains a core militia function to this day.[64]

However, we identified only one instance of an information warfare militia unit training for air defense functions.[65]

Another area of importance would be greater insight into the incentives or mandates that lead to the creation of information warfare militia units. China's 2004 defense white paper claimed, "It is the glorious duty of the Chinese citizens to . . . join militia organizations according to law."[66] Perhaps so, but much remains unknown about how these specific militia units generally come to be. Additional information about the conditions that cause localities to establish information warfare militia units, private firms (especially foreign firms) to host them, and individual employees to join them, would be illuminating for the analysis of both information warfare militia units specifically and civil-military integration more generally. The fact that certain provincial MLP implementation plans referenced "high-tech militias" raises the interesting possibility that companies may, for example, form information warfare militia units as a quid pro quo for access to a High-Tech Development Zone or other forms of preferential treatment. That is purely speculative, but the premise bears further examination.[67]

Policy Implications

The most critical question facing policymakers on this topic is the issue of information warfare militia units located within China's telecommunications industry. The *Financial Times* reported that "[a]n employee of China Telecom in the coastal province of Jiangsu said the state-owned carrier's local affiliate had an information warfare militia unit, and he believed similar groups had been set up in other provinces."[68] We found evidence that several branches of both China Telecom and China Mobile each host a number of information warfare militia units.[69] This is clearly undesirable from the perspective of US and other non-Chinese Internet service providers that maintain peering arrangements with these large carriers. The matter is particularly questionable in the case of China Telecom in light of past instances of questionable Internet traffic stewardship.[70]

Also of potential concern is the presence of information warfare militia units in certain Chinese universities and businesses, which raises important questions about the desirability of US interactions with these institutions. For example, as "prominent American universities are racing to build closer ties to China," in the words of one recent report, perhaps computer sciences-related programs should adopt a cautious risk profile so as not to inadvertently assist in the development of Chinese computer network operations capabilities.[71]

Finally, in an age of almost inconceivably fragmented supply chains, the presence of militiamen in information technology firms casts doubt on the sanctity of components and systems produced or assembled therein. For example, one militia in our sample was associated with Yin He Electronics Development Company, a firm that apparently has a role in the development of supervisory control and data acquisition (SCADA) systems.[72] Although we were not able to find specific information on this firm's activities, the connection raises two troubling possibilities. First, SCADA developers are uniquely qualified to identify SCADA-related attack vectors—and not necessarily just in the context of their own products. Second, SCADA-related manufacturers or assemblers could have ample opportunity to execute supply chain attacks.[73] Therefore, foreign companies ought to conduct a reasonable level of due diligence to avoid sourcing components and systems—particularly those destined for sensitive applications—from firms with information warfare militia units.

Table 8.A1 INFORMATION WARFARE MILITIA UNITS AND SUBUNITS

Cited Name	Year	Affiliation	Location
Network Warfare Militia Subunit[1]	2005	Nanhao Beijing Science and Technology Co. Ltd.	Beijing (Beijing MR)
Network Warfare Militia Subunit[2]	2009	Beijing University of Aeronautics and Astronautics	Beijing (Beijing MR)
Network Attack and Defense Militia Subunit[3]		Central South University	Changsha, Hunan (Guangzhou MR)
Network Militia Subunit[4]	2004	Changsha High Tech Development Zone	Changsha, Hunan (Guangzhou MR)
Computer Network Militia Battalion[5]	2002	Changzhou City, Tianning District	Changzhou, Jiangsu (Nanjing MR)
Information Network Militia Subunit[6]	2010	Changzhou High-Tech Development Zone	Changzhou, Jiangsu (Nanjing MR)
Communications Technology Militia Sub-Unit[7]	1999	Chongqing University	Chongqing (Chengdu MR)
Computer Technology Militia Subunit[7]	1999	Chongqing University	Chongqing (Chengdu MR)
Special Network Attack Militia Subunit[8]	2000	Chongqing Garrison	Chongqing (Chengdu MR)

(Continued)

Cited Name	Year	Affiliation	Location
Network Warfare Militia Special Subunit[9]	2000	Chongqing University of Posts and Telecommunications	Chongqing (Chengdu MR)
Computer Network Attack and Defense Militia Subunit[10]	2006	Liaoning Shihua Engineering University	Fushun, Liaoning (Shenyang MR)
Information Warfare Militia Subunit[11]		Fuyuan County Defense Mobilization Network Information Center	Fuyuan, Yunnan (Chengdu MR)
Network Attack and Defense Militia Subunit[12]	2004	Fuzhou University	Fuzhou, Fujian (Nanjing MR)
Emergency Communications Security Militia Subunit[13]	2010	China Mobile, Guangyuan Branch	Guangyuan, Sichuan (Chengdu MR)
Network Warfare Militia Subunit[14]		South China Normal University	Guangzhou, Guangdong (Guangzhou MR)
Network Warfare Militia Subunit[15]	2012	Guangdong Telecom	Guangzhou, Guangdong (Guangzhou MR)
Information Warfare Militia Subunit[15]	2012	Guangdong Telecom	Guangzhou, Guangdong (Guangzhou MR)
Communications Security Militia Subunit[15]	2012	Guangdong Telecom	Guangzhou, Guangdong (Guangzhou MR)
Electronic Warfare Militia Subunit[15]	2012	Guangdong Telecom	Guangzhou, Guangdong (Guangzhou MR)
Network Warfare Militia Subunit[15]	2012	Guangdong Provincial Government Digital Communications Bureau	Guangzhou, Guangdong (Guangzhou MR)
Information Warfare Militia Training Base[16]	2002	Guiyang Garrison (partnering with local universities)	Guiyang, Guizhou (Chengdu MR)
Network Attack and Defense Militia Subunit[17]	2005	Guiyang City, Wudang District	Guiyang, Guizhou (Chengdu MR)
Emergency Communications Militia Subunit[17]	2005	Guiyang City, Wudang District	Guiyang, Guizhou (Chengdu MR)

(Continued)

Cited Name	Year	Affiliation	Location
Electronic Warfare Militia Subunit[17]	2005	Guiyang City, Wudang District	Guiyang, Guizhou (Chengdu MR)
Information Warfare Militia Subunit[17]	2005	Guiyang City, Wudang District	Guiyang, Guizhou (Chengdu MR)
Information Warfare Militia Sub-unit[18]	2005	Guiyang University	Guiyang, Guizhou (Chengdu MR)
Network Militia Subunit[19]		Hainan University	Haikou, Hainan (Guangzhou MR)
Psychological [Network] Warfare Militia Subunit[19]		Hainan University	Haikou, Hainan (Guangzhou MR)
Information Warfare Militia Subunit[20]		Handan City	Handan, Hebei (Beijing MR)
Information Warfare Militia Subunit[21]		Zhejiang Agricultural and Forestry University	Hangzhou, Zhejiang (Nanjing MR)
Informatized Network Militia Subunit[22]	2012	Zhejiang University	Hangzhou, Zhejiang (Nanjing MR)
Information Warfare Militia Group, Network Warfare Battalion[23]	2001	Guangzhou People's Armed Forces Department	Hubei (Guangzhou MR)
Information Warfare Militia Group, Electronic Warfare Battalion[23]	2001	Guangzhou People's Armed Forces Department	Hubei (Guangzhou MR)
Information Warfare Militia Group, Psychological Warfare Battalion[23]	2001	Guangzhou People's Armed Forces Department	Hubei (Guangzhou MR)
Information Warfare Militia Group, Intelligence Warfare Battalion[23]	2001	Guangzhou People's Armed Forces Department	Hubei (Guangzhou MR)
Information Warfare Militia Subunit[24]		China Telecom	Jiangsu (Nanjing MR)
Informatized Electronic Warfare Militia Subunit[25]	2011	Jiyuan Technical Institute	Jiyuan, Henan (Jinan MR)
Information Warfare Militia Subunit[26]	Prior to 2005	Lanzhou University	Lanzhou, Gansu (Lanzhou MR)

(*Continued*)

Table 8.A1 (Continued)

Cited Name	Year	Affiliation	Location
Electronic Information High-Tech Militia Subunit[27]	2002	Luoyang Gao Xin Hong Ye Technology Company	Luoyang, Henan (Jinan MR)
Information Warfare Militia Subunit[28]	2004	Southwest University of Science and Technology	Mianyang, Sichuan (Chengdu MR)
Network Attack and Defense High-Tech Specialized Militia Subunit[29]	2000	Southeast University	Nanjing, Jiangsu (Nanjing MR)
Informatized Warfare Militia Unit[30]	2005	Nanjing City, Baixia District	Nanjing, Jiangsu (Nanjing MR)
Computer Network Attack and Defense Militia Subunit[30]	2005	Nanjing City, Baixia District	Nanjing, Jiangsu (Nanjing MR)
Network Militia Subunit[31]	2003	Nanyang City	Nanyang, Henan (Jinan MR)
Network Warfare Militia Subunit[32]	2006	Yanshan University	Qinhuangdao, Hebei (Beijing MR)
Information Network Militia Subunit[33]	2007	Shanghai Jiao Tong University Information Security Institute	Shanghai (Nanjing MR)
Information Network Militia Subunit[33]	2007	Shanghai Jiao Tong University Radar Laboratory	Shanghai (Nanjing MR)
Network Militia Subunit[34]	2011	Shanghai, Hongkou District	Shanghai (Nanjing MR)
Network Warfare Militia Subunit[35]	2010	Shaoxing County	Shaoxing, Zhejiang (Nanjing MR)
Information Warfare Militia Subunit[36]		China Mobile	Shijiazhuang, Hebei (Beijing MR)
Information Warfare Militia Subunit[37]		China Telecom	Shijiazhuang, Hebei (Beijing MR)
Emergency Communications Security Militia Unit[38]	2010	Sichuan province	Sichuan (Chengdu MR)
Network Attack and Defense Militia Subunit[39]	2012	Soochow University	Suzhou, Jiangsu (Nanjing MR)
Network Militia Subunit[40]		Taiyuan High-Tech Development Zone	Taiyuan, Shanxi (Beijing MR)

(Continued)

Table 8.A1 (Continued)

Cited Name	Year	Affiliation	Location
Computer Development and Application Militia Subunit[40]	2000	Yin He Electronics Development Company	Taiyuan, Shanxi (Beijing MR)
Information Warfare Militia Subunit[41]	2003	Taiyuan City, Zuoyun County	Taiyuan, Shanxi (Beijing MR)
Information Warfare Militia Unit[42]	2004	Taizhou City	Taizhou, Jiangsu (Nanjing MR)
Electronic Deception Militia Subunit[42]	2004	Taizhou City	Taizhou, Jiangsu (Nanjing MR)
GPS Jamming Militia Subunit[42]	2004	Taizhou City	Taizhou, Jiangsu (Nanjing MR)
Photoelectric Jamming Militia Subunit[42]	2004	Taizhou City	Taizhou, Jiangsu (Nanjing MR)
Network Attack and Defense Militia Subunit[42]	2004	Taizhou City	Taizhou, Jiangsu (Nanjing MR)
Psychological Warfare Militia Subunit[42]	2004	Taizhou City	Taizhou, Jiangsu (Nanjing MR)
Electromagnetic Attack Militia Subunit[42]	2004	Taizhou City	Taizhou, Jiangsu (Nanjing MR)
Network Warfare Militia Subunit[43]		Tianjin City, Beichen District, Education Department	Tianjin (Beijing MR)
Network Warfare Militia Subunit[44]		Tianjin Technical University	Tianjin (Beijing MR)
Electronic Warfare Militia Subunit[45]	2008	Tianjin University of Technology	Tianjin (Beijing MR)
Network Warfare Militia Subunit[46]	2008	Tianjin City Information Center	Tianjin (Beijing MR)
Network Militia Subunit[47]	2006	Weihai City	Weihai, Shandong (Jinan MR)
Network Security Militia Subunit[48]	2009	Weinan City	Weinan, Shaanxi (Lanzhou MR)
Information Network Militia Subunit[49]	2005	Hunan University of Science and Technology	Xiangtan, Hunan (Guangzhou MR)
Network Mobilization Militia Subunit[50]	2004	Yantai City	Yantai, Shandong (Jinan MR)
Electronic Network Militia Subunit[51]	2007	Yinchuan City	Yinchuan, Ningxia (Lanzhou MR)
Psychological Warfare Militia Subunit[51]	2007	Yinchuan City	Yinchuan, Ningxia (Lanzhou MR)
Information Warfare Militia Subunit[52]	2008	Yongning City	Yongning, Ningxia (Lanzhou MR)

(Continued)

Table 8.A1 (Continued)

Cited Name	Year	Affiliation	Location
Network Warfare Militia Detachment[52]	2008	Yongning City	Yongning, Ningxia (Lanzhou MR)
Information Collection and Processing Militia Detachment[52]	2008	Yongning City	Yongning, Ningxia (Lanzhou MR)
Network Defense Militia Detachment[52]	2008	Yongning City	Yongning, Ningxia (Lanzhou MR)
Network Warfare Militia Subunit[53]		Zhengzhou Hongyuan Electronics Company	Zhengzhou, Henan (Jinan MR)
Network Warfare Militia Subunit[54]	2008	Sichuan Atlantic Welding Corporation	Zigong, Sichuan (Chengdu MR)
Network Warfare Militia Subunit[54]	2008	ZiGong YingZhi HeJin Co. Ltd.	Zigong, Sichuan (Chengdu MR)

Note: For brevity, sourcing of militia units identified will include only the URL of the Chinese website which lists it.

[1] http://jpkc.nciae.edu.cn/dxjsj/shownews.asp?id=14.
[2] http://www.ft.com/cms/s/0/33dc83e4-c800-11e0-9501-00144feabdc0.html; http://www.nhii.cn/UploadFiles/20111019172746740.jpg.
[3] http://cne.csu.edu.cn/Html/news/2008/2008/1305.html.
[4] http://www.pladaily.com.cn/big5/pladaily/2004/06/28/20040628001033.html.
[5] www.pladaily.com.cn/item/zgmb/200206/txt/02.htm.
[6] http://epaper.loone.cn/site1/czrb/html/2010-12/30/content_374814.htm.
[7] http://wuxizazhi.cnki.net/Search/XNMB199902029.html.
[8] http://web.archive.org/web/20050509013608/http://www.yesky.com/NewsChannel/72902018968059904/20000829/109310.shtml.
[9] www.pladaily.com.cn/item/zgmb/200206/txt/02.htm.
[10] http://tuanwei.lnpu.edu.cn/neirong.jsp?urltype=news.NewsContentUrl&wbtreeid=4641&wbnewsid=75942.
[11] http://news.sohu.com/20060609/n243649107.shtml.
[12] http://www.66163.com/fujian_w/news/fzd/fzrb/20020918/GB/fzrb%5E1449%5E01%5ERb011002.htm; http://news.xinhuanet.com/mil/2004-12/16/content_2342389.htm.
[13] http://www.c114.net/news/118/a689563.html.
[14] http://www2.scnu.edu.cn/wzb/jslljxview.asp?id=90.
[15] http://chn.chinamil.com.cn/zgmb/2012-02/13/content_4788912.htm.
[16] http://gzrb.big5.gog.com.cn/system/2007/07/24/010093755.shtml.
[17] http://mil.news.sina.com.cn/2005-08-07/1723311224.html.
[18] http://dsa.gzu.edu.cn/szw/news/xuegongjianxun/2008/62/921019019653.html.
[19] http://www.hainu.edu.cn/stm/zy_wuzhuangbu/2009422/10210841.shtml.
[20] http://www.hainu.edu.cn/stm/zy_wuzhuangbu/2009422/10210841.shtml.
[21] http://bwc.zjfc.edu.cn/articles/93/46/.
[22] http://www.adyun.com/news/detail/?news_id=2257.
[23] http://news.xinhuanet.com/mil/2003-06/12/content_916888.htm.
[24] http://www.ft.com/intl/cms/s/0/33dc83e4-c800-11e0-9501-00144feabdc0.html.
[25] http://www.jyvtc.com/news/show.asp?b_class=%D4%BA%CF%B5%D0%C2%CE%C5&id=1326; http://www.dvdhn.com/heshihuchoujing/84.html; http://www.jyvtc.com/jsj/showi.asp?b_class=%CF%B5%B2%BF%D0%C2%CE%C5&id=620.
[26] http://news.lzu.edu.cn/c/200505/lmc2195.html.
[27] http://www.hongye.com.cn/web/news/ShowArticle.asp?ArticleID=94.
[28] http://www.my.gov.cn/MYGOV/144683669963931648/20040303/903.html.
[29] http://mil.eastday.com/epublish/gb/paper2/20000916/class000200012/hwz102778.htm.
[30] http://news.sina.com.cn/o/2005-07-07/08516372393s.shtml.
[31] http://news.sina.com.cn/c/2004-04-26/07292402697s.shtml. http://wenku.baidu.com/view/1c2b3fef102de2bd96058824.html; http://www.docin.com/p-685414389.html.
[32] http://mil.qianlong.com/4919/2007/05/21/135@3847946.htm.
[33] http://chn.chinamil.com.cn/xwpdxw/mbybyxw/2011-02/21/content_4388059.htm.
[34] www.zit.zj.cn/news/201005/2385.shtml.

[35] http://shijiazhuang.mofcom.gov.cn/column/print.shtml?/gaikuang/200509/20050900484468.
[36] http://121.28.35.251/content.jsp?code=000224522/2010-03791&name=.
[37] http://shijiazhuang.mofcom.gov.cn/column/print.shtml?/gaikuang/200509/20050900484468.
[38] http://www.c114.net/news/118/a689563.html.
[39] http://gf.jsgjxh.cn/news_view.asp?id=220.
[40] http://mil.news.sina.com.cn/2003-11-03/160125.html.
[41] http://www.zuoyun.gov.cn/news.php?id=604.
[42] http://www.law-lib.com/law/law_view.asp?id=91407.
[43] http://www.tj.gov.cn/zwgk/wjgz/szfwj/201001/t20100125_112096.htm.
[44] http://www.tjpu.edu.cn/News/general/2009/4/1221284636.html; http://www.eyw.edu.cn/www/a/eyuantupian/shetuanhuodong/eyuanwangzhan/2010/0809/7475_13.html.
[45] http://www.tjut.edu.cn/qiushinews/article_view.jsp?id=3084.
[46] http://www.tjic.cn/XXLR1.ASP?ID=7930.
[47] http://www.chinamil.com.cn/site1/zbxl/2006-10/02/content_605872.htm.
[48] http://www.chinamil.com.cn/site1/xwpdxw/2009-03/26/content_1703268.htm.
[49] http://www1.hnust.cn/Show.asp?78.
[50] http://mil.news.sina.com.cn/2004-11-22/1355245169.html.
[51] http://news.qq.com/a/20070609/001013.htm.
[52] http://cif.mofcom.gov.cn/cif/html/sheng/xwkx/zxxx/2008/3/1205896154568.html.
[53] http://news.yktchina.com/2009-11/a1aaf58132ac4b91827c1a1cec596eae.html.
[54] http://www.zgda.gov.cn/news/articles/2008/09/08/20080908160330-585750-00-000.aspx.

NOTES

1. Tai Ming Cheung, *Fortifying China: The Struggle to Build a Modern Defense Economy* (Ithaca, NY: Cornell University Press, 2009).

2. Ibid., 197.

3. Ibid., 199.

4. These programs are described in Bryan Krekel, Patton Adams, and George Bakos, *Occupying the Information High Ground: Chinese Capabilities for Computer Network Operations and Cyber Espionage* (Washington DC: U.S-China Economic and Security Review Commission, 2012), 70.

5. See LeighAnn Ragland, Joe McReynolds, and Debra Geary, "China's Defense Electronics Industry," paper presented at the 2012 IGCC Annual Conference on China's Defense Science, Technology, and Industrial Base, La Jolla, CA.

6. Krekel, Adams, and Bakos, *Occupying the Information High Ground*, 61.

7. Research institutes engaged in traditional weapons development, about which considerably more information is available, may provide insight into the processes by which network warfare capabilities are developed and eventually matriculate to the PLA arsenal. This area merits further investigation.

8. Bryan Krekel et. al., *Capability of the People's Republic of China to Conduct Cyber Warfare and Computer Network Exploitation* (Washington, DC: U.S.-China Economic and Security Review Commission, 2009), 45–49, http://www.uscc.gov/research-papers/2009/NorthropGrumman_PRC_Cyber_Paper_FINAL_Approved%20Report_16Oct2009.pdf.

9. Dennis J. Blasko, *The Chinese Army Today: Tradition and Transformation for the 21st Century*, 2nd ed. (New York: Routledge, 2012), 112.

10. Philip C. Huang, "'Public Sphere'/'Civil Society' in China? The Third Realm between State and Society," *Modern China* 19, no. 2 (April 1993): 216–40.

11. David Shambaugh, *Modernizing China's Military: Progress, Problems, and Prospects* (Berkeley: University of California Press, 2004), 174.

12. Xu Jingen and Wang Yong, *National Defense Mobilization Practice, Organization and Implementation* (Beijing: PLA Press, 2010), 88–89, 152.

13. Those with an affinity for Marxist language will prefer the definition used in China's 2002 defense white paper: "The militia is an armed mass organization not released from production."

14. Information Office of the State Council, *China's National Defense in 2004* (Beijing, 2005).

15. Blasko, *The Chinese Army Today*, 29.

16. Ibid., 29.

17. Ibid., 29–32.

18. Information Office of the State Council, *China's National Defense in 2004*.

19. Information Office of the State Council, *China's National Defense in 2010* (Beijing, 2011).

20. Information Office of the State Council, *China's National Defense in 2008* (Beijing, 2009).

21. Blasko, *The Chinese Army Today*, 29.

22. Krekel et al., *Capability of the People's Republic of China to Conduct Cyber Warfare*, 33.

23. Specifically, the Militia Bureau of the Mobilization Department. See Shambaugh, *Modernizing China's Military*, 129.

24. Information Office of the State Council, *China's National Defense in 2006* (Beijing, 2007).

25. Blasko, *The Chinese Army Today*, 41.

26. Quote from Information Office of the State Council, *China's National Defense in 2002* (Beijing, 2003). See also Krekel et al., *Capability of the People's Republic of China to Conduct Cyber Warfare*, 35–36.

27. Cheung, *Fortifying China*, 241.

28. "Guidelines for the Medium- and Long-Term National Science and Technology Development Program (2006–2020)," Xinhua News Agency, February 9, 2006, OSC ID: CPP20060209005001.

29. "China Unveils Plan for Developing Defense Technologies," Xinhua News Agency, May 25, 2006, OSC ID: CPP20060525079027.

30. For more detail on these points, see Joe McReynolds, "Chinese Thinking on Deterrence and Escalation in the Network Domain," presentation at the 2013 CAPS-RAND Conference on the PLA.

31. Ye Youcai and Zhou Wenrui, "建设一支高素质的民兵信息技术分队" [Building a High-Quality Militia Information Technology Element], Guofang (国防), September 15, 2003, OSC ID: CPP20031002000138. Cyber militia organizational groupings and staffing levels are not always described consistently and are possibly in flux. A 2004 report described information militia subunits as being staffed by eight to twelve militiamen each (Guo Yan, 民兵预备役部队维稳研究 [*Research on Militias and Reserve Units' Role in Maintaining Stability*] (Jiangsu: PLA Publishing, 2004).). A 2007 source stated that there were approximately fifteen militiamen per unit, divided among a "Network Support Group," a "Surveillance Group," a "Network Defense Group," and a "Comprehensive Support Group." Zhang Zhilun, "军分区如何精编活训网络战民兵分队" [How Can Military Subregions Pay Careful Attention to the Training of Network Militias?] *Southwestern Militia*, January 2007.

32. Ye and Zhou, "Building a High-Quality Militia Information Technology Element."

33. As far as we were able to tell, the only way that information warfare militias differ from other "primary" militia units is with respect to relaxed fitness requirements, presumably to enable the participation of the most technically skilled operators. See Krekel et al., *Capability of the People's Republic of China to Conduct Cyber Warfare*, 36.

34. Zhou Xing and Wang Xiong, "Guiyang City to Actively Explore Joint Civil-Military Training Mechanism," *PLA Daily*, July 10, 2006, http://mil.news.sina.com.cn/2006-07-10/0913382545.html.

35. Mark Stokes, Jenny Lin, and L. C. Russell Hisao, *The Chinese People's Liberation Army Signals Intelligence and Cyber Reconnaissance Infrastructure* (Arlington, VA: Project 2049 Institute, 2011).

36. "Cyber Cooperation Needed," *China Daily*, November 22, 2011.

37. Zheng Gang and Wang Jun, "民兵网络分队建设要有"撒手锏" [The Construction of Network Militias Must Have an Assassin's Mace], *Southwestern Militia*, May 2005.

38. Zhang, "How Can Military Subregions Pay Careful Attention to the Training of Network Militias?"

39. Guo, *Research on Militias and Reserve Units' Role in Maintaining Stability*.

40. Zhang, "How Can Military Subregions Pay Careful Attention to the Training of Network Militias?"

41. Yuan Bailing and Shi Senlin, "网络尖兵挑大梁—河北省唐山军分区民兵网络分队参加演示速描" [The Leading Role of the Network Vanguard: Attending an Exercise of the Hebei Province Tangshan Region Network Militia], *Northern Militia* 12 (2005). Yuan and Shi recount a Hebei-based militia drill in which operators access "top secret documents" on an enemy computer.

42. Krekel, Adams, and Bakos, *Occupying the Information High Ground*, 54. While the term "interlocking fields of fire" is an imperative on the battlefield, it has a potentially less positive connotation in network exploitation operations in which stealth might be the highest priority. However, there are certainly indications that, even in peacetime, the PLA is willing to sacrifice stealth for volume.

43. Ibid., 55.

44. Mandiant Corporation, "M-Trends: An Evolving Threat," 2012.

45. Krekel et al., *Capability of the People's Republic of China to Conduct Cyber Warfare*, 56.

46. Our best sense of our sample's comprehensiveness is that the data we have collected is only a fraction of the total number of information warfare militia units and subunits that exist in China today. If reports are accurate and China's militia system is comprised of thousands of units and 8 million people—and some 60% of new units focus on high-tech tasks (see Blasko, *The Chinese Army Today*, 112)—it appears that we only identified a small percentage.

47. China Mobile, "China Mobile Limited Announces 2012 Interim Results," August 16, 2012, http://www.chinamobileltd.com/en/media/press/p120816.pdf, and China Mobile, "Overview," http://www.chinamobileltd.com/en/about/overview.php.

48. C114.net, "China Mobile Participates in Earthquake Relief Emergency Drill with Efforts to Build a Communication Safety Net," May 13, 2012, http://www.c114.net/news/118/a689563.html.

49. CN Hubei, "Hubei Information Protection Militia Large Unit Established, China Mobile's Informatization Strengthening of the Military Opens a New Chapter," May 15, 2012, http://news.cnhubei.com/gdxw/201205/t2070033.shtml.

50. Luo Guoying, "Looking Back at 2005: The Rise of the National Defense Reserve Force and Scholars and Expert Matrix," *3MT*, December 30, 2005, http://ido.3mt.com.cn/pc/200512/20051230315480.shtm.

51. Tianjin Polytechnic University News, "Our School Holds a 2009 Demonstration Where an Entire Militia Accepts Training in Network Attack and Defense Subjects," April 4, 2010, http://www.tjpu.edu.cn/News/general/2009/4/1221284636.html.

52. Hainan University, "Meilan District People's Armed Forces Department Inspection Department Group Comes to Our Units for a Complete Militia Inspection," April 21, 2006, http://www.hainu.edu.cn/stm/zy_wuzhuangbu/2006421/26618.shtml. See

also Hainan University, "Hainan Province First College Student Militia Organized at Hainan University Is Established," May 5, 2004, http://www.hainu.edu.cn/stm/zy_wuzhuangbu/2004519/1591.shtml.

53. See South China Normal University, "Military Strategy Research on Militias in Local Wars under Informationalized Conditions," May 17, 2011, http://www2.scnu.edu.cn/wzb/jslljxview.asp?id=90; and North China Institute of Aerospace Engineering, "Joint Efforts of the Military and Masses in Computer Systems Builds Cyber Militias," April 9, 2011. http://jpkc.nciae.edu.cn/dxjsj/shownews.asp?id=14.

54. Blasko, *The Chinese Army Today*, 29.

55. Dennis Blasko, "Chinese Strategic Thinking: People's War in the 21st Century," *China Brief*, 2010.

56. Krekel et al., *Capability of the People's Republic of China to Conduct Cyber Warfare*, 20–21.

57. Kunming Harbor, "Kunming Military Personnel and Civilians Develop a Series of Reports," August 28, 2011, http://www.km.gov.cn/structure/sylm/kmx-wxx_167826_1.htm.

58. Sinodefence.com, "PLA General Staff Department," August 24, 2008, accessed February 28, 2014, http://www.sinodefence.com/overview/organisation/gsd.asp.

59. Sinodefence.com, "PLA General Staff Department," August 24, 2008, http://www.sinodefence.com/overview/organisation/gsd.asp.

60. Jan Van Tol et al., "AirSea Battle: A Point-of-Departure Operational Concept," Center for Strategic and Budgetary Assessments, Washington, DC, April 1, 2010.

61. Krekel et al., *Capability of the People's Republic of China to Conduct Cyber Warfare*, 28–41.

62. Shambaugh, *Modernizing China's Military*, 175.

63. Rumors of successful network attacks on enemy air defense networks have surfaced periodically since the First Gulf War, perhaps most persuasively in the context of Israel's September 2007 air strike on the Syria's nascent nuclear reactor. More recently, the US military reportedly considered the use of a network attack on Libya's air defense systems at the outset of Operation Odyssey Dawn.

64. Blasko, *The Chinese Army Today*, 112.

65. Zhou and Wang, "Guiyang City to Actively Explore Joint Civil-Military Training Mechanism."

66. Information Office of the State Council, *China's National Defense in 2004*, chapter 5.

67. In addition to the topical areas for additional research identified above, the further study of information warfare calls for a complementary methodological approach: fieldwork. Although the authors were unable to travel China to conduct interviews for the purposes of this chapter, many of the unanswered questions could probably be answered through questioning both local government officials and militia members themselves. Here, the "civil" aspects of militia system (versus the strictly military nature of the PLA) bodes well for the prospects of outsiders obtaining real information.

68. Kathrin Hille, "Chinese Military Mobilises Cybermilitias," *Financial Times*, October 12, 2011.

69. Shijiazhuang Ministry of Commerce, "Information Warfare Unit Formed in Shijiazhuang City," September 29, 2005, http://shijiazhuang.mofcom.gov.cn/column/print.shtml?/gaikuang/200509/20050900484468.

70. US-China Economic and Security Review Commission, *Annual Report to Congress* (Washington, DC: Government Printing Office, 2010), 243–44.

71. David Barboza, "Berkeley Reveals Plan for Academic Center in China," *New York Times*, November 16, 2011. Although not treated here, a related concern is ties to Chinese universities conducting general CNO-related research. Prominent examples are listed in Krekel, Adams, and Bakos, *Occupying the Information High Ground*, 111–12.
72. Yang Hong, "Taiyuan, Shanxi Province Military Sub-district to Deepen Reform of the Urban Militia," *PLA Daily*, November 3, 2003.
73. The authors did not examine the extent to which the United States procures SCADA systems from Chinese firms, or the extent to which US or other foreign SCADA suppliers source their components or systems from China. This example is intended to be illustrative.

PART III
National Cybersecurity Policy

CHAPTER 9

China's Cybersecurity Situation and the Potential for International Cooperation

LI YUXIAO AND XU LU

China and the United States maintain an important and complex relationship that spans diplomatic, economic, and military spheres. Cyberspace cuts across all levels of the bilateral relationship, and it is important to understand both the new challenges it introduces as well as the opportunities to improve relations. As China's ambassador for disarmament affairs Wang Qun has said,

> Information and cyber networks have linked all of us closely together, making distance among countries a matter of microseconds in many cases. Let us work together to intensify our exchanges and cooperation in the field of information and cyberspace security and reach an early consensus on the Code [of Conduct] with the objective of building a peaceful, secure, and equitable information and cyber space.[1]

Today, cyberspace serves an important role in China's continued development efforts. Interconnecting basic infrastructures such as electric power, telecommunications, transportation, water supply, financial, disaster relief, education, and government service, cyberspace has become the fifth domain of human activity, joining land, sea, air, and outer space, and has an increasingly profound influence on every aspect of human life. Despite similarities in terms of technological production and allocation, cyberspace is very different from the other four domains. First, unlike its natural counterparts, the development of cyberspace as a domain is nearly completely free of time and space constraints. Furthermore, in the cyber domain, there are virtually no limitations on the distribution, transmission, and exchange of information. Technological innovation continues to overcome barriers in storage, bandwidth, and processing times. These unique characteristics require that cyberspace be treated with a newer and more comprehensive perspective in order to establish policies, legislation, and regulation.

Although cybersecurity awareness has increased over time, many countries still lack a comprehensive understanding of cybersecurity at the government, business, and social levels. The considerable degree of resistance to cooperation among countries leads to the persistence of various cybersecurity issues. The United States, where the Internet was developed, still holds major power with respect to Internet technology, while China has developed significant influence in the realm of Internet applications. Given the important roles these two countries play in the future of cyberspace development, promoting cooperation on cybersecurity is increasingly significant. As Chinese president Xi Jinping stated during the 2013 Sino-US summit, "China and the United States must find a new path, one that is different from the inevitable confrontation and conflict between the major countries of the past."[2] By discussing and analyzing current cybersecurity issues, this chapter explores the importance of Sino-US cooperation on cybersecurity and proposes recommendations to promote cooperation.

THE STATE OF CHINESE CYBERSPACE SECURITY

The development of the Internet in China has been rapid and comprehensive, not only in terms of numbers of users and network information resources, but also in terms of industrial development and foreign investment. By the end of June 2013, the number of Internet users (or netizens) in China reached 591 million with a total Internet penetration rate of 44.1%. At the same time, the number of mobile Internet users has reached 464 million and the annual growth rate has reached over 18%, surpassing that of the traditional Internet. In 2013, a "Broadband China" strategy was promoted to extend full rural and urban coverage by 2020, Chinese network infrastructure services were greatly enhanced, and a 3G network was finally deployed throughout the country.

The Internet has brought great changes to Chinese society. Expanded access has increased political openness and transparency, promoted economic growth, improved production efficiency and capacity, and changed traditional ways of thinking. Overall, the Internet has increased access to information and strengthened communication. However, alongside the unquestionable benefits brought by the rapid development of the Internet, cybersecurity has emerged as a daunting challenge. Through the joint efforts of government departments, Internet service providers, network security companies, and Internet users, the overall security of Chinese networks appears relatively stable. The level of basic network protection has gradually improved, resulting in fewer government website security events. But although the government has made progress on ensuring network security while increasing network speed, there is still a series of outstanding problems and threats.

In general, there is a lack of basic network protection capability in China, and there are myriad information security vulnerabilities. According to the National Computer Network Emergency Response Technical Team Coordination Center of China (CNCERT/CC), basic network operations ran smoothly in 2012, but loopholes in information security were still prevalent. Incidents of virus infections numbered about 4 million per month, most of which were botnets and worms. Manipulation of users, Trojan horses, implanted backdoors, and counterfeit websites represent the main threats to Chinese domestic websites. The 2013 data collected in the China National Vulnerability Database revealed 156 information security vulnerabilities; of these 32 were high-risk, and more than 140 of the vulnerabilities could be used to implement remote attacks.

On the whole, there are still significant threats to network security, and there have been frequent leaks of personal information in China.[3] Since network security protection measures are weak, mainland Chinese websites have a higher chance of being tampered with or hacked than in other countries. Website security issues lead to threats to personal information and data security. Major breaches of personal information have occurred on the China Software Developer Network (CSDN), Tianya, and other Chinese community websites. In 2011, twenty-six databases were suspected of having leaked personal information, involving 278 million accounts and passwords.[4] This was the largest information leakage in Chinese Internet history, as reported by the media. Publicity about incidents such as these has sparked widespread concern about threats to Internet users' right to privacy as well as Internet security itself. Meanwhile, instances of online banking phishing threats, malicious mobile device programs, applications with software vulnerabilities, Trojan horse attacks, and Distributed Denial of Service (DDoS) attacks are growing. The diversity of threats and rapidly evolving cybercrime technology, as well as the complex and volatile network environment which supports them, have had definite impacts on

Chinese network security. The 2012 Internet Security Report released by the company Qihu 360 shows that phishing fraud increased by 21.7% over 2011 and has become the main security threat faced by Chinese netizens.

Multiple factors contribute to these network security issues. At the national level, information insecurity has aided the development of a relatively mature cybercrime black market in China.[5] It is important to recognize that these activities are driven by economic interests, use a variety of technical means, and take advantage of the weak protection of personal identifiable information and network security.[6] Cybercriminals have organized an underground industrial chain with a clear division of roles and economic linkages. Through the use of a variety of illegal profit chains, cybercriminals reap large gains while endangering the security of Internet users' personal information. With the development and growth of the black market, cybercriminals have set up a large number of underground communities that facilitate the provision of illegal goods, as well as platforms for communication that serve as the backbone for the operation of the online underground economy.

At the international level, attacks on Chinese networks from foreign areas are severe. In the first half of 2013, according to the data reported by CNCERT, intrusions from nearly 28,000 different foreign IPs hit 7.8 million computers in China. Of those attacks, 24% originated in the United States, 17.2% in Japan, and 11.4% in South Korea. In June 2013, the *Guardian* and *Washington Post* newspapers exposed the PRISM secret surveillance program of the US National Security Agency (NSA) and the Federal Bureau of Investigation (FBI). According to documents leaked by NSA contractor Edward Snowden, the NSA invaded a Chinese telecommunications company to obtain mobile phone messages and repeatedly attacked the backbone network of Tsinghua University and computers of the telecommunications company Pacnet in their Hong Kong headquarters.[7] As we can see, the situation of cyberattacks from abroad has become even worse. Consequently, China continues to seek improvement in network security and prioritize its cyber defenses.

THE DEVELOPMENT OF CHINA'S CYBERSECURITY POLICY

In its early stages of network development, China invested heavily in Internet infrastructure. In just a dozen years, the popularity of the Internet has increased rapidly, and China has the largest number of users around the world. However, network security policies have not developed quickly enough to catch up. Until recently, society's enthusiasm for novel Internet applications has far outweighed concerns about security. After a series of network security incidents, especially the PRISM revelations, the Chinese government, enterprises, and Chinese citizens have gained an increased awareness of cybersecurity issues and have begun to take measures to improve the situation.

At the governmental level, the State Informatization Leading Group released its "View of National Informatization Leading Group on Strengthening Information Security Work" in 2003, a report that proposed some general overall requirements for network security.[8] During the fourth plenary session of the Sixteenth Central Committee in 2004, Chinese leaders proposed measures to enhance awareness of national security, improving national security strategy, effectively preventing and responding to a variety of risks and challenges, and ensuring the country's political, economic, cultural, and information security. As incidents have increased, the government has developed a new understanding of the importance of network security and has begun to speed up the development of cybersecurity policies and regulations. In 2012, for example, cybersecurity issues were discussed in the "Twelfth Five-Year National Strategic Development Plan on Emerging Industry," and they were also included in the five-year plans for the communications and Internet industries. On December 12, 2012, the Standing Committee of the National People's Congress passed its "Decision on the Strengthening of Network Information Protection," which established the basic principles of network information protection at the national level.[9] This policy decision reflects the Chinese government's awareness of the importance of the network information protection, and it is gradually beginning to take additional measures.

Since the Eighteenth National Congress of the Communist Party of China, China's new leadership has shown unprecedented attention to cyberspace security. During the Sino-US Summit held July 7–8, 2013, President Xi publicly said that the "Chinese government is committed to the maintenance of network security, and holds major concerns about network security." During this summit, leaders on both sides agreed to strengthen dialogue, coordination, and cooperation in the field of network security through the main channel of the United Nations in order to promote the establishment of a fair, democratic, and transparent international Internet administration mechanism and to build a peaceful, secure, open, and cooperative cyberspace. On November 15, 2013, the Third Plenary Session of the Eighteenth Committee of the Communist Party of China published "The Decision on Major Issues Concerning Comprehensively Deepening Reforms." In this important document, it was emphasized that China must "strengthen the governance of the Internet in accordance with the law, accelerate the improvement of the management system and leadership, and ensure the security of national networks and information." When discussing the decision right after it was announced, President Xi commented that "network and information security is related to national security and social stability. It is a new comprehensive challenge we face." He also outlined the disadvantages of the current management system, online media management, and industrial management.[10] On February, 28, 2014, the national Cybersecurity and Informatization Leading Group was formally established, with President Xi as group leader, and Politburo members Li Keqiang and Liu Yunshan as deputy group leaders, indicating that network security has risen to the highest national security strategy level.

At the enterprise level, it was not until the early 1990s that Chinese enterprises began to appreciate the threat posed by network viruses; even then, security measures were limited to internal administration systems. With the emergence of interconnected information technology infrastructures and the development of sophisticated network attack techniques, enterprise data loss became common. Many enterprises have gradually become aware of the impact of network security on their potential for survival. As a result, technology and management strategies are developing rapidly. These include virtual private networks, intrusion detection and prevention systems, encryption technology, identification, network access control systems, and employee behavior management.

At the academic research level, Chinese efforts toward increasing network security continue to develop. Scholars have begun to research technical regulations, as well as service standards, and their application to the legal system from the viewpoints of political, military, and social systems. Ma Minhu, a Chinese information security expert and director of the Institute of Information Security Governance and Law of Xi'an JiaoTong University, cites foreign legislative experiences and proposes the creation of legislation on network information security emergencies. Ma argues that China should strengthen legislation for the protection of network security through an information network security protection law, which should

> set prevention and mitigation of risks to safety and combating information and cyberspace criminal and terrorist activities as the main target, set establishing a mechanism of quick response as the core, set implementing security protection level engineering as the basic content, and set mobilization of social information from security service institutions as the regulatory strategy, in order to ensure the development of industrialization with informatization and achieve a great-leap-forward development on social productivity.[11]

Qi Aimin, an expert on information law and networking and e-commerce law, proposes the concept that personal information is not equivalent to individual privacy, and has called on China to enact specific personal information protection laws as soon as possible.[12]

DEFICIENCIES IN CHINESE CYBERSPACE SECURITY PROTECTION

When compared to the relatively high level of attention to cybersecurity realized by the United States, Chinese policy measures are not fully in place, and there is a lack of consistency in the guidelines and implementation of cybersecurity. Particularly, China has yet to establish national or international strategies on cyberspace, and it lacks systematic systems for decision-making, processes and standards for handling network security issues, and a clear network security coordination mechanism. Furthermore, China lacks Internet security personnel who are often unable to contend with the openness and flexibility of the Internet. These problems have resulted in the current environment of network security incidents.

Lags in the Development of Cybersecurity Technology

China did not start to research cybersecurity technology until 1994, which has resulted in a weak cybersecurity foundation. China's current information security system consists of passive defense measures and does not include active defense or integrated prevention technologies. China's information security system relies on firewalls, intrusion detection, and virus prevention. Conventional security on the network layer blocks unauthorized users from accessing the network to prevent attacks but does not issue controls on visitor sources and the information layer. The method for patching vulnerabilities relies on characteristics of known attacks and malware and other lagged information. With the evolving sophistication of malicious attacks, cybersecurity experts can only build stronger firewalls, more specified intrusion detection systems, and larger malicious code bases, which at a point could render the maintenance and management too hard and too complex to be feasibly implemented. Because of the continuously evolving technical sophistication of attacks, cybersecurity issues cannot be completely solved at a technical level.

The Chinese network is also vulnerable because China relies heavily on foreign countries for core network security technology, which ranges from computer hardware to network security products. Given this dependence on foreign core network technologies, Chinese networks remain vulnerable to potential subversion by foreign actors. According to national statistics, 80% of Chinese chips, high-end components, universal protocols, and standards depend on imports, and 65% of firewall, encryption machines, and other kinds of information security products are also imports. At present, attacks aimed at important information systems and industrial control networks continue to rise. The launch of network attacks could lead to the breakdown of important information and industrial control systems, which would seriously challenge China's economic development and industrial security.

In September 2012, the Ministry of Industry and Information Technology and the State Electricity Regulatory Commission claimed that Canada's RuggedCom grid equipment contained preset backdoors and required the Chinese electrical power sector to develop contingency plans and risk management to deal with potential problems posed by this technology.[13] To achieve security in the long run, China must domestically produce chip technology, operating systems, and cryptographic techniques with independent intellectual property. Only with these steps can China guarantee the real safety of national networks.

Lack of a Legal Foundation for Cybersecurity

Since 1994, China has promulgated a series of laws and regulations related to Internet governance, including the "National People's Congress Standing Committee's Decision on Safeguarding Internet Security," "Telecommunications Regulations of the People's Republic of China," "Internet Information Services Management Measures," "Computer Information System Security Protection Ordinance of the People's Republic of China," "Regulations on the Administration of Foreign-Invested Telecommunications," "International Networking of Computer Information Network Security Management Approach," "National People's Congress Standing Committee's Decision on Strengthen the Network Information Protection," and other rules.

Despite these laws and regulations, there are still problems regarding the construction of a legal framework. First, legal principles applicable to the new domain are underdeveloped. The law often applies the logic of jurisprudence from the physical world to cyberspace, which in many cases cannot be justified and is then poorly implemented. Second, network legislation lacks an overall plan, thus emergency, trailing, and local legislation are common to make up for the gap; departmental rules and regulations are often redundant and contradictory and have low legal enforceability. Third, network monitoring mainly focuses on precaution, which lays emphasis on approval procedures, not management. Different departments make different regulatory policies and implementation guidelines, which ignores the involvement of social parties. Fourth, cyber law resources are insufficient, nascent network rights are not recognized by law, and it is difficult to find applicable laws. Emphasis is laid on the responsibility of network service providers and Internet users; prohibitive norms are common and the protection of network rights is ineffective. Fifth, society has not established a trustworthy foundation of legal regulation. When it comes to the problem of lies and rumors on the Internet, it is hard for law enforcement to gather evidence and fully deal with the problem. Finally, the study of network law is weak, since it has yet to clarify the impact of the qualitative change of network characteristics on traditional law.

Problems at the Commercial Enterprise Level

While China's Internet enterprises are developing rapidly, their desire to maximize profit results in underinvestment in network security. The purchase and maintenance costs of network protection devices are high, as those devices require professional operators. Websites, particularly e-commerce websites, tend to trade off information security for system expansion to achieve faster growth. Insufficient investment in website security leads to severe vulnerabilities. Social websites and e-commerce websites generally do not disclose the leak of user information, and almost none of them publish actual security investment figures.[14]

Chinese enterprises exploit loopholes in personal information protection and treat user data as a kind of proprietary resource belonging to the enterprise. Enterprises often use the collected customer data for targeted advertising campaigns, or analyze consumer behaviors, particularly on online game and social networking websites, which hold the largest amount of customers' personal data. Moreover, some enterprises sell their customers' personal data for profit. According to industry estimates, 100 million game users' information is valued at more than 10 million yuan.[15] Even given these misuses, Internet users cannot revoke a registered account or guarantee that their information is deleted.

Challenges at the Societal Level

Due to a lack of systematic Internet security education, the Chinese public does not pay enough attention to protecting their privacy and personal data. In addition, the public lacks knowledge of network security protection technologies, methods, and standards. According to the survey data of iResearch, 68% of netizens said they would actively pay attention to network security. But in terms of knowledge about network security, only 52.6% of netizens had a clear understanding while the other 47.4% are unfamiliar with basic precautions.[16]

The security habits of netizens are risky. For example, Internet users often use the same user names and passwords for various website accounts or use weak passwords that do not provide sufficient protection. Once one password is leaked, other important accounts like online payment, e-mail, and chat accounts that share the same password become vulnerable, thereby causing much larger losses. Some netizens carry out network attacks or expose corruption or embarrassing details freely through "human flesh search" (人肉搜索), a form cyberbullying by an online crowd that insults other people's dignity and, more importantly, infringes on others' personal information security. The absence of sufficient regulation of cyberspace results in the proliferation of cybercrime.

Despite the many problems with cybersecurity, it is still possible to see some progress in increasing awareness of cybersecurity issues with respect to both the development of China's economic and information network as well as China's law and social development. As discussed in the previous section, top Chinese leaders are now making cybersecurity an important priority, so there should be more progress in this area in the future.

NETWORK SECURITY PROBLEMS BETWEEN CHINA AND THE UNITED STATES

The Sino-American relationship is one of the most important bilateral relationships in the world. Both countries play a leading role in major global issues such as peace and security, finance and trade, and the environment. Whether the two countries can achieve progress in cybersecurity cooperation will have great influence, not only on each country's national interests, but also on global network security as a whole. However, due to the lack of mutual trust and the inconsistency of network regulation mechanisms, thus far China and the United States have not had effective communication or cooperation with respect to cybersecurity issues.[17]

China and the United States suspect each other of committing major cyberattacks against their domestic networks. In reality, many of these attacks may originate from third-party hackers who abuse IPs in China and the United States in order to commit further attacks. When facing such attacks from third parties, both sides make judgments that might compromise the interests of the other due to the lack of mutual trust and communication mechanisms.

It appears that US concerns about China's threat to US cybersecurity are at an all-time high. A 2011 Office of the National Counterintelligence Executive report stated that China is the "most active and persistent" perpetrator of cyberattacks against the United States.[18] In its report "Strategy for Operating in Cyberspace" the US Department of Defense also named China as the source of network security threats, although without detailing specific evidence.[19] This kind of distrust in the field of cybersecurity has even spread to international trade. In 2008, Huawei attempted to purchase the American telecom company 3Com, but gave up due to the US government's "national security" concerns. In August 2010, eight US senators, all Republicans, wrote to President Barack Obama asking him to investigate Huawei's sale of equipment to an American telecom operator, Sprint Nextel, in order to evaluate a possible threat to national security. In the same year, Huawei again tried to purchase some American telecom enterprises like 3Com and the network equipment department of Motorola, but was impeded by similar security concerns.[20] On October 8, 2012, the US House of Representatives Intelligence Committee started an investigation against Huawei and ZTE because of their alleged ties to the Chinese military, which they claimed could have threatened US national security.[21]

At the same time, China names the United States as a source of its cyber insecurity because of cyberattacks originating in the United States.[22] China also feels insecure about US dominance in the field of global network infrastructure and its influence on network science and technology. For example, the entire Internet depends on thirteen root servers, most of which are managed by entities in the United States. We have already mentioned Edward Snowden's disclosure of NSA and FBI cyber espionage in China, which is a very serious concern. The government of China is also seriously concerned about the influence of companies like Microsoft and Oracle and is considering curtailing their use for government applications.

The first step after putting cybersecurity cooperation on the international agenda is to reconcile differences between Chinese and American terminology. China and the United States must reach a consensus on various terms involved in cybersecurity issues ranging from basic terms and concepts to highly technical aspects. Because the two countries lack a common vocabulary for key terms, they can take on different meanings in different political and cultural situations. Therefore, definitions and terminology are extremely important in policy discussions, as the actors may use in the same words but with completely different meanings.[23] In the China-US Track II Bilateral on Cybersecurity in 2013, the network working group had published a report titled "Frank Communication and Sensible Cooperation to Stem Harmful Hacking." In this report, some key concepts are defined, such as "hack," "hacker," and "compromise."[24] However, achieving consensus on these key concepts is not enough. A common, extensive vocabulary list should be built to strengthen future Sino-US dialogue and further joint research on cybersecurity, especially on what kind of "network attack" constitutes a "use of force" and what amounts to a "military attack." These issues should be discussed by both countries in earnest to build a consensus.

There is too much ambiguity in cybersecurity management mechanisms, and cooperation mechanisms are largely absent. Because of the sensitivity and ambiguity of cybersecurity, the two countries lack communication at the national level. Although there are many US government departments that are responsible for network security, the leads are the Department of Defense and the White House Cybersecurity Coordinator. As a leading department, the Department of Defense is able to organize, manage, and investigate cybersecurity issues. The Cybersecurity Coordinator ensures the coordination of the various departments in special periods, including the increasingly important Department of Homeland Security. In China, the departments involved in Internet security management are the State Internet and Information Office (also known as the Cyberspace Administration of China), the Ministry of Industry and Information Technology, the Ministry of Public Security, the Ministry of Foreign Affairs, and the military. However, there is no clear coordination mechanism for network security between these different agencies, nor is there an effective means of transnational communication when network security events occur. This internal ambiguity makes it difficult for the United States and China to cooperate reliably in every case.

THE ROLE OF NONGOVERNMENTAL ORGANIZATIONS

Although the United States and some other countries have benefited from the contributions of the Internet Corporation for Assigned Names and Numbers (ICANN) and other organizations in the development of Internet practices and other more technical rules, the scope of these contributions is still incomplete. Cyberspace will not be fully developed until people and countries all over the world are able to fully enjoy the benefits of the Internet. A safe, trustworthy, reliable network now extends beyond just technology and has become a common goal of human society. Narrowing the digital gap and enhancing national network literacy in every country has become an international concern and an important issue for international cooperation.

The establishment of common standards and norms requires the cooperation of all countries. The "virtual society" is closely linked with social reality, so it is inevitable for it to be associated with existing social organizational structures. It is necessary to rely on existing social norms while establishing new social rules for cyberspace. Therefore, in this field, all countries need to cooperate with each other; particularly, developed countries and countries with high Internet use should cooperate to allow cyberspace to truly become a platform for all of mankind's growth and development.

In addition, the healthy development of a networked society requires countries to carry out effective cooperation. Network security is a fundamental part of networked society and even an indispensable part of human development. People should try their best and fully use the limited funds and abilities they have to enhance their own capacity and to further develop human society. Thus network attacks should be strictly prohibited. Due to the increasing complexity of cyberspace, cybersecurity problems are becoming similarly complicated. For example, cybercrime is not limited by a country's border. One country's citizens can use servers in other countries to execute Internet fraud against a third country's residents. It is almost impossible to solve such cases without some basis for international cooperation. To build this foundation, it is necessary to strengthen the power of relevant international organizations and consider transferring necessary powers to those organizations to resolve these problems. However, the perception of what rights are fundamental ones differs between countries and thus serves as an obstacle to delegating authority to these organizations. It is possible to imagine a scenario where a cybercrime investigation violates a citizen's constitutional rights in one country, but not in another. This implies that international cooperation on cybersecurity may violate a country's sovereignty, so China and the United States must work together to determine how to the ensure rights and interests of all countries, while also promoting the security of their own networks.

The United States and China have strong complementary Internet technologies and applications that could form a huge testing ground for network attack and defense. The two countries should consider working together to carry out cooperation, experiments, and exchanges in academia, industry, and government to establish a long-term, effective mechanism for dialogue that faces the challenges of network security. Cooperation on network security will promote global informatization.

THE FORMATION OF A CONSENSUS ON THE BASIC LEVEL OF CYBERSECURITY

Differences in ideology and political system between the United States and China have resulted in different understandings of basic concepts of cybersecurity and have impeded effective communication and cooperation. Examples of issues that could be readily clarified include basic principles of bilateral communication on network security, the definition and recognition of network security hazards, the classification of cyberattacks, the definition and punishment of network crimes, and the understanding of network attacks that are unrelated to national security. Therefore, the United States and China should first establish effective academic communication in order to study these basic concepts of network security and reach a consensus on a set of terms suitable for the communication and decision-making process between the two governments.

Although cooperation on cybersecurity issues may not seem as vital as, say, nuclear disarmament negotiations, establishing a China-US cybersecurity communication mechanism is important to improve mutual trust and enhance research and defense capabilities. Chinese defense minister Liang Guanglie emphasized the importance of bilateral military ties and stated, "The two sides should, within the framework of building a China-US cooperative partnership, advance a new type of military tie featuring equality, reciprocity, and win-win cooperation in an active and pragmatic way."[25] Therefore, China and the United States should establish an agenda for cybersecurity cooperation and a complete multilevel communication mechanism, on both governmental and civilian levels. Exchanges at the civilian level, particularly between academic institutions, could smooth communication and cooperation between the two countries, as well as support the construction of a mechanism for a China-US cybersecurity dialogue.

First, China should establish a mechanism for cybersecurity coordination with the highest institutional authority, similar to the US National Cybersecurity Committee and the White House Cybersecurity Coordinator mechanism. This mechanism is necessary to ensure that cybersecurity events can be handled quickly, comprehensively, and effectively. At the same time, the cybersecurity communication channel for the government should be kept smooth in order to increase mutual trust between China and the United States.

Second, China and the United States should clarify basic principles and the basis for a bilateral cybersecurity communication. Within bilateral discussions, the two governments need to standardize the criteria for judgments of network attacks and set an approved attack state buffer zone. In this zone, agencies from both sides can conduct attack tests, but the bottom line and the limit should be set in advance in order to determine accurately whether the attacks are from each other or terrorist organizations.

Third, a long-term China-US civil communication mechanism should be established. For example, research institutions owning advanced technologies should assemble expert groups led by civil organizations to carry out regular academic discussions and exchanges. At present, China and the United States have launched a Sino-US nongovernmental level dialogue on network security, and published the "China-U.S. Anti-Hacking Report," in which they exchange ideas on current trends in network security and issues of cooperation and put forward specific, practical recommendations on how to build trust between China and the United States on cybersecurity in order to ensure the security of cyberspace together. In the future, we should also deepen nongovernmental-level dialogue. A mechanism through which civil organizations can share research results effectively should be established, so that these organizations can provide effective support to the government. Furthermore, a coordination mechanism between networking groups, nongovernmental organizations, and commercial organizations should be established to ensure that the results of their dialogue and research can be applied to enterprises and social organizations.

CONCLUSION

With the rapid development of cyberspace technology, information networks will play an increasingly significant role in the national economy and social development of China. The dependence of the government, culture, society, and national defense on these technologies increases every day. The importance of cyberspace to national and political security will continue to expand and the political and strategic position of cybersecurity will become increasingly evident.

Because of their ideological and institutional differences, there is wide divergence between China and the United States on basic concepts of cybersecurity. This divergence hinders communication between the two. The lack of a dialogue mechanism makes it difficult to establish mutual trust between the two countries in the field of network security, which has become a serious issue affecting China-US relations. The two countries should accelerate the establishment of China-US bilateral dialogue mechanisms on network security and build a set of common rules for the network society in order to promote the process of global informatization. In the meantime, issues like the protection of personal information, construction of a social credit system, and the boundaries between social public power and individual rights should be made clear. Together, China and the United States should carefully consider their changing social relationship, treat cyberspace as an ecosystem, and build common rules for the network society.

NOTES

1. "China Proposes 'Traffic Rules' for Information, Cyberspace Security," October 21, 2011, http://www.gov.cn/misc/2011-10/21/content_1975109.htm.
2. Quoted in Jackie Calmes and Steven Lee Myers, "U.S. and China Move Closer on North Korea, but Not on Cyberespionage," *New York Times*, June 8, 2013.
3. China Internet Network Information Center, 2013 年中国网民信息安全状况研究报告 [2013 Chinese Cyber Citizen Information Security Research Report], Beijing, September 2013.
4. Cha Rui and Guan Jian, "CSDN网站被曝用户信息泄露 600万用户邮箱密码被公开" [CSDN Website Was Exposed to Leak User Information; 6 Million Users' Passwords Were Disclosed], *Phoenix Online*, December 23, 2011; Liu Jia, "CSDN密码泄露事件升级互联网上亿用户信息 "裸奔"" [CSDN User Password Leakage Escalated; Millions of Internet Users' Information Got No Protection], China.com.cn, January 1, 2012.
5. See Zhuge et al., chapter 4 in this volume.
6. See Xu, chapter 10 in this volume.
7. "斯诺登：美国曾入侵中国电讯公司及清华主干网络" [Snowden: The United States Had Attacked Tsinghua Backbone Network], *Phoenix Online*, June 23, 2013.
8. General Office of the CPC Central Committee, 国家信息化领导小组关于加强信息安全保障工作的意见 [National Informatization Leading Group's Opinions on Strengthening Information Security], [2013] 27, Beijing, 2003.
9. Ministry of Industry and Information Technology of the People's Republic of China, "全国人民代表大会常务委员会关于加强网络信息保护的决定" [National People's Congress Standing Committee's Decision on Strengthening Network Information Protection], December 28, 2012.
10. "关于《中共中央关于全面深化改革若干重大问题的决定》的说明" [About "The CPC Central Committee's Decision on Deepening Reform on A Number of Major Issues"], *Sina News*, November 16, 2013.
11. Ma Minhu, "网络安全法律的困惑与对策" [Puzzles and Countermeasures in the Cyber Security Law], 中国人民公安大学学报(社会科学版) [*Journal of the Chinese People's Public Security University: Social Science Edition*], 2007/1.

12. Qi Qiangjun, Qi Aimin, Chen Kun, "论我国个人信息保护立法的权利基础" [Basis of Legislation of China's Personal Information Protection], 青海社会科学 [*Qinghai Social Science*], 2010/1.

13. State Electricity Regulatory Commission Shanxi Regulatory Office, 关于转发国家电监会"关于做好对存在预置后门风险的罗杰康产品防范应对工作的通知"的通知 [Forwarding SERC's Notification on Prevention and Responses to RuggedCom's Products with Potential Backdoor Risk], (2012) 136, Shanxi, September 28, 2012.

14. "用户资料泄密原因起底: 网站安全投入低" [Reasons of User Data Leakage: Low Investment in Website Security], 中国电子商务研究中心 [China e-Business Research Center], December 31, 2011.

15. Tang Xunfang, "安全支出不足1%: 互联网用户信息"裸奔"揭秘" [Less Than 1% in Security Spending: Revisited Protection of Internet User Information], iceo.com. cn, December 27, 2011.

16. iResearch, "2011年下半年个人网络安全报告" [2011 Second Half-Year Personal Internet Security Research], January 2012.

17. Kenneth G. Lieberthal and Peter W. Singer, *Cybersecurity and U.S.-China Relations* (Washington, DC: Brookings Institution, 2012).

18. US Department of Defense, "Strategy for Operating in Cyberspace," July 2011.

19. Ibid.

20. "美国会借口国家安全调查华为" [US Congress Uses National Security as an Excuse to Investigate Huawei], Xinhua Net, November 18, 2011.

21. Chen Yiming, "美国众议院认定华为中兴可能危害其国家安全" [US House of Representatives Found Huawei and ZTE Might Jeopardize Its National Security], *Phoenix Online*, October 8, 2012.

22. China Internet Network Information Center, "第30次中国互联网络发展状况调查统计报告" [Thirtieth China Internet Network Development Condition Investigation Statistics Report], Beijing, July 2012.

23. Jerry Brito and Tate Watkins, "Loving the Cyber Bomb: The Dangers of Threat Inflation in Cyber Policy," Mercatus Center Working Paper, April 2011.

24. "中美网络反黑客攻击报告在全球网络空间合作峰会上发布" [US-China Antihacker Attacks Report Published on the Global Cyberspace Cooperation Summit], 国家互联网应急中心 [The National Computer Network Emergency Response Technical Team Coordination Center of China], November 7, 2013.

25. "China Looks to Promote Military Ties with U.S.," GOV.cn, September 18, 2012.

CHAPTER 10

Evolving Legal Frameworks for Protecting the Right to Internet Privacy in China

XU JINGHONG

When discussing the Internet in China, most Western audiences only hear about espionage or Internet control portrayed by their media. They do not understand China's social and economic Internet challenges. Since the advent of the Internet, China has witnessed rapid development, and this has created many security and privacy problems for Chinese Internet users (netizens). To improve the security, reliability, and economic potential of its networks, China now also must improve Internet privacy. Generally speaking, Internet privacy is an important consideration in China's national cybersecurity situation.

On December 28, 2012, China's Standing Committee of the National People's Congress adopted its Decision on Strengthening Information Protection on Networks.[1] Its main purpose was to enhance the protection of online personal information and to safeguard the public interest. The Decision was an important milestone in Chinese law and the regulation of Internet privacy. To elucidate why the Congress took this step, this chapter argues that a recent Internet regulation represents a critical turning point in this effort of reconceptualization, in which "privacy" has been replaced by "information security." The chapter traces the historical and cultural background of Internet privacy in China, the evolving legal frameworks for protecting the right to privacy and Internet privacy, and problems with the existing legal framework, and will offer suggestions for improvement.

ORIGINS OF PRIVACY RIGHTS IN CHINA

In traditional Chinese society and culture, there is a notable absence of what those in the West (especially the United States) would describe as the "right to privacy." This does not mean, however, that the Chinese have no concept of a right to privacy. If we trace Chinese history in detail, we find that the Chinese people do care about the right to privacy, but they operate with a different understanding and definition than in the West, where privacy standards often seem to equate to the right to be left alone.[2]

The scholar He Daokuan has argued that the concept of collective family privacy is the key to understanding traditional Chinese culture.[3] Thus the Chinese concept of privacy is better explained as group privacy rather than individual privacy. Historically, Chinese notions about privacy have focused on shameful or embarrassing things and could involve safeguarding family secrets around indecent or unethical acts (such as rape or molestation). In traditional Chinese society the concept of privacy rights lacked a positive connotation, and this persisted even after the founding of the People's Republic of China (PRC) in 1949. Moreover, the implementation of a planned economic system after the founding of the PRC resulted in much government involvement in an individual citizen's "private" life, to the extent that the government played a role in providing employment and influencing marital decisions.[4]

Cardinal Guides and the Five Constant Virtues

According to Liang Zhiping, "In ancient Chinese society, we could not find a similar distinction between the public law and private law as in ancient Rome, but could only find the 'Single Standard'—Li—which governed almost everything and linked the family and the nation."[5] This link is manifested through three cardinal guides and the five constant virtues. The three cardinal guides are these: the ruler guides the subject, the father guides the son, and the husband guides the wife. The five constant virtues are benevolence, righteousness, propriety, knowledge, and sincerity. These concepts have had a strong influence on Chinese culture, creating a strict social hierarchy and limiting personal life.

Yang Kuo-Shu has noted that "Chinese familism constitutes the core of familistic orientation. In Chinese society, it is the family, rather than the individual, that is the basic structural and functional unit."[6] The Chinese concept of "public" and "private" is more about the relationship between the public and the family, and not so much between the public and the individual. Thus, as far as traditional Chinese understanding goes, the privacy of an individual is not as important as the privacy of the whole family, the latter being a special kind of group privacy or collective privacy for the entire family.

In ancient China, the respect and protection of the right to privacy mainly applied to the ruling class, and the violator of this privacy was cruelly punished. The first feudal legal code, the Book of Law, states that those who peep into the imperial palace should be punished by cutting their kneecaps and those who talk about royal affairs may be sentenced to death. The emperor, however, could arbitrarily gain access to the private affairs of others.[7]

Legal Roots

Progress toward a right to privacy was minimal until the middle of the twentieth century. Both the Civil Law Draft of the Qing Dynasty (completed in 1911) and the Civil Law Draft of the Republic of China (completed in 1925) contain a very general protection of the right to personality without any specific regulations about the right to privacy. The two drafts were not put into practice for complicated reasons. The first civil code in Chinese history, the Civil Law Code of the Republic of China, enacted between 1929 and 1932, contains the first reference to privacy rights in national law.[8] The idea was not strongly emphasized, as it was listed with many other rights. By the end of October 2010, however, there were twenty-two laws, fifteen administrative regulations, hundreds of departmental rules, and other normalizing documents of law that use the word yǐn sī (隐私, privacy).[9] In their analysis of these rules and laws, Zhou Hanhua and Su Miaohan concluded that after the foundation of the People's Republic of China, the legislative history of the right to privacy can approximately be divided into three periods.[10]

The first period was roughly from 1949 to 1981, when legislation used the word yīn sī (阴私, shameful or embarrassing private affairs) rather than yǐn sī (隐私, privacy). The first law was the Decision of the Standing Committee of the National People's Congress on Cases Not to Be Heard in Public (issued in 1956 and in effect until 1987), which was actually a reply to the question raised by the Supreme People's Court, What kind of cases could not be heard in public raised by the Supreme People's Court? The answer was "Cases involving state secrets, individual's shameful or embarrassing private affairs and crimes committed by minors younger than eighteen years may not be heard in public by People's courts." This provision set the core principle of legal privacy, which lasted to the early 1980s. Article 19 of the Criminal Procedure Law of the People's Republic of China and Article 7 of the Law of the People's Republic of China on the Organization of the People's Courts, both issued in 1979, use a similar definition of privacy.[11] Reinforcing this was the Preliminary Opinions of the Supreme People's Court on Judicial Openness according to Law in the People's Courts (issued in 1981), which defined the specific meaning of *yīn sī* as the following: "Generally speaking, cases involving individual's shameful or embarrassing private affairs refer to those involving sex behavior and humiliating women." The laws and regulations concerning the right to privacy of this period are strictly limited to the aspect of shameful or embarrassing private affairs, based on the strong historical and cultural traditions and influences noted earlier.

The second period was roughly from 1982 to 2002, during which *yǐn sī* began to appear and to gradually replace *yīn sī*. The Civil Procedure Law of the People's Republic of China for Trial Implementation issued in 1982 was the first law to use privacy. Its article 45 provides:

> With the permission of the people's court, the parties may consult the materials relating to the court proceedings of the case and may request that copies of the materials and other legal documents be made at their own expense. However, materials involving state secrets and individuals' privacy shall be exceptions.

During the first years of this period, the traditional *yīn sī* (shameful or embarrassing private affairs) and *yǐn sī* (privacy) were used at the same time when issuing new laws or amending old laws.[12] The main drivers of the switch to *yǐn sī* were China's reform and opening-up policy, cultural exchanges, and Chinese scholars' research on privacy. During the first period, there was sort of definition of *yīn sī* (shameful or embarrassing private affairs), but during the second period *yǐn sī* (privacy) was not well defined.

In the third period (from roughly 2003 to 2012), the idea of personal information began to appear in laws and regulations. The Law of the People's Republic of China on the Identity Card of Residents (issued in 2003) was the first law to use the word "personal information."[13] The Passport Law of the People's Republic of China (issued in 2006) has two articles using the concept of personal information.[14]

On December 28, 2012, the Standing Committee of the National People's Congress adopted the Decision on Strengthening Information Protection on Networks. To enhance the protection of online personal information and to safeguard the public interest, the decision goes even further by focusing on the protection of personal electronic information or online personal information. Thus, it is more accurate to say that a new fourth period has begun, from roughly 2012 to the present. The recent Internet regulation represents a critical turning point in this effort of reconceptualization, in which "privacy" is replaced by "information security," focusing more on information security or cybersecurity related to privacy.

In short, we can see a clear transition from protecting the ruler's right to privacy to protecting a citizen's shameful or embarrassing affairs to protecting the privacy of personal information, and now to ensuring the safety of online personal information.

INTERNET PRIVACY

As a result of the above-mentioned system, the Chinese people's expectation of privacy rights was minimal. Wang Liming's (1994) definitions of privacy and right to privacy are easily generalizable and share some common characteristics with American interpretations: "The right to privacy is a natural person's right of personality, which endows the natural person with the right to control his or her personal information, personal activities, and personal spaces that have nothing to do with the public interest."[15]

Considering this, there should be at least four basic forms of Internet privacy. First, privacy should include all kinds of private information of a natural person (including Internet users and nonusers) on the Internet. Second, an Internet user's online activities that have no bearing on the public interest should be considered private. Third, an Internet user's personal online spaces, which have nothing to do with the public interest, should be considered private. Finally, and most important, is the Internet user's autonomous right to his or her online personal information. The last piece includes the right to know how his or her personal information is being collected, the right to revise his or her personal information, the right to ask for the security of his or her personal information, the right to benefit from his or her personal information, and the right to select and decide how his or her personal information is used.[16]

As the right to Internet privacy is the newest form of the right to privacy, it is understandable that Chinese Internet users usually care little about it. According to the Fifteenth Statistical Report on Internet Development in China issued in 2005 by China Internet Network Information Center

(CNNIC), 3.7% of Internet users strongly agreed that it is easy to expose a user's privacy information when surfing the Internet, 23.2% somewhat agreed, 15.2% half disagreed and half agreed, 45.2% somewhat disagreed, and 12.5% strongly disagreed; of non-Internet users, 9.4% strongly agreed, 18.6% somewhat agreed, 10.2% half disagreed and half agreed, 38.1% somewhat disagreed, and 23.7% strongly disagreed.[17] The strong disagreement reflects a poor understanding of the risks to information on the Internet. According to the Seventeenth Statistical Report issued in 2006 by CNNIC, with regard to the same viewpoint, 5% of interviewees (including both Internet users and nonusers) strongly agreed, 32% somewhat agreed, 11% half agreed and half disagreed, 33% somewhat disagreed, 6% strongly disagreed, and 15% had no idea.[18] Both reports showed that most Internet users and non-Internet users do not think that it is easy to expose a user's privacy information while surfing the Internet.

According to the 2012 Research Report on Chinese Netizens' Usage of Social Networking Sites, more than 62% of users expressed trust in the way social networking sites secure their personal information even after the large-scale leakage of users' information at the end of 2011. It should not be inferred that social networking sites have done very well in protecting their user's privacy, but rather that the users care little about the related information security issue.[19]

THE PRESENT LEGAL FRAMEWORK FOR PROTECTING THE RIGHT TO INTERNET PRIVACY

By the end of April 2013, China had twenty-seven laws, eleven administrative regulations, and more than four hundred departmental rules and other normative documents of law that use the term "personal information." The main reason for the inclusion of "personal information" under privacy law is informationization and the advent of the Internet. During this period, *yīn sī* (shameful or embarrassing private affairs) has been completely replaced by either *yǐn sī* (privacy) or "personal information" in the laws and regulations. Most of the time, "privacy" and "personal information" are regarded as the same and are used interchangeably.

Since privacy rights on the Internet are an extension of standard privacy rights, all laws and regulations protecting privacy rights should apply equally. Although the laws and regulations pertaining to privacy rights are too numerous to list separately, they can be described by two distinct categories: laws protecting standard privacy rights and the laws that directly protect privacy rights on the Internet.[20] Generally speaking, many Chinese laws and regulations such as the Constitution of the People's Republic of China, General Principles of the Civil Law of the People's Republic of China, and Criminal Law of the People's Republic of China, have articles that protect the right to privacy. Amendment (VII) to the Criminal Law of the People's Republic of China and the Decision on Strengthening Online Information Protection, among others, have articles directly protecting the right to privacy on the Internet.

The Constitution of the People's Republic of China

Articles 39 and 40, and even article 38, of the constitution can be interpreted as protecting the right to privacy. Article 38 states that the personal dignity of citizens of the People's Republic of China is inviolable.[21] As Zhang Xinbao has pointed out, the personal dignity of citizens is a very basic and broad category that includes not only reputation, but also name, likeness, and privacy.[22] Article 39 prohibits two kinds of activities that infringe on privacy rights—unlawful search of and intrusion into a citizen's residence.[23] Article 40 protects two aspects of correspondence of citizens—both the freedom and the privacy of correspondence of citizens.[24]

Chinese Civil Law

In the civil law system, the General Principles of the Civil Law of the People's Republic of China (issued in 1986 and revised in 2009) and the Tort Law of the People's Republic of China (issued in 2009 and effective in 2010) have important implications for privacy rights. Article 101 of General Principles of the Civil Law of the People's Republic of China does not clearly define the right to privacy as a concrete principle, but in juridical practices, the right to privacy has been protected indirectly by expanding the explanation of the right of reputation.[25] Several articles of the Tort Law of the People's Republic of China protect the right to privacy, and it was the first law to use the phrase "the right to privacy" in mainland China.[26]

The Criminal Law of the People's Republic of China

Articles 245, 252, 253, and 284 criminalized the illegal search of a person and intrusion into his residence, infringement upon the citizen's right of communication freedom, postal workers opening, hiding, or destroying mail or telegrams without authorization, and the use of special monitoring or photographing equipment and causing grave consequences respectively.[27] All the crimes are related to infringing on the right to privacy. Amendment (VII) to the Criminal Law of the People's Republic of China (issued in 2009) criminalized the acquisition and sale of citizens' personal information.

Chinese Procedure Law

Chinese Procedure Law can be divided into three categories: Civil Procedure Law, Criminal Procedure Law, and Administrative Procedure Law. The Civil Procedure Law of the People's Republic of China (issued in 1991 and revised in 2007 and 2012) has several articles mainly stating that the facts of certain cases and evidence should not be made public.[28] The Criminal Procedure Law of the People's Republic of China (issued in 1979 and revised in 1996 and 2012) provides several conditions when evidence and parties involving individual's privacy shall be kept confidential.[29] The Administrative Procedure Law of the People's Republic of China (1989) also contains two articles protecting the right to privacy.[30]

Chinese Administrative Law

The People's Police Law of the People's Republic of China (issued in 1995 and revised in 2012) contains two articles protecting the right to privacy.[31] Article 42 of the Law of the People's Republic of China on Administrative Penalty (issued in 1996) states that hearings involving private affairs shall be kept confidential.[32] The Administrative Reconsideration Law of the People's Republic of China (issued in 1999 and revised in 2009) provides that the administrative organ for reconsideration (appeal) may refuse a request to view a judgment as written or the evidence, grounds, and other relevant materials that involve individual private affairs.[33] Several articles of the Regulation of the People's Republic of China on the Disclosure of Government Information (issued in 2007) also provide the conditions for disclosing government information involving individual privacy.[34]

Local Rules and Regulations

In China, provinces, autonomous regions, and municipalities have some rules and regulations protecting the right to privacy. For example, the

Regulation of Shanghai City on the Protection of Consumer Rights and Interests (issued in 2002) has two articles protecting consumers' right to privacy in their purchases, use of commodities, or receipt of services.[35] Provisions of Anhui Province on Prohibiting the Identification of the Gender of a Fetus and Aborting a Pregnancy Based on the Gender of a Fetus without Medical Needs (issued in 2000 and revised in 2004) also protect the privacy of the parties concerned.[36]

EXPLAINING INTERNET PRIVACY DEVELOPMENTS

The enactment of the Decision of the Standing Committee of the National People's Congress on Strengthening Online Information Protection illustrates the considerable progress that has been made in China's legal protection of Internet privacy. Before that, China lagged far behind the United States and the European Union in the protection of Internet privacy rights. The newly enacted Decision brought China to the forefront as one of the few countries with a specific legal protection for citizen's Internet privacy and online information. Furthermore, there is a growing body of jurisprudence encouraging the Chinese people to rely on laws to protect their right to Internet privacy.

Among them, the first case of the right to Internet privacy and the first case of "human flesh search" (the use of the Internet to find embarrassing information about a person and harass them) are the most well-known cases in China. On April 9, 1996, graduate student Xue Yange at Peking University received an e-mail from University of Michigan, telling her that she would be granted a full scholarship of USD 18,000. She was very happy and waited for the formal notification. But on April 12, 1996, University of Michigan received an e-mail in her name that she would decline the grant because she had already accepted an invitation from another university. Later she found out that the imposter was her classmate and roommate, with whom she had shared the e-mail from University of Michigan. In the end, the two came to an accommodation with the help of court mediation, and Xue received compensation of RMB 12,000. The first case of human flesh search began at the end of 2007, when Jiang Yan wrote a death blog and committed suicide. Her friend Zhang Leyi published an online condemnation of her unfaithful husband Wang Fei, containing his personal information. Angry netizens searched out Wang Fei's personal information and his lover's personal information and made it public, which forced them both to quit their jobs. Some netizens insulted him online and some even went to his house to harass him and his parents. Later he accused his wife's friend Zhang Leyi and three websites, and he won the case.

There are several factors that impelled China to speed up its protection of Internet privacy and personal electronic information. First, e-commerce is developing very rapidly in China, accounting for 4.5 trillion yuan in 2010.[37] The development of this market demands the quick establishment of related laws and regulations, including those that protect Internet privacy. Second, with the rapid development of Internet technologies and applications have come increased instances of online fraud, online disclosure of personal information, selling citizen's personal information, and spam.

Third, Internet service providers and the Internet industry seldom self-regulate concerning protection of personal information. An analysis of five online privacy statements revealed that these statements imposed virtually no restrictions on how these websites could collect and use netizens' information for their own profit. Instead, they tricked users into offering more personal information.[38] For instance, the heated battle between China's two top Internet firms, Tencent QQ and Qihoo 360, triggered a public outcry in 2010 when they accused each other of spying, hacking, and leaking users' private information, affecting thousands of users. The event demonstrated that without effective legislation Internet firms completely ignore the right to Internet privacy. The battle lasted from 2010 to 2012 and China's Ministry of Industry and Information Technology (MIIT), Ministry of Public Security, and the Internet Society of China had to intervene. At the beginning of 2011, MIIT unveiled on its website two draft regulations that were intended to deter unfair competition on the Internet, and solicited feedback from the public. The Decision of the Standing Committee of the National People's Congress on Strengthening Online Information Protection is, to some extent, based on the two draft regulations.

Fourth, the behavior of individual employees of industries who collect citizens' personal information can infringe upon the privacy of users' electronic information. According to Haidian District Procuratorate of Beijing City, an analysis of thirty-one cases handled in 2010 concluded that industries such as automobile sales, estate agents, banks, telecommunications, and hospitals and their employees have access to and collect huge amounts of citizens' personal information. These industries tend to be the source of leaks of citizens' personal information because they lack a system to protect citizens' personal information and monitor the behavior of their employees.[39]

CONCLUSION: CHALLENGES FOR INTERNET PRIVACY

Despite the progress made to date, the protection of Internet privacy and online information in China still faces problems. First, laws and regulations protecting the right to Internet privacy are too general and do not define the specific contents of citizen's personal electronic information. The laws also do not specify governing institutions and their specific duties and functions in enforcing the regulations. All these need to be explored and provided in detail in the future.

Second, among the three core concepts, *yīn sī* (shameful or embarrassing private affairs), *yǐn sī* (privacy), and "personal information," only *yīn sī* has been explained in detail by national laws. The other two more important, but difficult to explain, concepts are ignored or are defined differently in different laws and regulations. More research must be done to define and distinguish between concepts such as personal electronic information, online personal information, online personalized information data, online personal privacy data, online personal data, online information privacy, and online personal data.

Third, hundreds of laws and regulations have been enacted to protect the right to online privacy, but they are quite unsystematic and hard to put into practice. Future amendments to constitutional law, civil law, criminal law, procedure law, and administrative law, rules of the departments under the State Council, and local laws and regulations should strengthen the protection of the right to online privacy. For example, the right to privacy should be included in the Constitution of the People's Republic of China. The right to privacy should be protected separately as an independent right to personality, and the ways of infringing the right to privacy and their specific responsibility and liability should be clearly provided in civil law. The crime of infringing on privacy rights and the specific punishments for different kinds of infringements should be clearly defined in criminal law without using the ambiguous typical qualification: "if the case is serious." In administrative law, special provisions should be enacted for the organs of power to protect the right to Internet privacy.

Fourth, exchange and cooperation should be strengthened. At present, the United States and the European Union cooperate in the field of protecting privacy rights and the transborder flow of personal data, while China lags behind. It is more practical for Mainland China to cooperate first with Hong Kong and Taiwan and then with the European Union and United States.

APPENDIX: DECISION OF THE STANDING COMMITTEE OF THE NATIONAL PEOPLE'S CONGRESS ON STRENGTHENING INFORMATION PROTECTION ON NETWORKS

(Adopted at the Thirtieth Session of the Standing Committee of the Eleventh National People's Congress on December 28, 2012.)

To protect the information security on networks, maintain the lawful rights and interests of citizens, legal persons and other organizations, and safeguard the national security and public interest, this Decision is made as follows:

I. The state protects electronic information by which individual citizens can be identified and which involves the individual privacy of citizens. All organizations and individuals may not obtain electronic personal information of citizens by theft or any other illegal means and may not sell or illegally provide others with electronic personal information of citizens.

II. Network service providers and other enterprises and institutions shall, when gathering and using electronic personal information of citizens in business activities, adhere to the principles of legality, rationality and necessarily, explicitly state the purposes, manners and scopes of collecting and using information, and obtain the consent of those from whom information is collected, and shall not collect and use information in violation of laws and regulations and the agreement between both sides. Network service providers and other enterprises and institutions shall, when gathering and using electronic personal information of citizens, publish their collection and use rules.

III. Network service providers and other enterprises and institutions and their personnel must strictly keep confidential and may not divulge, alter, damage, sell, or illegally provide others with the electronic personal information of citizens gathered in business activities.

IV. Network service providers and other enterprises and institutions shall take technical measures and other necessary measures to ensure information security and prevent electronic personal information of citizens gathered in their business activities from being divulged, damaged or lost. When any information divulgence, damage or loss occurs or may occur, remedial actions shall be taken immediately.

V. Network service providers shall strengthen management of information released by their users and, when discovering any information prohibited by laws and regulations from being released or transmitted, immediately stop the transmission of such information, take elimination and other handling measures, preserve relevant records, and report to the relevant competent authorities.

VI. Network service providers which provide the website access service for users, handle landline or mobile phone network access procedures for users or provide the information publishing service for users shall, when signing agreements with users or confirming the provision of services, require users to provide their true identity information.

VII. No organizations and individuals may, without the consent of or the request from the recipients of electronic information or with an explicit refusal from the recipients of electronic information, send commercial electronic information to their landline or mobile phones or personal e-mail boxes.

VIII. Citizens who discover any network information divulging their personal identities, disseminating their individual privacy or otherwise infringing upon their lawful rights and interests or who are annoyed by unwanted commercial electronic information shall have the right to require network service providers to delete relevant information or take other necessary prohibitive measures.

IX. All organizations and individuals shall have the right to report or allege any theft, obtainment by other illegal means, sale, or illegal provision to others of electronic personal information of citizens and other violations of law and crimes involving information on networks to the relevant competent authorities; the authorities receiving such reports or allegations shall handle them in a timely manner as legally required. The victims of infringement may file lawsuits in accordance with law.

X. The relevant competent authorities shall perform duties within the scope of their respective functions in accordance with law and take technical measures and other necessary measures to prevent, stop, investigate and punish theft, obtainment by other illegal means, sale, or illegal provision to others of electronic personal information of citizens and other violations of law and crimes involving information on networks. When the relevant competent authorities perform duties in accordance with law, network service providers shall provide cooperation and technical support. State organs and their personnel shall keep confidential the electronic personal information of citizens known in their performance of duties and may not divulge, alter, damage, sell, or illegally provide others with such information.

XI. For violations of this Decision, punishment shall be imposed in accordance with law, such as warning, fine, confiscation of illegal income, license forfeiture or cancellation of recordation, closure of website, or prohibition of relevant liable persons from engaging in network services, which shall be recorded into the violators' social credit files and disclosed to the public; if the public security administration is violated, public security administration punishment shall be imposed in accordance with law. Those suspected of a crime shall be punished in accordance with law. Those infringing upon the civil rights and interests of others shall assume civil liability in accordance with law.

XII. This Decision shall come into force on the date of issuance.

NOTES

1. See the appendix for the text of the entire decision, translated by the database pkulaw.cn.
2. Samuel D. Warren and Louis D. Brandeis, "The Right to Privacy," *Harvard Law Review* 4, no. 5 (1890): 193–220.
3. He Daokuan, "On the Chinese Concept of Privacy," *Journal of Shenzhen University (Humanities and Social Sciences)* 13, no. 4 (1996): 83 [in Chinese].
4. Wang Xiuzhe, *Constitutional Protection of the Right to Privacy* [in Chinese] (Beijing: Social Sciences Academic Press, 2007), 229.
5. Liang Zhiping, *Seeking the Harmony of Natural Order: Chinese Traditional Legal Culture Study* [in Chinese] (Beijing: China University of Political Science and Law Press, 1997), 19.
6. Kuo-Shu Yang, "Chinese Social Orientation: An Integrative Analysis," in *Chinese Societies and Mental Health*, ed. Tsung-Yi Lin, Wen-Shing Tseng, and Eng-Kung Yeh (Hong Kong: Oxford University Press, 1995), 22.
7. Xu Xianming, "Personal and Personality Rights," in *Comparative Study of Constitutions* [in Chinese], ed. Buyun Li (Beijing: Law Press, 1998), 486.
8. Article 195 on compensation for non-property damages to body, health, reputation, or freedom provides that " . . . if the victim is illegally injured regarding his or her right to body, right to health, right to reputation, right to freedom, right to credit, right to privacy, right to chastity or any other legal interests and rights of personality with serious consequences, the victim shall have the right to demand a certain amount of money as compensation even if he or she hasn't suffered property loss. When his or her reputation is infringed upon, the victim shall have the right to demand that his reputation be rehabilitated with certain appropriate punishments."
9. Zhou Hanhua, "Analyzing the Related Legal Problems of 360 Privacy-Protector and QQ Bodyguard [in Chinese]," http://www.iolaw.org.cn/showArticle.asp?id=2766.
10. Zhou Hanhua and Su Miaohan, "Sixty Years of Constructing Chinese Informationization Laws and Regulations," *E-Government*, no. 10 (2009): 53–54 [in Chinese].

11. Article 19 provides that "Cases of first instance in a people's court shall be heard in public. However, cases involving state secrets or individual's shameful or embarrassing private affairs shall not be heard in public. No cases involving crimes committed by minors who have reached the age of 14 but not the age of 16 shall be heard in public. Generally, cases involving crimes committed by minors who have reached the age of 16 but not the age of 18 shall also not be heard in public. The reason for not hearing a case in public shall be announced in court." Article 7 provides that "All cases in the people's courts shall be heard in public, except for those involving state secrets, individual's shameful or embarrassing private affairs and the crimes committed by minors."

12. For example, when the Law of the People's Republic of China on the Organization of the People's Courts was revised in 1983, its Article 7 remained the same and kept *yīn sī* (shameful or embarrassing private affairs). Until its 1986 revision, the law changed and began to use *yǐn sī* (privacy).

13. Article 6 provides: "The personal information of the citizens learnt of by the public security organs and the people's policemen in the course of making, issuing, checking and detaining of the identity cards shall be kept confidential." Article 19 provides that "a policeman who infringes upon the legal rights and interests of the citizens to disclose the personal information of the citizens learnt of in the course of the making, issuing, checking, and detaining of the identity cards, shall be given an administrative sanction in accordance with the law according to the circumstances; if a crime is constituted, he shall be prosecuted for criminal responsibilities."

14. Article 12 provides: "The passport issuance departments and their functionaries shall keep confidential citizens' personal information they know or have access to due to making or issuing passports." Article 20 provides: "Any functionary of a passport issuance department impairing the legitimate rights and interests of any citizen due to divulging the personal information of the citizen which he knows or has access to in the course of making or issuing a passport during the process of handling the affairs relating to passports-related matter, he shall be given an administrative sanction. If any crime is constituted, he shall be subject to criminal liabilities."

15. Wang Liming, *New Discussion on Right to Personality Law* [in Chinese] (Changchun: Jilin People's Publishing House, 1994), 487.

16. Xu Jinghong, *The Right to Privacy and Its Protection during the Course of Internet Communication* [in Chinese] (Beijing: Beijing Yanshan Press, 2010), 15.

17. CNNIC, "Fifteenth Statistical Report on Internet Development in China," http://www.cnnic.cn/hlwfzyj/hlwxzbg/hlwtjbg/201206/P020120612484930004462.pdf.

18. CNNIC, "Seventeenth Statistical Report on Internet Development in China," http://www.cnnic.cn/hlwfzyj/hlwxzbg/hlwtjbg/201206/P020120612484933207194.pdf.

19. CNNIC, "2012 Research Report on Chinese Netizens' Usage of Social Networking Sites," http://www.cnnic.net.cn/hlwfzyj/hlwxzbg/mtbg/201302/P020130219611651054576.pdf.

20. Xu, *The Right to Privacy*, 195–211.

21. Article 38 provides: "The personal dignity of citizens of the People's Republic of China is inviolable. Insult, libel, false accusation, or false incrimination directed against citizens by any means is prohibited."

22. Zhang Xinbao, *The Law of Torts in China,* 2nd ed. [in Chinese] (Beijing: China Social Sciences Press, 1998), 365.

23. Article 39 provides: "The residences of citizens of the People's Republic of China are inviolable. Unlawful search of, or intrusion into, a citizen's residence is prohibited."

24. Article 40 provides: "Freedom and privacy of correspondence of citizens of the People's Republic of China are protected by law. No organization or individual may, on any ground, infringe upon citizens' freedom and privacy of correspondence, except in cases where, to meet the needs of state security or of criminal investigation, public security or procuratorial organs are permitted to censor correspondence in accordance with procedures prescribed by law."

25. Article 101 provides: "Citizens and legal persons shall enjoy the right of reputation. The personality of citizens shall be protected by law, and the use of insults, libel, or other means to damage the reputation of citizens or legal persons shall be prohibited."

26. Article 2 provides: "Those who infringe upon civil rights and interests shall be subject to the tort liability according to this Law. 'Civil rights and interests' used in this Law shall include the right to life, the right to health, the right to name, the right to reputation, the right to honor, right to self image, right of privacy, marital autonomy, guardianship, ownership, usufruct, security interest, copyright, patent right, exclusive right to use a trademark, right to discovery, equities, right of succession, and other personal and property rights and interests." Article 62 provides: "A medical institution and its medical staff shall keep confidential the privacy of a patient. If any privacy data of a patient is divulged or any of the medical history data of a patient is open to the public without the consent of the patient, causing any harm to the patient, the medial institution shall assume the tort liability."

27. Article 245 provides: "Those illegally physically searching others or illegally searching others' residences, or those illegally intruding into others' residences, are to be sentenced to three years or fewer in prison, or put under criminal detention.

Judicial workers committing crimes stipulated in the above paragraph by abusing their authority are to be severely punished."

Article 252 provides: "Those infringing upon the citizen's right of communication freedom by hiding, destroying, or illegally opening others' letters, if the case is serious, are to be sentenced to one year or less in prison or put under criminal detention." Article 253 provides: "Postal workers who open, hide, or destroy mail or telegrams without authorization are to be sentenced to two years or less in prison or put under criminal detention. Those committing crimes stipulated in the above paragraph and stealing money or other articles are to be convicted and severely punished according to article 264 of this law." Article 284 provides: "Whoever illegally uses special monitoring or photographing equipment and causes grave consequences is to be sentenced to not more than two years of fixed-term imprisonment, criminal detention, or control."

28. Article 68 provides: "Evidence that involves state secrets, trade secrets, or individual privacy shall not be presented in an open court session." Article 134 provides: "Civil cases adjudicated by people's courts shall usually be heard publicly, except for the cases that involve state secrets or the private affairs of individuals, or are otherwise provided by law. A divorce case or a case involving trade secrets may not be heard publicly if a party so requests." Article 156 provides: "The public may consult legally effective written judgments and verdicts, except for those judgments and verdicts that involve state secrets, trade secrets or the private affairs of individuals."

29. Article 52 provides: "Evidence involving state secrets, trade secrets or individual's privacy shall be kept confidential." Article 109 provides: "If the informant, complainant or accuser wishes to remain anonymous and keep his informing, complaining and accusing action secret, his name and action shall be kept confidential." Article 118 provides: "The defendant shall answer the investigatory personnel's questions truthfully, but he shall have the right to refuse to answer any questions that are irrelevant to the case." Article 153 provides: "State secrets, trade secrets or the private affairs of individuals obtained during the course of technical investigation by investigator personnel shall be kept confidential; information obtained during the course of technical investigation but irrelevant to the case should be destroyed timely; information obtained during the course of technical investigation should only be used for investigation, prosecution and trial and should not be used for any other purposes; while public security organs taking technical investigation measures, the units and individuals concerned should cooperate in the action and should keep the related information confidential." Article 183 provides: "Cases of first instance in a People's Court shall be heard in public. However, cases involving State secrets or private affairs of individuals shall not be heard in public."

30. Article 30 provides: "A lawyer who serves as an agent ad litem may consult materials pertaining to the case in accordance with relevant provisions, and may also investigate among and collect evidence from the organizations and citizens concerned. If the information involves state secrets or the private affairs of individuals, he shall keep it confidential in accordance with relevant provisions of the law. With the approval of the people's court, parties and other agents ad litem may consult the materials relating to the court proceedings of the case, except those that involve state secrets or the private affairs of individuals." Article 45 provides: "Administrative cases in the people's courts shall be tried in public, except for those that involve state secrets or the private affairs of individuals or are otherwise provided for by law."

31. Article 22 provides: "People's policemen may not commit any of the following acts: . . . (5) to unlawfully deprive other people of, or restrict, their freedom of the person, or illegally search a person, his or her belongings, residence or place." Article 48 provides: "A people's policeman who commits any of the acts specified in Article 22 of this Law shall be given an administrative sanction; if a crime is constituted, he shall be investigated for criminal responsibility according to law."

32. Article 42 provides: "(3) The hearing shall be held openly, except where State secrets, business secrets, or private affairs are involved."

33. Article 23 provides: "The applicant and the third party may consult the reply as written and the evidence, grounds, and other relevant materials, on the basis of which the specific administrative act has been undertaken, and the administrative reconsideration organ shall not refuse the requirement except that those involve State secrets, business secrets, or the private affairs of individuals."

34. Article 14 provides: "No administrative organ may disclose any government information involving state secrets, commercial secrets or individual privacy. But in case the obligee approves or the administrative organ believes that the failure to disclose such information would result in great influence on public interests, such government information may be disclosed." Article 23 provides: "Where an administrative organ believes that the government information applied to be disclosed involves any business secret or individual privacy and that its disclosure may damage the legal rights and interests of a third party, the organ shall solicit the third

party's opinion in written form; if the third party disagrees with the disclosure, the organ may not disclose such information, unless it believes that failure to disclose such information would exert great influence on public interests, and under such circumstance, the organ shall notify the third party of the content of the government information to be disclosed and the corresponding reasons in written form." Article 25 provides: "A citizen, legal person, or any other organization applying to the administrative organ for providing the government information related to his/its tax payment, social security, medical care and health, etc., shall produce his/its valid identity certificate or evidentiary documents. Where a citizen, legal person, or any other organization has evidence to prove that the related government information provided by the administrative organ is inaccurate, he/it is entitled to request the administrative organ to correct. If the administrative organ has no right to correct such information, it shall transfer it to the administrative organ entitled to correct and notify the applicant of the situation."

35. Article 14 provides: "Consumers shall, in their purchasing and using commodities or receiving services, have the right to demand compensations from the operator in accordance with the law if their such personal rights as right to life and health, right of name, right of portrait, right of reputation, right to honor right of privacy, etc.—are infringed upon." Article 29 provides: "The operators should not, in providing commodities or services, ask the consumers to provide personal information that is irrelevant to their consuming; the operators should not, under any pretext, disclose consumers' personal information to any third party without the consent of the consumers, except where otherwise provided for in laws or regulations.

 The aforesaid personal information in this article includes consumers' name, sex, occupation, education, contact information, marital status, income and property status, finger print, blood type, medical history, etc., which is closely related to consumer and his family."

36. Article 29 provides: "The working body of Family Planning and authorized operating institution should protect the privacy of the parties concerned in accordance with law."

37. "E-commerce Development in China," http://www.askci.com/news/201203/28/174919_81.shtml.

38. Xu Jinghong, "Undermining the Real Functions of Online Privacy Statements: Text Analysis of Five Online Privacy Statements," *Contemporary Communications*, no. 6 (2008): 67–70 [in Chinese].

39. Economic Information, "How to Seize the Evil Backstage Manipulators Who Leak Our Personal Information?" http://news.xinhuanet.com/politics/2011-06/20/c_121556359_6.htm.

CHAPTER 11

"Foreign Hostile Forces"

The Human Rights Dimension of China's
Cyber Campaigns

SARAH MCKUNE

In July 2012, the international community took a crucial step toward recognizing the importance of human rights in the online environment. The United Nations (UN) Human Rights Council adopted by consensus a resolution "affirm[ing] that the same rights that people have offline must also be protected online, in particular freedom of expression, which is applicable regardless of frontiers and through any media of one's choice."[1] The resolution, which China did not oppose, also "call[ed] upon all States to promote and facilitate access to the internet."[2] Yet simmering below the surface lie conflicting values and interests concerning the appropriate governance of and restrictions upon cyberspace. As Chinese citizens increasingly use the Internet to organize, influence, and advocate change, the Chinese Communist Party (CCP) reacts through a complex system of offensive and defensive measures in the name of securing domestic stability.[3] To the Chinese government, security is rooted in domestic stability, and as President Xi Jinping asserts, "No internet safety means no national security."[4]

This chapter examines China's activity in and policies concerning cyberspace from a human rights-based perspective. As a responsible member of the international community, China is obliged to protect the exercise of human rights under international and domestic law. Accordingly, human rights such as freedom of expression and privacy, including through digital media, are supposed to be respected in China. Pushing for greater respect for human rights in China, however, has often resulted in crackdown, with the government exerting authoritarian control to prevent domestic "instability." With respect to cyberspace, this reality has translated into robust online content control measures in the domestic space, measures to limit foreign influence through digital means in China, and negative impacts on the security of the international cyber environment as a whole.

The Chinese government's treatment of human rights and its approach to security are fundamentally intertwined, in cyberspace and beyond. The government has characterized efforts to promote and protect human rights, particularly civil and political rights, as a front to undermine CCP control and domestic stability. Great concern exists among the CCP leadership over erosion of its ideology and policy through the Internet and other means, which could weaken regime control. The CCP considers the propagation or assertion of "Western" ideologies and "universal" values, including human rights principles, in China as a calculated effort of "foreign hostile forces" and "internal dissidents" to challenge its authority. As a result, rights-related advocacy may serve as a basis on which the government identifies threat actors or targets of value. Authorities may consider not only foreign governments but also civil society groups and other nonstate actors working on rights issues as legitimate targets for offensive cyber activity. It is therefore unsurprising that entities compromised by China-based cyber activity include civil society actors such as Tibetan and Uighur nongovernmental organizations (NGOs) as well as Western media outlets reporting on sensitive rights-related issues, alongside better-known targets such as government and private industry.

Despite their prevalence, cyberthreats against civil society—namely, those individuals and entities working on public interest issues outside of private enterprise or government, such as activists, NGOs, exile groups, political movements, and other not-for-profit coalitions—are an often-overlooked subset of the broader cybersecurity problem.[5] Discussions of how to ensure cybersecurity in the United States, for example, have largely focused on threats to industry and government, without addressing the crucial matter of ever-increasing civil society compromise. This third prong, however, implicates important factors affecting the cyber policies and practices of China and other nations well into the future. Official legitimization of the targeting of civil society groups raises serious questions regarding China's ability and willingness to distinguish among targets in cyberspace, as well as its compliance with international human rights law and development of appropriate norms of restraint in this strategic domain. Diplomacy regarding cyberspace requires a holistic understanding of the Chinese government's approach to cybersecurity, including its views on threats to security in the guise of human rights. For as cyberspace binds the international community closer together, the result is the internationalization of domestic political control at the expense of human rights.

HUMAN RIGHTS IN AN ONLINE WORLD

Importantly, human rights are not a concept alien to China; they are recognized in international law, including a number of international treaties ratified by China,[6] as well as in the Chinese constitution[7] and the country's National Human Rights Action Plan,[8] and are asserted by Chinese citizens in a variety of contexts.[9] The Chinese government has itself flagged the importance of the international system and international law in many situations that suited its policy prerogatives, including with respect to cyberspace.[10] It has regularly sought a seat on the UN Human Rights Council, and was elected to that body most recently for the 2014–16 term.[11] However, as citizens in recent years have increasingly relied upon the elaboration of human rights to call for change within China—including through a significant movement among *weiquan* (rights defense) lawyers,[12] popular support for "Constitutionalism,"[13] and the growth of the "New Citizens Movement"[14]—the Chinese government has backpedaled on its human rights commitments and cracked down on activists, emphasizing domestic stability and Party control.[15]

Even as Xi Jinping has implemented sweeping reforms since coming to power,[16] the government has employed a heavy hand to prevent public grievances from giving rise to "mass incidents" such as riots, civil unrest, and protests.[17] Authorities regularly detain or otherwise restrict the movement of activists and others who speak out or organize against the government; impose significant limitations on freedom of expression and association at large; and criminally charge and imprison those deemed to have seriously challenged official authority, such as Xu Zhiyong and other members of the New Citizens Movement.[18] Indeed, China's annual domestic security budget was increased in 2013 by 8.7%, to 769.1 billion yuan (approximately US$125 billion), exceeding even the national defense budget (740.6 billion yuan).[19] The message conveyed to the public is to "sit tight": the CCP, and *only* the CCP, will deliver required economic and social changes, without the need for significant political change.

This approach has manifested itself online as surely as it has in other areas of Chinese life. China's massive online censorship apparatus, encompassing comprehensive legal, regulatory, and technical measures to control content and monitor activity online, is perhaps the most well-known element of the Chinese government's cyber-related domestic stability efforts.[20] The "Great Firewall" has for many years restricted access to information in China through automated monitoring, blocking, and filtering of network traffic.[21] The government has also mandated and relied heavily on industry-based enforcement of content control measures. Internet companies operating in China are subject to numerous and evolving regulatory requirements and penalties, and many establish entire departments devoted to surveillance and censorship of their users.[22] Research suggests that censorship efforts focus on content representing, reinforcing, or encouraging social mobilization (rather than content that is critical of the government in general).[23] China state media have reported that over two million people are employed to monitor such web activity.[24] Authorities have also required companies to implement real name registration for use of microblogs and other online services (as described in Zhuge et al., chapter 4 in this volume).[25] Since 2013, authorities have arrested hundreds of bloggers, and the use of the Sina Weibo microblog platform as a vehicle for free expression appears to have declined.[26] While some reports suggest that discussion of sensitive topics is moving to mobile messaging applications such as WeChat, that platform remains subject to laws governing "online rumors" and is not without its own challenges, including keyword censorship and possible server-side surveillance.[27]

THE IDEOLOGICAL UNDERPINNINGS OF SECURITY IN CHINA

Cyberspace has enhanced the proximity of the West to China, and the CCP views increased information flows as a potential source of instability and ideological contestation. As the director of the Information Office of the State Council and the External Propaganda Department of the CCP explained:

> As long as our country's internet is linked to the global internet, there will be channels and means for all sorts of harmful foreign information to appear on our domestic internet. As long as our internet is open to the public, there will be channels and means for netizens to express all sorts of speech on the internet.[28]

It is not an uncommon belief among Chinese leadership that governments of the West are attempting to undermine CCP control and interfere in China's internal affairs by advancing a contrary ideology of "universal values," a term used pejoratively by Chinese officialdom to broadly cover such concepts as human rights, democracy promotion, and Internet freedom, which are cast as incompatible with China's circumstances and ultimately destabilizing.[29] According to a senior propaganda official, "Universal values and red culture are in conflict."[30]

At the UN Human Rights Council Universal Periodic Review of China in 2013, the Chinese government noted its "respect" for "the principle of universality of human rights," while also asserting the need for "equal attention to the achievement of civil and political rights, economic, social, and cultural rights, and the right to development"[31]—given that China has made more progress in the latter two areas than on civil and political rights. Nevertheless, government officials have soundly rejected Western criticism of the country's rights record as an "attack" of which the "real purpose is not to help China improve human rights, but to change China's political system and reroute China's development path."[32] Deep-rooted suspicion appears to exist within the government that internationally recognized human rights will serve as a lever for Western-backed regime change in China.

In April 2013, the General Office of the Central Committee of the CCP issued "A Communiqué on the Current State of the Ideological Sphere" (also referred to as "Document No. 9"), a directive approved by the central leadership and circulated among Party members, instructing them to counter foreign influence and other subversive currents in the ideological sphere.[33] The document affirms, inter alia, that espousing "universal values"—described as "Western freedom, democracy, and human rights"— is an attempt to supplant the values of socialism advocated by the Party. It describes civil society as a "political tool" "adopted by Western anti-China forces" and "some people with ulterior motives within China," amounting to a "serious form of political opposition." It further asserts that "foreign hostile forces" and "internal 'dissidents'" pose an ongoing threat to Party ideology and regime control: "Western embassies, consulates, media operations, and NGOs operating inside China under various covers are spreading Western ideas and values and are cultivating so-called anti-government forces." "'Dissidents' and people identified with 'rights protection' are active. Some of them are working together with Western anti-China forces, echoing each other and relying on each other's support."[34] Official linkage of civil society and human rights initiatives to security threats has thus colored the interactions between China's domestic constituencies, Western entities, and the Chinese government on either issue.

Document No. 9 cites a number of purported major efforts of "Western anti-China forces and internal 'dissidents'" to challenge the CCP, one of which is "accelerating infiltration of the internet."[35] The notion that foreign actors together with "internal dissidents" will attempt to acquire influence in and through cyberspace to the detriment of the CCP has strengthened in light of the events of the Arab Spring, the international movement around "Internet freedom" (a concept championed by the United States and other Western governments), and the Snowden disclosures of 2013.

Much debate has emerged in the wake of the Arab Spring regarding the potential of information and communication technologies (ICTs) to prompt regime change.[36] ICTs—social media in particular—are widely acknowledged to have served as important tools in mobilizing protests and activism on the ground in the Middle East and North Africa, as they helped overcome information barriers and collective action dilemmas.[37] At the same time, a number of other factors beyond ICT usage, including economic and geopolitical factors, affected the dynamics of the Arab Spring, and it is by no means evident that similar dynamics could evolve in China.[38] Even so, the Chinese government attempted to contain and shape news of the events of the Arab Spring, took severe steps to limit dissent inspired by them (see discussion of Jasmine Rallies later in this chapter), and reacted harshly to the prospect of the use of the Internet and ICTs to promote change in China—particularly as such change was deemed to advance the values and interests of the West.[39]

Ironically, it is possible that the Internet freedom agenda, which emerged as official US policy approximately one year before the developments of the Arab Spring, may have fed the belief that greater access to information and freedom of expression online will proceed hand-in-glove with foreign infiltration of China. In a January 2010 speech, then-US secretary of state Hillary Clinton laid out the US commitment to Internet freedom as a fundamental tenet of its foreign policy, stating that the United States would "devot[e] the diplomatic, economic, and technological resources necessary" to advance the freedom to connect through technology around the world.[40] She identified US funding for circumvention and other technological tools as an important part of that effort, to develop "new tools that enable citizens to exercise their rights of free expression by circumventing politically motivated censorship. . . . We want to put these tools in the hands of people who will use them to advance democracy and human rights."[41] While funding has varied over time, estimates place total support channeled through the US State Department and USAID from 2008 to 2012 for Internet freedom-related initiatives at approximately US$100 million, including a 2012 allocation of $23 million.[42]

The Chinese government has interpreted this effort, with its emphasis on technologies designed to circumvent the information controls put in place by the state and enable dissidents and other civil society entities, as destabilizing and hostile interference in internal affairs, asserting that "practicing power politics in cyberspace in the name of cyber freedom [is] untenable."[43] And with US funding channeled to civil society in line with a government-endorsed policy of Internet freedom, threat actors on China's radar appear to include not only governments but also those nonstate entities supported by them or associated with "Western" ideological precepts such as human rights, democracy promotion, and Internet freedom initiatives.[44]

Moreover, the Chinese government likely considers Internet freedom and assertion of human rights in the cyber environment as one more manifestation of US hegemony in and exploitation of cyberspace, which is growing increasingly intolerable to China.[45] China, along with a number of other countries, has highlighted its relative strategic disadvantage vis-à-vis the United States in Internet development and governance, particularly given the US origins of the Internet Corporation for Assigned Names and Numbers and the most important private companies driving the ICT industry (including Microsoft, Google, Apple, and Intel).[46] Indeed, the Shanghai Cooperation Organization has identified one of the "main threats in the field of ensuring international information security" as "use of the dominant position in the information space to the detriment of the interests and security of other States."[47] China has likewise voiced its concern with US initiatives to enhance offensive cyber capabilities, while attempting to bolster its own capacity in that area.[48] US emphasis on cyberattacks as a primary security threat, involvement in the Stuxnet cyberattack against Iranian nuclear facilities, and active pursuit of other cyber weapons such as zero-day exploits, have led to rising tensions over the possibility of cyberwarfare.[49]

The 2013 disclosures by Edward Snowden of US National Security Agency mass-surveillance programs reinforced the Chinese government stance that the United States will use its "dominant position" in the cyber domain to achieve its own agenda, thereby necessitating state action to prevent interference in China's internal affairs.[50] The two governments had exchanged serious accusations regarding cyber espionage and network attack capabilities even prior to the Snowden disclosures that summer, as the US government for the first time explicitly named China a paramount source of such cyberthreats.[51] The Snowden disclosures, however, undermined US criticism of China and other countries for engagement in cyber espionage and lack of Internet freedom, and encouraged other countries to develop protective countermeasures, if not advanced cyber surveillance programs of their own. Snowden's assertions that US intelligence agencies targeted entities in China and Hong Kong, including Tsinghua University, the Chinese University of Hong Kong, and Chinese mobile phone companies, incensed the leadership and citizenry, which accused the United States of double standards.[52] It was subsequently reported that authorities would engage in probes of major US technology companies providing services in China.[53] Chinese authorities have emphasized the need to develop homegrown, advanced cyber capabilities.[54]

CHINA'S CONCEPT OF "FOREIGN HOSTILE FORCES"

In the perceived contest for ideological dominance being waged online as well as offline, the government has used the phrase "foreign hostile forces" (or "Western anti-China forces") to describe the nebulous threat actors and principles challenging CCP doctrine and authority, resulting in security compromise. This concept sidesteps the fact that many incidents attributed to foreign hostile forces stem from legitimate grievances raised by individuals *within* China concerning the realization of their human rights. Pegging critical domestic problems affecting stability as threats involving foreign hostile forces, however, allows the government to avoid addressing the underlying root causes of those problems. Such attribution may attempt to create an enemy mentality in society, transferring public attention and anger from the government's own policy failures and shortcomings to vague external threats allegedly motivated by "anti-China" sentiment. Depending on the circumstances, such an approach may also expose individuals within China's jurisdiction to criminal charges for state security-related crimes, such as incitement to or subversion of state power.[55]

Indeed, one can almost consider the authorities' use of the term "foreign hostile forces" as a bellwether, signifying strong concern by the government with a particular domestic incident or issue. The concept has evolved along with the increased connectivity afforded to China's population through technology, as well as mounting domestic discontent, and reached a critical threshold after the events of the Arab Spring demonstrated the mobilizing force of ICTs.[56] Former president Hu Jintao first used the phrase in a speech at the 2011 annual policy meeting of the CCP Central Committee, in which he stated, "We must clearly see that international hostile forces are intensifying the strategic plot of westernizing and dividing China, and ideological and cultural fields are the focal areas of their long-term infiltration."[57] The designation of "soft power" factors such as ideology and culture as a focal point of the alleged infiltration signals the importance to the government of information flows through media and ICTs as a means of influence of the domestic population.[58]

The "foreign hostile forces" concept appears set to play a defining role in the Chinese government's approach to the cyber environment. In 2010, Wang Chen, director of the Information Office of the State Council, specifically linked the free flow of information on the Internet to exploitation by foreign threat actors:

> We will perfect our system to monitor harmful information on the internet, and strengthen the blocking of harmful information from outside China, to effectively prevent it from being disseminated in China through the internet, and to *withstand infiltration of the internet by overseas hostile forces*. We will strictly regulate the orderly dissemination of information on the internet, improve our efficiency in handling harmful information on the internet, strictly prevent the large-scale dissemination and proliferation of harmful information on the internet, and maintain social harmony and stability [emphasis added].[59]

In responding to such perceived threats the government not only employs the online censorship apparatus previously described, but also proactively shapes public discourse on sensitive issues. Wang Chen noted the significance of initiatives undertaken "to guide public opinion related to major emergency incidents, hot topics related to people's welfare, and key ideological issues," and identified as examples the government's handling of the March 2008 unrest in Tibet and the July 2009 unrest in Urumqi (described in a later section).[60] According to Wang, "Those efforts provided powerful public opinion support for unifying thinking, consolidating strength, assisting in our diplomatic battles, and safeguarding our national interests."[61] Document No. 9 reiterated the importance of information control, indicating that "mistaken views and ideas" from overseas "penetrate China through the internet," and urging officials to "reinforce our management of all types and levels of propaganda on the cultural front, perfect and carry out related administrative systems, and allow absolutely no opportunity or outlets for incorrect thinking or viewpoints to spread."[62]

Recent incidents attributed by the Chinese government to foreign hostile forces include the following:

Unrest in and related to the Xinjiang Uyghur Autonomous Region (XUAR): On July 5, 2009, widespread rioting broke out in Urumqi, capital of XUAR.[63]

Official estimates stated that the riots and subsequent backlash resulted in 197 lives lost, 1,700 injuries, and extensive property damage.[64] Rather than addressing the pervasive ethnic tension underlying events in XUAR and its root causes, however, the government asserted that the riots "were masterminded by terrorist, separatist, and extremist forces both inside and outside China."[65] It attributed the violence and other plotting to "'East Turkistan' forces" (East Turkestan is the name used by many Uighurs to refer to Xinjiang), a nebulous threat actor allegedly "supported by hostile foreign forces."[66]

Notably, the government linked these "'East Turkistan' forces" to the World Uyghur Congress (WUC), a US-based NGO and critic of Chinese government policies in XUAR.[67] In doing so, the government made an explicit connection with the group's human rights advocacy, stating, "In recent years, the 'East Turkistan' forces have continued separatist activities under the banners of 'democracy,' 'human rights' and 'freedom,' trying to escape strikes against them or to clear themselves of the name of terrorism."[68] Official media also drew connections between the funding of WUC by the National Endowment for Democracy, which is itself funded by the US Congress, and support by foreign governments of terrorism, extremism, and separatism in China.[69]

Numerous violent and deadly incidents in and related to XUAR have continued to take place since 2009, including a horrific attack at a train station in Kunming, Yunnan province, in March 2014 that resulted in thirty-three deaths and 143 people injured.[70] The government has consistently attributed these incidents to foreign-linked groups without confronting the root causes of discontent and hostility among the Uighur community in China. It assigned responsibility for the Kunming attack to "Xinjiang separatist forces" instigated from overseas, who allegedly used VPNs to access jihadi videos through the Internet.[71]

Call for Jasmine Rallies: In February 2011, inspired by the unfolding events of the Arab Spring, calls began to circulate online for "Jasmine Rallies"—peaceful protests in the form of "strolls" in designated areas within thirteen cities in China, meant to signify support for an end to corruption and a government supervised by the people.[72] With official sensitivity particularly high in light of the events in the Middle East and North Africa, the Chinese government responded severely to these calls, rapidly censoring information online, detaining activists and rights defense lawyers, deploying police in locations designated for the rallies, and restricting foreign media coverage, with physical violence used against some journalists.[73] Chinese officials alleged a "conspiracy of certain hostile forces in the West to westernize China and split the country. . . . They're waving the banner of rights defense but are looking for opportunities to meddle in domestic conflicts and are deliberately creating all kinds of disturbances."[74]

Calls for greater press freedom: In January 2013, the *Southern Weekly*, a well-reputed newspaper based in Guangdong province and known for its more critical and independent investigative journalism, published a "New Year's Greeting" editorial, the original version of which "called for a bold realization of the 'dream of constitutionalism in China.'"[75] That version, however, never went to print; instead, without the knowledge of the *Southern Weekly* editorial staff, propaganda officials directly censored the editorial prior to its publication, replacing critical elements with empty reiteration of the Party line. This sparked outcry, an eventual strike from the paper's staff, significant online criticism regarding the lack of press freedom in China, and large protests staged outside the offices of publisher Southern Media Group.[76] As the incident progressed, the Central Propaganda Department issued a notice to media outlets and Party committees instructing not only that "Party control of the media is an unwavering basic principle," but also that "external hostile forces are involved in the development of the situation."[77] Chinese netizens responded incredulously to the assertion of interference by foreign hostile forces.[78]

Self-immolations in Tibet: In March 2008, numerous protests in Lhasa and beyond against Chinese rule—some of which escalated to violence and rioting—resulted in fatalities, detentions, and an ongoing crackdown by the authorities.[79] Events since that time have underscored Tibetans' widespread discontent with official policies in the region and toward the Tibetan ethnic group. Self-immolations—controversial manifestations of Tibetan opposition to Chinese government policies—have swept the region, and government suspicion of and efforts to control Tibetans have only increased. As of April 2014, it is estimated that at least 131 Tibetans have self-immolated since 2009, most of whom died as a result.[80]

The Chinese government's official response to the events has developed and become increasingly hardline as the practice has become more widespread, culminating in assertions that the practice is instigated by foreign hostile forces, including "overseas Tibetan separatist forces" and the Dalai Lama.[81] The Tibetan government-in-exile has insisted that "exiled Tibetan leadership did not encourage self-immolations," and that it does not seek to challenge China's sovereignty or territorial integrity.[82] Yet in a joint "Opinion on Handling Self-Immolation Cases in Tibetan Areas in Accordance with the Law," the PRC Supreme People's Court, Supreme People's Procuratorate, and Ministry of Public Security reportedly stated that "the recent self-immolations that have occurred in Tibetan areas are cases of significant evil that result from collusion between hostile forces inside and outside our borders whose attempts to use premeditated, organized plots to incite splittism, undermine ethnic unity, and seriously disrupt social order."[83] Authorities have launched a crackdown in Tibet against self-immolators and those who are alleged to incite them, with the aforementioned Opinion instructing that "anyone who organizes, plots, incites, coerces, entices, abets, or assists others to commit self-immolations shall be held criminally liable for intentional homicide."[84] This effort has already resulted in numerous detentions and severe criminal sentences for some individuals, based in part on alleged evidence of their digital contact with overseas groups.[85]

TARGETING "FOREIGN HOSTILE FORCES" IN CYBERSPACE

Perhaps the most concerning element of China's invocation of "foreign hostile forces" is the apparent inability or unwillingness to distinguish between actual state-linked aggression, intelligence, or destabilization efforts in the cyber environment, and the legitimate exercise or protection of internationally recognized human rights, including freedom of expression, by civil society, media, and other nonstate actors. This is a critical issue, as China's information operations are not exclusive to controlling domestic access to information, nor are they simply concerned with assessing the positions of foreign governments or companies on strategic and China-related issues. Rather, they also appear to incorporate offensive activity designed to extinguish what they cast as orchestrated efforts to undermine the Chinese government and its hold on power and domestic stability in China through advancement of ideological principles such as human rights.

The proximity afforded by cyberspace cuts both ways. While international connectivity has enhanced information flows to and from the country, strengthening civil society initiatives for the advancement of rights in China, it has also allowed China to proactively compromise those external entities cast as the source of threats to its domestic control through the conduct of cyber operations directly against those it has labeled foreign hostile forces. Overseas entities such as human rights NGOs and exile groups, previously beyond the direct reach of the Chinese government, as well as international media outlets and other nonstate actors working on rights-related issues, are increasingly subject to surveillance, espionage, and obstruction. Compromise of these entities may likewise result in collateral compromise of those individuals inside China with whom they are in contact. Cyber espionage and other more overt forms of targeted attack against these entities, such as defacement and denial of service attacks against organizations' websites, have flourished, resulting in resource drain, information compromise, and curtailing of the rights to freedom of expression and privacy.

Attribution of cyberthreats is an ongoing challenge—particularly for civil society actors, which may lack the resources necessary for full-scale technical investigation of an attack or compromise. Some attacks can be traced only as far as a command-and-control server, which itself could be controlled from another location entirely. However, while it is often impossible to attribute these attacks to specific actors with certainty, the choice of target, timing, social engineering employed, and operation of malware (including the content it delivers to the command-and-control server) together establish a strong likelihood that certain attacks are political in nature and related to issues of concern to the Chinese government. At a minimum the Chinese government has provided tacit support for such attacks, as it has encouraged them through its rhetoric regarding foreign hostile forces and has not publicly investigated or otherwise attempted to control such cyber intrusions against foreign actors.

Additionally, some investigations have gathered evidence linking attacks and campaigns to particular individuals or institutions in China.[86] For example, in February 2013, security company Mandiant released its report *APT1: Exposing One of China's Cyber Espionage Units*, which detailed evidence gathered over multiple years from 141 companies that were targets of cyber espionage to conclude that China is the source of a sophisticated cyber espionage operation referred to as Advanced Persistent Threat 1 (APT1).[87] The report further drew the conclusion that the operation is based out of a People's Liberation Army (PLA) unit, and is therefore an official government effort to covertly obtain sensitive and valuable information from targets that include critical industries within the United States.[88] While the connection between APT1 and the PLA is disputed, additional reporting suggests that the PLA is active in recruiting patriotic hackers, and collaborates on cybersecurity research and development with computer science and engineering departments at elite universities within China.[89] Moreover, since the release of the Mandiant report, the US government has asserted that its computer systems are "targeted for intrusions, some of which appear to be attributable directly to the Chinese government and military."[90] While the Chinese government has denied these assertions, it has thus far declined to publicly refute the substantive facts associated with the claims against it, including the details of the Mandiant report.[91]

These cyber espionage efforts raise some critical questions about appropriate targeting of external actors in cyberspace. With CPC official rhetoric and ideological positions surrounding foreign hostile forces, the government has cast nonstate entities such as media outlets, journalists, NGOs, think tanks, and other civil society actors as legitimate adversarial targets. Government officials may even believe they are within their right to self-defense and justified in launching or condoning these campaigns in order to preserve the ideological conditions necessary for CPC control and domestic stability. Whether or not that is the case, the fact that nonstate actors linked to rights-related issues are extensively targeted for cyber espionage merits additional scrutiny and discussion.

The actual operation of a number of China-linked cyber espionage campaigns has made little distinction among government versus private or civil society actors, suggesting that, at least at the level of collection, those backing the intrusions perceive the chosen targets as presenting security concerns of similar importance and/or providing information of similar value.[92] While variations exist in the sophistication of malware deployed against targets—perhaps adjusted to the level of difficulty of the intrusion—certain commonalities among attacks linked to China suggest that targets from government, the private sector, and civil society are chosen and handled together within the same campaigns. Similarities across campaigns exist as well.

For example, multiple analyses of the cyber espionage activity of the "Comment Group"—also known as APT1—indicate widespread targeting of NGOs, think tanks, the energy industry, governments including the United States and European Union, and others.[93] The Citizen Lab at the Munk School of Global Affairs, University of Toronto, has likewise confirmed that APT1 targets civil society actors alongside the "higher profile" companies and organizations on its roster: Citizen Lab's investigation of a malicious e-mail targeting a Tibetan NGO found that the malware used in the attack incorporated much of the same code and employed one of the same command-and-control servers as the APT1 attacks documented by Mandiant, indicating the malware came from the same source.[94] That malware was distributed through a link in an e-mail sent to the head of the organization, with the subject line "save my Tibetan wife."[95] Similarly, the Luckycat campaign, active since at least June 2011, targeted Tibetan activists as well as entities in the aerospace, energy, engineering, and shipping industries, and military research, in Japan and India, with a total of 233 computers compromised.[96] The Luckycat campaign also employed a malware family previously utilized in the ShadowNet campaign, which itself targeted entities associated with the Indian government as well as Tibetan activists and raised significant concerns over collateral compromise.[97]

The seeming equivalence of priority assigned to such targets in cyber espionage campaigns suggests that China has strategic interest in cyber infiltration of not only governments (for intelligence purposes) and industry (for competitive advantage) but also civil society groups and others working on human rights or ideological issues that are considered to present security threats; that is, qualify as foreign hostile forces. Noteworthy examples of targeting of nonstate actors that may be included within the rubric of "foreign hostile forces" include information operations against Tibetans and Uighurs, and cyber espionage campaigns against high-profile Western media outlets.

Targeting Tibetans

Citizen Lab has studied information operations against Tibetan groups and other civil society entities for a number of years. It participated in investigations of cyber espionage networks that culminated in the 2009 report *Tracking GhostNet: Investigating a Cyber Espionage Network*, and the 2010 follow-on report *Shadows in the Cloud: Investigating Cyber Espionage 2.0.*[98] The GhostNet investigation documented evidence of infiltration into at least 1,295 computers in 103 countries: within the private offices of the Dalai Lama and other Tibetan entities, as well as among other diplomatic, political, economic, and military entities, including ministries of foreign affairs and embassies of a number of states. The Shadows investigation tracked a cyber espionage network that compromised government, business, and academic computer systems in the Office of the Dalai Lama as well as in India, the United Nations, and other locations. That cyber espionage campaign resulted in the theft of classified and sensitive documents, as well as collateral compromise among affected entities. While these investigations did not generate conclusive evidence of Chinese government backing, the interest and/or involvement of the Chinese state is probable in light of the targeted entities and technical forensics indicating China as the location of the command-and-control servers employed. Citizen Lab has since explored additional cyberthreats leveraged against Tibetan groups that have incorporated targeted social engineering, including content related to self-immolations.[99]

Since 2011, the Chinese government's concerns with and attempts to enforce stability in Tibet have intensified in the wake of self-immolations among the Tibetan population. Efforts to control Tibetans have ramped up in the digital realm, which is perceived as a primary conduit for hostile foreign influence. Among Tibetans, however, overseas connections have been fed for many years by migration in pursuit of greater freedoms or flight from persecution. The domestic, international, and exile communities are deeply intertwined, given the diaspora nature of the community and the importance of familial relationships within the Tibetan culture. As a result, the entire community has become suspect and subject to criminal prosecution based on the deep-rooted overseas contact that stems from the very nature of the community.

The government has enacted sweeping information controls alongside other strict security policies in Tibetan regions in an apparent attempt to isolate Tibetans from overseas contact and other perceived sources of support. In October 2012, authorities circulated notices offering substantial sums of money, as well as assurances of anonymity and security, for information "on the people who plan, incite to carry out, control, and lure people to commit self-immolation."[100] The notices also banned "any forms of communication or information judged as being used for 'criminal purposes,'" including "'speech and the distribution of written information,' 'cartoons,' 'homemade materials,' 'videos,' 'websites,' 'emails, and audio files,' or 'SMS text messages.'"[101] Reports have emerged regarding disruptions to Internet access, and authorities have also confiscated satellite dishes and receivers to restrict the ability of Tibetans to access channels originating from overseas (described as "anti-China" channels).[102]

The focus on digital mediums in control efforts is noteworthy, as foreign contact from inside China (where travel to Tibet by Westerners is effectively precluded) necessarily takes place through satellites, mobile devices, and the Internet—with mobile devices in particular the primary means of connection for individuals in rural areas.[103] Hence, who controls the device controls the purported foreign interference. In March 2013, a notice listing additional prohibited acts was circulated in Tibetan regions, reportedly "based on points made by an unnamed senior Chinese official at a recent provincial-level meeting."[104] The list included "inciting self-immolation protests"; "sending images or information about self-immolations to 'outside separatist forces'"; "'taking pictures and filming the actual scene of self-immolation and mass gatherings' and 'providing secret information to separatist forces,' apparently referring to Tibetan exile groups."[105] In apparent enforcement of this prohibition, authorities have conducted security sweeps of mobile phones in monasteries in Lhasa and surrounding areas, "searching for images and writings deemed politically sensitive."[106] Photos, video, messages, and contacts stored in digital devices have thus become a basis for criminal liability and crackdown.

Reports regarding sentencing of Tibetans in 2013 have confirmed the authorities' focus on overseas contact by digital means as a basis for liability, with judicial bodies linking such contact to separatism. In one case publicized by official media, Lobsang Konchok, a monk from Sichuan province, was sentenced to death with a two-year reprieve—tantamount to life imprisonment—while his nephew Lobsang Tsering was sentenced to ten years' imprisonment, on charges of intentional homicide for allegedly inciting eight people to self-immolate.[107] Prosecutors heavily emphasized contact between the defendants and overseas entities during the trial, asserting that Lobsang Konchok revealed the following during police interrogation:

> He received a phone call from Samtan, an old acquaintance living abroad, after a Kirti Monastery monk named Tapey self-immolated in 2009. Samtan asked Lorang [Lobsang] Konchok to goad more people to self-immolate and collect and send information about self-immolation abroad . . . [Samtan] is a key figure of an overseas "Kirti Monastery media liaison team"—a "Tibet independence" organization of the Dalai Lama clique.[108]

Prosecutors also cited police evidence of "95 calls to various foreign numbers, including Indian ones using a mobile phone from January to August in 2012. . . . Lorang Konchok had called his foreign contacts after each of the five self-immolation cases happened in Aba during these months" and had allegedly promised to spread news of the self-immolations abroad using those contacts.[109] The court found that the actions of the defendants amounted to intentional homicide and that the information disseminated by Lobsang Konchok "was used by some overseas media as a basis for creating secessionist propaganda."[110]

In a notable corollary to the government's use of digital evidence from mobile devices in support of its crackdown on self-immolations purportedly linked to foreign hostile forces, Citizen Lab research into targeted threats against the Tibetan community has confirmed the use of mobile malware.[111] The malware at issue was circulated in January 2013 and designed to surreptitiously transmit detailed information from mobile devices to an attacker. It modified a legitimate Android Application Package File (APK) for a mobile application called Kakao Talk used by many Tibetans for chat and media sharing that was originally circulated as an attachment to a genuine e-mail from a Tibetan information security expert based in Dharamsala, India. The original APK was modified by the attacker to include additional permission requests while preserving the core chat functionality and user interface of the application.[112] With the added permissions in place the malware operates to send a user's contacts, call history, SMS messages, and cellular network configuration to an attacker.

Importantly, the cellular network configuration information gathered includes the base station ID, tower ID, mobile network code, and mobile area code of the phone in question. As Citizen Lab noted in its report, such information would only be useful

> to actors with access to the cellular communications provider and its techni-
> cal infrastructure, such as large businesses and government. It almost certainly
> represents the information that a cellular service provider requires to initiate
> eavesdropping, often referred to as "trap and trace." Actors at this level would
> also have access to the data required to perform radio frequency triangulation
> based on the signal data from multiple towers, placing the user within a small
> geographical area.[113]

This kind of functionality, combined with the use of social engineering specifically targeting Tibetans, strongly suggests that mobile malware is deployed for the purpose of collecting digital evidence on and curtailing Tibetans' communications, including with individuals or entities overseas.

Targeting Uighurs

A similar emphasis on digital communications as enabling foreign hostile forces has emerged in the authorities' handling of unrest in XUAR among the Uighur ethnic group. Digital mediums have factored heavily in court sentences, as authorities asserted "the accused were 'seduced by ideas of religious extremism and terrorist violence' and 'used the internet, mobile phones and digital storage devices to organize, lead and participate in ter-ror organizations, provoke incidents, and incite separatism.'"[114] After a violent clash in April 2013 that left twenty-five people dead in Siriqbuya, XUAR—which the government attributed to terrorism but eventually admitted lacked any link to foreign forces—Uighur students were detained for alleged connections with overseas contacts, and authorities intensi-fied efforts to enforce real-name registration requirements for purchase of SIM cards for use in mobile phones.[115] And in 2014, outspoken Uighur scholar Ilham Tohti was detained, charged with separatism, and accused of colluding with overseas forces, apparently based in part on his fielding of interviews from foreign media and his news and commentary website Uighurbiz.net.[116] Meanwhile, XUAR Party secretary Zhang Chunxian was reported to link the Kunming attacks to jihadi materials accessed online.[117]

While cyberattacks against Uighur civil society groups are well docu-mented, it is noteworthy that mobile malware discovered to have targeted

Tibetans itself incorporates social engineering and other elements related to the Uighur ethnic group.[118] Forensic techniques suggest that this type of mobile malware and targeted attack may be used against multiple civil society groups and activists representing Uighurs, Tibetans, and others.[119] It therefore appears that authorities are increasingly relying on digital evidence and digital crackdown to manage discontent and possible unrest among ethnic groups, a security threat associated in official policy with foreign hostile forces. Cyberattacks and other information controls may facilitate this effort.

Targeting Western Media Outlets

High-profile Western media outlets and journalists associated with them have also experienced cyber espionage campaigns that appear to have originated in China. Targets of such campaigns that have gone public include the *New York Times*, the *Wall Street Journal*, *Bloomberg News*, and the *Washington Post*. The *New York Times* released significant details concerning its experience, which provide insight into such campaigns.

Ongoing cyber infiltration of the *New York Times* began in mid-September 2012, as its work on an article regarding the wealth of relatives of then-prime minister Wen Jiabao was underway.[120] The cyber espionage campaign specifically targeted the work of David Barboza, Shanghai bureau chief for the *Times*, who wrote the Wen article, and Jim Yardley, the former bureau chief in Beijing, rather than attempting to bluntly obstruct the *Times*'s operations at large. According to the *New York Times*, the attackers "created custom software that allowed them to search for and grab Mr. Barboza's and Mr. Yardley's e-mails and documents from a Times e-mail server."[121] The effort appeared to include a focus on obtaining information on contacts in China who might have served as sources for the Wen article—despite the fact that the *New York Times*'s research "was based on public records, including thousands of corporate documents through China's State Administration for Industry and Commerce" that "were used to trace the business interests of relatives of Mr. Wen."[122] The cyber espionage effort began over a month prior to the publication of the Wen article on October 25, 2012, suggesting that the operation was informed by other intelligence regarding the trajectory of the *Times*'s China reporting. This covert cyber espionage effort was only supplemented by more traditional and obvious information control efforts of the authorities after October 25, when China blocked all domestic access to the *New York Times* website and censored online references related to the Wen article, including on Sina Weibo.[123]

Ultimately, this cyber espionage campaign appeared to serve a purpose beyond that of simply managing the Chinese government's public image, given the informed, highly targeted, prepublication roots of the campaign, and the effective censorship mechanisms already available to the government. Indeed, despite the fact that publication had already occurred and the reporting was effectively blocked domestically, the espionage activity of the attackers intensified in the period after the October 25 publication date—in the lead-up to the highly sensitive Eighteenth National Congress of the CCP, which began on November 8 and at which the once-a-decade Chinese leadership transition took place. The cyber espionage campaign as a whole advanced the interests of the Chinese government in surveilling and undermining specific activity of foreign media that it viewed as hostile to the regime—including suspected contact with domestic informants—during a period of time critical to domestic stability.

Document No. 9 and other official statements confirm that the CCP views foreign media as a strategic threat.[124] The cyber efforts detailed above thus appear to complement (and perhaps inform) existing Internet censorship as well as ongoing regulatory restrictions over foreign media and journalists, including media regulations banning the use of "contents from overseas without permission," and refusals to issue or renew foreign journalist visas, thereby limiting in-country media coverage.[125]

IMPLICATIONS FOR INTERNATIONAL CYBERSECURITY

China's long-standing human rights problems are playing out in the cyber realm, and constitute a major catalyst for cyber insecurity. The motivations behind the Chinese government's actions in and policies toward cyberspace go beyond economic or military advantage. Domestic stability is the first priority of the Chinese government, and that stability relies as much on ideology and the management of dissent as it does on continued economic growth and military prowess. Indeed, cyber campaigns linked to China to date suggest some parity between economic, military, and rights-related interests in terms of methods employed, targets chosen, and type of resources allocated. From the perspective of the Chinese government, exfiltrated information regarding civil society plans to advance human rights issues may be considered just as valuable to stability efforts as information on foreign defense industries. Further consideration of cyberthreats against the full spectrum of targets, including civil society actors, may provide additional insights into the operation of China's cyber espionage activities.

It is probable that cyber intrusions against civil society and other non-state actors working on issues with ideological implications will continue to increase. Such activity has the potential to compromise the freedom of expression, privacy, and, depending on the data exfiltrated, even the physical security of targeted individuals. These circumstances may also lead to collateral compromise of entities in other sectors, further drive the development of cyber offensive capabilities as a whole, and widen the normative gap between China and the West on the protection of rights online.

Genuine progress on international cybersecurity will thus require recognition and airing of some fundamental disagreements between countries that are based on ideology and human rights principles—not only those of China but also those of Western countries, particularly the United States. If liberal democracies are to make progress on this issue, diplomatic efforts must credibly address the Chinese government's assertions that Western governments seek to use ICTs for regime destabilization, and that civil society actors, including the media and NGOs, are backed by hostile foreign interests in a bid to interfere with China's internal affairs. The Internet freedom agenda and questions of US hegemony in and exploitation of cyberspace will need to be addressed and perhaps further elucidated to distinguish encouragement of freedom of expression and access to information from incitement and material support of threats to public security. It is imperative to delink the legitimate exercise by civil society of freedom of expression, privacy, and other rights from genuine security threats, and to develop objective criteria on which to do so. Consensus must be built around the premise that civil society actors are not legitimate targets of cyber espionage and cyberattacks. That, in turn, requires the political will of states to prioritize civil society concerns, rather than focus exclusively on cyberthreats against government and industry. Only when these points are engaged can the international community effectively confront issues of cyber insecurity at their roots.[126]

Governments seeking to promote a rights-based approach to cyber norms would do well to contest the notion of "foreign hostile forces" and cyber espionage against nonstate, civil society actors in international forums,[127] as well as in bilateral engagements, such as the US-China working group on cybersecurity that met for the first time in July 2013.[128] Though the conduct of cyber espionage against civil society actors is not a typical element of debates surrounding "cyberwarfare," and is not governed by the law of armed conflict, it is of sufficient importance that a norm similar to the principle of distinction embodied in the law of armed conflict should be developed to address such targeting.[129] The principle of distinction holds that states should distinguish between targets that are genuine participants in hostilities, such as the military, and civilians or other noncombatants.[130] Similarly, principles should be developed that recognize states must refrain from and prevent entities within their jurisdiction from targeting legitimate civil society actors through cyber espionage or other cyberthreats. Such actors should be considered "off-limits" if they operate according to principles of international human rights law (including freedoms of expression and association), and have not themselves engaged in activity against the state that would qualify as hostile and illegal under international law.

The Snowden disclosures have affected any possible diplomacy around this issue. The US government is limited in what it can now credibly assert constitutes appropriate behavior in cyberspace, and the main issue raised in its bilateral discussions with China continues to be theft of intellectual property rather than other forms of cyber espionage.[131] At the same time, however, the Snowden affair may have encouraged greater awareness and advocacy of human rights in cyberspace among other countries. For example, in December 2013, the UN General Assembly unanimously approved a resolution that recognized the negative impact of surveillance and interception of communications—both domestic and extraterritorial—and called on states to "respect and protect the right to privacy, including in the context of digital communication."[132] The resolution was coordinated by Brazil and Germany specifically in response to US surveillance.[133] Such efforts to advance digital privacy and limit surveillance serve as an important foundation on which to address cyber espionage against civil society actors. It remains to be seen, however, whether the Snowden disclosures will catalyze rights in cyberspace or further polarize states on the issue of cyberthreats.

While it is important for governments to engage on these issues, this is also an area in which involvement of civil society is crucial. Perhaps the greatest irony of China's "foreign hostile forces" concept is that, while civil society initiatives have been equated with foreign government interference, civil society actors are largely without the resources available to the government or the private sector for defense against and prevention of cyber compromise. An improved infrastructure of support to civil society, including political support as well as enhanced research, collaboration, and technical assistance, is essential in the face of these cyberthreats.[134]

NOTES

1. UN Human Rights Council, "The Promotion, Protection and Enjoyment of Human Rights on the Internet," Res. 20/8, UN Doc. A/HRC/RES/20/8, July 5, 2012, para. 1, http://www.un.org/Docs/journal/asp/ws.asp?m=A/HRC/RES/20/8.

2. Ibid., para. 3.

3. See Gao Wenqian, "The Internet Is a Natural Enemy to Authoritarian China," translation by Human Rights in China, *China Rights Forum: "China's Internet": Staking Digital Ground*, no. 2 (2010), http://www.hrichina.org/crf/article/3246; see also "The Machinery of Control: Cat and Mouse," *Economist*, April 6, 2013, http://www.economist.com/news/special-report/21574629-how-china-makes-sure-its-internet-abides-rules-cat-and-mouse; OpenNet Initiative, "Country Profiles: China," August 9, 2012, http://opennet.net/research/profiles/china.

4. "Xi Jinping Leads Internet Security Group," Xinhua, February 27, 2014, http://news.xinhuanet.com/english/china/2014-02/27/c_133148273.htm.

5. Ron Deibert and Sarah McKune, "Civil Society Hung Out to Dry in Global Cyber Espionage," CircleID, March 4, 2013, http://www.circleid.com/posts/20130304_civil_society_hung_out_to_dry_in_global_cyber_espionage/.

6. China has signed or ratified core international human rights treaties, including treaties addressing torture, racial discrimination, civil and political rights, and economic, social, and cultural rights. See United Nations Treaty Collection, "Chapter IV: Human Rights," http://treaties.un.org/Pages/Treaties.aspx?id=4&subid=A&lang=en. China has signed, but not yet ratified, the International Covenant on Civil and Political Rights, but as a signatory is still "obliged to refrain from acts which would defeat the object and purpose of the treaty." Vienna Convention on the Law of Treaties, 1155 UNT.S. 331, 8 I.L.M. 679 (1969), entered into force May 23, 1969, Art. 18, http://untreaty.un.org/ilc/texts/instruments/english/conventions/1_1_1969.pdf.

7. See Constitution of the People's Republic of China, National People's Congress, at chap. 2: The Fundamental Rights and Duties of Citizens, Art. 33 et seq., http://www.npc.gov.cn/englishnpc/Constitution/2007-11/15/content_1372964.htm.

8. See Information Office of the State Council of the People's Republic of China, National Human Rights Action Plan of China (2012–2015), June 11, 2012, http://news.xinhuanet.com/english/china/2012-06/11/c_131645029.htm; Information Office of the State Council of the People's Republic of China, National Human Rights Action Plan of China (2009–2010), April 13, 2009, http://english.gov.cn/official/2009-04/13/content_1284128.htm.

9. For example, in February 2013, a group of more than one hundred academics, journalists, lawyers, former Party officials, and others circulated an open letter calling on the government to ratify the International Covenant on Civil and Political Rights. See David Bandurski, "Open Letter to NPC on Human Rights," China Media Project, February 26, 2013, http://cmp.hku.hk/2013/02/26/31531/ (providing an English translation of the open letter).

10. See, e.g., UN Department of Public Information, "Unregulated Information Highway is Non-traditional Security Threat with Too Many 'Traffic Accidents,' China Tells First Committee, Warning of Security Breaches," October 20, 2011, http://www.un.org/News/Press/docs/2011/gadis3442.doc.htm.

11. "General Assembly Elects 14 Members to UN Human Rights Council," UN News Center, November 12, 2013, http://www.un.org/apps/news/story.asp/story.asp?NewsID=46476&Cr=human+rights&Cr1.

12. See generally Committee to Support Chinese Lawyers, "Background and Cases," http://www.csclawyers.org/cases/; Committee to Support Chinese Lawyers, *Legal Advocacy and the 2011 Crackdown in China: Adversity, Repression, and Resilience*, November 2011, http://www.csclawyers.org/letters/Legal%20Advocacy%20and%20the%202011%20Crackdown%20in%20China.pdf.

13. See, e.g., "China's Constitutional Crisis," *Atlantic*, September 3, 2013, http://www.theatlantic.com/china/archive/2013/09/chinas-constitutional-crisis/279285/.

14. The "New Citizens Movement," of which legal activist Xu Zhiyong is a prominent member, "drew up to 5,000 members dedicated to fighting government graft and education policies restricting the children of rural migrants from attending big city schools," and engaged in informal meetings and peaceful protests. See Andrew Jacobs and Chris Buckley, "China Sentences Legal Activist to 4 Years for Role in Protests," *New York Times*, January 26, 2014, http://cn.nytimes.com/china/20140126/c26xuzhiyong/dual/; see also Xu Zhiyong, "China Needs a New Citizens' Movement," May 29, 2012. English translation available at http://www.hrichina.org/en/crf/article/6205.

15. See generally Malcolm Moore, "China's Human Rights Situation 'Worst in Decades,'" *Telegraph*, March 2, 2014, www.telegraph.co.uk/news/worldnews/asia/china/10670520/Chinas-human-rights-situation-worst-in-decades.html.

16. See generally "A Blueprint for Reform: The Xi Manifesto," *Economist*, November 23, 2013, http://www.economist.com/news/china/21590499-chinas-president-unveils-most-striking-plans-reform-two-decades-they-mix-unusual.

17. See Jeremy Goldkorn, "Legal Daily Report on Mass Incidents in China in 2012," Danwei, January 6, 2013, http://webcache.googleusercontent.com/search?q=cache:i6DYkMyQ_WcJ:www.danwei.com/a-report-on-mass-incidents-in-china-in-2012/+&cd=1&hl=en&ct=clnk.

18. See Andrew Jacobs and Chris Buckley, "Chinese Activists Test New Leader and Are Crushed," *New York Times*, January 16, 2014, http://cn.nytimes.com/china/20140116/c16citizen/dual/; Beijing Municipal No. 1 Intermediate People's Court, Criminal Division, First-Instance Verdict No. 5268 (2013), January 26, 2014, English translation by the China Law Translate Community available at Human Rights in China, "Xu Zhiyong's First-Instance Verdict (English translation)," January 26, 2014, http://www.hrichina.org/en/citizens-square/xu-zhiyongs-first-instance-verdict-english-translation; Moore, "China's Human Rights Situation."

19. Ben Blanchard and John Ruwitch, "China Hikes Defense Budget, to Spend More on Internal Security," Reuters, March 5, 2013, http://www.reuters.com/article/2013/03/05/us-china-parliament-defence-idUSBRE92403620130305.

20. See generally "The Machinery of Control: Cat and Mouse"; and OpenNet Initiative, "Country Profiles: China."

21. See James Fallows, "'The Connection Has Been Reset,'" *Atlantic*, March 1, 2008, http://www.theatlantic.com/magazine/archive/2008/03/-the-connection-has-been-reset/306650/; "The Numbers behind the Great Firewall of China," Backgroundcheck.org, http://www.backgroundcheck.org/the-numbers-behind-the-great-firewall-of-china/.

22. For an overview, see Jedidiah R. Crandall et al., "Chat Program Censorship and Surveillance in China: Tracking TOM-Skype and Sina UC," *First Monday* 18, no. 7 (July 1, 2013), http://firstmonday.org/ojs/index.php/fm/article/view/4628/3727. See also Rebecca MacKinnon, "China's Censorship 2.0: How Companies Censor Bloggers," *First Monday* 14, no. 2 (February 2, 2009), http://firstmonday.org/htbin/cgiwrap/bin/ojs/index.php/fm/article/view/2378/2089; Rebecca MacKinnon, "Google's China Troubles Continue; Congress Examines U.S. Investment in Chinese Censorship," June 29, 2010, http://rconversation.blogs.com/rconversation/2010/06/index.html.

23. Gary King, Jennifer Pan, and Margaret Roberts, "How Censorship in China Allows Government Criticism but Silences Collective Expression," 2012, http://gking.harvard.edu/files/censored.pdf.

24. "China Employs Two Million Microblog Monitors, State Media Say," BBC, October 4, 2013, http://www.bbc.co.uk/news/world-asia-china-24396957; see also Li Hui and Megha Rajagopalan, "At Sina Weibo's Censorship Hub, China's Little Brothers Cleanse Online Chatter," Reuters, September 11, 2013, http://www.reuters.com/article/2013/09/11/net-us-china-internet-idUSBRE98A18Z20130911; Tao Zhu, David Phipps, Adam Pridgen, Jedidiah R. Crandall, and Dan S. Wallach, "The Velocity of Censorship: High-Fidelity Detection of Microblog Post Deletions," http://arxiv.org/pdf/1303.0597.pdf.

25. See Beijing Municipal Government, Central Provisions on the Administration of Microblog Development, Art. 9, http://digicha.com/index.php/2011/12/translation-of-beijings-new-weibo-regulations/; National People's Congress Standing Committee, Decision Concerning Strengthening Network Information Protection, 2012, Art. 6, http://chinacopyrightandmedia.wordpress.com/2012/12/28/national-peoples-congress-standing-committee-decision-concerning-strengthening-network-information-protection/.

26. See Murong Xuecun, "Busting China's Bloggers," *New York Times*, October 15, 2013, http://www.nytimes.com/2013/10/16/opinion/murong-busting-chinas-bloggers.html; Malcolm Moore, Joel Gunter, and Mark Oliver, "China Kills Off Discussion on Weibo after Internet Crackdown," *Telegraph*, February 3, 2014, http://www.telegraph.co.uk/news/worldnews/asia/china/10608245/China-kills-off-discussion-on-Weibo-after-internet-crackdown.html (estimating posts fell by 70%); "From Weibo to WeChat: After a Crackdown on Microblogs, Sensitive Online Discussion Has Shifted," *Economist*, January 18, 2014, http://www.economist.com/news/china/21594296-after-crackdown-microblogs-sensitive-online-discussion-has-shifted-weibo-wechat.

27. Moore, Gunter, and Oliver, "China Kills Off Discussion"; "From Weibo to WeChat"; Citizen Lab, "Asia Chats: Analyzing Information Controls and Privacy in Asian Messaging Applications," November 14, 2013, https://citizenlab.org/2013/11/asia-chats-analyzing-information-controls-privacy-asian-messaging-applications/.

28. Wang Chen, "Concerning the Development and Administration of Our Country's Internet," translation by Human Rights in China, *China Rights Forum: "China's Internet": Staking Digital Ground*, no. 2 (2010), http://www.hrichina.org/crf/article/3242, at Section II.

29. Notably, in its most recent National Human Rights Action Plan, the Chinese government emphasized that the plan was formulated in accordance with, inter alia, "The principle of pursuing practicality. The Chinese government respects the principle of universality of human rights, *but also upholds proceeding from China's national conditions and new realities to advance the development of its human rights cause on a practical basis.*" Information Office of the State Council of the People's Republic of China, *National Human Rights Action Plan of China (2012–2015)*, June 11, 2012, http://english.gov.cn/2012-06/11/content_2158183_3.htm (emphasis added).

30. John Garnaut, "The Children Devour the Revolution," *Foreign Policy*, November 10, 2012, http://www.foreignpolicy.com/articles/2012/11/09/the_children_devour_the_revolution.

31. UN Human Rights Council, "National Report Submitted in Accordance with Paragraph 5 of the Annex to Human Rights Council Resolution 16/21: China," Working Group on the Universal Periodic Review, Seventeenth Session, UN Doc. A/HRC/WG.6/17/CHN/1*, August 5, 2013, http://www.un.org/Docs/journal/asp/ws.asp?m=A/HRC/WG.6/17/CHN/1, at para. 4.

32. Permanent Mission of the People's Republic of China to the UN, Statement by Ambassador Wang Min at the Third Committee of the Sixty-Eighth Session of the General Assembly on Human Rights, October 31, 2013, http://www.fmprc.gov.cn/eng/wjb/zwjg/zwbd/t1094826.shtml.

33. Central Committee of the Communist Party of China's General Office, "Communiqué on the Current State of the Ideological Sphere," April 22, 2013, English translation by ChinaFile available at https://www.chinafile.com/document-9-chinafile-translation; see also Chris Buckley, "China's New Leadership Takes Hard Line in Secret Memo," *New York Times*, August 20, 2013, http://cn.nytimes.com/china/20130820/c20document/dual/.

34. Ibid.

35. Ibid.

36. See, e.g., "On Topic: Arab Spring," *MIT Technology Review*, http://www2.technologyreview.com/ontopic/arabspring/; Philip N. Howard and Muzammil M. Hussain, *Democracy's Fourth Wave? Digital Media and the Arab Spring* (New York: Oxford University Press, 2013).

37. See Zeynep Tufekci, "New Media and the People-Powered Uprisings," *MIT Technology Review*, August 30, 2011, http://www.technologyreview.com/view/425280/new-media-and-the-people-powered-uprisings/.

38. See, e.g., Richard Javad Heydarian, "The Economics of the Arab Spring," Foreign Policy in Focus, April 21, 2011, http://www.fpif.org/articles/the_economics_of_the_arab_spring.

39. See James Fallows, "Arab Spring, Chinese Winter," *Atlantic*, July 24, 2011, http://www.theatlantic.com/magazine/archive/2011/09/arab-spring-chinese-winter/308601/.

40. Hillary Rodham Clinton, "Remarks on Internet Freedom," The Newseum, Washington, DC, January 21, 2010, http://www.state.gov/secretary/rm/2010/01/135519.htm.

41. Ibid.

42. Fergus Hanson, "Internet Freedom: The Role of the U.S. State Department," Brookings Institution, October 25, 2012, http://www.brookings.edu/research/reports/2012/10/25-ediplomacy-hanson-internet-freedom.

43. UN Department of Public Information, "Unregulated Information Highway is Non-traditional Security Threat."

44. See Baogang He, "Working with China to Promote Democracy," *Washington Quarterly* 36, no. 1 (2013): 37–53, http://csis.org/files/publication/TWQ_13Winter_He.pdf.

45. See, e.g., Zhao Haijian, "Cyberspace Hegemony: The New U.S. Strategy Commanding Heights," *Guangzhou Ribao Online*, May 29, 2011, translation by Open Source Center, https://www.opensource.gov/portal/server.pt/gateway/PTARGS_0_0_200_203_0_43/content/Display/PRINCE/CPP20110604338002?printerFriendly=true (on file with author) ("In fact, as a 'superpower' in cyberspace, to consolidate and expand its own hegemonic position, the United States is extending its reach to every corner of the online world. Nonetheless, it has often

done so in the name of 'maintaining the information freedom in the Internet' or any other deceptively charming cover").

46. See generally Zhao Haijian, "Cyberspace Hegemony: The New U.S. Strategy Commanding Heights" ("Few people of more than one billion Internet users in the world may know that . . . in every key aspect in the Internet industry chain are all controlled basically by US companies. . . . '[I]n the Internet realm, the United States has the absolutely hegemony'").

47. SCO, Agreement Between the Governments of the Member States of the Shanghai Cooperation Organization on Cooperation in the Field of International Information Security, June 16, 2009 (on file with author) (describing sources and characteristics of the threat of information dominance at Annex 2, para. 4).

48. See "China Calls U.S. the 'Real Hacking Empire' after Pentagon Report," Reuters, May 8, 2013, http://news.yahoo.com/china-calls-u-real-hacking-emp ire-pentagon-report-024829833.html.

49. In 2013 the US intelligence community noted cyberthreats as a matter of first priority in its worldwide threat assessment. See Senate Select Committee on Intelligence, "Worldwide Threat Assessment of the U.S. Intelligence Community," Statement for the Record of James R. Clapper, Director of National Intelligence, March 12, 2013, http://www.intelligence.senate.gov/130312/clapper.pdf; Office of the Director of National Intelligence, Remarks as delivered by James R. Clapper, Director of National Intelligence, "Worldwide Threat Assessment to the Senate Select Committee on Intelligence," March 12, 2013, http://www.dni.gov/files/doc-uments/Intelligence%20Reports/WWTA%20Remarks%20as%20delivered%20 12%20Mar%202013.pdf. On Stuxnet, see David E. Sanger, "Obama Order Sped Up Wave of Cyberattacks against Iran," *New York Times*, June 1, 2012, http://www.nytimes.com/2012/06/01/world/middleeast/obama-ordered-wave-of-cyberattacks-against-iran.html?pagewanted=all. General Keith Alexander of US Cyber Command has publicly declared US development of offensive cyber capabilities. See "Pentagon Creates 13 Offensive Cyber Teams for Worldwide Attacks," RT, March 13, 2013, http://rt.com/usa/alexander-cyber-command-offensive-209/. The US government is also a major buyer in the market for computer exploits. See Joseph Menn, "Special Report: U.S. Cyberwar Strategy Stokes Fear of Blowback," Reuters, May 10, 2013, http://www.reuters.com/article/2013/05/10/us-usa-cyberweapons-specialreport-idUSBRE9490EL20130510.

50. See generally "The NSA Files," *Guardian*, http://www.theguardian.com/world/the-nsa-files.

51. See, e.g., Steve Holland, "Obama, China's Xi Discuss Cybersecurity Dispute in Phone Call," Reuters, March 14, 2013, http://www.reuters.com/arti-cle/2013/03/14/us-usa-china-obama-call-idUSBRE92D11G20130314; Office of the Secretary of Defense, *Annual Report to Congress: Military and Security Developments Involving the People's Republic of China 2013*, May 2013, http://www.defense.gov/pubs/2013_china_report_final.pdf; David E. Sanger, "U.S. Blames China's Military Directly for Cyberattacks," *New York Times*, May 6, 2013, http://www.nytimes.com/2013/05/07/world/asia/us-accuses-chinas-military-in-cyberattacks.html.

52. Zachary Keck, "Snowden: US Spies on China's Universities and Mobile Firms," *Diplomat*, June 23, 2013, http://thediplomat.com/2013/06/snowden-us-spies-on-chinas-univ ersities-and-mobile-firms/; Helen Gao, "Chinese Hail Edward Snowden as a Hero," *Guardian*, June 17, 2013, http://www.theguardian.com/commentisfree/2013/

jun/17/chinese-hail-edward-snowden-hero; Warren Murray, "Edward Snowden's NSA Surveillance Revelations Strain China-US Relations," *Guardian*, June 13, 2013, http://www.theguardian.com/world/2013/jun/13/snowden-revelations-nsa-china-relations?guni=Article:in%20body%20link.

53. "China Seen Probing IBM, Oracle, EMC after Snowden Leaks," Reuters, August 16, 2013, http://www.reuters.com/article/2013/08/16/us-china-ioe-idUSBRE97F02720130816.

54. William Wan, "After Snowden Revelations, China Worries about Cyberdefense, Hackers," *Washington Post*, September 4, 2013, http://www.washingtonpost.com/world/after-snowden-revelations-china-worries-about-cyberdefense-hackers/2013/09/04/0b5ae97e-ff62-11e2-9711-3708310f6f4d_story.html; "Central Leading Group for Internet Security and Informatization Established," China Copyright and Media, March 1, 2014, http://chinacopyrightandmedia.wordpress.com/2014/03/01/central-leading-group-for-internet-security-and-informatization-established/.

55. Criminal Law of the People's Republic of China, issued by the National People's Congress, promulgated July 1, 1979, effective January 1, 1980; revised March 14, 1997, effective October 1, 1997, Art. 105, http://www.npc.gov.cn/englishnpc/Law/2007-12/13/content_1384075.htm.

56. Garnaut, "The Children Devour the Revolution."

57. See Gillian Wong, "Hu: Hostile Forces Seek to Westernize, Split China," Associated Press, January 3, 2012, http://www.guardian.co.uk/world/feedarticle/10022027.

58. See, e.g., Joseph S. Nye Jr., "China's Soft Power Deficit," *Wall Street Journal*, May 8, 2012, http://online.wsj.com/article/SB10001424052702304451104577389923098678842.html.

59. Wang Chen, "Concerning the Development and Administration of Our Country's Internet," translation by Human Rights in China, *China Rights Forum: "China's Internet": Staking Digital Ground*, no. 2 (2010), http://www.hrichina.org/crf/article/3242, at para. III.6.

60. Ibid.

61. Ibid.

62. "Communiqué on the Current State of the Ideological Sphere," supra n. 33.

63. Edward Wong, "Riots in Western China Amid Ethnic Tension," *New York Times*, July 5, 2009, http://www.nytimes.com/2009/07/06/world/asia/06china.html.

64. Information Office of the State Council of the People's Republic of China, "Development and Progress in Xinjiang," September 21, 2009, section 7, http://english.people.com.cn/90001/90776/90785/6763708.html.

65. Ibid.

66. Ibid.

67. Ibid.

68. Ibid.

69. "China Urges Other Countries to Stop Funding 'East Turkistan Terrorists,'" Xinhua, July 14, 2009, http://english.cctv.com/20090714/109041.shtml.

70. Jonathan Kaiman, "China Knife Massacre Culprits Wanted to Wage Jihad Abroad, Official Says," *Guardian*, March 5, 2014, http://www.theguardian.com/world/2014/mar/05/china-knife-massacre-wage-jihad-abroad; Didi Tang, "Separatists Blamed for China Knife Attack; 33 Dead," Associated

Press, March 1, 2014, http://abcnews.go.com/International/wireStory/knife-wielding-men-attack-sw-china-train-station-22730405.

71. "Kunming Terrorist Attack Orchestrated by Xinjiang Separatists," Xinhua, March 2, 2014, http://news.xinhuanet.com/english/china/2014-03/02/c_133152815.htm; "Xinjiang Chairman Blames Overseas Forces for Separatist Activities," Xinhua, March 6, 2013, http://news.xinhuanet.com/english/special/2014-03/06/c_133166794.htm; Hannah Beech, "The Internet Helped Cause the Kunming Terrorist Attack, Says China," *Time*, March 6, 2014, http://time.com/14234/china-kunming-xinjiang-terror/.

72. Human Rights in China, "Jasmine Organizers Call for Rallies Every Sunday," February 22, 2011, http://hrichina.org/content/4895.

73. See Paul Mooney, "Why Does the CCP Fear the Jasmine Rallies?" *China Rights Forum: China at a Crossroads*, nos. 1–2 (2011), http://www.hrichina.org/crf/article/5419; Andrew Jacobs and Jonathan Ansfield, "Well-Oiled Security Apparatus in China Stifles Calls for Change," *New York Times*, February 28, 2011, http://www.nytimes.com/2011/03/01/world/asia/01china.html; Damian Grammaticas, "Calls for Protests in China Met with Brutality," British Broadcasting Corporation, February 27, 2011, http://www.bbc.co.uk/news/world-asia-pacific-12593328; Human Rights in China, "Lawyers and Activists Detained, Summoned, and Harassed in 'Jasmine Rallies' Crackdown," February 23, 2011, http://hrichina.org/public/contents/192623.

74. See Ku Yang, "Beijing Intensifies Pressure as Jasmine Smile Hits China," *China Rights Forum: China at a Crossroads*, nos. 1–2 (2011), http://www.hrichina.org/crf/article/5420.

75. David Bandurski, "A New Year's Greeting Gets the Axe in China," China Media Project, January 3, 2013, http://cmp.hku.hk/2013/01/03/30247/.

76. See Freedom House, "Special Feature: The 'Southern Weekly' Controversy," China Media Bulletin, January 18, 2013, http://www.freedomhouse.org/cmb/2013_southern_weekly; David Bandurski, "Inside the Southern Weekly Incident," China Media Project, January 7, 2013, http://cmp.hku.hk/2013/01/07/30402/.

77. China Digital Times, "Ministry of Truth: Urgent Notice on Southern Weekly," January 7, 2013, http://chinadigitaltimes.net/2013/01/ministry-of-truth-urgent-notice-on-southern-weekly/#.UOuww4cl77k.twitter; see also Abby, "China Blames 'Foreign Forces' for Press Freedom Protests," Global Voices, January 8, 2013, http://globalvoicesonline.org/2013/01/08/chinas-blames-foreign-forces-for-press-freedom-protests/.

78. Ibid.

79. See International Campaign for Tibet, *Tibet at a Turning Point: The Spring Uprising and China's New Crackdown*, August 6, 2008, http://72.32.136.41/files/documents/Tibet_at_a_Turning_Point.pdf.

80. International Campaign for Tibet, "Self-Immolations by Tibetans," April 16, 2014, http://www.savetibet.org/resource-center/maps-data-fact-sheets/self-immolation-fact-sheet.

81. See Gillian Wong, "As Tibet Burns, China Makes Arrests, Seizes TVs," Associated Press, January 18, 2013, http://news.yahoo.com/tibet-burns-china-makes-arrests-seizes-tvs-074227574.html; Hannah Beech, "As Tibetans Burn Themselves to Protest Chinese Rule, Communists in Beijing Stress Happiness in Tibet," *Time*, November 10, 2012, http://world.time.com/2012/11/10/as-tibetans-burn-themselves-to-protest-chinese-rule-communists-in-beijing-stress-happiness-in-tibet/; Gillian Wong, "China Rebukes Monastery at Heart of Fiery Protests," Associated Press, March 7, 2013, http://news.yahoo.

com/china-rebukes-monastery-heart-fiery-protests-063345759.html; see also "Communiqué on the Current State of the Ideological Sphere," supra n. 33 (listing "manipulating and hyping the Tibetan self-immolations" as one of the major efforts of "Western anti-China forces").

82. "Exiled Tibetans Accept Beijing's Rule, says PM-in-Waiting," Agence France-Presse, May 10, 2013, http://www.scmp.com/news/china/article/1233531/exiled-tibet-pm-lobsang-sangay-not-challenging-china-communists.

83. Dui Hua, "China Outlines Criminal Punishments for Tibetan Self-Immolations," *Human Rights Journal*, December 5, 2012, http://www.duihuahrjournal.org/2012/12/china-outlines-criminal-punishments-for.html.

84. Ibid.; "China to Press Murder Charges for Inciting Tibet Immolations," Agence France-Presse, December 6, 2012, http://sg.news.yahoo.com/china-press-murder-charges-inciting-tibet-immolations-194717384.html.

85. Calum MacLeod, "China Jails 8 Tibetans in Self-immolation Cases," *USA Today*, January 31, 2013, http://www.usatoday.com/story/news/world/2013/01/31/china-tibet-immolations/1880677/; "Feature: Monk Goads People to Commit Suicide," Xinhua, January 29, 2013, http://english.sina.com/china/2013/0128/554724.html.

86. See generally Laura Saporito and James A. Lewis, *Cyber Incidents Attributed to China*, Center for Strategic and International Studies, March 11, 2013, https://csis.org/publication/cyber-incidents-attributed-china.

87. Mandiant, *APT1: Exposing One of China's Cyber Espionage Units*, February 2013, http://intelreport.mandiant.com/.

88. Ibid.

89. "Cyber-Hacking: Masters of the Cyber-Universe," *Economist*, April 6, 2013, http://www.economist.com/news/special-report/21574636-chinas-state-sponsored-hackers-are-ubiquitousand-totally-unabashed-masters; Barbara Demick, "China Hacker's Angst Opens a Window onto Cyber-Espionage," *Los Angeles Times*, March 12, 2013, http://articles.latimes.com/2013/mar/12/world/la-fg-china-hacking-20130313; Melanie Lee, "Top China College in Focus with Ties to Army's Cyber-Spying Unit," Reuters, March 24, 2013, http://www.reuters.com/article/2013/03/24/net-us-china-cybersecurity-university-idUSBRE92N01120130324.

90. Office of the Secretary of Defense, *Annual Report to Congress: Military and Security Developments Involving the People's Republic of China 2013*; see also Sanger, "U.S. Blames China's Military Directly for Cyberattacks."

91. See Keith Bradsher, "China Blasts Hacking Claim by Pentagon," *New York Times*, May 7, 2013, http://www.nytimes.com/2013/05/08/world/asia/china-criticizes-pentagon-report-on-cyberattacks.html.

92. It is unknown how the copious amounts of information collected in cyber espionage campaigns linked to China are ultimately analyzed and escalated. The process employed for such analysis, including incorporation of data mining or other techniques, is an important area for further research.

93. Brian Krebs, "Chinese Hackers Blamed for Intrusion at Energy Industry Giant Telvent," Krebs on Security, September 26, 2012, http://krebsonsecurity.com/2012/09/chinese-hackers-blamed-for-intrusion-at-energy-industry-giant-telvent/#more-16936; Michael Riley and Dune Lawrence, "Hackers Linked to China's Army Seen From EU to D.C.," Bloomberg, July 26, 2012, http://www.bloomberg.com/news/2012-07-26/china-hackers-hit-eu-point-man-and-d-c-with-byzantine-candor.html; Dmitri Alperovitch, *Revealed: Operation Shady RAT*, McAfee (2011), http://www.mcafee.com/us/resources/white-papers/wp-operation-shady-rat.pdf.

94. Seth Hardy, "APT1's GLASSES: Watching a Human Rights Organization," Citizen Lab, February 25, 2013, https://citizenlab.org/2013/02/apt1s-glasses-watching-a-human-rights-organization/.

95. Ibid.

96. Trend Micro, *Luckycat Redux: Inside an APT Campaign with Multiple Targets in India and Japan*, March 2012, http://www.trendmicro.com/cloud-content/us/pdfs/security-intelligence/white-papers/wp_luckycat_redux.pdf.

97. Information Warfare Monitor and Shadowserver Foundation, *Shadows in the Cloud: Investigating Cyber Espionage 2.0*, April 2010, http://www.scribd.com/doc/29435784/SHADOWS-IN-THE-CLOUD-Investigating-Cyber-Espionage-2-0.

98. Information Warfare Monitor, *Tracking GhostNet: Investigating a Cyber Espionage Network*, March 2009, http://www.scribd.com/doc/13731776/Tracking-GhostNet-Investigating-a-Cyber-Espionage-Network.

99. See Citizen Lab: "Human Rights Groups Targeted by PlugX RAT," September 28, 2012, https://citizenlab.org/2012/09/human-rights-groups-targeted-by-plugx-rat/; "Recent Observations in Tibet-Related Information Operations: Advanced Social Engineering for the Distribution of LURK Malware," July 26, 2012, https://citizenlab.org/2012/07/recent-observations/; "Spoofing the European Parliament: An Analysis of the Repurposing of Legitimate Content in Targeted Malware Attacks," June 20, 2012, https://citizenlab.org/2012/06/spoofing-the-european-parliament/; "Information Operations and Tibetan Rights in the Wake of Self-Immolations: Part I," March 9, 2012, http://citizen-lab.org/2012/03/information-operations-and-tibetan-rights-in-the-wake-of-self-immolations-part-i/.

100. Jeff Seldin, "Reward Posters Part of Beijing's Immolation Crackdown," October 25, 2012, http://www.voanews.com/content/reward-posters-part-of-beijings-immolation-crackdown/1533250.html; see also "Rewards for Burning Tip-offs," Radio Free Asia, October 24, 2012, http://www.rfa.org/english/news/tibet/rewards-10242012141110.html.

101. "China Expands List of Activities Forbidden to Tibetans," Radio Free Asia, March 28, 2013, http://www.rfa.org/english/news/tibet/forbidden-03282013163454.html.

102. "Threat to Cut Aid over Burnings," Radio Free Asia, November 22, 2012, http://www.rfa.org/english/news/tibet/aid-11222012174527.html; Ananth Krishnan, "China: Will 'Crush Dalai Lama Clique,'" *Hindu*, March 2, 2012, http://www.thehindu.com/news/international/article2954854.ece; "Authorities Restrict Cellphone Use in Lhasa," Radio Free Asia, March 11, 2013, http://www.rfa.org/english/news/tibet/restrict-03112013145602.html; "China Plan Information Blackout in Eastern Tibet, Burn Satellite Dishes," Phayul, January 10, 2013, http://www.phayul.com/news/article.aspx?id=32815&t=1; "China Seizes TVs, Satellite Equipment in Tibetan Area," Reuters, December 27, 2012, http://www.reuters.com/article/2012/12/27/us-china-tibet-idUSBRE8BQ02O20121227.

103. See, e.g., Isaac Stone Fish, "China's Black Hole," *Foreign Policy*, April 26, 2013, http://www.foreignpolicy.com/articles/2013/04/26/china_s_black_hole_tibet_xinjiang.

104. Radio Free Asia, "China Expands List of Activities Forbidden to Tibetans."

105. Ibid.

106. "Authorities Restrict Cellphone Use in Lhasa," Radio Free Asia, March 11, 2013, http://www.rfa.org/english/news/tibet/restrict-03112013145602.html.

107. Xinhua, "Feature: Monk Goads People to Commit Suicide"; MacLeod, "China Jails 8 Tibetans in Self-Immolation Cases."

108. Xinhua, "Feature: Monk Goads People to Commit Suicide."

109. Ibid.

110. "China Sentences 2 Tibetans over Self-immolation," Xinhua, January 31, 2013, http://www.globaltimes.cn/content/759358.shtml.

111. Citizen Lab, "Permission to Spy: An Analysis of Android Malware Targeting Tibetans," April 18, 2013, https://citizenlab.org/2013/04/permission-to-spy-an-analysis-of-android-malware-targeting-tibetans/.

112. Ibid.

113. Ibid.

114. Chris Buckley, "China Convicts and Sentences 20 Accused of Militant Separatism in Restive Region," New York Times, March 27, 2013, http://www.nytimes.com/2013/03/28/world/asia/china-sentences-20-for-separatists-acts-in-restive-region.html.

115. "China Says No Foreign Link in Xinjiang Violence," Associated Press, May 2, 2013, http://www.scmp.com/news/china/article/1228260/china-says-no-foreign-link-xinjiang-violence; "Uyghur Students Detained in Regionwide Crackdown," Radio Free Asia, May 9, 2013, http://www.rfa.org/english/news/uyghur/crackdown-05092013114334.html; "Xinjiang Cell Phone Users Forced to Register with Real Names," Radio Free Asia, April 30, 2013, http://www.rfa.org/english/news/uyghur/register-04302013134824.html.

116. "Xinjiang Official Nur Bekri Says Evidence against Uygur Academic Ilham Tohti 'Irrefutable,'" Agence France-Presse, March 6, 2014, http://www.scmp.com/news/china/article/1442049/xinjiang-official-nur-bekri-says-evidence-against-uygur-academic-ilham; Macolm Moore, "China Silences Last Voice of Dissent on Xinjiang," Telegraph, February 26, 2014, http://www.telegraph.co.uk/news/worldnews/asia/china/10661998/China-silences-last-voice-of-dissent-on-Xinjiang.html; Andrew Jacobs, "China Accuses Uighur Intellectual of Separatism for His Advocacy Work," New York Times, January 25, 2014, http://www.nytimes.com/2014/01/26/world/asia/china.html.

117. Beech, "The Internet Helped Cause the Kunming Terrorist Attack, Says China."

118. See, e.g., "Hackers Target Uyghur Groups," Radio Free Asia, September 6, 2012, http://www.rfa.org/english/news/uyghur/hackers-09062012153043.html; Costin Raiu and Kurt Baumgartner, "Cyber Attacks against Uyghur Mac OS X Users Intensify," Securelist, February 13, 2013, https://www.securelist.com/en/blog/208194116/Cyber_Attacks_Against_Uyghur_Mac_OS_X_Users_Intensify.

119. In its investigation of the malicious Kakao Talk APK, Citizen Lab found that the actual sender email employed to distribute the malware was "uygur52@gmx.com," and the command-and-control domain used in the attack was "android.uyghur.dnsd.me." Citizen Lab, "Permission to Spy: An Analysis of Android Malware Targeting Tibetans," April 18, 2013, https://citizenlab.org/2013/04/permission-to-spy-an-analysis-of-android-malware-targeting-tibetans/. Moreover, in March 2013 Kaspersky Lab reported on a separate malicious APK sent to a Tibetan activist, which referenced a World Uyghur Congress conference in the APK filename as well as the body of the e-mail message to which the APK was attached. That malware harvested contacts, call logs,

SMS messages, geolocation, and phone data. Costin Raiu, Kurt Baumgartner, and Denis Maslennikov, "Android Trojan Found in Targeted Attack," Securelist, March 26, 2013, https://www.securelist.com/en/blog/208194186/Android_Trojan_Found_in_Targeted_Attack.

120. Nicole Perlroth, "Hackers in China Attacked the Times for Last 4 Months," *New York Times*, January 30, 2013, http://www.nytimes.com/2013/01/31/technology/chinese-hackers-infiltrate-new-york-times-computers.html.

121. Ibid.

122. Ibid.

123. Ibid.

124. See, e.g., "Head of Xinhua Says Western Media Pushing Revolution in China," Reuters, September 4, 2013, http://www.reuters.com/article/2013/09/04/us-china-media-idUSBRE9830DW20130904.

125. "China Tightens Media Regulations," *Economic Observer*, April 17, 2013, http://www.eeo.com.cn/ens/2013/0417/242711.shtml; William Wan, "China Renews Western Journalists' Visas after Months-Long Standoff," *Washington Post*, January 9, 2014, http://www.washingtonpost.com/world/china-renews-western-journalists-visas-after-months-long-standoff/2014/01/09/fde67b9c-792c-11e3-8963-b4b654bcc9b2_story.html.

126. It is noteworthy that in past US-China dialogues on cybersecurity, the Chinese side has indicated willingness to engage most fully on matters of cybercrime, while an impasse persists on more sensitive issues influenced by ideology. See Adam Segal, "U.S. and China in Cyberspace: Uneasy Next Steps," Council on Foreign Relations, June 18, 2012, http://blogs.cfr.org/asia/2012/06/18/u-s-and-china-in-cyberspace-uneasy-next-steps/; China Institute of Contemporary International Relations and Center for Strategic and International Studies, "Bilateral Discussions on Cooperation in Cybersecurity," June 2012, http://www.cicir.ac.cn/chinese/newsView.aspx?nid=3878.

127. Work within the UN's First Committee (Disarmament and International Security Committee) on cybersecurity, including meetings of the UN Group of Governmental Experts on Developments in the Field of Information and Telecommunications in the Context of International Security, is of relevance to this issue. See generally Eneken Tikk-Ringas, *Developments in the Field of Information and Telecommunication in the Context of International Security: Work of the UN First Committee 1998–2012*, 2012, available at https://citizenlab.org/wp-content/uploads/2012/08/UN-GGE-Brief-2012.pdf.

128. See "US-China Cybersecurity Working Group Meets," BBC, July 9, 2013, http://www.bbc.co.uk/news/world-asia-china-23177538.

129. See, e.g., Nils Melzer, *Cyberwarfare and International Law*, UNIDIR, 2011, http://unidir.org/pdf/activites/pdf2-act649.pdf, 28.

130. Ibid., 29.

131. See Paul Eckert and Anna Yukhananov, "U.S.-China Talks Cover Cyber Issues, Currency, Chinese Reform," July 10, 2013, http://www.reuters.com/article/2013/07/10/us-usa-china-dialogue-idUSBRE9690T520130710; see also Dan Roberts and Suzanne Goldenberg, "US-China Summit Ends with Accord on All but Cyber-Espionage," *Guardian*, June 9, 2013, http://www.theguardian.com/world/2013/jun/09/us-china-summit-barack-obama-xi-jinping.

132. UN General Assembly, "The Right to Privacy in the Digital Age," UN Doc. A/C.3/68/L.45/Rev.1, November 20, 2013, http://www.un.org/Docs/journal/asp/ws.asp?m=A/C.3/68/L.45/Rev.1.

133. "General Assembly Backs Right to Privacy in Digital Age," UN News Center, December 19, 2013, http://www.un.org/apps/news/story.asp?NewsID=46780& Cr=privacy&Cr1.

134. For further elaboration, see Sarah McKune, "Improving the Infrastructure of Support to Civil Society Actors in Confronting Cyber Threats," Stockholm Internet Forum on Internet Freedom for Global Development, April 19, 2012, http://www.stockholminternetforum.se/wordpress/wp-content/uploads/2012/03/OnePager_McKune.pdf.

PART IV

Practical and Theoretical Implications

CHAPTER 12

China and Information Security Threats

Policy Responses in the United States

FRED H. CATE

INTRODUCTION

"Cybersecurity" has come to dominate newspaper headlines in the United States and elsewhere as society's reliance on digital data and data-based systems increases and successful threats to those systems escalate. Until June 2013, when Edward Snowden disclosed activities of the National Security Agency (NSA) and shifted considerable attention to the United States, much of that attention focused on threats allegedly posed by China.

In 2013, administration officials began publicly identifying the Chinese government as the source of many cyberattacks—a tactic the *Economist* described as "naming and shaming."[1] In May, the US Department of Defense for the first time specifically named the Chinese government and military as the source of significant cyberattacks against the United States.[2] On May 7, the *New York Times*, typical of many US newspapers, editorialized about "China and Cyberwar," arguing that "there seems little doubt that China's computer hackers are engaged in an aggressive and increasingly threatening campaign of cyber espionage directed at a range of government and private systems in the United States."[3]

Despite the mounting attention to cybersecurity and the growing awareness that law and policy are critical to providing the appropriate incentives for effective defensive measures, there has been little action by US legislators. Proposed cybersecurity legislation has repeatedly died in Congress, with one telling exception: In March 2013 Congress adopted an appropriations bill, section 516 of which bars the Departments of Commerce and Justice, the National Aeronautics and Space Administration, and the National Science Foundation from acquiring information technology systems unless "the head of the entity, in consultation with the Federal Bureau of Investigation or other appropriate Federal entity" has made a risk assessment of potential "cyber espionage or sabotage . . . associated with such system being produced, manufactured, or assembled by one or more entities that are owned, directed or subsidized by the People's Republic of China."[4]

For its part, the Obama administration has been surprisingly bipolar in its approach to cybersecurity. During its first term, on the civilian or cyber defense side of the equation, the administration opposed legislation or regulation to enhance cybersecurity in the private sector or to address the perceived threat from China. Instead, it created a cybersecurity coordinator position with no authority or budgetary control over cybersecurity assets. On cyber offense, the administration expanded the use of cyberattacks as a national security tool and reportedly launched successful cyberattacks against Iran's uranium-processing facilities.[5]

In its second term, the administration appeared to be stepping up its efforts on both defensive and offensive fronts. While still failing to provide a central cybersecurity authority, the government issued a long-awaited executive order providing a road map for incentivizing better cybersecurity in the private sector, at least for providers of "critical infrastructure."[6] At the same time, it issued a classified executive order that press reports indicate instructed national security officials to consider other possible targets for offensive cyberattacks.[7] In February 2014, the US National Institute of Standards and Technology, following a yearlong collaborative process involving government agencies, industry, and others, released its "Framework for Improving Critical Infrastructure Cybersecurity."[8]

Complicating all of this has been a steady stream of disclosures in the popular press, often based on material provided by Edward Snowden, revealing the extent of US surveillance and the role of the NSA in allegedly creating, hiding, and exploiting cybersecurity vulnerabilities.[9] Moreover, according to unverified documents provided by Snowden, the NSA has been attacking "hundreds" of targets in Hong Kong and mainland China, as part of the agency's attacks on 61,000 targets worldwide.[10]

This chapter examines some of the key characteristics of digital data and networked control systems, as well as of the cybersecurity threats that target them; the US regulatory and policy approach to defending against cyberattacks; and the role of China in influencing that approach. It concludes by addressing some critical but unresolved issues about the essential role of law and policy and of the relationship between the United States and China in the fight to secure data and networks.

THE PROLIFERATION OF DIGITAL DATA AND NETWORKED CONTROL SYSTEMS

The Digital Data Avalanche

We are living through a deluge of digital data that we generate as we engage in everyday activities, that we increasingly volunteer to remote servers, that are observed by a growing explosion in sensor networks, and that ubiquitous networks, applications, and government regulations are conspiring to ensure are collected, stored, and shared. "With the rise of new networks," *BusinessWeek* wrote in its August 28, 2008, cover story, we are "channeling the details of our lives into vast databases. Every credit-card purchase, every cell-phone call, every click on the computer mouse [feeds] these digital troves. Those with the tools and skills to make sense of them [can] begin to decipher our movements, desires, diseases, and shopping habits—and predict our behavior."[11] The phenomenon that *BusinessWeek* was describing in 2008 has become even more routine and all-embracing today.

The vast collections of these data serve many important purposes—from law enforcement to medical research—but it is also true that the data can be revealing. "Our biographies are etched in the ones and zeros we leave behind in daily digital transactions," former Stanford Law School dean Kathleen Sullivan has written.[12] Those zeros and ones identify, describe, and increasingly define us to others.

There is a huge demand for these data and the services that generate them by individuals, industry, universities, the not-for-profit sector, political campaigns, and governments. Moreover, technology has not only contributed to an explosion in data, but also the range of parties with physical access to those data, and the practical and economic ability of those parties to collect, store, share, and use those digital footprints. According to the *New York Times*, one corporation—Acxiom—records 50 *trillion* data transactions a year.[13]

While the government has long made use of large datasets for many purposes, such as administering taxes and the distribution of public benefits, providing oversight of regulated industries, protecting borders, and investigating crime, it is the private sector that increasingly leads the way in creating and developing innovative uses for "big data." In fact, the government increasingly relies on data that industry collects and stores for commercial reasons or as required by regulatory compulsion for a wide variety of uses, including surveillance of US and foreign institutions and individuals. Whether held by public or private entities, such large datasets pose an increasingly attractive target for cyberattacks.

The Proliferation and Importance of Cyber Infrastructure

Our world is experiencing not only an avalanche of data, but also the proliferation of new networked data-based control systems. In this vast data-based infrastructure, software increasingly substitutes for what previously would have been controlled by hardware. Control systems for airplanes, trains, and natural gas pipelines all use the Internet, sometimes with wireless switches. And software control systems—sometimes referred to as SCADA systems for "Supervisory Control and Data Acquisition"—are joined by thousands of other data-based systems that rely on the Internet. We are moving to a smart grid for electricity—controlled by the Internet. Just-in-time supply chains are increasingly common, and all rely on the Internet. ATM networks and financial transactions use the Internet, as do credit and debit card transactions.

These systems increasingly are prevalent in every aspect of our lives. They constitute a "cyber infrastructure" that increasingly pervades every aspect of society. They almost all connect via the Internet, which means they are accessible globally and vulnerable to whatever viruses or other attacks are proliferating online. Moreover, they usually interconnect with each other and with other networks, which makes them difficult to isolate or protect. By eliminating physical controls managed by humans, they make malfunctions easier to obscure and potentially more likely to result in serious damage when they do occur. As with all data-based systems, they generate and store information that is also vulnerable to attack or misuse. The stakes are vast—not just to data but to the networks and control systems on which modern economies depend.

THE NATURE OF CYBERTHREATS

The Breadth of Threats

The extraordinary volume and variety of personal and other data accessible online and the expanding range of networked control systems face significant risks of being compromised—accidentally or deliberately. They create a vast attack surface that is increasingly being targeted. In the first six weeks of 2013, Apple, Facebook, Twitter, the *New York Times*, the *Wall Street Journal*, and the *Washington Post* all reported that they were among the "thousands of American corporations" attacked over the last three years.[14] In December 2013, Target, the United States' second largest retailer, was infected with malware that exposed credit card and personal data of more than 110 million customers.[15] In April 2014, researchers discovered perhaps the greatest security vulnerability in the Internet's history, the Heartbleed bug, which exposed the memory of systems protected by vulnerable versions of OpenSSL, a widely used encryption system used to protect online traffic and data.[16]

US government officials plainly recognize the threat. One of President Obama's first actions upon becoming president was to order a top-to-bottom review of cyberthreats and responses. The final report of that review could hardly be clearer:

> The architecture of the Nation's digital infrastructure, based largely upon the Internet, is not secure or resilient. Without major advances in the security of these systems or significant change in how they are constructed or operated, it is doubtful that the United States can protect itself from the growing threat of cybercrime and state-sponsored intrusions and operations. Our digital infrastructure has already suffered intrusions that have allowed criminals to steal hundreds of millions of dollars and nation-states and other entities to steal intellectual property and sensitive military information.[17]

Former US NSA director Mike McConnell wrote in the *Washington Post* in February 2010: "The United States is fighting a cyber-war today, and we are losing. It's that simple. As the most wired nation on Earth, we offer the most targets of significance, yet our cyber-defenses are woefully lacking. . . . The stakes are enormous."[18] In 2014, for the first time, cyberthreats headed the US Intelligence Community's Worldwide Threat Assessment.[19]

The breadth of the perceived threat is noteworthy. This was evident in President Obama's May 29, 2009, East Wing press statement on cybersecurity, at which he released the report produced by the White House cybersecurity review. In the context of that statement he identified as "digital infrastructure" risks the following: "cyber thieves trolling for sensitive information," "the disgruntled employee on the inside," "the lone hacker a thousand miles away," "organized crime," "the industrial spy," "foreign intelligence services," "cybercrime" (by which I think he meant identity theft), "hackers gain[ing] access to emails and . . . campaign files," "stealing money from ATM networks," theft of "corporate intellectual property," "cyber intruders . . . prob[ing] our electrical grid and in other countries . . . plung[ing] entire cities into darkness," "constant attack[s] . . . [against] our defense and military networks," "Al Qaeda and other terrorist groups . . . [threatening to] unleash a cyber attack on our country—a weapon of mass disruption," "malicious software—malware," "a glimpse of the future of war," and "Mumbai terrorists rel[ying] not only on guns and grenades but also on GPS on phones using voice-over-the-Internet."[20]

The breadth of cyberthreats, while adding to their importance, also interferes with efforts to address them effectively both within institutions and as a matter of national policy.

The Perceived Role of China

Much of the US political debate over cyberthreats has focused on threats allegedly posed by China, not just during the Obama administration, but many years earlier. In 2005, the *Washington Post* first published details of "Titan Rain," a series of attacks originating in China against computer networks in the Department of Defense, NASA, Lockheed Martin, and Sandia National Laboratories.[21] As the attacks continued, there were rechristened "Byzantine Hades," and were followed in 2009 by reports of "GhostNet," a series of attacks originating in China against significant targets in 103 countries, including the Dalai Lama's Tibetan exile centers in India, London, and New York City (see McKune, chapter 11 in this volume). Then came disclosures in 2010 about "Operation Aurora," in which Chinese hackers attacked Google, Adobe Systems, Juniper Networks, Rackspace, Yahoo, Symantec, Northrop Grumman, Morgan Stanley, and Dow Chemical, among other US companies. The press carried reports in 2011 about "Operation Shady RAT," which targeted dozens of organizations including the Department of Defense and defense contractors, the United Nations, and the International Olympic Committee. That same year, stories began circulating about "Night Dragon," a series of cyberattacks originating in China that targeted energy companies. The one thing all of these reports had in common was the alleged source of the attacks—China—although the press was careful to note that despite the fact that the attacks originated within China's borders it was not clear whether they were sponsored by the Chinese government.

That changed in 2013, when Obama administration officials and others began publicly identifying the Chinese government as the source of many cyberattacks. In February 2013, cybersecurity consulting firm Mandiant published a report linking attacks against US companies to a unit of the Chinese government.[22] The Mandiant report attributed to Unit 61398 of the People's Liberation Army successful hacks into 141 companies (115 in the United States) that exfiltrated terabytes of data. That same month, the *Washington Post* reported that the classified new National Intelligence Estimate identified China as "the country most aggressively seeking to penetrate the computer systems of American businesses and institutions to gain access to data that could be used for economic gain" through a "massive, sustained cyber-espionage campaign."[23]

In May, the Department of Defense for the first time specifically named the Chinese government and military as the source of significant cyberattacks against the United States.[24] May also saw publication of the report of the Commission on the Theft of American Intellectual Property, which stated boldly that "China is the world's largest source of IP theft," and pointed to cyber incursions as the primary method through which such theft occurred.[25] In the days leading up to the first summit meeting between Chinese president Xi Jinping and President Obama June 7–8, 2013, cybersecurity headed the US agenda. Ultimately, leaks by Snowden about the US government's own cyberattacks and online surveillance activities allegedly dampened the vigor with which the US president pressed the topic.[26] Ironically, the Chinese delegation refused to stay at the Sunnylands estate where the summit was held, reportedly out of fear that the US government would spy on them.

It is impossible to verify independently US claims about Chinese cyber activity, or Chinese claims about US spying. What is clear is that the evidence about Chinese activity is mounting to the degree that US companies and government agencies are increasingly willing to charge not only that significant attacks originate from China, but also that at least some of those attacks are connected with the Chinese government. Those allegations are playing an increasingly visible and potent role in the US debate over cybersecurity. This is evidenced by the fact that the only piece of cybersecurity legislation to pass Congress in the first half of 2013 was section 516 of an appropriations bill that restricts the ability of certain federal agencies to procure information technologies "produced, manufactured, or assembled by one or more entities that are owned, directed, or subsidized by the People's Republic of China."[27]

The Perceived Role of the United States

The leaks that began immediately prior to the US-China summit, and have continued ever since then, have largely revealed US surveillance activities around the world (including within the United States). But those leaks have also exposed cyber exploits by the NSA designed to facilitate surveillance, launch cyberattacks, and interfere with online transactions. According to documents provided by Snowden and widely reported in the press, the United States was actively hacking Chinese telecommunications companies, the owner of China's most extensive fiber-optic submarine cable network, and Beijing University.[28] One prominent target, according to documents reviewed by the *New York Times*, was telecommunications giant Huawei. The NSA installed backdoors into networks operated by Huawei, which reportedly serve a third of the world's population, not merely to collect information from the Chinese, but to surveil users in other countries that used Huawei's networks and to conduct offensive cyber operations.[29]

According to leaked NSA documents, US intelligence services carried out 231 offensive cyber operations in 2011.[30] "Load stations" operated by US intelligence agencies around the world—including at least two in China—allowed those agencies to interdict computers and related accessories, load malware or hardware components onto them, and then arrange for the delivery of the now-compromised equipment to their intended recipients.[31] In addition, the NSA's Tailored Access Operations (TAO) group uses "covert implants"—"sophisticated malware transmitted from far away, in computers, routers, and firewalls on tens of thousands of machines every year," with plans to expand exponentially.[32] According to officials interviewed by *BusinessWeek*, TAO implants access 2 petabytes of data an hour, "the equivalent of hundreds of millions of pages of text."[33]

The scope of the attacks is so vast that they are managed by an automated system—codenamed "Turbine"—intended, according to leaked NSA documents, to provide "intelligent command and control capability" for "industrial-scale exploitation" by the NSA.[34] The NSA documents tout Turbine as a tool for increasing the agency's capability to both gather intelligence and disrupt, damage, or destroy systems through "potentially millions of implants."[35] The documents detail the agency's ability to use the implants to covertly "take over a targeted computer's microphone and record conversations taking place near the device"; "take over a computer's webcam and snap photographs"; "record[] logs of Internet browsing histories and collect[] login details and passwords used to access websites and email accounts"; "log keystrokes"; and "exfiltrate[] data from removable flash drives that connect to an infected computer."[36] Leaked NSA documents also describe the NSA infecting computers with malware to infiltrate data from through "man-in-the-middle" attacks in which NSA servers impersonated real websites.[37]

Even machines never connected to the Internet can be compromised, according to Snowden's revelations, thanks to miniature technologies US intelligence agencies install on target computers, which then transmit information by radio to nearby briefcase-sized relay stations.[38] And targets include not only traditional computers, but mobile phones and large network servers, including those made by the Chinese.[39] Among frequent targets of the NSA's sophisticated attacks reportedly is the Chinese army, which the United States accuses of launching cyberattacks.[40]

Documents provided by Snowden also reveal that the NSA "has circumvented or cracked much of the encryption, or digital scrambling, that guards global commerce and banking systems, protects sensitive data like trade secrets and medical records, and automatically secures the e-mails, Web searches, Internet chats and phone calls of Americans and others around the world."[41] The NSA is not merely breaking encryption keys; it was obtaining them through "coercion" from industry, avoiding them through software implants in computers and encryption chips so that information is collected prior to being encrypted, and even introducing vulnerabilities into international encryption standards.[42] As a result, the NSA has the ability to "decode most of the billions of calls and texts that travel over public airwaves every day."[43] This ability was put to practical effect through listening stations atop eighty US embassies and other facilities, one of which, at the US embassy in Berlin, allowed the NSA to collect the calls of German chancellor Angela Merkel.[44]

The Increasingly Complex Relationship between the United States and China over Cybersecurity

While the cybersecurity dialogue promised during the June 2013 summit between Presidents Xi and Obama has sputtered along, the Obama administration has reduced efforts to "name and shame" the Chinese over cyber issues in large part because of the difficulty of doing so credibly while defending itself from domestic and foreign charges that it is engaged in similar attacks in China and other countries. US officials have tried to argue that it only conducts cyber operations against governments for military and other government information, while the Chinese are hacking businesses for trade secrets and commercial information, but this has proved a tough sell. Revelations about US cyber operations against Huawei and other networks in China and elsewhere, as well as leaked information about US efforts to obtain information on Indonesian trade negotiations and Brazil's largest energy company Petrobas, are seen as casting doubt on the veracity of US claims. As Jack Goldsmith, former assistant attorney general and special counsel to the Department of Defense during the George W. Bush administration, has noted, "the Huawei revelations are devastating rebuttals to hypocritical U.S. complaints about Chinese penetration of U.S. networks, and also make USG protestations about not stealing intellectual property to help U.S. firms' competitiveness seem like the self-serving hairsplitting that it is."[45]

It is also clear that the Chinese (and officials from other nations as well) do not always see the clear divide that the United States is trying to articulate between national security and industrial espionage. Peter Singer of the Brookings Institution has observed that "to the Chinese, gaining economic advantage is part of national security."[46] Moreover, the US campaign against Huawei not only prohibits the company from operating in the United States, but by pressing US companies not to purchase Huawei equipment and lobbying other countries to exclude the company from foreign markets, has clear competitive and economic effects, whether or not it is motivated by national security concerns.[47]

There is also the question of whether the distinction matters, especially in terms of international law. "Economic espionage is expressly prohibited by US domestic law, but is not prohibited by international law, written or unwritten, and it is widely practiced," Jack Goldsmith argues.[48] US complaints about China engaging in the wrong type of espionage "amount to the claim that the Chinese are not playing by the rules that suit the USG [US government]."[49]

Finally, as many cybersecurity experts have noted, activities designed to create or exploit security vulnerabilities for one purpose, no matter how important or well defined, are certain to weaken networks and expose them to attacks for other purposes. As security guru Bruce Schneier has argued, "the NSA not only develops and purchases vulnerabilities, but deliberately creates them through secret vendor agreements. These actions go against everything we know about improving security on the internet."[50] The reason why is clear: weakened encryption standards, covert backdoors, new hacking tools, compromised hardware, or undisclosed security vulnerabilities can be exploited by bad guys as well as good. According to Schneier, the risk "isn't hypothetical. We already know of government-mandated backdoors being used by criminals in Greece, Italy, and elsewhere."[51]

Whatever the merits of the United States' arguments, the unavoidable reality is that in the wake of Snowden revelations about US surveillance and cyber operations, those arguments just are not playing well. When President Obama raised the topic of hacking at the June 2013 summit, President Xi reportedly cited the *Guardian*'s first report on Snowden's revelations as "proof that America should not be lecturing Beijing about abusive surveillance."[52] After the revelations about US intrusions into Huawei's networks, William Plummer, a senior Huawei executive, observed "the irony is that exactly what they are doing to us is what they have always charged that the Chinese are doing through us."[53] Irrespective of distinctions about targeting government versus corporate information and even of the underlying accuracy of the Chinese response, revelations about NSA activities have compromised both the credibility and the effectiveness of US claims about Chinese hacking, even as those attacks are reportedly increasing.[54] "Snowden changed the argument from one of 'The Chinese are doing this, it's intolerable' to 'Look, the U.S. government spies, so everybody spies,'" according to Richard Bejtlich, former chief security officer at Mandiant.[55] Jason Healey, director of the Cyber Statecraft Initiative at the Atlantic Council, has observed: "no one cares anymore about our whining about Chinese espionage. The time we had for making the case on that is long gone. Internationally, I don't see how we recover."[56]

KEY ISSUES FACING POLICYMAKERS

Achieving effective cybersecurity is not easy, and US policymakers—as well as leaders of other countries—face critical issues, including the cyber activities of both China and the United States, that must be addressed if that goal is to be reached.

Need for Appropriate Incentives

Cybersecurity is a field in need of better incentives. At present it suffers from a "tragedy of the commons" phenomenon by which many key players assume someone else is providing for security, combined with a sense of despair about the size and complexity of the challenge that often frustrates significant investment. While it is often preferable to allow markets to create appropriate incentives for desired behaviors, there are occasions where government intervention is necessary. Information security is one of those instances. The threats are too broad, the actors too numerous, the knowledge levels too unequal, the risks too easy to avoid internalizing, the free-rider problem too prevalent, and the stakes too great to believe that markets alone will be adequate to create the right incentives or outcomes. Too many entities and individuals assume that someone else will take care of cybersecurity threats, or that the problems are too vast for individual responses to be meaningful, or that it is economically rational to leave the problem to somebody else on the basis that the actions of others will benefit everyone.

These are not unreasonable conclusions, but they are fundamentally incorrect or incomplete. For example, despite system-wide improvements in cyber defenses, individuals and institutions continue to act in ways that undermine even the best cyber protection. We connect to broadband networks and install home wireless routers with no security and little awareness of how to provide adequate security or the importance of doing so. We visit unsecured websites, download suspect files (even installing peer-to-peer software to facilitate doing so and also providing the world with unhindered access to our machines), fail to install or update antivirus software, connect to insecure wireless networks, and install unverified programs and equipment in our homes and offices, often in violation of corporate policies.

Behavior around passwords is an especially good example of the ways in which individual actors unwittingly defeat even strong security systems. A surprising number of people select easy passwords (including the word "password"), use them across dozens of sites, never change them, and the share them with family members and colleagues. In July 2012, Yahoo! confirmed that more than 450,000 Voices users had their usernames and passwords compromised and posted online by an anonymous group of hackers. An analysis of those passwords demonstrates that users continue to be our own worst nightmare when it comes to cybersecurity risks. CNET found 2,295 Yahoo! passwords where a sequential list of numbers was used (160 used "111111"). An astonishing 780 users had the word "password" as their password. Users chose the word "welcome" as part of their password in 437 cases; 161 used the word "freedom" as their password; the same number used another f-word. "Baseball" appeared 133 times, more than any other sport.[57] Analyses of prior breaches show similar results, with an astonishing number of users choosing simple, ineffective passwords—often first names, cities, days or months, sports team names, and other common words. Two percent of eHarmony users selected the names of the twelve months to protect their most sensitive personal information.[58]

The failure of both individuals and institutions to internalize and act to prevent cybersecurity losses also reflects a common inability to appreciate the full cost of those losses.[59] Unsecured networks, computers, and data threaten us all. Unsecured computers are used as "bots" to attack other systems as part of vast "botnets." Unsecured data are used for targeted phishing attacks that rely on personal data to make the fraudulent e-mail messages look more genuine. In addition, stolen data is combined with other stolen or publicly available data to piece together valuable intellectual property, create synthetic identities, and launch other attacks.

Moreover, individuals and institutions may be distanced from the impact of their poor security through other means. For example, Congress has limited the liability of credit card holders for fraudulent transactions to $50, and credit card companies rarely assess even that minimum charge, so credit card users have little economic incentive to protect their cards and related information.[60] Similarly, various forms of insurance may reduce the economic impact of cyberattacks.

For all of these reasons, few institutions adequately value the cost of lost or missing data, unless it concerns their own trade secrets or proprietary information. Too many businesses sell digital products and services that are not secure and use personal information in ways that make it vulnerable to error and abuse. While cyberattacks are growing increasingly sophisticated and malicious, many of the most successful take advantage of our simple failure to do the things that individuals and institutions know they should do to protect themselves. Consider that despite possessing sensitive personal information on more than 100 million Americans, Sony did not even have a chief information security officer when it suffered its serious breaches in 2011.[61] Neither did LinkedIn, the social network that lost 6.5 million of its members' passwords in 2012.[62] Amazingly, neither did RSA, the security company that had 40 million SecureID authentication tokens stolen in 2011.[63] Clearly, the market was not providing adequate incentives for appropriate cybersecurity preparedness.

Where markets fail to produce appropriate incentives, we usually look to law, yet, as economists Bruce Berkowitz and Robert Hahn observe, the government has largely rejected "regulation, government standards, and use of liability laws to improve cybersecurity in toto. These are all basic building blocks of most public policies designed to shape public behavior, so one must wonder why they are avoided like a deadly virus (so to speak)."[64]

Initially, the Obama administration was plainly in the camp of those who opposed regulation as a tool to enhance cybersecurity in the private sector. In his May 2009 cybersecurity announcement, even though he acknowledged that "the vast majority of our critical information infrastructure in the United States is owned and operated by the private sector," President Obama was adamant that his administration would "collaborate with industry to find technology solutions," rather than "dictate security standards for private companies."[65] These comments suggested to many that the administration intended to focus its cybersecurity efforts on new technologies, rather than creating legal and economic incentives for the private sector to invest in better security. In the days following that announcement, business leaders spoke openly about having "dodged the bullet" of cybersecurity regulation.

On February 12, 2013, the president issued an executive order on "Improving Critical Infrastructure Cybersecurity," which marks a clear reversal of the no-regulation policy.[66] Although worded in terms of "consultation" and "voluntary" adoption of a cybersecurity framework, which the National Institute of Standards and Technology released in February 2014, the executive order also calls for federal agencies to consider incentives, including changes to the federal acquisition regulations, for encouraging adoption of the framework.[67] It requires agencies to report on the extent to which the private sector is complying with the framework.[68] And, most significantly, the executive order directs agencies to "determine if current cybersecurity regulatory requirements are sufficient given current and projected risks"; to report on "whether or not the agency has clear authority to establish requirements based upon the Cybersecurity Framework to sufficiently address current and projected cyber risks to critical infrastructure, the existing authorities identified, and any additional authority required"; and, if current regulatory requirements are deemed to be "insufficient," to "propose prioritized, risk-based, efficient, and coordinated actions . . . to mitigate cyber risk."[69]

It is not at all clear that the administration can go far down the road of imposing cybersecurity requirements on industry without legislation. In repeated statements, administration spokespeople and cybersecurity experts have argued that congressional action was necessary. In his February 12, 2013, State of the Union address, the president himself called on Congress to "act . . . by passing legislation to give our government a greater capacity to secure our networks and deter attacks."[70] It remains to be seen whether Congress will take up the invitation, but in the absence of congressional action, the president's authority to regulate the private sector is limited.

However, incentives can take many forms other than direct regulation. Tax advantages, standard setting, investment, safe harbors from liability, and preferred status when competing for government contracts and grants are among the many tools available to the government to incentivize desired behavior. Some of these and similar measures can be undertaken without specific congressional authorization, but some form of direct regulation, authorized by Congress, seems necessary to achieve the broad accountability that effective cybersecurity requires. The big challenge is to target regulation and other incentives well to avoid overregulating, misregulating, or penalizing responsible businesses that are trying and may, on occasion, fail.

The proper scope of that regulation is also still uncertain. The executive order focused on "critical infrastructure," an approach that is understandable, but appears outdated in light of the increasing interconnections among networks and data—irrespective of industry sector or national boundaries—and the ever-expanding definition of the phrase. As detailed in the presidential policy directive that accompanied the executive order, "critical infrastructure" includes virtually the entire economic infrastructure of the United States, including chemical, commercial facilities, communications, critical manufacturing, dams, defense industrial base, emergency services, energy, financial services, food and agriculture, government facilities, healthcare and public health, information technology, nuclear reactors, materials, and waste, transportation systems, and water and wastewater systems.[71] The critical infrastructure approach may reflect divisions among federal agencies and congressional committees more than a rational assessment of cybersecurity threats and vulnerabilities. The addition of the concept of "critical infrastructure at greatest risk" in the executive order further complicates this approach.[72] In any event, the critical infrastructure approach seems unlikely to exclude many private-sector enterprises, even while it singles out some for extra federal scrutiny.

Irrespective of the scope of legislation or regulation, it is increasingly clear that law is increasingly vital to provide appropriate incentives, create meaningful oversight, and protect individual rights that are often implicated by security measures. Even the computer scientists organized by the US National Science Foundation to provide input into the White House's 2009 cybersecurity review stressed the need for a deeper understanding of "law, investment policies, [and] economics," and recommended creating a "small Trustworthy Systems Research Advisory Board, populated by researchers in systems and software sitting side by side with experts in law, public policy, and economics."[73] The executive order reflects a long-overdue, but important step to focus on the role of law in enhancing cybersecurity.

THE NEED FOR A COMPETENT CENTRAL AUTHORITY FOR CYBERSECURITY

Cybersecurity is an inherently broad topic; the vulnerabilities, threats, attackers, attack vectors, and motivations are all numerous and cut across jurisdictions and industry sectors. This breadth inherently challenges governments, which are generally organized along sectors. One of the critical foundational issues, therefore, is determining how the government (and private-sector organizations) should be organized to address cyberthreats and what powers it should have. There is mounting evidence that some central authority is necessary to articulate a strategy for cybersecurity, to oversee implementation of that strategy, and to take responsibility for failures.

To date, however, the US government has eschewed this approach. Responsibility for cybersecurity—defense and offense—is initially divided between military and civilian sectors. On the military side, US Cyber Command was stood up in 2009. It shares facilities, staff, and leadership with the NSA, thus raising the question about how the missions and resources of the two organizations differ. (The President's Review Group on Intelligence and Communications Technology, appointed by President Obama in light of the Snowden disclosures, in fact recommended splitting the NSA from Cyber Command, but the president rejected this advice.)[74] Despite this apparent centralization, cybersecurity in the military and national security context is still shared across all of the uniformed commands and apparently all of the intelligence agencies.

On the civilian side, which is more relevant to this discussion, rather than ensuring that someone has both the authority and the responsibility for overseeing efforts, the federal government has pursued a collaborative or competitive approach. Instead of a cybersecurity "czar," the White House has a "cybersecurity coordinator," and the recent executive order and accompanying presidential policy directive are largely consumed with parceling out and coordinating authority among dozens of "sector-specific agencies."

When it comes to keeping its own house in order, much less assisting the private sector, the civilian side of the federal government lacks a single point of leadership. At many private-sector organizations, by contrast, the chief information officer has the authority to take whatever measures he or she believes are necessary to secure the network, including the power to remove machines or users instantly if they are compromising the network. Surprisingly, no one in the civilian side of the federal government has that authority.

The disarray among cybersecurity authorities in the federal government is suggested by the fact that when Google announced in January 2010 that it had been the subject of a "highly sophisticated and targeted attack" that originated in China, later called "Operation Aurora," it turned to the NSA for assistance.[75] This was surprising given the NSA's location in the Department of Defense; its historical focus on securing government, not private-sector infrastructure; and the fact that the latter mission was the responsibility of the Department of Homeland Security. This move also worried many civil libertarians that the NSA would take advantage of

Google's extensive data and networks to assist in the agency's offensive use of cyberattacks.

The agencies sought to provide greater coordination among the military and civilian resources with the creation in 2010 of a Joint Coordination Element between DHS and NSA.[76] The Joint Coordination Element is based at the NSA, but includes staff from both agencies. To date, while it may have smoothed internal coordination between the two agencies, it has done little to provide any increased sense of leadership or direction to the civilian private sector on cybersecurity.[77] The Joint Coordination Element is not mentioned in the Critical Infrastructure Executive Order.

More significantly, the US Federal Trade Commission (FTC) does not appear in that order either, which is ironic since the agency has emerged as the primary cybersecurity regulator for the private sector. The FTC has explicit authority over cybersecurity only in limited sectors (e.g., protecting children under thirteen online), but it has applied its broad general authority under section 5 of the act that created it to target poor cybersecurity measures as "deceptive" or "unfair" practices affecting commerce.[78] While claims of deception require that the targeted company made some promise of good cybersecurity that it ultimately failed to live up to, the claim of unfairness is much broader and does not require any promises to customers. Instead, under federal law, to be unfair a practice must result in an injury to consumers that is "substantial," "not outweighed by any countervailing benefits to consumers or competition," and not something they could "reasonably have avoided."[79] Over the past decade, the FTC has brought more than fifty cybersecurity cases, about one-third of which involved a claim of unfairness. In almost all of those cases, the targets of the FTC's suits have settled—usually for consent decrees that involve no fine or admission of wrongdoing, but subject the companies to twenty years of FTC oversight. On April 7, 2014, the US District Court for New Jersey ruled that the FTC authority extends to cybersecurity.[80] This was the first (and only) judicial determination on this issue, and it occurred in the context of deciding a motion to dismiss, rather than following a full trial, and has yet to be endorsed by any appellate court, so it is only the first step in resolving the scope of the FTC's authority relating to cybersecurity.

However, because the FTC is an "independent" agency, not part of the administration as such, the administration has ignored it and other independent regulators that had sought to impose modest security requirements. As a result, coordination of cybersecurity in the federal government is not only divided between military and civilian agencies, but among dozens of agencies on each side, including independent agencies that are not directly subject to the administration's control but nevertheless play a leading role in enforcing cybersecurity standards. The administration's so-called cybersecurity coordinator appears to play little role and also is not mentioned in the Critical Infrastructure Executive Order. It seems clear that a more organized, if not centralized, approach will be necessary to achieve a higher level of cybersecurity.

The Need for Appropriate National and Multinational Frameworks for Pursuing and Responding to Cyberattacks

On October 11, 2012, then-US secretary of defense Leon Panetta delivered the first in a series of major administration policy addresses on cybersecurity. He warned:

> As director of the CIA and now Secretary of Defense, I have understood that cyberattacks are every bit as real as the more well-known threats like terrorism, nuclear weapons proliferation, and the turmoil that we see in the Middle East.
>
> And the cyber threats facing this country are growing. With dramatic advances, this is an area of dramatic developments in cyber technology. With that happening, potential aggressors are exploiting vulnerabilities in our security.[81]

One of the key steps he outlined as necessary for effective cybersecurity was for the government to put "in place the policies and organizations we need to execute our mission."[82]

The policies Secretary Panetta describe are indeed critical, not just for one department, but for the entire government and, ultimately, for governments working collaboratively. Consider, for example, the role of the US Department of Defense in launching Stuxnet, a computer virus that successfully targeted Iranian uranium centrifuges in an effort to slow that nation's development of weapons-grade fissionable material. As reported in the *New York Times*, the development of Stuxnet was a major initiative of both the Bush and Obama administrations.[83] Irrespective of whether the use of Stuxnet was appropriate or effective, it clearly occurred outside of an agreed-upon legal framework as to the legality of such an attack. Moreover, it has made the United States vulnerable to charges that it participated in deploying another virus, Flame, which has similarities to Stuxnet, and to attacks that use the Stuxnet "vehicle" to carry other malicious payloads that target US resources. It appears to have contributed to retaliatory attacks by Iran against US banks and other targets.[84] Together with subsequent disclosures by Edward Snowden, it raises questions about the US government taking advantage of, or even contributing to, undisclosed vulnerabilities in commercial operating systems to achieve national policies (as opposed to disclosing or helping to remedy those vulnerabilities). Perhaps most significantly, it limits the legitimacy of US claims that other countries violate norms of international law when they engage in cyberattacks, if the US government itself perpetrates such attacks.

As noted, the US officials claim that cyberattacks for political and national security purposes are totally different in terms of legal and diplomatic acceptability than if conducted for commercial advantage. It is not clear that this view is universally accepted, and even if it is, in a world of rapidly evolving and increasingly dual-use technologies, its application requires agreement on key terms and resolution of complex issues, such as how to handle attacks on commercial networks used to support both industrial and governmental activities.

National governments working separately and together need to begin the process of developing legal frameworks for when and under what circumstances cyberattacks may be used, and how to avoid causing collateral damage that could cost lives and lead to retaliatory attacks with cyber or other weapons. Until those frameworks are in place, cyberattacks are likely to cause harm beyond their direct impact by contributing to destabilizing an already fragile cyber environment.

In October 2008, the US National Academy of Sciences released its long-awaited report on information-based programs for fighting terrorism. The report was the product of a three-year study chaired by former secretary of defense William Perry and Academy of Engineering president and former president of MIT Chuck Vest. The report included a recommended framework for vetting new national security programs to ensure that they were both legal and consistent with US values and also effective and efficient. That framework would seem equally applicable for evaluating new cybersecurity tools as well.[85]

As Richard Clarke, former national coordinator for security, infrastructure protection, and counterterrorism, wrote in the *Washington Post* in February 2013: "There has been an enormous rush in the United States and abroad to create an army of cyberwarriors. Nations would be wise to consider a new cadre of cyber-diplomats, too."[86]

The Need to Prioritize Threats, Responses, and Resources

Information security has been dominated in recent years by a sense of unreality. Businesses make unrealistic promises in an effort to attract consumers or sell security solutions. State and federal agencies have been preoccupied with breach notices to the extent that they feel like a solution in search of a problem. Politicians have made bold statements about the importance of data security, while appropriating a pittance to fund a herculean task. Meanwhile data breaches continue apparently out of control, suggesting that even if they are not the direct cause of broad harm to individuals and the economy, they are at least a symptom of a larger-scale problem with institutions being stewards of data rather than merely users of it. And individuals behave with an almost breathless irresponsibility toward the security of their own and other's data and systems, largely insulated from the practical effects of their carelessness by laws and competitive businesses practices that shift financial responsibility to banks and retailers.

Policymakers and industry leaders need to develop a more realistic view of information security threats and of the steps and resources necessary to combat them. This requires prioritizing threats and vulnerabilities, and strategically deploying scarce resources to address them.

Security often tends to be backward-looking, responding to the most recently deployed threat. To a certain degree that is inevitable, but to succeed we need to not only reduce the time between attack and response, but also, where possible, anticipate and counter attacks even before they are witnessed. One key step is enhancing collaboration with the research community, which often identifies, or even predicts, threats before they are witnessed in the wild. Another, described in greater detail below, is to enhance data sharing, so that systems can begin actively combating new threats even before they experience them. A more aggressive, anticipatory approach is necessary, to replace our reactive, perimeter-based approach to information security.

In a very real sense, society is in an arms race against security threats. It is a race that we realistically cannot win—there will always be lost and stolen data; there will always be new threats—but that we cannot afford to lose. Staying in the race will require effective strategies, substantial investment, continual reevaluation of tactics and objectives, and sustained commitment—all things that governments are historically not very good at.

The Need to Enhance Data Sharing

The response to security threats has not kept up with the sophistication and efficient organization of many of those attacks. The United States, like most other countries, lacks good data about the frequency and severity of attacks. Organizations that successfully fend off an attack are not required to notify similarly situated entities, even though evidence shows that attacks driven off from one site just move to a less well-protected, similar site. US consumers receive billions of breach notices, but there is neither centralized reporting nationally (much less globally) of attacks and attack strategies, nor is there broad-based collaboration to identify and repel attackers.

Two-way information sharing between the private sector and the government has proven controversial in the United States because of fear that the government would obtain inappropriate access to private information. As a result, the Obama administration limited its February 2013 executive order to encouraging the government to share more data with the private sector, while remaining silent on the reporting and disclosure obligations of the private sector. Fears about inappropriate access to information or misuse of information by the government are common throughout much of the world and highlight the importance, discussed elsewhere, of having both a framework of laws and oversight tools to facilitate responsible information sharing and cyber activities in general and clear, legal protections for privacy to enhance public confidence.

The government needs to facilitate the information-sharing and collaboration necessary to enhance security effectively. At a minimum this means reducing barriers to collaboration wherever they occur, but it probably also requires mandatory reporting to the government or some other central clearinghouse of threats.

The Need for Clearer Statutory Protection for Privacy

As noted, concerns about privacy have led to resistance to effective cybersecurity measures in the United States and elsewhere. As a result, enhancing cybersecurity requires addressing those privacy concerns.

The Constitution

In the United States, privacy in the cybersecurity context is protected through three primary legal provisions. The first of these is the Fourth Amendment to the US Constitution, which prohibits "unreasonable searches and seizures," and has been interpreted by the Supreme Court to require judicial warrants to authorize searches.[87] This broad protection is narrowed through a series of exceptions adopted by the Supreme Court.

The Court has determined, for example, that warrants are not required to search or seize items in the "plain view" of a law enforcement officer,[88] for searches that are conducted incidental to valid arrests,[89] or to obtain records held by a third party, even if those records are held under a promise of confidentiality.[90] (The "third party" doctrine is addressed in greater detail below.)

In addition, the Fourth Amendment poses no limits on how the government may use information. As a result, personal data seized by the government in compliance with the Fourth Amendment may later be used in a context for which the data could not have been obtained lawfully.

The Fourth Amendment applies to searches and surveillance conducted for domestic law enforcement purposes within the United States, and those conducted outside of the United States if they involve US citizens. In a 1972 case commonly referred to as the *Keith* decision, the Supreme Court held that the Fourth Amendment also applies to searches and surveillance conducted for national security and intelligence purposes within the United States if they involve US persons who do not have a connection to a foreign power.[91] The Court, however, recognized that "different policy and practical considerations" might apply in the national security context than in traditional law enforcement investigations, and specifically invited Congress "to consider protective standards for . . . [domestic security] which differ from those already prescribed for specified crimes in Title III."[92]

Electronic Communications Privacy Act

The second significant legal protection for privacy likely to be relevant to cybersecurity issues is the Electronic Communications Privacy Act (ECPA). Title I of ECPA—the Wiretap Act—enacted in 1968, deals with the interception of communications in transmission.[93] It applies to "wire communications," although not to video unaccompanied by sound. To intercept wire communications in transit requires a "'super' search warrant," which can only be sought by designated federal officials and requires probable cause, details about the communication to be intercepted, minimization of any nonrelevant communications inadvertently intercepted, and termination immediately upon completion.[94] Information obtained in violation of these requirements is subject to the exclusionary rule so that it cannot be used in a subsequent criminal prosecution.

Title II of ECPA—the Stored Communications Act—was adopted in 1986 and deals with communications in electronic storage, such as e-mail and voice mail.[95] Traditional warrants are required to obtain access to communications stored 180 days or less. To obtain material stored for more than 180 days, the government need only provide an administrative subpoena, a grand jury subpoena, a trial subpoena, or a court order, all of which are easier to obtain. Information about a customer's account maintained by a communications provider can be obtained by the government merely by providing "specific and articulable facts showing that there are reasonable grounds to believe that . . . the records or other information sought are relevant and material to an ongoing criminal investigation."[96]

Title III—the Pen Register Act—also adopted in 1986, applies to "pen registers" (to record outgoing call information) and "trap and trace" devices (to record incoming call information).[97] To obtain information akin to what is contained in a phone bill or revealed by caller ID, e-mail header information (the "To," "From," "Re," and "Date" lines in an e-mail), or the IP address of a site visited on the Web, then government need only obtain a court order. The court must provide the order—there is no room for judicial discretion—if the government has certified that "the information likely to be obtained by such installation and use is relevant to an ongoing investigation."[98]

Foreign Intelligence Surveillance Act

ECPA is concerned with collecting electronic information for domestic law enforcement purposes. The third relevant legal provision concerns the collection of information—electronic or otherwise—for foreign intelligence or national security purposes—traditionally areas subject to the president's discretion. Following the Supreme Court's 1972 invitation to Congress in the *Keith* decision to "consider protective standards" in this area, Congress enacted the Foreign Intelligence Surveillance Act of 1978 (FISA).[99] The act created a statutory regime governing the collection of "foreign intelligence" from a "foreign power" or "agent of a foreign power" within the borders of the United States. The act established a special court—the Foreign Intelligence Surveillance Court—of seven (now eleven) federal district court judges. The court meets in secret and hears applications from the Department of Justice for ex parte orders authorizing surveillance or physical searches. All that the government must show is that there is "probable cause to believe that the target of the electronic surveillance is a foreign power or agent of a foreign power"[100] and that gathering foreign intelligence is "the purpose" of the requested order.[101] In 2001, the USA PATRIOT Act changed this standard to "a significant purpose."[102]

Congress substantially amended FISA in the Protect America Act of 2007 and the FISA Amendments Act of 2008.[103] The laws were enacted in response to a number of Bush administration programs involving warrantless searches of telephone conversations. These laws permit the attorney general and the director of national intelligence to "authorize jointly, for a period of up to one year from the effective date of the authorization, the targeting of persons reasonably believed to be located outside the United States to acquire foreign intelligence information," even if all or part of the communication occurs within the United States.[104] Applications for mass surveillance of persons reasonably believed to be located outside of the United States ("mass acquisition orders") must be submitted to the FISA court, but the court's role is "narrowly circumscribed" and extends only to reviewing such applications to ensure compliance with procedural requirements.[105] The FISA Amendments Act of 2008 also effectively granted immunity to the telecommunications providers for "providing any information, facilities, or assistance" to assist the government with warrantless surveillance.[106]

Section 215 of the USA PATRIOT Act amended an existing statutory provision to allow the Foreign Intelligence Surveillance Court to grant secret orders requiring the production of "any tangible things (including books, records, papers, documents, and other items) for an investigation to protect against international terrorism or clandestine intelligence activities."[107] Section 215 was amended in 2006 to require that an application establish "reasonable grounds to believe that the tangible things are relevant to an authorized investigation," but presuming relevance in the case of foreign powers, agents of foreign powers, subjects of authorized counterintelligence or counterterrorism investigations, and individuals known to associate with the subjects of such investigations.[108]

Privacy Law Reform

These are not the only protections for privacy in US law, but they are the most relevant for cybersecurity initiatives. In practice, these laws are marked by what Professor Daniel Solove, an expert in privacy law, has described as "profound complexity."[109] Courts have "described surveillance law as caught up in a 'fog,' 'convoluted,' 'fraught with trip wires,' and 'confusing and uncertain.'"[110] As a result, privacy is often not protected and public and legislative concerns about the proper line between privacy and security have led to political firestorms over proposed security programs and created great uncertainty and even a sense of personal risk among security professionals in the government.

That ambiguity and its consequences were amply demonstrated by documents provided by Edward Snowden and later by the Obama administration revealing that the Foreign Intelligence Surveillance Court had granted secret orders authorizing the collection of "metadata" about all US domestic and international calls despite the absence of any "authorized investigation" to which such a sweeping set of data could be relevant.[111] Subsequent disclosures that the NSA was using authorized access to data about non-US persons collected abroad to obtain data on US persons, was exploiting ambiguity about whether or not data concerned a US person to collect and retain the data, and was retaining for up to five years data about US persons erroneously collected have only furthered calls for clarifying and strengthening US privacy law.[112] Added to this was the revelation that officials from the intelligence community had misled the Foreign Intelligence Surveillance Court and Congress, even when appearing under oath,[113] thus casting further doubt on the effectiveness of existing oversight mechanisms and leading to calls for sweeping improvements from two panels charged with reviewing NSA activities.[114]

In addition, under the US Supreme Court's "third-party doctrine," sensitive personal data held by third parties is denied any protection under the Fourth Amendment. The doctrine originated in 1976 in *United States v. Miller*, where the Court held that there can be no reasonable expectation of privacy in information shared with a third party.[115] The case involved canceled checks, to which, the Court noted, "respondent can assert neither ownership nor possession."[116] Such documents "contain only information voluntarily conveyed to the banks and exposed to their employees in the ordinary course of business,"[117] and therefore the Court found that the Fourth Amendment is not implicated when the government sought access to them:

> The depositor takes the risk, in revealing his affairs to another, that the information will be conveyed by that person to the Government. This Court has held repeatedly that the Fourth Amendment does not prohibit the obtaining of information revealed to a third party and conveyed by him to Government authorities, even if the information is revealed on the assumption that it will be used only for a limited purpose and the confidence placed in the third party will not be betrayed.[118]

The Court reinforced its holding in *Miller* in the 1979 case of *Smith v. Maryland*, involving information about (as opposed to the content of) telephone calls.[119] The Supreme Court found that the Fourth Amendment is inapplicable to telecommunications "attributes" (e.g., the number dialed, the time the call was placed, the duration of the call, etc.), because that information is necessarily conveyed to, or observable by, third parties involved in connecting the call.[120] "[T]elephone users, in sum, typically know that they must convey numerical information to the phone company; that the phone company has facilities for recording this information; and that the phone company does in fact record this information for a variety of legitimate business purposes."[121] Title III of ECPA was enacted to help fill the hole created by this decision.

Excluding data held by third parties from the protection of the Fourth Amendment is problematic today because of the extraordinary increase in both the volume and sensitivity of information about individuals necessarily held by third parties. The Supreme Court's exemption from the Fourth Amendment for records held by third parties today means that virtually all personal information is removed from the protection of the Fourth Amendment. As a result, individuals feel more exposed than ever to government scrutiny, and thus are less accepting of measures that might implicate personal information in the quest for better information security.

Imposing some order on the law applicable to privacy and security could go a long way toward building public support for important security measures, while also providing everyone with clearer congressional guidance about the proper protection of privacy. In the absence of that support, legislation designed to enhance cyber preparedness, such as bills debated in the US Congress during 2012, will continue to fail due to fears over the power they would give the federal government.

This issue is of more than merely domestic importance. Provinces in Canada and a growing range of national governments in the European Union have cited the US government's broad access to private-sector records as a basis for blocking the export of personal data to the United States.[122] Addressing this issue is critical to building stronger, more cooperative relationships with our allies in the quest for better security.

The Technology and Privacy Advisory Committee, the blue-ribbon bipartisan committee then-secretary of defense Donald Rumsfeld appointed to examine privacy and security issues, reported in 2004 that "[l]aws regulating the collection and use of information about US persons are often not merely disjointed, but outdated." They "fail to address extraordinary developments in digital technologies, including the Internet." As a result, "It is time to update the law to respond to new challenges."[123] The National Academy of Sciences echoed the call for updating laws in 2008, again to no avail.[124]

THE NEED TO ENGAGE CHINA—AND OTHER NATIONS—
MORE EFFECTIVELY

Given the prevalence of cyberattacks from other countries and the intrinsically multinational character of data flows, it would seem obvious that the United States and other nations must do more to engage their allies and their adversaries if they are to have any hope of improving cybersecurity (or address other digital issues). The need is especially great in light of what appears to be growing nationalism around information. The United States targets China (and, to a lesser degree, Russia) on cybersecurity issues; following the Snowden leaks, much of the world is criticizing the United States for its cyber incursions. Europe and Canadian provinces target the United States on privacy issues. China, India, the United States, and other countries focus on national origin of critical components of cyber infrastructure in an effort to better secure that infrastructure. India has sought to require the disclosure of encryption keys by US and Canadian telecommunications and Internet service providers and of transaction data by US credit card and other financial institutions as part of its antiterrorism initiatives. Brazil, Iran, and other countries have announced plans to build their own Internets.

This petty nationalism compromises rather than enhances security. Cybercriminals, like the data and networks themselves, move freely across national borders that restrain national laws and enforcement. No efforts to enhance cybersecurity will be truly effective if they do not involve international cooperation. This seems especially true and important in the case of the United States and China.

There are a number of policy steps that the United States could take alone, or could seek to facilitate multinationally, to enhance cybersecurity, US credibility about cybersecurity, and the global environment for addressing cybersecurity in the future. Some of these are described above and some are already underway. Whatever their domestic value, however, these measures would facilitate critical bilateral and multilateral efforts to enhance cybersecurity. Moreover, these measures interrelate, so it will be difficult to achieve any of the broader goals of enhancing cybersecurity, US credibility, or global cooperation without making some significant progress in each of these areas.

Policy Steps

Be careful about rhetoric, especially if the rhetoric is going to make the United States appear hypocritical. This does not require shying away from calling out bad behavior, but it does require both appreciation of the diplomatic niceties of dealing with another sovereign nation and the importance of not appearing inconsistent in either words or deeds. The tone of communications has also been repeatedly demonstrated to be very important, so while "naming" may be appropriate in appropriate circumstances, "shaming" may not be the best approach to dealing with China over cybersecurity.

It is vital that the United States not weaken through its cyber activities the very cyber infrastructure it is claiming to be seeking to protect. This does not mean that it should not conduct lawful surveillance, but rather that it should not create, distribute, or hide vulnerabilities that broadly weaken security in the private sector or civilian infrastructure. Moreover, as described in greater detail below, it should support the creation of legal restraints on government activities that threaten cybersecurity, structures, and processes to ensure appropriate oversight, and both domestic and multinational efforts to define acceptable offensive cyberattacks and the contexts in which they may lawfully be employed. Those efforts likely would benefit from splitting the NSA into two agencies so that its intelligence-gathering mission is not seen as overriding its cyber assurance mission.

The United States should enact necessary legal changes to provide oversight and protect privacy. This is necessary because of the degree to which technological capabilities have outstripped US law, and it is essential both to protect constitutional rights at home and to build credibility with international partners. For the same reasons, the United States should work to ensure, and to be able to demonstrate, that it follows its own laws and that when senior officials speak, especially before Congress, that they tell the truth or suffer consequences for failing to do so. The recent revelations about senior intelligence officials misleading Congress and the Foreign Intelligence Surveillance Court are not nearly as surprising, and harmful to US interests, as the apparent unwillingness of the president to take action against them for doing so.

Another important step is to increase transparency about government cyber activities. This may seem like an impossible goal in an area so intertwined with national security, but a key place to start is transparency within government, so that different agencies are not speaking or acting inconsistently. In addition, transparency about processes and goals need not threaten national interests, and can do much to enhance them. The United States managed to establish a high degree of transparency about key elements of its nuclear arsenal in dealing with arms control with the Soviet Union. Former Secretary of Defense Chuck Hagel has offered initial steps toward transparency about the US cyber arsenal in talks with the Chinese.[125] These are important beginnings on which both the United States and China would do well to follow through.

Finally, there is a critical need to expand efforts to define multinational norms, and ultimately reach multinational agreements, about appropriate types, uses, targets, and purposes of cyberattacks. Disagreements over these issues have been a hallmark of the relationship between China and the United States in recent years. While a solution to those disagreements may be far away, a key first step toward finding it, and enhancing cybersecurity, is to focus on common ground and shared goals. In the long run, presumably neither China nor the United States benefits from cyber activities that destabilize the networks that support trade and commerce. The importance of those networks and the economic and political impact of any interruption to them is only increasing. Another key early step would be to define key terms and concepts to help clarify disagreements and provide a vocabulary for moving forward.

CONCLUSION

The risks posed by cyberthreats are rapidly escalating as our dependence on stored digital data and digital networks expands. Cyberattacks identified as originating in China, and in some cases alleged to have been launched by the Chinese government itself, are playing an increasingly influential role in motivating US responses. Meanwhile, disclosures about US behavior have significantly weakened US credibility. The focus on Chinese threats, combined with the political and diplomatic inability to deal effectively with those perceived threats, is undesirable both because it leaves significant threats unaddressed and because it contributes to US policymakers losing sight of the broad range of cyberthreats and their many sources, which include, but certainly are not limited to, China. Technologies contribute both to the threat and to potential responses, but technology alone will never offer adequate protection. A workable, effective strategy inevitably requires the judicious use of law and policy to provide real incentives for better security, establish rules for the use of forensic investigations and "counterattacks" in cyberspace by governments and businesses, prioritize threats and responses, protect privacy, and facilitate information sharing and meaningful cooperation within nations and across national borders. Law and policy will also be critical in strengthening cybersecurity everywhere, enhancing US credibility and ability to lead on cyber issues, and to building a multinational framework for addressing differences over cybersecurity in the future.

NOTES

1. "Admit Nothing and Deny Everything," *Economist*, June 8, 2013.
2. Ellen Nakashima, "Confidential Report Lists U.S. Weapons System Designs Compromised by Chinese Cyberspies," *Washington Post*, May 27, 2013, A1, http://articles.washingtonpost.com/2013-05-27/world/39554997_1_u-s-miss ile-defenses-weapons-combat-aircraft.
3. Editorial, "China and Cyberwar," *New York Times*, May 7, 2013, http://www. nytimes.com/2013/05/08/opinion/china-and-cyberwar.html?ref=stuxnet&_r=0.
4. Consolidated and Further Continuing Appropriations Act for Fiscal Year 2013, Pub. L. No. 113-6, § 516 (2013).
5. David Sanger, "Obama Order Sped Up Wave of Cyberattacks against Iran," June 1, 2012, A1, http://www.nytimes.com/2012/06/01/world/middleeast/ obama-ordered-wave-of-cyberattacks-against-iran.html.
6. The White House, Improving Critical Infrastructure Cybersecurity (Executive Order), February 12, 2013, http://www.whitehouse.gov/the-press-office/2013/02/12/ executive-order-improving-critical-infrastructure-cybersecurity.
7. Seth Rosenblatt, "Revealed: U.S. Compiled Secret Cybertargets List," CNet, June 7, 2013, http://news.cnet.com/8301-1009_3-57588291-83/revealed-u.s-compi led-secret-cybertargets-list/.
8. U.S. National Institute of Standards and Technology, "Framework for Improving Critical Infrastructure Cybersecurity," February 12, 2014, http://www.nist.gov/ cyberframework/upload/cybersecurity-framework-021214-final.pdf.
9. See "Timeline of Edward Snowden's Revelations," Aljazeera America, http://amer-ica.aljazeera.com/articles/multimedia/timeline-edward-snowden-revelations. html.
10. Kelvin Chan, "Leaker Snowden Alleges NSA Hacking on China, World," *South China Morning Post*, June 18, 2013, http://www.scmp.com/news/hong-kong/ article/1260074/leaker-snowden-alleges-nsa-hacking-china-world.
11. "Introduction to Book Excerpt: The Numerati by Stephen Baker," *Businessweek*, August 28, 2008, http://www.businessweek.com/stories/2008-08-27/book-excerpt-the-numerati-by-stephen-baker. Ironically, the 2008 story is actually referring to a January 23, 2006, cover story, "Math Will Rock Your World."
12. Kathleen M. Sullivan, "Under a Watchful Eye: Incursions on Personal Privacy," in *The War on Our Freedoms: Civil Liberties in an Age of Terrorism*, ed. Richard Leone and Greg Anrig Jr. (New York: Public Affairs, 2003), 128, 131.
13. Natasha Singer, "You for Sale: Mapping, and Sharing, the Consumer Genome," *New York Times*, June 16, 2012, http://www.nytimes.com/2012/06/17/ technology/acxiom-the-quiet-giant-of-consumer-database-marketing. html?pagewanted=all.
14. Nicole Perlroth, "Some Victims of Online Hacking Edge into the Light," *New York Times*, February 20, 2013, http://www.nytimes.com/2013/02/21/technology/ hacking-victims-edge-into-light.html?pagewanted=all&_r=0.
15. "Sources: Target Investigating Data Breach," Krebs on Security, December 13, 2013, http://krebsonsecurity.com/2013/12/sources-target-investigating-data-breach/; "Target: Names, Emails, Phone Numbers on up to 70 Million Customers Stolen," Krebs on Security, January 14, 2014, http://krebsonsecurity. com/2014/01/target-names-emails-phone-numbers-on-up-to-70-million-customers-stolen/; "Email Attack on Vendor Set Up Breach at Target,"

Krebs on Security, February 14, 2014, http://krebsonsecurity.com/2014/02/email-attack-on-vendor-set-up-breach-at-target/.

16. Brian X. Chen, "Q. and A. on Heartbleed: A Flaw Missed by the Masses," *New York Times*, April 9, 2014, http://bits.blogs.nytimes.com/2014/04/09/qa-on-heartbleed-a-flaw-missed-by-the-masses/?_php=true&_type=blogs&_r=0.

17. White House, *Cyberspace Policy Review: Assuring a Trusted and Resilient Information and Communications Infrastructure* (2009), I, http://www.whitehouse.gov/assets/documents/Cyberspace_Policy_Review_final.pdf.

18. Mike McConnell, "We're Losing the Cyber-War: Here's the Strategy to Win It." *Washington Post*, February 28, 2010, B01, http://www.washingtonpost.com/wp-dyn/content/article/2010/02/25/AR2010022502493.html.

19. James R. Clapper, "Worldwide Threat Assessment of the U.S. Intelligence Community," Statement for the Record before the Senate Select Committee on Intelligence, January 29, 2014, http://www.dni.gov/files/documents/Intelligence%20Reports/2014%20WWTA%20%20SFR_SSCI_29_Jan.pdf.

20. White House, "Remarks by the President on Securing Our Nation's Cyber Infrastructure," Washington, DC, May 29, 2009, http://www.whitehouse.gov/the-press-office/remarks-president-securing-our-nations-cyber-infrastructure.

21. Bradley Graham, "Hackers Attack via Chinese Web Sites," *Washington Post*, August 25, 2005, A1.

22. Mandiant, *APT1: Exposing One of China's Cyber Espionage Units*, 2013, http://intel-report.mandiant.com/.

23. Ellen Nakashima, "U.S. Said to be Target of Massive Cyber-Espionage Campaign," *Washington Post*, February 10, 2013, A1, http://articles.washingtonpost.com/2013-02-10/world/37026024_1_cyber-espionage-national-counterintelligence-executive-trade-secrets.

24. Nakashima, "Confidential Report Lists U.S. Weapons System Designs Compromised by Chinese Cyberspies."

25. Commission on the Theft of American Intellectual Property, *The IP Commission Report*, 2013, 2, http://ipcommission.org/report/IP_Commission_Report_052213.pdf.

26. Tim Walker, "'Positive' US-China Summit Stumbles over Cyber Security," *Independent* (London), June 9, 2013, http://www.independent.co.uk/news/world/americas/positive-uschina-summit-stumbles-over-cyber-security-8651256.html.

27. Consolidated and Further Continuing Appropriations Act for Fiscal Year 2013.

28. Kurt Eichenwald, "How Edward Snowden Escalated Cyber War with China," *Newsweek*, November 1, 2013, http://www.newsweek.com/how-edward-snowden-escalated-cyber-war-1461.

29. David E. Sanger and Nicole Perlroth, "N.S.A. Breached Chinese Servers Seen as Security Threat," *New York Times*, March 22, 2014, http://www.nytimes.com/2014/03/23/world/asia/nsa-breached-chinese-servers-seen-as-spy-peril.html?_r=0.

30. Barton Gellman and Ellen Nakashima, "U.S. Spy Agencies Mounted 231 Offensive Cyber-Operations in 2011, Documents Show," *Washington Post*, August 30, 2013, http://www.washingtonpost.com/world/national-security/us-spy-agencies-mounted-231-offensive-cyber-operations-in-2011-documents-show/2013/08/30/d090a6ae-119e-11e3-b4cb-fd7ce041d814_story.html.

31. David E. Sanger and Thom Shanker, "N.S.A. Devises Radio Pathway into Computers," *New York Times*, January 14, 2014, http://www.nytimes.com/2014/01/15/us/

nsa-effort-pries-open-computers-not-connected-to-internet.html; "Inside TAO: Documents Reveal Top NSA Hacking Unit," *Der Spiegel*, December 29, 2013, http://www.spiegel.de/international/world/the-nsa-uses-powerful-toolbox-in-effort-to-spy-on-global-networks-a-940969.html.

32. "Inside TAO."
33. Michael Riley, "How the U.S. Government Hacks the World," *Businessweek*, May 23, 2013, http://www.businessweek.com/articles/2013-05-23/how-the-u-dot-s-dot-government-hacks-the-world.
34. Ryan Gallagher and Glenn Greenwald, "How the NSA Plans to Infect 'Millions' of Computers with Malware," *The Intercept*, March 12, 2014, https://firstlook.org/theintercept/article/2014/03/12/nsa-plans-infect-millions-computers-malware/.
35. Ibid.
36. Ibid.
37. Gallagher and Greenwald, "How the NSA Plans to Infect 'Millions' of Computers."
38. Sanger and Shanker, "N.S.A. Devises Radio Pathway into Computers."
39. Ibid.
40. Ibid.
41. Nicole Perlroth, Jeff Larson, and Scott Shane, "N.S.A. Able to Foil Basic Safeguards of Privacy on Web," *New York Times*, September 5, 2013, http://www.nytimes.com/2013/09/06/us/nsa-foils-much-internet-encryption.html?pagewanted=all&_r=0.
42. Ibid.
43. Craig Timberg and Ashkan Soltani, "By Cracking Cellphone Code, NSA Has Capacity for Decoding Private Conversations," *Washington Post*, December 13, 2013, http://www.washingtonpost.com/business/technology/by-cracking-cellphone-code-nsa-has-capacity-for-decoding-private-conversations/2013/12/13/e119b598-612f-11e3-bf45-61f69f54fc5f_story.html.
44. Ibid.
45. Jack Goldsmith, "The NYT on NSA's Huawei Penetration," Lawfare, March 22, 2014, http://www.lawfareblog.com/2014/03/the-nyt-on-nsas-huawei-penetration/.
46. Quoted in Sanger and Shanker, "N.S.A. Devises Radio Pathway into Computers."
47. Sanger and Perlroth, "N.S.A. Breached Chinese Servers Seen as Security Threat."
48. Jack Goldsmith, "Why the USG Complaints against Chinese Economic Cyber-Snooping Are So Weak," Lawfare, March 25, 2013, http://www.lawfareblog.com/2013/03/why-the-usg-complaints-against-chinese-economic-cyber-snooping-are-so-weak/#.UtZzldJDuSo.
49. Jack Goldsmith, "More Questions about the USG Basis for Complaints about China's Cyber Exploitations," May 30, 2013, http://www.lawfareblog.com/2013/05/more-questions-about-the-usg-basis-for-complaints-about-chinas-cyber-exploitations/.
50. Bruce Schneier, "Why the NSA's Attacks on the Internet Must Be Made Public," *Guardian*, October 4, 2013, http://www.theguardian.com/commentisfree/2013/oct/04/nsa-attacks-internet-bruce-schneier.
51. Ibid.
52. Eichenwald, "How Edward Snowden Escalated Cyber War with China."
53. Quoted in Sanger and Perlroth, "N.S.A. Breached Chinese Servers Seen as Security Threat."
54. Ibid.
55. Quoted in Eichenwald, "How Edward Snowden Escalated Cyber War with China."
56. Quoted in Eichenwald, "How Edward Snowden Escalated Cyber War with China."

57. Roger Cheng and Declan McCullagh, "Yahoo Breach: Swiped Passwords by the Numbers," CNET, July 12, 2012, http://news.cnet.com/8301-1009_3-57470878-83/yahoo-breach-swiped-passwords-by-the-numbers/.

58. "eHarmony Password Dump Analysis," Trustwave SpiderLabs, June 25, 2012, http://blog.spiderlabs.com/2012/06/eharmony-password-dump-analysis.html.

59. See generally Paul Rosenzweig, "Cybersecurity and Public Goods: The Public/Private 'Partnership,'" An Emerging Threats Essay, Hoover Institution, Stanford University, 2012, http://media.hoover.org/sites/default/files/documents/EmergingThreats_Rosenzweig.pdf.

60. 15 U.S.C. § 1643.

61. "Sony Appoints Philip Reitiner as CISO after Data Breach Hits 100m Customers," *InfoSecurity*, September 6, 2011, http://www.infosecurity-magazine.com/view/20552/sony-appoints-philip-reitinger-as-ciso-after-data-breach-hits-100m-customers/.

62. Eric Chabrow, "LinkedIn Has Neither CIO nor CISO," *BankInfo Security*, June 8, 2012, http://www.bankinfosecurity.com/blogs/linkedin-has-neither-cio-nor-ciso-p-1289.

63. Eric Chabrow, "RSA Explains Duties of New CSO," InfoRisk Today, June 10, 2011, http://www.inforisktoday.com/rsa-explains-duties-new-cso-a-3733.

64. Bruce Berkowitz and Robert Hahn, *Cyber Security: Who's Watching the Store?* AEI-Brookings Joint Center for Regulatory Studies, Regulatory Analysis 03-5, (2003), 6.

65. White House, "Remarks by the President on Securing Our Nation's Cyber Infrastructure."

66. The White House, Improving Critical Infrastructure Cybersecurity (Executive Order), February 12, 2013.

67. Ibid., § 8.

68. Ibid., § 8(c).

69. Ibid., § 10.

70. President Barack Obama, State of the Union Address, February 12, 2013, http://www.whitehouse.gov/state-of-the-union-2013.

71. The White House, Critical Infrastructure Security and Resilience (Presidential Policy Directive 21), February 12, 2013, http://www.whitehouse.gov/the-press-office/2013/02/12/presidential-policy-directive-critical-infrastructure-security-and-resil.

72. Improving Critical Infrastructure Cybersecurity (Executive Order), § 9.

73. "Notes for White House 60-Day Cyber-Policy Review," March 25, 2009, http://www.whitehouse.gov/files/documents/cyber/National%20Science%20Foundation%20-%20Notes%20for%20White%20House%2060-day%20Cyber-Policy%20Review%20-%20March%2025%202009.pdf.

74. President's Review Group on Intelligence and Communications Technologies, *Liberty and Security in a Changing World* (2013), http://www.whitehouse.gov/sites/default/files/docs/2013-12-12_rg_final_report.pdf.

75. Rosenzweig, "Cybersecurity and Public Goods," 1.

76. Memorandum of Agreement between the Department of Homeland Security and the Department of Defense Regarding Cybersecurity, September 27, 2010, http://www.gwu.edu/~nsarchiv/NSAEBB/NSAEBB424/docs/Cyber-037.pdf.

77. See, e.g., Robert M. Gates, *Duty: Memoirs of a Secretary at War* (New York: Knopf, 2014), 451.

78. 15 U.S.C. § 45(a).

79. Ibid., § 45(n).
80. *FTC v. Wyndham Worldwide Corporation*, Civil Action No. 13-1887 (ES) (D.N.J. Apr. 7, 2014), http://ashkansoltani.files.wordpress.com/2014/04/ftc-v-wyndham-opinion.pdf.
81. Department of Defense, "Remarks by Secretary Panetta on Cybersecurity to the Business Executives for National Security, New York City," October 11, 2012, http://www.defense.gov/transcripts/transcript.aspx?transcriptid=5136.
82. Ibid.
83. Sanger, "Obama Order Sped Up Wave of Cyberattacks against Iran."
84. Siobhan Gorman and Danny Yadron, "Banks Seek U.S. Help on Iran Cyberattacks," *Wall Street Journal*, January 15, 2013, http://online.wsj.com/article/SB1000142 4127887324734904578244302923178548.html; Daniel Politi, "Officials: Iran Stepping Up Cyberattacks against U.S. Targets," *Slate*, October 13, 2012, http://www.slate.com/blogs/the_slatest/2012/10/13/iran_cyberattacks_against_american_targets_on_the_rise.html; "Remarks by Secretary Panetta."
85. Committee on Technical and Privacy Dimensions of Information for Terrorism Prevention and Other National Goals, *Protecting Individual Privacy in the Struggle against Terrorists: A Framework for Assessment* (Washington, DC: National Academy of Sciences, 2008), http://epic.org/misc/nrc_rept_100708.pdf. See also http://www8.nationalacademies.org/onpinews/newsitem.aspx?RecordID=10072008A.
86. Richard A. Clarke, "A Global Cyber-Crisis in Waiting," *Washington Post*, February 7, 2013, http://articles.washingtonpost.com/2013-02-07/opinions/36973008_1_cybercrime-fly-away-teams-espionage.
87. U.S. Constitution amend. IV.
88. *Coolidge v. New Hampshire*, 403 U.S. 443 (1971).
89. *United States v. Edwards*, 415 U.S. 800 (1974).
90. *United States v. Miller*, 425 U.S. 435 (1976).
91. *United States v. U.S. District Court for the Eastern District of Michigan*, 407 U.S. 297 (1972).
92. Ibid., 322.
93. Wiretap Act, Pub. L. No. 90-351, 82 Stat. 197 (1968) (codified as amended at 18 U.S.C. §§ 2510–22).
94. Orin S. Kerr, "Internet Surveillance Law after the USA Patriot Act: The Big Brother That Isn't," *Northwestern University Law Review* 97 (2003): 607, 621.
95. Stored Communications Act, Pub. L. No. 99-508, Title II, § 201, 100 Stat. 1848 (1986) (codified as amended at 18 U.S.C. §§ 2701–11).
96. 18 U.S.C. § 2703(d).
97. Pen Register Act, Pub. L. No. 99-508, Title III, § 301(a), 100 Stat. 1868 (1986) (codified as amended at 18 U.S.C. §§ 3121–27).
98. 18 U.S.C. § 3123(a).
99. Pub L. No. 95-511, 92 Stat. 1783 (1978) (codified at 50 U.S.C. § 1801–11).
100. 50 U.S.C. § 1805(a)(3)(A).
101. Ibid. § 1804(7) (prior to being amended in 2001).
102. Uniting and Strengthening America by Providing Appropriate Tools Required to Intercept and Obstruct Terrorism Act of 2001, Pub. L. No. 107-56, § 204, 115 Stat. 272 (codified at 50 U.S.C. § 1804(a)(7)(B)).
103. Pub. L. No. 110-55, § 105A (2007); Pub. L. No. 110-261, § 702(a) (2008).
104. Pub. L. No. 110-261, § 702(a) (2008) (codified at 50 U.S.C. § 105B(a)).
105. Ibid.
106. 50 U.S.C. § 105B(l).

107. 50 U.S.C. § 1861.

108. USA PATRIOT Improvement and Reauthorization Act of 2005, Public Law No. 109-177, 120 Stat. 192 (Mar. 9, 2006) (codified at 50 U.S.C. § 1861(b)(2)).

109. Daniel J. Solove, "Reconstructing Electronic Surveillance Law," *George Washington Law Review* 72 (2004): 1264, 1292, http://papers.ssrn.com/sol3/papers.cfm?abstract_id=445180.

110. Ibid., 1293.

111. *In re Application of the FBI for an Order Requiring the Production of Tangible Things from Verizon Bus. Network Serv., Inc. on Behalf of MCI Commc'n Serv., Inc. D/B/A Verizon Bus. Serv.*, Dkt. No. BR 13-80 (RV) at 1-2 (FISA Ct. Apr. 25, 2013); Glenn Greenwald, "NSA Collecting Phone Records of Millions of Verizon Customers Daily," *Guardian*, June 5, 2013, http://www.theguardian.com/world/2013/jun/06/nsa-phone-records-verizon-court-order; Office of the Director of National Intelligence, "Foreign Intelligence Surveillance Court Renews Authority to Collect Telephony Metadata," July 19, 2013, http://www.dni.gov/index.php/newsroom/press-releases/191-press-releases-2013/898-foreign-intelligence-surveillance-court-renews-authority-to-collect-telephony-metadata.

112. "U.S. Confirms Warrantless Searches of Americans," *USA Today*, April 2, 2014, http://www.usatoday.com/story/news/politics/2014/04/01/us-confirms-warrantless-searches-nsa/7176749/; Edward Moyer, "NSA Taps into Google, Yahoo Clouds, Can Collect Data 'At Will,' Says Post," CNET, October 30, 2013, http://www.cnet.com/news/nsa-taps-into-google-yahoo-clouds-can-collect-data-at-will-says-post/; James Risen and Laura Poitras, "N.S.A. Gathers Data on Social Connections of U.S. Citizens," *New York Times*, September 28, 2013, http://mobile.nytimes.com/2013/09/29/us/nsa-examines-social-networks-of-us-citizens.html; Glenn Greenwald and James Ball, "The Top Secret Rules that Allow NSA to Use US Data without a Warrant," *Guardian*, June 20, 2013, http://www.theguardian.com/world/2013/jun/20/fisa-court-nsa-without-warrant.

113. Sean Lawson, "Did Intelligence Officials Lie to Congress about NSA Domestic Spying?" *Forbes*, June 6, 2013, http://www.forbes.com/sites/seanlawson/2013/06/06/did-intelligence-officials-lie-to-congress-about-nsa-domestic-spying/; Charlie Savage and Scott Shane, "Secret Court Rebuked N.S.A. on Surveillance," *New York Times*, August 21, 2013, http://www.nytimes.com/2013/08/22/us/2011-ruling-found-an-nsa-program-unconstitutional.html?_r=0.

114. President's Review Group, *Liberty and Security in a Changing World;* Privacy and Civil Liberties Oversight Board, *Report on the Telephone Records Program Conducted under Section 215 of the USA PATRIOT Act and on the Operations of the Foreign Intelligence Surveillance Court* (2014), http://www.pclob.gov/SiteAssets/Pages/default/PCLOB-Report-on-the-Telephone-Records-Program.pdf.

115. *United States v. Miller*, 425 U.S. 435 (1976).

116. Ibid., 440.

117. Ibid., 442.

118. Ibid., 443 (citation omitted).

119. 442 U.S. 735 (1979).

120. Ibid., 743.

121. Ibid.

122. See Fred H. Cate, James X. Dempsey, and Ira S. Rubinstein, "Systematic Government Access to Private-Sector Data," *International Data Privacy Law* 2, no. 4 (2012): 195, 196, http://idpl.oxfordjournals.org/content/2/4/195.full.pdf+html.

123. U.S. Department of Defense, Technology and Privacy Advisory Committee, *Safeguarding Privacy in the Fight against Terrorism* 6 (2004), http://epic.org/privacy/profiling/tia/tapac_report.pdf.
124. Committee on Technical and Privacy Dimensions of Information, *Protecting Individual Privacy in the Struggle against Terrorists*.
125. Tom Bowman, "In China, Hagel Outlines U.S. Approach to Cybersecurity," NPR, April 8, 2014, http://www.npr.org/2014/04/08/300477952/hagel-outlines-to-china-u-s-approach-to-cyberattacks.

CHAPTER 13

Conclusion

The Rise of China and the Future of Cybersecurity

JON R. LINDSAY AND DEREK S. REVERON*

Morality tales abound in cybersecurity discourse. Chinese hackers are pillaging intellectual property and creating asymmetric threats. The National Security Agency (NSA) is jeopardizing civil liberties and weakening the Internet. Communist censorship is undermining the democratic promise of information technology, even as American firms unfairly dominate its development. Cybercrime is costing everyone trillions of dollars. Yet at the same time cyberspace continues to be a major catalyst for economic growth, technological innovation, and social development around the world. There is a grain of truth in all of these claims, which means that the phenomenon as a whole must be more complicated than any one of them suggests.

Computers and data networks are invaluable in every sector of modern society. As a result, the security of digital systems both affects and reflects economic, military, and political factors at the domestic and international levels. The breadth and complexity of cybersecurity as a practical and intellectual domain is readily apparent across the chapters in this volume. The authors—a diverse mix of scientists, scholars, and policy analysts from China, the United States, Canada, and the United Kingdom—bring a balance of political, economic, legal, and strategic perspectives to get beyond the media hype. They do not always agree with one another, which is itself an important point and should encourage humility in anyone seeking to understand cybersecurity in China, or anywhere. Some consider cyber-threats to be extremely dangerous, while others downplay their dangers, and some see deliberate state efforts to exploit user trust in the Internet, while others see a government struggling to come to grips with the pace of change in the digital era. These authors are part of an ongoing interdisciplinary and international conversation that is still in its infancy.

AN INTERSECTION OF CONCEPTUAL DEBATES

Secrecy regarding the technical facts about cyber operations and the political facts about government intentions is a considerable barrier to understanding. Likewise, companies have incentives to hide data losses and compromises, but also encourage governments to protect intellectual property losses. Some of the confusion, however, is not just about facts but also about how to interpret them. Among scholars and policymakers there exist fundamental disagreements about the magnitude of risk posed by threats in cyberspace and the trajectory of China's rise in international politics. It should hardly be surprising that there is confusion where these debates and assumptions intersect.

In the technological debate, there is a wide spread of opinion about the strategic implications of the Internet.[1] Many view cyberspace as a new "domain" of conflict in addition to air, sea, land, and outer space. Top intelligence officials in the United States have claimed that "Cyber-attacks and cyber-espionage pose a greater potential danger to U.S. national security than Al Qaeda and other militants that have dominated America's global focus since Sept. 11, 2001."[2] Cyber weapons with the power to disrupt, confuse, or deceive are thought to provide powerful asymmetric tools for political upstarts. Skeptics counter that outbursts of aggression from nationalist mobs and computer criminals have little effect on the course of politics, while powerful states stand to gain even more through cyber variants of signals intelligence and electronic warfare. As Erik Gartzke argues, "the mere ability to cause harm over the internet does not suffice to predict that cyberwar will substitute for terrestrial conflict, or even that it will be an important independent domain for the future of warfare."[3]

In the political debate, there is disagreement about the political and economic implications of the rise of China. Many analysts describe heightened potential for conflict as China grows wealthier, modernizes its military, and becomes more assertive in the region. Analysts in the realist school of international relations point to the potential for security dilemmas, arms races, and escalation-prone crises as China closes the still considerable gap between it and the United States. Rising levels of popular nationalism combined with insecurity in Chinese Communist Party leadership could exacerbate pressures to respond aggressively to international crises or perceived slights. Liberalist and constructivist schools, by contrast, counter that increasing levels of commercial, financial, and institutional interdependence between China and the world, as well as changing global norms regarding the utility of force, will enable these states to eschew conflict and realize mutual gains. Military "hard power" is seen to be of decreasing utility in world politics, while economic and cultural "soft power" becomes more important. Both strains of thought coexist in tension in state policies, reflecting the complexity and mixed incentives of the Sino-American relationship.[4]

The subject of this book falls at the nexus of these two contentious debates. The interaction between their extreme positions gives rise to four different interpretations of the political character of cyberspace (see figure 13.1). Optimists on both dimensions can point out that Asian international relations have been more or less peaceful for decades and the majority of observable Internet abuse is cybercrime, espionage, and "hacktivism," more of an irritant than a revolution. Pessimists foresee a grimmer future in which antagonistic Chinese or American diplomacy erupts into cyberwarfare, paralyzing critical infrastructure or undermining competitive advantage. Yet between the sanguine Internet status quo and unlikely scenarios of cyberwarfare, there are two other possibilities. One is a world in which nations cooperate on arms control arrangements and normative frameworks to rein in the destabilizing

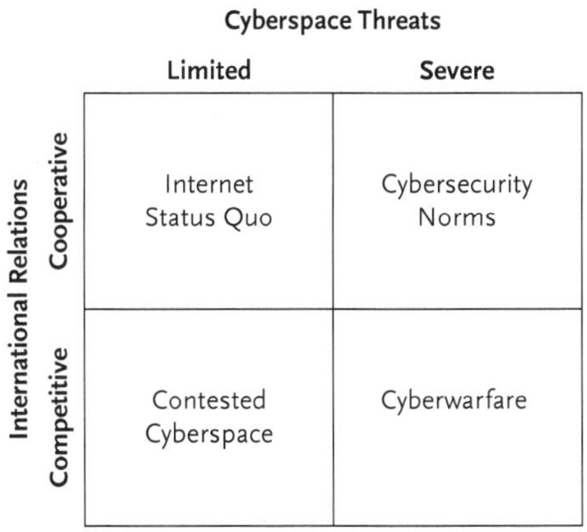

		Cyberspace Threats	
		Limited	Severe
International Relations	Cooperative	Internet Status Quo	Cybersecurity Norms
	Competitive	Contested Cyberspace	Cyberwarfare

Figure 13.1 The Political Organization of Cyberspace

potential of cyber weapons and data losses by cybercriminals. The other is a world in which international relations are highly competitive and cyber operations enable, but do not fundamentally transform, that competition. Contested cyberspace is subject to frequent abuse, high levels of cybercrime, an erosion of user trust, and growing barriers between national networks, but the resulting loss of openness and efficiency falls far short of more disruptive visions of cyberwarfare. In sum, assumptions about technology and politics inform assertions about the scope and magnitude of cyber challenges and the feasibility of solutions to address them.[5]

Cyberspace has long been characterized by minor threats and widespread agreement about the usefulness of the Internet. Yet there are already tendencies moving cyberspace toward less cooperation and greater competition. China's emergence onto the global stage has contributed to Internet insecurity as economic imperatives promote espionage abroad and political domination imperatives of a single political party promote exploitation at home. The United States, meanwhile, a global and potentially declining hegemon, has not hesitated to use its considerable resources and expertise to leverage American firms for intelligence and military advantage. In China and the United States, as in every advanced industrial nation, rifts between government bureaucracies who would regulate security and industrial actors who invent and operate information technology exacerbates Internet insecurity even further.

The chapters in this volume explore cyber issues that span these four different categories. Many authors acknowledge the benefits of the Internet status quo as a point of departure for describing the risks it creates. Zhuge Jianwei and his team point out that cybercrime is a problem in China as it is elsewhere. Xu Jinghong, Li Yuxiao and Xu Lu, and Fred Cate describe the challenges of devising effective governance regimes to balance competing values of security, privacy, and economic productivity, even as the latter two are also concerned about more dangerous developments. Other chapters venture into the realm of contested cyberspace, including those by Jon Lindsay and Tai Ming Cheung on economic espionage, Nigel Inkster on national intelligence, and Sarah McKune on political control. The four chapters on the Chinese military by Ye Zheng, Kevin Pollpeter, Mark Stokes, and Robert Sheldon and Joe McReynolds, respectively, explore strategic and organizational considerations that could affect more severe competition or cyberwarfare. A number of authors, particularly Li and Xu, Cate, McKune, and Ye, also cycle back to discuss the desirability or feasibility of international norms to regulate these dangers.

The distribution of this material across the four categories gives us an opportunity to use the case of China to evaluate more general claims about cybersecurity and world politics. This book has taken a mostly descriptive approach simply because there is so little scholarship available on this topic. Some chapters also offer evaluative and normative analyses of how effectively various policies are functioning and how they might be reformed. In this section we leverage their collective insights to explain what accounts for the types of cyberthreats and responses we observe in this important case.

While it is beyond our scope to develop refined theoretical propositions, we can consider three broad approaches to explaining cyber phenomena: technologist, liberalist, and realist. The first of these is wildly popular and considers information technology to be a transforming force in political and economic affairs. Technological determinism comes in optimistic and pessimistic varieties, assuming either that the Internet empowers individuals and promotes democracy or that it creates dire threats to safety and stability. As we have seen, there is considerable disagreement over whether cyberthreats are evolutionary or revolutionary in nature. The availability of multiple but contradictory determinist narratives makes all of them seem unsatisfying. Moreover, a constant (the Internet) cannot by itself explain the variety of cyber activity—crime, espionage, warfare, political control, and public policy for defense—that we observe within and across countries. The simplistic technologist approach is insufficient to account for the range of phenomena the chapters describe for the case of China.

By contrast, liberalist and realist approaches use politics to explain technology rather than vice versa.[6] Liberalist explanations focus on domestic factors within states as well as trade and governance among states. Strong domestic institutions for the protection of property and the rule of law, norms of democracy and nonviolent conflict resolution, and open and robust trade across borders are thought to enhance mutual gains for all parties. These all provide incentives to adopt open Internet protocols and enforce laws to limit predation, to include mutually agreeable norms and regulatory institutions at the international level. States with weak or undemocratic institutions in this view fall short of this ideal and Internet security should suffer accordingly, potentially inflicting negative externalities on others. Even so, the common benefits of trade and the common challenges of terrorism or transnational groups that threaten the international system should incentivize states to cooperate to establish mutually beneficial, and mutually constraining, norms for cybersecurity.

Realist explanation focuses instead on the anarchic nature of the international system. States (or any autonomous political groups) pursue power and wealth because there is nothing to stop them, which in turn compels others to look out for their own security. Moreover, the measures they take to defend themselves from perceived threats can leave others feeling even more threatened. The more severe the security dilemma between states like China, Japan, India, the United States, and Russia, the less likely they will be to pursue cooperative approaches to cyber challenges, which they themselves have incentives to create. Cyberthreats are constrained not by a consensual decision to pursue only peaceful transactions but rather through the implicit threat of retaliation by cyber or other means. Yet the covert nature and complexity of cyber operations greatly complicate strategies of cross-domain deterrence.[7] The rest of this section evaluates these approaches across the four conceptual categories introduced above.

The Unstable Internet Status Quo

In the last three decades cybercrime has evolved from a minor blight caused by thrill-seeking amateurs into a complicated economy of specialized products and services, although this economic drag is still dwarfed by the contribution of the Internet to global economic growth. The chapter by Zhuge Jianwei, Gu Lion, Duan Haixin, and Taylor Roberts describes the organization of the Chinese online underground economy with its dozens of profit models deriving from four different value chains. By analyzing illicit transactions on Chinese social media, they estimate losses to cybercrime in 2011 of over RMB 5.36 billion ($852 million), affecting 110.8 million users and 1.1 million websites. This large underground market targets virtual goods such as video game accounts and currencies in which both the criminals and the victims are Chinese. By contrast, cybercrime from Eastern Europe targets victims in Western Europe and the United States, avoiding domestic predation. This difference points to a relative neglect of consistent law enforcement in the case of China. Other online irritants besides financial cybercrime include Distributed Denial of Service Attacks (DDoS) and website defacement during political crises and outbreaks of "human flesh search" (*renrou sousuo*), when thousands of vigilante "netizens" seek out humiliating information about individuals or seek to expose corrupt government officials.

Li Yuxiao and Xu Lu observe that these institutional imperfections undermine China's defense against cyberthreats of both domestic and international origin:

When compared to the relatively high level of attention to network security by the United States, Chinese policy measures are not in place, and there is a lack of consistency in the guidelines and implementation of cybersecurity. Particularly, China has yet to establish national or international strategies on cyberspace, and lacks systematic systems for decision-making, processes and standards for handling network security issues, and a clear network security coordination mechanism. Furthermore, China lacks Internet security personnel and is often unable to contend with the openness and flexibility of the Internet. These problems have resulted in the current environment of network security incidents.[8]

China's struggle to reconcile its many bureaucratic stakeholders in cybersecurity has some resonance with the governance challenges in the United States described by Fred Cate. Another overlap between US and Chinese policy concerns the protection of privacy. Cate points out how technological progress has steadily undermined privacy protection in the United States, most recently by massive Internet surveillance against both foreign and domestic users revealed by Edward Snowden. Xu Jinghong shows that China also has developed a legal regime for privacy protection, which might come as surprising news for Western readers. Enforcement is uneven and the meaning of privacy in China is evolving as the boisterous Internet brings the issue to prominence for Chinese netizens. Yet there is a marked difference in national approaches: Cate describes the foundations of American privacy law as rooted in the protection of individual privacy *from* government intrusion, while Xu describes protection of netizens *by* the government from other unscrupulous users or companies. The contrast between American democracy and Chinese socialism has even more far-reaching implications.

Mark Stokes underscores that "information security can be viewed within the broadest context as ensuring CCP [Chinese Communist Party] legitimacy, enhancing the Party-state's ability to consolidate power, defending national networks against internal and external threats, and supporting economic development. Therefore, security of the Party and state requires mastery of the global cybersphere."[9] Sarah McKune shows how Chinese domestic politics have international consequences because of the global Internet. China's politically motivated cyber exploitations use many of the same techniques and appear to involve some of the same specialist groups involved in economic and national security espionage campaigns. For example, Canadian investigators reported extensive penetration of Tibetan expatriate computers as well as diplomatic and military networks around the world.[10] In early 2013, the *New York Times*, *Wall Street Journal*, and *Washington Post* all reported that Chinese hackers had infiltrated their networks in response to journalistic investigation into China's 2012 leadership transition.[11] Empirical measurement of Chinese censorship of social media sites suggests that the government places its greatest emphasis on suppressing collective action challenges to CCP legitimacy while allowing simple criticism to occur.[12] The latter may actually provide an informational feedback to CCP elite by enabling them to intervene in potential political challenges or censure corrupt officials before popular resentment metastasizes.

Technologists can enlighten the enabling conditions for all this activity. Clearly, the growth of computer networks makes new forms of crime and government surveillance possible, and these present netizens and policymakers alike with new challenges. Yet a means-based explanation says little about the motivation for this growth or the absence of impediments to threats. Liberalist explanations perform much better. Indeed, China's pursuit of economic growth and commercial globalization explains a great deal of its embrace of the Internet, even with the risks of more open communication among netizens. Yet the CCP has sought, with some success, to separate economic from political openness. Illiberalism has exacerbated cyber insecurity in two ways, first through direct state efforts to restrict Internet freedom and second through the state's relative neglect of technical network security in favor of information content security. Uncoordinated governance among state organs reinforces a commercially driven mode of Internet operation without effectively protecting against exploitative threats at home and abroad. The liberalist perspective explains China's economic embrace of the Internet, its authoritarian divergence from the libertarian status quo, and the inefficiency of its cyber defenses. Realists might expect a state, especially an authoritarian one, to better attend to its defenses, but the institutional challenges in doing so are considerable for China.

Increasingly Contested Cyberspace

Realism is better at explaining Chinese cyber offense than defense. In economic and political competition against a hegemonic United States, and facing territorial disputes with other regional powers, a rising China can use espionage as a shortcut for economic development and military modernization, as well as to gather intelligence on perceived state and nonstate threats. Any improvement through fair means or foul, as long as it does not trigger retaliation, would enhance Chinese relative power. Realists expect a state to do whatever it can get away with to enhance its wealth and power.

Technologist explanation again only provides conditions for the possibility of enhanced espionage, although in this case the sophistication of advanced persistent threat (APT) activity and the expansion of Internet attack surfaces requires more technical savvy to assess. Liberal norms have proved inadequate to check this behavior, as will be discussed later.

The chapter by Nigel Inkster points out that the Chinese intelligence services have gradually taken a turn toward incorporating cyber exploitation into their tradecraft. Many questions remain about Chinese ability to sort through and analyze what is collected, but it is at least clear that the Ministry of State Security has decided to emphasize Internet collection in conjunction with traditional forms of human intelligence. Mark Stokes in his chapter points out that the People's Liberation Army (PLA) has similarly transformed its signals intelligence (SIGINT) apparatus into a formidable cyber collection platform. Inkster finds "that the modus operandi of China's intelligence agencies in respect of foreign collection has evolved from one of great caution and risk aversion to one of greater operational self-confidence commensurate with China's rising status and influence in the world."[13] As China's foreign policy deepens to match its international economic activity, we can expect its confidence and activity in cyberspace to grow.

National policies to stimulate economic growth like China's 863 Program have long stressed the importance of acquiring foreign expertise, and Chinese intelligence services have long singled out Western industrial targets. The approach to industrial espionage is tied to Chinese economic development that relies on introducing acquired intellectual property, digesting it, absorbing it into Chinese companies, and re-innovating it to produce the original for Chinese purposes. There is now a large body of individually circumstantial but collectively convincing evidence that the Chinese state is engaged in a broad campaign of cyber espionage against Western commercial targets. The means, motives, and history of Chinese espionage trump the weak alibi of Internet anonymity often offered by Chinese ripostes to Western allegations. However, given the inefficiency of China's national innovation system, as described in the chapter by Jon Lindsay and Tai Ming Cheung, there is reason to doubt that prodigious Chinese espionage does in fact amount to "the greatest transfer of wealth in history." Technologist accounts of cyber espionage tend to ignore the formidable institutional challenges associated with discovering and absorbing stolen data and applying it in competitive interactions. Moreover, Chinese overreliance on espionage risks hobbling its ambitions to become a leading innovator in the global economy if it is dependent on the prior existence of leading firms to pilfer.

Few issues have become as contentious in Sino-American relations as cyber espionage. In response to a cyber operation with Chinese origins dubbed "Byzantine Candor" by US intelligence, a former FBI official called it "the biggest vacuuming up of U.S. proprietary data that we've ever seen."[14] The US government has been increasingly willing to single out China by name for its large-scale industrial espionage campaigns. For example, the United States named and indicted five officers of the PLA in May 2014 alleging they conspired to steal trade secrets to benefit Chinese companies. The filed criminal charges were the first time state actors were indicted for hacking.

China, meanwhile, has counterattacked by complaining of cyberattacks originating from the United States. A Chinese Defense Ministry spokesman said in early 2013, "The Defense Ministry and China Military Online websites have faced a serious threat from hacking attacks since they were established, and the number of hacks has risen steadily in recent years . . . attacks from the U.S. accounted for 62.9%."[15] Investigative journalists have described a secretive unit within the NSA focused on penetrating sensitive Chinese networks.[16] Edward Snowden has alleged that the NSA tapped Chinese communications through a civilian university backbone and thoroughly penetrated the headquarters of telecommunications conglomerate Huawei.[17] Li Haidong, quoted in the *China Daily*, captured this view: "For months, Washington has been accusing China of cyber espionage, but it turns out that the biggest threat to the pursuit of individual freedom and privacy in the U.S. is the unbridled power of the government."[18] At the same time, revelations about the role that US companies play in intelligence collection (both legally compelled and unknowingly exploited) are shutting companies out of international markets, potentially costing hundreds of billions of dollars.[19]

US officials distinguish between US hacking of targets in China for national security or counterintelligence motivations and Chinese hacking of civilian targets for industrial espionage. As chairman of the Joint Chiefs General Martin Dempsey said, "All nations on the face of the planet always conduct intelligence operations in all domains . . . [but] China's particular niche in cyber has been theft and intellectual property. . . . Their view is that there are no rules of the road in cyber, there's nothing, there's no laws that they are breaking, there's no standards of behavior."[20] In fact, after the Snowden revelations, President Obama issued Presidential Policy Directive 28 (PPD-28), which forbids "the collection of foreign private commercial information or trade secrets . . . to afford a competitive advantage to U.S. companies and U.S. business sectors commercially."[21] This distinction attests to the marginal influence of liberal norms on US cyber policy.

These nuances are often lost in both debate and diplomacy, however, given the intensity and pervasiveness of US exploitation against political and military targets abroad.

American espionage against China, to include Chinese information technology companies, is unlikely to abate just because of public indignation in Chinese media or diplomatic protest without more serious consequences. Likewise, the cybersecurity firm Mandiant notes that "recent observations of China-based APT activity indicate that the PRC has no intention of abandoning its cyber campaigns, despite the Obama administration's specific warnings that China's continued cyber espionage 'was going to be [a] very difficult problem in the economic relationship' between the two countries."[22] This situation highlights a major obstacle to the establishment of international norms. It is hard to establish an agreement over activities that the parties do not admit to conducting. It is hard to enforce compliance with an agreement when the proscribed activity is intentionally designed to be undetectable. Many governments have the technical means and expertise to conduct covert operations online and have thus far shown little restraint in doing so when it serves national interests. Realism is useful for explaining both the incentives for espionage and the inability of liberal norms and institutions to contain it.

The Ambiguity of Cyberwarfare

Realism would further expect states to pursue not only espionage but also capabilities for more disruptive forms of cyberwarfare. Military cyber operations are a natural extension of electronic warfare and SIGINT, which has been around for a century, but it uses logical code rather than beams of electromagnetic energy to monitor, disrupt, and deceive enemy radars and datalinks. Because advanced industrial militaries depend heavily on C4ISR (command, control, communication, computers, intelligence, surveillance, and reconnaissance), their wars should be expected to have a cyber dimension. As PLA senior colonel Ye Zheng writes in his chapter, "Cyberwarfare is still in its early stages, yet most countries and armies are quickening their preparations of cyber arms to avoid being the losers in this competition. Under these circumstances, China has also turned more attention to cyberspace security."[23] Ye discusses cyber operations including intelligence collection, paralysis of an opponent's systems, integration of cyber and electronic warfare with broader military operations, psychological persuasion and the manipulation of crowds, and defense against all of the above.

Cyberwarfare might seem especially attractive to weaker or rising powers that seek to develop a means to counter the traditional military advantages of stronger rivals. Kevin Pollpeter in his chapter reveals that many Chinese strategists believe that cyberwarfare is an affordable way to reach out to affect or even paralyze a sophisticated C4ISR-dependent adversary like the United States. The Chinese assumption of asymmetric advantage is widely shared in Western technologist accounts, perhaps unsurprisingly as China has been a voracious reader of recent Western military writings on the "revolution in military affairs." Yet cyberwarfare is also attractive for strong powers like the United States, which can use it to supplement the exercise of military power (e.g., as a substitute for electronic warfare against defense radars to create a window for an air strike) or to expand the range of covert action options. Moreover, experienced and advanced militaries may have more experience managing complex network operations, possessing institutional advantages in cyber capacity that technologists tend to overlook. Senior Colonel Ye argues that other countries are pursuing cyber capabilities in response to the hegemon's head start, as realists would expect: "Today the United States has established the world's first dedicated Cyber Command and fully functional cyberwarfare units in order to establish a controlling position over cyber power. Following this example, other countries are developing their own cyber power in competition with one another."[24]

Mark Stokes shows that open sources can reveal some detail about the PLA's organization for intelligence gathering through the General Staff Department, Third Department (3/PLA). Yet the relationship between Chinese intelligence and PLA organizations, and between the intelligence and operational branches of the PLA, remains murky. The Fourth Department (4/PLA) for electronic warfare may take more responsibility in time of war, or cyberattack functions may reside within the more experienced 3/PLA. In the United States, the NSA and Cyber Command are co-located and have the same commander because cyber exploitation and attack share technical methods and require similar human expertise for network intrusion. The importance of human capital in the cyber domain raises serious questions for any analysis of PLA competency. Lindsay and Cheung note that Chinese operators have displayed sloppy tradecraft, enabling Western investigators to confidently attribute espionage to China and the PLA. Similar mistakes in more sensitive crisis situations could mean the critical failure of a cyber operation.

Furthermore, the PLA has no recent combat experience with the serious operational and organizational challenges of C4ISR, while the US military, by contrast, has discovered that reality often departs from the ideals of network-centric warfare.[25] While the PLA has shown much interest in cyberwarfare—inspired in no small part by American writing and demonstrated ability in the field—it still faces considerable challenges implementing strategic concepts. Moreover, as Robert Sheldon and Joe McReynolds argue in their chapter, the PLA's enigmatic civilian "cyber militias" appear to be peripheral to PLA cyberwarfare capacity rather than some sort of postmodern People's War, as often feared. The PLA conducts exploitation campaigns against Western interests with vigor, to be sure; however, contrary to technologist expectations, the ability to successfully create large-scale cyber disruption cannot and should not be easily inferred. In cyberwarfare, as in espionage, the PLA appears to be playing catch-up to the United States.

A realist perspective accounts for why countries would want to pursue cyber capabilities. However, this does not mean that all can do so to the same extent or that the result is a revolutionary threat. Cyberwarfare requires a great deal of intelligence, preparation, and engineering integration to attack physical infrastructure successfully. Pragmatic complications generate uncertainty and potential for mistakes, which undermines commanders' confidence in cyber weapons and their utility for coercion. Technologist worries about a "digital Pearl Harbor" or "cyber 9/11" are unrealistic on both operational and strategic grounds.[26] Yet for the same reason, there is troubling potential for misperception and miscalculation in the cyber domain. Pollpeter shows that Chinese cyber strategists emphasize striking first, rapidly, and widely in order to paralyze the enemy's ability to think or act. This mindset recalls the "ideology of the offensive" shared by the Great Powers in 1914: belief in the potency of infantry élan over machine guns and barbed wire contributed to the outbreak and stalemate of World War I.[27] A mistaken belief in cyber offense dominance could similarly lead to inadvertent escalation in a crisis.[28]

Disagreement over Cybersecurity Norms

The perceived severity of the threats above has generated numerous calls for improved international cooperation on cybersecurity. Jason Healey, for example, sees a "flurry of organized and unorganized violence" in the cyber domain but anticipates new norms and regimes will keep cyberspace "generally as stable as the air, land, space, and maritime domains," containing localized conflict from disrupting the international system.[29] It is notable that the Chinese authors in this volume appear more optimistic about the potential for international cooperation than many of the Western authors.

Li Yuxiao and Xu Lu write that "a China-U.S. cybersecurity communication mechanism is important to improve mutual trust and enhance research and defense capabilities" and recommend working toward "a set of common rules for the network society in order to promote the process of global informatization."[30] Senior Colonel Ye similarly writes that "we have to reject the logic that there must be fierce hostilities between the traditional, established superpowers and rising powers," and instead recognize that "mutual respect, mutual understanding, and cooperation between nations should be the foundation of Asia-Pacific and world security, including cybersecurity."[31]

International cooperation on cybersecurity is desirable, but there are certain obstacles. Any notion of a cyber arms control treaty or the establishment of cyber norms must be reconciled with actual cyber activities and government interests in promoting or tolerating them. Sarah McKune points out that cyber exploitation of ethnic minorities and Internet censorship by the Chinese state stand in stark contrast to cosmopolitan visions of an open Internet with strong normative protections for human rights. The US Department of State "Internet freedom" agenda "works to advance Internet freedom as an aspect of the universal rights of freedom of expression and the free flow of information."[32] As part of this initiative, the US government and activists from nongovernmental organizations develop and deploy technologies that dissidents can use to subvert controls on Internet content. This essentially means hacking the "Great Firewall." China perceives this to be provocative interference in its domestic affairs and an attack on its information security architecture. China, together with Russia, would prefer to shift governance of the Internet to the United Nations with stronger norms of Internet sovereignty and noninterference; Europe and the United States prefer to maintain the current "multistakeholder" arrangement while strengthening norms of openness and human rights.[33] While there may be agreement that international norms are desirable, there is sharp disagreement on the content of those norms. The Obama administration's decision to transfer the Internet Assigned Name Authority (IANA) function from the Department of Commerce to the international community may be a sign of China's and Russia's effective diplomacy or at least a sign that the United States recognizes the damage done to its international reputation.

The challenge of international policy coordination is exacerbated by intrastate disorganization and disconnects between public and private actors. As Fred Cate writes, "The threats are too broad, the actors too numerous, the knowledge levels too unequal, the risks too easy to avoid internalizing, the free-rider problem too prevalent, and the stakes too great to believe that markets alone will be adequate to create the right incentives or outcomes."[34] Yet government remedies also can introduce problems. Unity of command is an American principle of warfare, but actual coordination of different organizations and agencies has proven to be extremely difficult, not least because cybersecurity is more about economic incentives than warfare. China's fragmented authoritarian system has fared little better and potentially worse in cyber policy integration, as discussed in the introduction. Furthermore, innovation in the commercial information technology sector moves far more rapidly than the pace of policymaking in any state. The opportunities for making mischief online emerge faster than government regulators can adjust to counter them, even if they were able to achieve normative agreement on the desirability of doing so.

The profusion of cyberthreats might appear to support technologist interpretations of cyberspace as an autonomous domain with its own deterministic logic. This interpretation overlooks a broad international consensus that the continuing buildout of the Internet economy is a good thing for commerce and development, consistent with liberalist expectations. Cyberspace is a man-made construct, after all, and connection to it is voluntary. Disconnection remains unattractive as long as the benefits of being online continue to be so great and the risks comparatively minor. Liberalists expect the repeated interaction and deep interdependence of cyberspace to act as a restraint on more severe forms of cyber harms: states stand to gain much from their Internet interdependence and much to lose from conflict. The fact that the Internet exists at all, a fabric of international interconnection, means that liberalist views should be taken seriously.

However, there are limits to this implicit liberal consensus, and explicit normative frameworks for international cyberspace may be beyond them. In an anarchic world, according to realists, there is nothing to prevent states and others from exploiting the Internet for espionage, political control, or more offensive applications. States are unlikely to agree to international legal arrangements if they have strong incentives to violate them, as both China and the United States do. The pressure to pursue cyber arms control is all the more diffuse if cyber operations tend toward the lower end of the spectrum (i.e., espionage and hacktivism), where there is less of a sense of common existential danger. Furthermore, traditional military deterrence provides a powerful disincentive for more extreme cyber harm. Thus while cyberspace appears to be well on its way toward increasing contestation, full-blown cyberwarfare remains unlikely. That shift, in any case, would depend more on politics than technology. If Chinese military spending continues to increase, while US military spending stagnates or declines, this would foreshadow a change in the current status of power dynamics in the terrestrial world as well as cyberspace.[35]

OPPORTUNITIES FOR FUTURE RESEARCH

Further research is needed to better understand which of these categories are most likely or how activity is likely to shift among them. With few English-language books providing empirical studies of cybersecurity, this volume has helped to bridge a gap between technology and area studies and thereby breaks some new ground. The examination of cybersecurity through the lens of China's rise puts both topics in a broader context. Our authors have revealed that China can both threaten cyberspace and feel threatened by it. They have also shown how the interplay of public and private actors within international and domestic spheres is essential for understanding cybersecurity. Yet many questions remain.

One major gap in the coverage of this volume is the political economy of civilian cybersecurity in China. The book's introduction and the chapter by Li Yuxiao and Xu Lu provide a high-level overview of Chinese policy apparatus, which has recently been reorganized by President Xi Jinping. The bureaucratic politics, progress, and prospects of this major reform remain something of a mystery at the time of this writing. Similarly, little is known (in English-language analysis) about the cyber role of commercial and other private-sector actors and their relations with regulatory and law enforcement entities. At a general level, do the patterns of market failure and policy inefficiency observed in Western cybersecurity also manifest in China's mixed economy? At a more descriptive level, what is the makeup of the indigenous cybersecurity market, and how much of its growth can be attributed to government versus private demand? Dependence on foreign technology and expertise is a common theme in Chinese political economy, but this also carries security risks in the cyber domain. How dependent are Chinese industries on foreign cybersecurity products, and how do they balance the security risks of foreign origins versus the security risks of inferior domestic technology? Multiple Chinese agencies impose certification requirements or outright restrictions on foreign vendors justified on cybersecurity grounds, but to what extent are these motivated by market protectionism as well?

A political economy framework could prove useful for global cybersecurity more broadly. American strengths in the national security and intelligence applications of cyberspace—and some would say vulnerabilities too—are partially a function of the dominance of American firms in the information technology global market. The constraints and dynamics in this relationship remain poorly understood, even as the Snowden leaks and Huawei hearings have highlighted its importance. How does public knowledge or suspicion about state-firm relationships affect market performance, and will market share shift away from American or Chinese firms? Security concerns could lead to barriers in trade that reduce welfare, or alternatively, they might enhance the demand for security products and risk mitigation that could improve both security and welfare. How will cyber dynamics change as China continues to rise, if it surpasses the United States, or if growth slows? What are the implications for security and economic productivity if China succeeds in reforming global Internet governance? Analysis of these and other alternatives might enlighten a policy debate mired in deadlock between "multistakeholder" and "cyber sovereignty" advocates.

As more evidence emerges of exfiltration of data across both sides of the Pacific, it remains unclear how these data are used. Further research is needed to examine the effectiveness of commercial espionage. It is unclear if and when Chinese espionage can be translated into Chinese economic breakthroughs. Specifically, which Western firms have been hurt and how? Which Chinese firms have benefited and which sectors have enhanced their competitiveness as a result? Similarly, what has been the marginal contribution of espionage to changes in the military balance? Would the emergence of new cyber norms, or a Chinese declaration similar to PPD-28 banning commercial espionage, or simply an overall strengthening of the rule of law in China be able to change its willingness to engage in economic exploitation? While it may be normal for countries to spy on one another for diplomatic and military advantage, Chinese intelligence services are further willing to spy on Western firms to benefit Chinese corporations. The details of intelligence-firm coordination in China are very murky. Given this portrayal of the security environment, it would be important to know how confidently technology companies like Apple can manufacture their products in China in the face of serious risks to their supply chain, or whether the benefits of outsourcing in fact outweigh the controlled risks of espionage.

In the military arena, many countries are developing organizations and doctrine for cyber operations. Over the next decade, it will be essential to research how these organizations develop and where they fit within each country's national security establishment. This will help to explain how cyber capabilities will integrate into warfighting and the role cyber will play in future conflicts. Both the United States and China have cyber elements within their militaries, but there is also a bureaucratic rivalry internally and with their intelligence services. More generally, there has been little work comparing national cyber defense postures, in no small part due to the absence of data on classified programs. Yet without some baseline it is hard to judge the effect on relative power of Xi Jinping's recent cybersecurity reforms, to take one example. As both countries attempt to integrate cyber capabilities in their strategic planning, it would be important to understand how virtual and physical capabilities are integrated. What is the potential for inadvertent escalation, signaling, or de-escalation? Can dominance in one area such as nuclear or space warfare provide "cross-domain deterrence" to discourage assaults on cyberspace? As we think about the national security implications of cyberspace, we may still need new ways to think about improving cybersecurity.

Less visible than traditional diplomatic, economic, and military activities, cyber operations have the potential to increase tensions rapidly. Establishing regular official communications between Washington and Beijing could moderate the impact of new cyber revelations, as Li Yuxiao and Xu Lu point out. However, it would be important to assess the extent to which formal relations between governments are impacted by activities of those in the private sphere. How might cyber militias, disgruntled insiders, and motivated "hacktivists" upset formal relations between China and the United States? How are their activities constrained or encouraged by the state, and how might online nationalist outbursts help or hinder coercive bargaining? How can both countries manage relations when confronted with subnational cyber challengers that create international challenges?

Lastly, students of cybersecurity must exercise caution to navigate between the hype of technologists and the bemusement of traditional security analysts. Disciplinary perspectives are prone to diverge: technologists risk misunderstanding the political, economic, and cultural factors that shape cyber operations in China, and China specialists risk misunderstanding the constraints and opportunities of fast-changing Internet technologies. As we have seen, both realist and liberalist perspectives can explain aspects of cyber behavior, but the complexity and ambiguity of the technology raises new questions that would benefit from more careful theoretical and empirical work specifying and evaluating mechanisms of influence. Eventually, academics and other researchers will need to gain access to classified, hidden governmental cyber activities in order to complete a full assessment. Given how sensitive cyber programs are, like intelligence generally, governments retain an information monopoly, leaving cyber analysts to rely on authorized and unauthorized public disclosures. While analysts can run experiments, make estimates, and exploit public Internet traffic (as successfully shown in several chapters), limited datasets narrow researchers' understanding of cyber challenges and contributions to cyber-security investigations. The limitations partly explain the ambiguity in our assessment of the drivers of cybersecurity.

CONCLUSION

It is increasingly clear that the United States and China, or any other advanced industrial countries for that matter, will not be able to separate cybersecurity from their diplomatic relations. To date, both states have attempted to find common ground against transnational criminal orga-nizations and have made modest progress on reconciling views on intel-lectual property. However, as cyber capabilities develop and deepen inside the national security establishments of both countries, it is difficult to ignore tensions created through cyber activities of all parties. Adam Segal, a participant in the multiyear "Sino-U.S. Cybersecurity Dialogue" spon-sored by the Center for Strategic International Studies and China Institute of Contemporary International Relations, noted that "When pressed for areas where China and the United States might cooperate, Chinese analysts pointed to protecting critical infrastructure and fighting crime, but also noted that cyber cooperation was a work in progress and the conditions might not be right for moving forward."[36]

One conclusion to draw from this volume is that it is futile to hope to eliminate cyber exploitation across national boundaries. It is simply too essential a tool for China's economic development and political stabil-ity strategy and for the national security strategy of the United States, although neither state likes to admit it publicly. Another conclusion to draw is that understanding cybersecurity in China requires attention to domestic institutions and incentives. Paradigms matter, and political economy might be as or more important than deterrence or warfighting for analyzing cybersecurity. Misunderstanding not only leads to over-simplification in analysis but also to potential miscalculation in strategic interaction. Therefore, while it might not be possible to completely elimi-nate cyberthreats through norms or formal agreements, we should be able to avoid making them worse through ignorance. "More transparency will strengthen China-U.S. relations," as former US Secretary of Defense Charles Hagel observed: "Greater openness about cyber reduces the risk that misunderstanding and misperception could lead to miscalculation."[37]

The authors in this volume hail from different national and disciplinary backgrounds, and they have different policy opinions. Yet together they have been able to deepen our insight into a subject rife with confusion and controversy. Li Yuxiao and Xu Lu write, "Differences in ideology and political systems between the United States and China have resulted in different understandings of some basic concepts of network security and have impeded effective communication and cooperation." Among their ideas for improving this situation, they recommend that "China and the United States should establish an agenda for cybersecurity cooperation and a complete multilevel communication mechanism, on both governmental and civilian levels. Exchanges at the civilian level, particularly between academic institutions, could smooth communication and cooperation between the two countries."[38] This volume exemplifies just this sort of collaboration to improve understanding.

NOTES

* The views expressed are those of the authors and do not reflect the official policy or position of the Department of the Navy, Department of Defense, or the U.S. Government.
1. Derek S. Reveron, *Cyberspace and National Security: Threats, Opportunities, and Power in a Virtual World* (Washington, DC: Georgetown University Press, 2012).
2. Ken Dilanian, "Cyber-Attacks a Bigger Threat Than Al Qaeda, Officials Say," *Los Angeles Times*, March 13, 2013.
3. Erik Gartzke, "The Myth of Cyberwar: Bring War in Cyberspace Back Down to Earth," *International Security* 38, no. 2 (2013): 57. On the revolutionary side of the debate see Richard A. Clarke and Robert Knake, *Cyber War: The Next Threat to National Security and What to Do about It* (New York: HarperCollins, 2010); Lucas Kello, "The Meaning of the Cyber Revolution: Perils to Theory and Statecraft," *International Security* 38, no. 2 (2013): 7–40. On the skeptical side see Jon Lindsay, "Stuxnet and the Limits of Cyber Warfare," *Security Studies* 22, no. 3 (2013): 365–404; Thomas Rid, "Cyber War Will Not Take Place," *Journal of Strategic Studies* 35, no. 1 (2011): 5–32.
4. Literature on the rise of China is vast. Overviews of the debate include Thomas J. Christensen, "Fostering Stability or Creating a Monster? The Rise of China and U.S. Policy toward East Asia," *International Security* 31, no. 1 (2006): 81–126; Avery Goldstein, "Power Transitions, Institutions, and China's Rise in East Asia: Theoretical Expectations and Evidence," *Journal of Strategic Studies* 30, no. 4 (2007): 639–82. For the pessimistic realist perspective see John J. Mearsheimer, *The Tragedy of Great Power Politics* (New York: Norton, 2003), chap. 10. For the optimistic liberal perspective see G. John Ikenberry, "The Rise of China and the Future of the West: Can the Liberal System Survive?" *Foreign Affairs*, January–February 2008; Edward S. Steinfeld, *Playing Our Game: Why China's Rise Doesn't Threaten the West* (New York: Oxford University Press, 2010).
5. Jon R. Lindsay, "Cybersecurity and International Relations," *International Security* (Forthcoming 2015).
6. Constructivist accounts that treat ideas and identity are often considered a third major school of international relations. For simplicity, constructivism and structural liberalism are merged here as "liberalist" accounts.

7. Erik Gartzke and Jon Lindsay, "Cross-Domain Deterrence: Strategy in an Era of Complexity," paper presented at the International Studies Association Annual Meeting, Toronto, March 25–29, 2014.

8. Li and Xu, chapter 9 in this volume.

9. Stokes, chapter 7 in this volume.

10. Information Warfare Monitor, *Tracking Ghostnet: Investigating a Cyber Espionage Network*, Secdev Group and University of Toronto Citizen Lab, March 2009.

11. Nicole Perlroth, "Hackers in China Attacked the Times for Last 4 Months," *New York Times*, January 31, 2013; Nicole Perlroth, "Wall Street Journal Announces That It, Too, Was Hacked by the Chinese," *New York Times*, January 31, 2013; Nicole Perlroth, "Washington Post Joins List of News Media Hacked by the Chinese," *New York Times*, February 1, 2013.

12. Gary King, Jennifer Pan, and Margaret E. Roberts, "How Censorship in China Allows Government Criticism but Silences Collective Expression," *American Political Science Review* 107, no. 2 (2013): 326–43.

13. Inkster, chapter 2 in this volume.

14. Quoted in Michael Riley and Dune Lawrence, "Hackers Linked to China's Army Seen from EU to D.C.," *Bloomberg*, July 26, 2012.

15. Quoted in "China Says U.S. Routinely Hacks Defense Ministry Websites," Reuters, February 28, 2013.

16. Matthew M. Aid, "Inside the NSA's Ultra-secret China Hacking Group," *Foreign Policy*, June 10, 2013.

17. Associated Press, "Leaker Snowden's Allegations about US Hacking Give China New Edge in Cyber War of Words," *Washington Post*, June 13, 2013; David E. Sanger and Nicole Perlroth, "N.S.A. Breached Chinese Servers Seen as Security Threat," *New York Times*, March 22, 2014.

18. Quoted in Didi Kirsten Tatlow, "Can N.S.A. Surveillance Be Likened to Chinese Spying?" *New York Times*, June 13, 2013.

19. James Staten, "The Cost of PRISM Will Be Larger Than ITIF," August 14, 2013, http://blogs.forrester.com/james_staten/13-08-14-the_cost_of_prism_will_be_larger_than_itif_projects.

20. David Alexander, "Top Officer Rejects Comparison of U.S., Chinese Cyber Snooping," Reuters, June 27, 2013.

21. White House, "Presidential Policy Directive 28," January 17, 2014.

22. Mandiant, "M-Trends: Beyond the Breach, 2014 Threat Report," April 2014, 21.

23. Ye, chapter 5 in this volume.

24. Ye, chapter 5 in this volume.

25. Jon R. Lindsay, "Reinventing the Revolution: Technological Visions, Counterinsurgent Criticism, and the Rise of Special Operations," *Journal of Strategic Studies* 36, no. 3 (2013): 422–53.

26. Lindsay, "Stuxnet and the Limits of Cyber Warfare"; Gartzke, "The Myth of Cyberwar."

27. Jack L. Snyder, *The Ideology of the Offensive: Military Decision Making and the Disasters of 1914* (Ithaca, NY: Cornell University Press, 1989); Stephen W. Van Evera, *Causes of War: Power and the Roots of Conflict* (Ithaca, NY: Cornell University Press, 1999).

28. David C. Gompert and Martin Libicki, "Cyber Warfare and Sino-American Crisis Instability," *Survival* 56, no. 4 (2014): 7–22.

29. Jason Healy, "The Five Futures of Cyber Conflict and Cooperation," Atlantic Council Issue Brief, 2011.

30. Li and Xu, chapter 9 in this volume.
31. Ye, chapter 5 in this volume.
32. U.S. Department of State, "Internet Freedom," http://www.state.gov/e/eb/cip/netfreedom/index.htm.
33. Alexander Klimburg, "The Internet Yalta," Center for a New American Security Commentary, February 5, 2013.
34. Cate, chapter 12 in this volume.
35. On this point Erik Gartzke writes, "If cyberwar functions not as an independent domain, but as part of a broader, coordinated military action, then the conventional military balance is the best indicator of where the most important threats exist in cyberspace." Gartzke, "The Myth of Cyberwar," 63.
36. Adam Segal, "U.S. and China in Cyberspace: Uneasy Next Steps," Council of Foreign Relations, Asia Unbound Blog, June 18, 2012.
37. Helene Cooper, "Hagel Spars with Chinese Over Islands and Security," *New York Times*, April 8, 2014.
38. Li and Xu, chapter 9 in this volume.

INDEX

3Com (U.S. telecommunications company), 235
418th Research Institute. *See* Beijing North Computing Center
863 Plan: Chinese technology development goals of, 34–35, 56; emphasis on acquiring foreign expertise and, 341; Expert Working Group on Computing and Software and, 167; Information Assurance Expert Working Group and, 170; information warfare militias funded by, 203; intelligence operations funded by, 57; origins of, 34

Academy of Military Science (People's Liberation Army), 195–197
active electronically scanned array (AESA) radar, 159n54
Acxiom, 299
Administrative Procedure Law of the People's Republic of China (1989), 249, 258n30
Administrative Reconsideration Law of the People's Republic of China (1999 and 2009), 249, 258n33
Adobe Systems, 302
advanced persistent threats from China (APTs): list of examples of, 58–60; measures to combat, 16, 63–64, 77–78; methods implemented by, 61, 64–66, 76, 81–82n28, 114, 163; military cyberespionage targeting requests and, 71, 75; organizational affiliations of, 200; targets by category of, 62
Afghanistan War (2001–), 18, 125, 128

Alexander, Keith: on China's cyberespionage against U.S. military targets, 43; on China's economic espionage against United States, 16, 46, 51–52; on cost estimates of global cybercrime, 52
Alibaba Group, 102
Al Qaeda, 302, 334
AMSC (U.S.-based wind turbine manufacturer), 46
Anderson, Ross, 52
Android operating system, 168, 171, 276–277
Anhui Province, 250
Ankara (Turkey), Chinese Embassy in, 33
Apple, 146, 266, 301, 349
APT-1 (Chinese cyberattack on Western targets), 13, 44, 60–61, 63
APT-12 (Chinese cyberattack group), 60
Arab Spring (2011), 124, 129–130, 265, 267, 269
Art of War (Sunzi), 29
Asia-Pacific regional security: China's role in, 123, 134–135, 346; cybersecurity and, 123–124, 133–134, 176, 346; international importance of, 123; United States and, 135, 346
Australia: China as target of trade restrictions in, 2–3, 12; China's cyberattacks and cyberespionage on targets in, 2–3, 33, 60; Chinese diaspora community in, 37; "Cyber Storm" exercises and, 131; Security Intelligence Organization in, 60
Aviation Industry Corporation of China, 57

law reform and, 320–322; realist approach to, 337–338, 340, 345, 347, 350; social networking sites and, 247; technologist approach to, 337, 340–341, 345; "tragedy of the commons" effect in, 307–308; United States policy regarding, 20–21, 44, 124, 130–131, 175–177, 199, 225–226, 231, 235–240, 250, 261, 280, 297–325, 333–334, 347, 350–352

Cybersecurity and Informatization Leading Group (CILG; China): creation of, 7, 10, 13, 164, 230; information security policies and, 11, 146, 230; membership list for, 14; Xi Jingping as chair of, 8–9, 13–14, 146, 164, 230

Cybersecurity Working Group (US-China Strategic and Economic Dialogue), 44, 280

Cyber-Sitter (Chinese cyberattack on U.S. targets), 59

Cyberspace Administration of China (SIIO), 9–11, 191, 236

"Cyber Storm" exercises (U.S. cybersecurity tests), 130–131

cyberwarfare. See also information warfare; network warfare: ambiguities of, 334, 343–345; asymmetrical nature of, 139, 344; botnets and, 127; China's capabilities and policies in, 3, 17–18, 42, 133, 138–157, 266, 343–345; cyber and electronic integration in, 128; cyber defense and, 130–131, 133; cyber espionage and, 125–126, 138; cyber paralysis and, 126–128, 138–139; cyber psychology and, 129–130; Distributed Denial of service attacks (DDoS) and, 127; as force multiplier, 139; nuclear warfare compared to, 17, 125, 140, 149, 154, 156; United States capacities and policies of, 17, 128, 133, 139, 146–147, 156–157, 266, 344–345; versatility of, 125

Dai Bingguo, 39

Dai Qingmin, 138, 145, 174

Dalai Lama: Chinese Ghost Net cyberattack (2009) on, 43, 58, 61, 274, 302; self-immolation protests in Tibet and, 270

Danilov, Valentin, 36

Datang Telecom, 191

"Decision of the Standing Committee of the National People's Congress on Cases Not to Be Heard in Public" (1956), 244–245

"Decision on Major Issues Concerning Comprehensively Deepening Reforms" (Chinese Communist Party, 2013), 229–230

"Decision on Strengthening Information Protection on Networks" (National People's Congress Standing Committee, 2012), 229, 232, 242, 246, 253–255

"Decision on Strengthening Online Information Protection" (National People's Congress Standing Committee), 248, 250–251

Delta IV rocket, 57

Dempsey, Martin E., 153, 342

Deng Xiaoping, 31–32, 34

Department of Commerce (United States), 58, 131, 298, 346

Department of Defense (United States), 58, 131, 235–236, 297, 302–303, 314

Department of Energy (United States), 131

Department of Homeland Security (United States), 130–131, 236, 312–313

Department of Justice (United States), 131, 298, 319

Department of State (United States), 58, 265–266, 346

Department of the Treasury (United States), 131

Department of Transportation (United States), 131

Distributed Denial of service attacks (DDoS): average price for commissioning of, 111; Chinese targets of, 227; as form of cyberwarfare, 127; as lesser form

Hoffman, Samantha, 40

Hong Kong and Macao Affairs Office (State Council), 39

Hong Kong and Macao Liaison Bureau (People's Liberation Army), 170

House of Representatives Intelligence Committee (United States), 235

Huawei: attempt to buy 3Com by, 235; Australian business restrictions on, 2–3, 12; Nortel's accusations regarding cyberespionage by, 46; People's Liberation Army and, 191; secure router business of, 3, 8; Sprint Nextel and, 235; U.S. business restrictions on, 2–3, 12, 349; U.S. cyberespionage on, 3, 13, 304–307

Hu Jintao: annual foreign policy assessment meeting of, 41; on cybersecurity, 3; on "foreign hostile forces," 267–268; intelligence services in China and, 38; internal security emphasized by, 39

"human flesh searches," 19, 234, 250–251, 338

human intelligence (HUMINT) operations, 16, 35–37, 47, 57

human rights in China: "foreign hostile forces" concept and, 261, 264–265, 267–270, 280–281; "internal dissidents" concept and, 261, 264–265; international law and, 262, 283n6, 283n9; National Human Rights Action Plan and, 262, 284n29; New Citizens Movement and, 262, 283n14; nongovernmental organizations (NGOs) and, 261; online dimensions of, 20, 260–268, 274–281, 346; United Nations 2013 review of, 264; *weiquan* (rights defense) lawyers and, 262

Hungary, 131

Hussein, Saddam, 35

ICBC (Chinese bank), 100–101

Icefog (Chinese cyberattack on Japanese and South Korean targets), 60

Improving Critical Infrastructure Cybersecurity (Obama Executive Order, 2013), 298, 310–311, 313–314

India: China's cyberattacks and cyberespionage on, 58, 60, 273–274; China's trade with, 134; cyberwarfare capabilities in, 133; Internet's contribution to economic productivity in, 1; plan to build national Internet in, 323; Tibet and, 276, 302

Indonesia, 33, 305

industrial espionage, 53. *See also* economic cyberespionage

Information Assurance Base (People's Liberation Army), 209

Information Engineering Academy Computer Network Attack and Defense section (People's Liberation Army), 171

Information Engineering University (People's Liberation Army), 169

information security. *See also* cybersecurity; network security: China's lack of legal foundations for, 232–233; China's levels of, 227; China's policies regarding, 8, 11, 16, 164–165, 167, 170, 229–234, 339–340; civil-military integration and, 191–192; as concept in privacy debates, 242, 246–247, 253; cyber militias and, 194, 200; need for more realistic views on, 315–316; "tragedy of the commons" effect in, 307; underground online markets and, 16

Information Security Certification Center (ISCCC), 9, 12

information warfare. *See also* cyberwarfare; network warfare: civil-military integration and, 189–190; "cyber militias" and, 192–206; electronic warfare and, 156; network warfare as a form of, 138, 151, 156; People's Liberation Army (PLA) doctrine on, 141–142

information warfare militias: case study analysis of, 206–208; civil-military integration and, 193; command

and control of, 198–199, 208;
cyber espionage and, 200;
electromagnetic warfare and,
197–198; geographic dispersion
of, 205–206; incentives for
creating, 211; information
domain and, 197–198; intelligence
operations and, 197; listed by
name, 203, 212–217; mobilization
of, 200–201; network defense
operations and, 10, 19, 190, 200,
202, 208–210; network warfare
and, 194–195, 197, 199–202,
207–208, 210; organizational
affiliations of, 19, 203–204;
peacetime operations of, 201;
policy implications regarding,
211–212; psychological warfare
and, 197; rate of creation of,
204–205; roles and missions of, 19,
199–200; size of, 194; structure of,
196–202; supply chain implications
from, 212; university-based
units of, 10, 207–208; wartime
operations of, 201–202
Inkster, Nigel, 11, 15, 57, 152, 190,
336, 341
Institute of Scientific and Technical
Information of China, 72
Institute on Global Conflict and
Cooperation (IGCC), 6
Intel, 3, 266
intellectual property theft, 2, 46, 303.
See also economic cyberespionage
intelligence agencies in China: academic
research on, 29; Chinese civil
war (1945–1949) and, 29–30;
Chinese diaspora populations and,
35, 37; Chinese policy community
and, 38–41, 47; cyber espionage
capabilities of, 42–47, 57; human
source techniques and, 35–37,
47, 57; intelligence analysis and, 38;
Leading Small Groups and, 38;
limited foreign collection in early
Communist era and, 30–32;
opposition groups located outside
China and, 45, 47; People's
Liberation Army and, 32–33;
science and technology collection

by, 34–35, 45; tradecraft of, 34–37;
World War II and, 29–30
International Code of Conduct for
Information Security, 176
International Department (Chinese
Communist Party), 39
International Liaison Department
(Chinese Communist Party), 30, 39
"International Networking of
Computer Information Network
Security Management Approach"
(Chinese government Internet
regulation), 232
International Olympic Committee, 43,
59, 302
international relations theory and
cybersecurity, 21, 334–335,
337–338, 340–341, 343, 345,
347, 350
"International Strategy for Cyberspace"
(United States, 2011), 124, 175
Internet. *See also* cybersecurity;
information security; network
security:
economic productivity and, 1–2, 333;
international governance of, 17, 19,
235–237, 266, 286n46, 325, 346;
international usage rates and, 1–2;
rapid technological advances and,
22, 225, 299–300, 347
Internet Assigned Name Authority
(IANA) function (United
States), 346
Internet Corporation for Assigned
Names and Numbers (ICANN), 3,
236, 266, 346
"Internet Information Services
Management Measures" (Chinese
law), 232
Internet Security and Informatization
Leading Small Group. *See*
Cybersecurity and Informatization
Leading Group (CILG)
Internet service providers (ISPs) in
China, 9, 11
Investigation Department of the
Central Committee of the Chinese
Communist Party (ID/CCP), 31–32
Iran: China's technological cooperation
with, 45; Israel's cyberwarfare

Lockheed-Martin, 58–59, 69, 125, 302
Lorenz, Edward, 129
Los Alamos Research Lab (United States), 35
Lou Jiwei, 14
Luckycat Campaign (Chinese cyberattack), 59, 273
Lurid (Chinese cyberattacks on Tibetan and Russian targets), 59
Lu Wei, 14

Madame Butterfly, 31
Ma Kai, 14
Ma Minhu, 230
Mandiant, reports on China's cyberattacks against United States from, 13, 44, 61, 63, 65, 272–273, 302–303, 343
Mao Zedong, 30, 135
Mattis, Peter, 40
McAfee, 43, 52
McCain, John, 58
McConnell, Michael, 17, 301
McKune, Sarah, 16–17, 20, 336, 339, 346
McReynolds, Joe, 10, 18–19, 336, 345
Meng Jianzhu, 14
Meng Xuezheng, 166
Merkel, Angela, 305
Miao Wei, 14
Microsoft, 3, 11, 235
Middle East and North Africa, Arab Spring (2011) events in, 124, 129–130, 265, 269
militias in China, 193–194. See also information warfare militias
Mill, John Stuart, 131
Ministry of Aviation (China), 57
Ministry of Commerce (China), 11
Ministry of Defense (China), 342
Ministry of Foreign Affairs (China), 30, 37, 39, 236
Ministry of Industry and Information Technology (MIIT; China): civil-military integration and, 191; cybersecurity policy and, 9–11, 236; Electronics Science and Technology Intelligence Research Institute and, 72; five-year plan for advanced manufacturing (2012)

of, 74; internet privacy regulations and, 251; RuggedCom network backdoor allegations and, 232
Ministry of Public Security (MPS; police in China): civil-military integration and, 191; cybersecurity policy and, 236; Eleventh Bureau of, 9, 11; intelligence operations and, 31–32; internet privacy regulations and, 251; Leading Small Groups for national security and, 39; as potential source of cyberattacks, 64
Ministry of Science and Technology, 72
Ministry of State Security (MSS; China): budget increases for, 39; Chinese Institute of Contemporary International Relations and, 32, 41; civil-military integration and, 191; cybersecurity policy and, 9, 11, 16, 175; intelligence operations of, 32, 36, 45, 341; internal security function of, 32; Leading Small Groups for national security and, 39; opposition groups located outside China and, 45; as potential source of cyberattacks, 64
Mongolia, 134
Morgan Stanley, 302
Motorola, 235
Munk School of Global Affairs (University of Toronto), 43, 65, 273
Mutter (Chinese cyberattack on South Asian targets), 60
Myanmar, 33

National Academy of Sciences (United States), 315, 322
National Aeronautics and Space Administration (NASA; United States), 61, 298, 302
National Defense University (China), 196
National Development and Reform Commission (China), 8–9, 12
National Endowment for Democracy, 269
National High Technology Research and Development Plan. See 863 Plan
National Human Rights Action Plan (China), 262, 284n29

National Information Network ("clean Internet" in Iran), 45–46, 323

National Information Security Industrial Bases, 167–168

National Institute of Standards and Technology (United States), 298, 310

National Intelligence Council (United States), 38

National Intelligence Estimate (United States, 2013), 2, 77–78, 303

National Medium- and Long-Term Plan for the Development of Science and Technology (MLP), 56–57, 63, 66–67, 73, 196

National People's Congress (China): Citizens' Personal Information Protection Law and, 115; Standing Committee's Decision on Cases Not to Be Heard in Public (1956), 244–245; Standing Committee's Decision on Strengthening Information Protection on Networks, 229, 232, 242, 246, 253–255; Standing Committee's Decision on Strengthening Online Information Protection, 248, 250–251

National Research Center for Anti-Computer Invasion and Virus Prevention (China), 11

National Science Foundation (United States), 298, 311

National Security Agency (NSA): China's cyberattacks and cyberespionage against U.S. targets and, 77; covert network backdoors installed by, 304, 306; cyberattacks and cyberespionage against China by, 3, 13, 266, 298, 303–306; data collection programs of, 124, 126, 228–229, 321, 333; Department of Homeland Security and, 313; encryption cracking by, 305; Google and, 77, 312–313; proposal to split intelligence gathering and cybersecurity functions of, 324; Quantum computer hardware espionage program of, 126; Snowden leaks regarding, 3, 13,

44, 126, 228, 235, 265–267, 281, 297–298, 303–307, 314, 321, 339, 342; Tailored Access Operations (TAO) group in, 304; Turbine coordination system of, 304; United States Cyber Command and, 312, 344

National Security Committee (China), 40–41

National Security Council (United States), 40–41

National Security Leading Small Group (China), 38–39

Naval War College (United States), 58

network security. *See also* cybersecurity; information security: academic research on, 5, 230; China's levels of, 227–228, 339; China's policies regarding, 6, 11, 167, 229–239, 339–340; commercial-oriented challenges to, 233; nongovernmental organizations' role in, 236–238; societal-level challenges to, 234; technological issues in, 231–232; underground online markets in China and, 87, 228

network warfare. *See also* cyberwarfare; information warfare: active offense strategy and, 143; assassin's mace weapons and, 149, 151; C4ISR systems (command, control, communication, computers, intelligence, surveillance, and reconnaissance) and, 143–145, 151–153, 156, 343; civil-military integration and, 189–190; computer network strikes and, 144–145; computer Renaissance and, 144, 152, 157; countermeasures against, 141; cyber coercion and, 139, 147–150, 153–155; definition of, 139–140; destructive capacity of, 140; deterrence and, 149–150, 153–154; doctrinal factors impacting China's strategies of, 139, 141–143; information warfare militias and, 19, 190, 194–195, 197, 199–202, 207–208, 210; integrated network electronic warfare (INEW)

and, 145; measuring efficacy
of, 155–156; mutually assured
destruction and, 154; network
defense and, 145–147; network
protocol deception and, 144–145;
network psychological warfare and,
150–151; societies' vulnerability to,
140, 151; targeting preferences and,
152–153

New Citizens Movement, 262, 283n14

New York Times: Chinese cyberattack on,
59, 278–279, 339–340; editorial on
Chinese cyberespionage by, 297

New Zealand, 42

Nigeria, 110

Night Dragon (economic cybercrime
attack, 2011), 58, 63, 302

Nitro (Chinese cyberattack in 2011), 59

Nixon, Richard, 31, 135

Norinco, 35

Nortel, 46

North Atlantic Treaty Organization
(NATO), 141

North China Institute of Aerospace
Engineering, 208

North Korea, 60

Northrop Grumman, 43–44, 302

Obama, Barack: China's cyberespionage
on campaign (2008) of, 58; on
cybersecurity, 2, 60, 175, 301–302,
310, 312, 343; cybersecurity policy
and, 298, 301, 305, 309–312, 317;
Internet governance and, 346;
Presidential Policy Directive 28
(PPD-28; United States), 342, 349;
State of the Union address (2013)
of, 310; Stuxnet cyberattack
and, 314; Xi Jingping's summit with
(2013) with, 13, 44, 229, 303, 305

Office of National Assessments
(Australia), 38

Office of the National
Counterintelligence Executive
(United States), 235

Operation Allied Force (Chinese
cyberattack on NATO systems,
1999), 141

Operation Aurora (Chinese cyberattack
on Internet companies): Google as

target of, 43, 58–59, 63, 77, 302,
312–313; Hillary Clinton's internet
freedom speech and, 58, 63; Shanghai
Jiaotong University and, 203

"Opinion on Handling Self-Immolation
Cases in Tibetan Areas in
Accordance with the Law" (Chinese
Supreme Court), 270–271

Oracle, 235

Orange Revolution (Ukraine), 129

Pacnet (Chinese telecommunications
company), 228

Pakistan, 70, 134

"Panda burning incense" case (2007),
95, 113

Panetta, Leon, 314

Passport Law of the People's Republic of
China (2006), 245, 256n14

Patriotic Education Campaign (Chinese
Communist Party), 29

Pen Register Act (Title III of Electronic
Communication Privacy Act; 1986),
319, 322

People's Air Defense units (China), 193

People's Armed Forces Departments, 195

People's Liberation Army (PLA). *See also
specific divisions and offices*: 863 Plan
and, 57;active defense strategy
and, 141; active offense strategy
and, 142–143, 153–154; ballistic
missile strike on weather satellite
(2007) by, 39; Central Military
Commission and, 40; Chinese
Communist Party control of, 7;
Chinese Institute for International
Strategic Studies and, 41;
civil-military integration and,
188–189, 191–196, 198–202, 206,
208–210, 345; computer network
operations (CNO) infrastructure
in, 18, 163–177; cyberattacks and
cyberespionage conducted by,
10, 13, 15, 18, 33, 44–45, 58, 60,
64–65, 72, 164–166, 168, 170–175,
199, 209, 272, 303, 341–342, 344;
cyberwarfare strategy and, 17–18,
42, 141; declining policymaking role
of, 40; formal outsourcing by, 192;
formal procurement relationships

Sixteenth Central Committee (Chinese Communist Party, 2004), 229

Sneaky Panda (Chinese cyberattack on U.S. targets), 59

Snowden, Edward: leaks on National Security Agency's intelligence gathering by, 126, 228, 235, 265–266, 281, 297, 314, 321, 339; leaks on the vulnerability of encryption technology by, 305; leaks on U.S. cyberattacks and cyberespionage against China by, 3, 13, 44, 266–267, 298, 303–307, 342; United States privacy rights debates and, 21, 321

Social Affairs Department (Chinese Communist Party), 31

social media: Arab Spring and, 265; privacy issues and, 247

Solid Oak Software, 59

Solove, Daniel, 320

Sony, 309

South China Normal University, 208, 213

South China Seas island disputes, 18, 135

South Korea, 60, 133–134, 171, 228

Southwest Institute of Electronics and Telecommunications Technology, 167

Soviet Union: China's break from, 31; collapse of, 67; economic espionage against the United States and, 78–79; United States nuclear arms agreements with, 324; World War II and, 30

space shuttle program (United States), 57

Special Action Plan for Governance of the underground economy (China, 2013), 115

Sprint Nextel, 235

Standing Committee of the Chinese Communist Party Politburo: Cybersecurity and Informatization Leading Group (CILG), 13–14; elite status of, 7; Leading Small Groups on national security issues and, 38;

People's Liberation Army and, 40; policymaking function of, 7

State Administration for Industry and Commerce (China), 278

State Administration for Science, Technology, and Industry for National Defense (SASTIND; China), 71

State Administration of Foreign Experts Affairs (China), 72–73

State Asset Supervision and Administration Commission (China), 12

State Council (China): bureaucratic coordination by, 7; Chinese Academy of Social Science and, 41; cybersecurity policy and, 9–10, 12; Hong Kong and Macao Affairs Office of, 39; Information Office (SCIO) of, 9, 11; Information Security Working Group of, 168–169; Internet privacy and, 252; National Medium- and Long-Term Plan for the Development of Science and Technology (MLP) and, 196

State Electricity Regulatory Commission (China), 232

State Encryption Bureau (Chinese Communist Party), 9–10

State Informatization Leading Group (SILG; China), 8–9, 14, 164, 229

State Internet Information Office (SIIO; China), 9–11, 191, 236

State Network and Information Security Coordination Group (SNISCG; China), 8–10, 14

State Secrecy Law (China), 10

State Secrets Protection Bureau (Chinese Communist Party), 8–9

State Security Committee (China), 40

Stokes, Mark, 10, 18, 61, 152, 336, 339, 341, 344

Stored Communications Act (Title II of Electronic Communications Privacy Act, 1986), 318–319

"Strategy for Operating in Cyberspace" (U.S. Department of Defense report), 235

Stuxnet cyberattack: Iran as the target of, 12, 124, 127–128, 152,

Printed in the USA/Agawam, MA
September 3, 2019

710360.009